*The wing is the corporeal element
which is most akin to the divine,
and which by nature tends to soar aloft and carry
that which gravitates downwards into the upper region,
which is the habitation of the gods.
The divine is beauty, wisdom, goodness, and the like;
and by these the wing of the soul is nourished,
and grows apace;
but when fed upon evil and foulness
and the opposite of good,
wastes and falls away.*

—Plato, *Phaedrus* (part II)

Books by George A. Panichas

Adventure in Consciousness:
The Meaning of D. H. Lawrence's Religious Quest (1964)

Epicurus (1967)

The Reverent Discipline:
Essays in Literary Criticism and Culture (1974)

The Burden of Vision: Dostoevsky's Spiritual Art (1977)

The Courage of Judgment:
Essays in Criticism, Culture, and Society (1982)

The Critic as Conservator:
Essays in Literature, Society, and Culture (1992)

Renaissance and Modern Essays: Presented to Vivian de Sola Pinto
in Celebration of His Seventieth Birthday,
edited with George R. Hibbard and Allan Rodway (1966)

Mansions of the Spirit: Essays in Literature and Religion, editor (1967)

Promise of Greatness: The War of 1914–1918, editor (1968)

The Politics of Twentieth-Century Novelists, editor (1971)

The Simone Weil Reader, editor (1977)

Irving Babbitt: Representative Writings, editor (1981)

Irving Babbitt in Our Time, edited, with Claes G. Ryn (1986)

Modern Age: The First Twenty-Five Years. A Selection, editor (1988)

In Continuity: The Last Essays of Austin Warren, editor (1996)

Growing Wings to Overcome Gravity

Criticism as the Pursuit of Virtue

George A. Panichas

MERCER UNIVERSITY PRESS
1979 – 1999
TWENTY YEARS OF PUBLISHING EXCELLENCE

ISBN 0-86554-606-1   (casebound)   MUP/H457
ISBN 0-86554-618-5   (perfectbound)   MUP/P177

Growing Wings to Overcome Gravity:
Criticism as the Pursuit of Virtue
by George A. Panichas
Copyright ©1999
Mercer University Press, Macon, Georgia 31210-3960 USA
All rights reserved
Manufactured in the United States of America

The paper used in this publication meets the minimum requirements
of American National Standard for Information Sciences—
Permanence of Paper for Printed Library Materials, ANSI Z39.48-1984.

∞

Library of Congress Cataloging-in-Publication Data

Panichas, George Andrew.
Growing wings to overcome gravity :
criticism as the pursuit of virtue / George A. Panichas.
p.   cm.
Includes bibliographical references and index.
ISBN 0-86554-606-1 (casebound : alk. paper).
ISBN 0-86554-618-5 (perfectbd. : alk. paper).
1. Criticism. 2. Literature—History and criticism. I. Title.
PN85.P36   1999
801'.95—dc21   98-33378
             CIP

Contents

Foreword

The title here is inspired by Plato's *Phaedrus*, its subtitle, *Criticism as the Pursuit of Virtue*, an extension of the same. And the author, George A. Panichas, the editor of *Modern Age: A Quarterly Review* and former professor of English at the University of Maryland, describes it as the *coda* to his critical trilogy, *The Reverent Discipline* (1974), *The Courage of Judgment* (1982), and *The Critic as Conservator* (1992). And in some ways, this collection of previously published essays and new ones as well, marks the supreme moment in his long and distinguished career—what he has dreamed of doing, what he has tried to do, and what he has actually done. Not criticism as a moral lesson but based on moral principles—something which sooner or later must resort to the words hardly heard in literary criticism today—"good" and "bad."

Again and again we hear words such as "order," "continuity," "tradition," "quality," "value," and such like. And we hear, on the other hand, the abhorrence with which such evaluations as "ideology," "relative," "pluralistic," and the like are spoken. Because Professor Panichas does believe that there are such in literature—as well as the Creation—which are fixed and not negotiable.

And he takes as some of the prime examples the works of Irving Babbitt, T. S. Eliot, Russell Kirk, Richard Weaver, Austin Warren—and these twentieth-century names are just a start. And sooner or later we find ourselves discussing values in many things besides literature and the other arts—the quality of life, the *whys* and *wherefores* of all such things here, which sooner or later must be evaluated. (And if I may do so, I'd like to interpolate here an exchange having to do with a freshman class I was teaching thirty years ago at Northwestern. I asked a young lady therein what she thought of a particular poem we were studying, and she smoothly replied that she didn't want to make a value judgment, whereupon I asked her what else was she there for!)

Well, that's what this distinguished book comes down to—beyond its impressive erudition and precise exposition: the *value* of criticism, of literature, and all the other arts, of all that makes our life higher than that of animals; how it enriches and gives to our lives what we hardly thought of as a desperate need, and of course the judgment needed for evaluating these commodities which finally know no price. Professor Panichas speaks here with firmness but also tact, in which capacity he strongly reminds me of his great friend, one of the greatest names here—Austin Warren, whose works and teaching, and above all, influence had inestimable value for several generations of students. Then there are Russell Kirk, the founder of *Modern Age*, and Henry Regnery, the publisher who brought so many of these recent names into print, Richard Weaver, philosopher and English professor for some years at the University of Chicago, and many other Chicago dwellers, such as the architect Louis Sullivan and, for some years, Frank Lloyd Wright. And there are others too, straight from the heart of the Midwest—Willa Cather, Hamlin Garland, and many more.

But all these are just a sample of what undergirds Professor Panichas's great achievement here—to restore and to understand what the arts are really for—not to teach, not to preach, but as Conrad said in the great preface to *The Nigger of the Narcissus*, to give us that glimpse of truth for which we have forgotten to ask. And finally, as I've tried to put into words myself, they somehow ask, in the midst of the weariness, the fever, and the fret we all must endure, what we propose to do about it all—what we will do for an encore.

Robert Drake
University of Tennessee

Author's Note

From the start and, it seems, always, as I was often reminded in the course of preparing the manuscript of this book for publication, my writings have focused on the moral imperative and the moral imagination, and, inevitably on the religious idea, on the search for order, and on the spiritual quest for transcendent reality. I do not hesitate in the least, then, to identify myself as a moralist critic and teacher—as one who, to recall the subtitle of this book, unhesitantly views criticism as the pursuit of virtue. The ongoing process of my critical interests and search, in forging a "singleness of vision," as one of my reviewers describes this process, has steadily defined and steered my choice of subjects and writers. This same reviewer goes on to observe, rightly, "It is a good, and rare, thing for a writer to know from early on what sort of shape one would like one's career to take. . . . "

Now, four decades after my first appearance in print, I can confidently say that the figures, and the themes, issues, problems, and concerns I have written on, chose me rather than I them, so to speak. Indeed, the particular novelists, poets, seers, critics, thinkers, philosophers, educators, and men and women of letters I celebrate in these pages are my intellectual and spiritual forebears and kinsmen. Without some internal awareness of, and dialogue with, these writers I do not think I would have ever written anything of substance or given concrete form and definition to my critical mission and ethos.

Instinctively, and unyieldingly, I have sought out exemplars and paradigms, and in turn standards and precepts and traditions worthy of emulation and loyalty, conducive to elevating life to its first principles, to making us better citizens in the life of the commonwealth, and to strengthening the life of the soul that resides in and distinguishes each one of us. The writers I esteem in this book, for the reasons I try to show in my commentaries, provide us with the moral and ethical life-stuff that helps to give us bearings, guidelines, sustenance. At the heart of this book, hence, is my belief that, in word and work, there exists a sacred communion of writers who redeem the time and enable us to discern and even to prevail over the abominations of the temporal self and the temporal realm. The present book is an unequivocal statement of a critic's faith, and undertakes to point the way beyond the fragmentation, the relativism, the disarray, and the secularism of contemporary times. D. H. Lawrence's words of promise and hope—"One must speak for life and growth, amid all the mass of destruction and disintegration"—aptly evoke my critical assumptions and yearnings here, and what I specifically call criticism as the pursuit of virtue, and of the place of virtues, of moral excellence, in the total scheme of human existence.

Growing Wings to Overcome Gravity—my main title (inspired by a passage from Plato's *Phaedrus*, which appears as the epigraph to this book)—serves as a coda to my critical trilogy, published over a span of nearly twenty years: *The Reverent Discipline* (1974), *The Courage of Judgment* (1982), and *The Critic as Conservator* (1992). My title here provides the encompassing poetic image—and the inspiration behind my critical intent—of ultimately overcoming the crises of modernism in which we agonize, and of attaining the promise of spiritual and moral order. The overarching critical emphasis is on human possibility, on the spiritual recovery and revitalization of American society and culture, in especial the republic of arts and letters. This coda contains, in essence, my literary, critical, and cultural affirmations, stressing as it does the flow of aspiration and the power of ascent. At the same time, it does not fail to confront the power of the abyss of negations, so pervasive and dominant in the modern world, and of the profane critical spirit that flourishes in the academy and the intellectual community.

If we are to move out of this abyss, which represents the absolute denial of virtues, and if we are to move beyond the secular prison house of ideology, as it has been conceived and built by "terrible simplifiers" endlessly inventing utopias and paradises on the quicksands of illusion, we must first be able to apprehend the negations that besiege and subvert contemporary life. Part 1 of this book attempts to identify variously and diagnostically the nature and purveyors of our affliction. Unless we become more fully aware of the dominion and powers of this affliction, we can hardly begin to take the upward path. But how can one turn from a life of negation to a life of virtue? How, in other words, can one grow wings to overcome gravity? These are basic questions that impel the plan and rhythm of this book and the questions it poses and sets out to answer.

Throughout, the individual parts, sections, and essays are sequentially and interconnectedly arranged so as to illustrate the lasting truth of Plato's image as it relates to man's quest for beauty, wisdom, goodness. In effect, they illustrate, too, how the critic himself traces his conception of criticism in direct relation to his particular understanding of the struggle for discovery, illumination, ascent. Each part of the book, and each essay, are thus placed in an order of ascent or growth, a galvanizing process that, according to Plato, "tends to soar aloft and carries that which gravitates downwards into the upper region." An ultimate goal of this book, thus, is simultaneously restorative and transcendent, and in active contention with those forces and conditions in modern civilization that, like the pull of gravity, diminish the moral life and the ethical life.

The economy of the book as a whole, it is hoped, has a kind of parabolic thrust, distinctly upwards, guiding the intellect to pathways of growth, to directions or turning points in terms of the good, of virtue. One could perhaps visualize the total structure of the book as a ladder to the higher self. The process of growth depicted here is one in which the critic portrays illuminations that become affirmations, that is to say, triumphs over the forces of gravity in human existence which Plato equates with "evil and foulness and the opposite of good." In particular, it is the purpose of part 3, "To See Again the Stars," to elucidate dimensions of acceptance and ascension—of an "orientation toward something higher," and of the values and virtues that the critic commends a reader to pursue and grasp.

Some final remarks remain to be said about part 2, "Shepherds of the Peoples," a title bestowed by the ancients on great visionary thinkers. This part serves, in select and significant ways, as the keystone of the book, that which locks together the parts that precede and follow it, and on which they depend. Of the necessity of paradigms and exemplars there is surely no end, especially if criticism as the pursuit of virtue is to be in any way effective and viable in a journey of intellectual and spiritual rebirth. We urgently need illuminators who can inspire illuminations; we need to be exposed to the *spoudaoi*, as Aristotle calls them, who challenge those "terrible simplifiers" who, if my assessment of the crisis of modernism has merit, have for too long exerted both a disproportionate and a destructive influence and control in our time. These *spoudaoi* are men of vision, excellence, and character, of insight and wisdom. They are helpers who can lead us out of the abyss of negations, and who can, in effect, rescue us from the crisis of modernism. They pay careful attention to the idea of value and the life of virtue, steadfastly "affirming the enduring order of things." Thus, they play a sapiential role in the community and have a sapiential influence. In their discriminations and judgments we find a categorical indictment of the legacy of the "terrible simplifiers"; this is a legacy in which the eclipse of God and the eclipse of excellence are dominant symptoms and consequences.

No one part of this book can be read as a single entity; the three parts, in their dialectical emanation and nexus, are interacting and interdependent, purposely generating a fusion which in the end makes all three parts act as one. The critical design of the book thus is holistic in its metaphysic and dynamic. Its principal aim is that of aiding the reader to approach more closely, and without distraction or deflection, higher civilizational truths; to revere the "permanent things"; to facilitate intellectual conversion; to encourage the search for virtue; in short, to emphasize the need for both recognizing and rising above the negations that defile and disorder the modern world and psyche. This is the world into which we are thrown, and with which we are constantly in collision. But however fearful our collision with this world happens to be, we need not be defeated by its might or perish under its wheel. The critic who gives his witness, as this book endeavors to demonstrate, can also play a beneficent role in the unceasing fight to quell the centrifugal condition and circumstances that Edmund Burke specifies in these words: "Vice is never so odious . . . as when it usurps and disgraces the place of virtue."

The following pages propose to validate both the view and the function of criticism as the pursuit of virtue. The book is addressed to those who are willing to acknowledge this view and to take part in this pursuit, and who dare not only to resist the way of negations, but also to contemplate the way of affirmation to its maximum point of ascension. At once critical and catechetical in scope and ambition, this book ventures to impart lessons in growing wings to overcome gravity.

Preface

The law of continuity, according to Leibnitz, underlines the principle that all change is continuous, that nothing passes from one state to another *per saltum*. Continuity identifies an unbroken, uninterrupted connection, or succession, and as such contributes to harmony and unity, to the inner and outer order of life and society. It is associated with other central qualities: with reverence, with discipline, with steadfastness. In continuity we seek to conserve those patterns and rhythms of existence that resist the volatile tendencies which make for disorder. But in a world in which fragments and quantum leaps characterize the disconnectedness, the disequilibrium of our times, it has meager appeal. Continuity is not a popular word with those who in increasing numbers instinctively side with the profane and destructive urge as it is found in the guise of supposedly progressive thinking and action. To speak for continuity in a predominantly secular society often invites derision. The idea of continuity, we are variously told, died in 1789, or in 1917, or at that point when, as Nietzsche announced, God died.

A rootless society clearly disdains the discipline of continuity, disdains, that is, what continuity both signifies and prescribes. The passage from discontinuity to Dis, it seems, is not unusual if one is to judge by the existent conditions of American (and Western) civilization. Indeed, it is the relentless speed with which this passage has been made that is so frightening. Little or nothing to contain the momentum is evident; no inner check, as it were, is deemed an appropriate measure to be applied correctively to our expansive temperament and mischievous habits. Not the continuous, in the sense of what is enduring and permanent, but the discontinuous, in the sense of wanton usurpation, elimination, cessation, denial, best describes the nature of things. And that fact, of course, helps to define our moral and spiritual sickness.

Continuity is a word that, with other words embodying moral value, has been gradually disappearing from our language, from the very language of life itself. We do not want to be reminded of anything that has a continuing line of development. "To be continued" is a phrase that no longer means anything in a world in which anything means everything and nothing. The only continuity we seem to know is the continuity of fragments, each acting as its own free agent. What we suffer from *ad infinitum* is the tyranny of fragmentation, with each fragment comprising an entropic quality. Perceiving things in connection, in a hierarchy, insofar as such a perception also dictates a causal relationship, involves the kind of judgmental and discriminating process of thought that demands close attention to matters that have a center, a location of values—of values that possess standards and posit paradigms.

The discipline of continuity revolves around fundamental certitudes, revolves around enduring principles of order and life and faith. The struggle between those who speak for continuity and those who assert change and expedience at any cost is the struggle between the substance of value, of verity, and the onus of fragmentation. That there are specific values of thought and behavior to be passed on, continued; that there are moral imperatives and constants that must be preserved and implemented; that there are ancient edifices and sacred texts, ideas, and laws (written and unwritten) to be honored and sustained in the midst of the assaults of change, of the lure of experimentation and innovation that all too easily become a quick fix—these are some of the disciplines of continuity that create the character of a civilization, of a culture, of a people. It is too often forgotten that these disciplines are precisely what make possible creativity itself and that instance, in the best active sense, the "rage for order."

Perhaps more than anything else it is the spiritual order of continuity that should concern us and inform our efforts. Only our acceptance of the continual presence of Spirit can finally resist the proliferating acts of "cosmic impiety" and "telluric revolt" that afflict the modern world and drive it toward a "traditionless future." In this respect, the idea of continuity acts as an antidote against those secular doctrines that, in turn, undermine the idea of transcendence. Continuity, as *sacra historia*, recognizes a hierarchic structure, affirms universals, dramatizes aspiration and ascent, sanctifies causal relationships. Continuity, as a virtue of memory, is the categorical answer to nominalist and relativist concepts and conditions which produce what is in the end static or mechanistic. Continuity, as a discipline of consciousness, predicates a process of development and alerts us to the perils of presentism.

What we have come to view as the great spiritual disaster of our time is the ascendancy of an inorganic view of the world that stresses not the whole but the self-subsisting parts and temporal phenomena. Such a view rejects the belief that successive parts exist in consequence and ultimately reveal a purpose in the world. The arrogant disavowal of the law of continuity, as we see it asserted in modern life, defines the extent of a fragmented world, without beginnings or endings, without value or purpose, without, that is, Order or Spirit. These absences encompass the broken world of modernity and also portray the shapeless, twisted, tormented, and arrested psyche of modern man, of human experience trapped within a parenthesis, having no connection and hence "no exit."

These reflections on the law of continuity, on both its mobilizing presence and its enervating absence, seek to identify the plight that paralyzes modern life as it exists in a vacuum of disinheritance, for increasingly we are cut off from roots, uncentered, unconnected. Yet, these are not only reflections on but also painful reminders of our predicament, which, notably among the intelligentsia, is hardly even registered, much less resisted. Especially disturbing is the blank acceptance of our plight among those who are in a position of command and influence.

The idea of continuity, and in effect its fateful consequences, is a moral one. It is one that, to quote Joseph Conrad, shows "that for life to be large and full, it must contain the care of the past and of the future in every passing moment of the present." The legacy, or burden, of "care" is what we find cruelly ignored or refuted; what elicits little concern at a time of moral and spiritual drifting. If the idea of continuity is to have any meaning or impact in our individual and collective life, if it is to exert the vigorous and consolidative kind of discipline that emerges as a moral discipline, then there can be no détente with any point of view unredeemed by deeper principles and loyalties. Moral anarchies and cynicism invade our national life, taint our thinking, compromise our conduct, distort our character. It is a point of view that imposes, in its paradoxical way, a manifest conformity in our society and culture, an "orthodoxy of enlightenment" as it has been termed.

Today the spiritual, intellectual, and political condition of society is both static and solipsistic, lacking as it does a sense of coherence and unity, lacking, above all, the moral character that emerges from moral effort and struggle. Particularly in the intellectual community and in the educational realm, this condition discloses a deteriorating situation, a perverse and nihilistic radicalization that now absorbs and dictates contemporary sense and sensibility. The astonishing swiftness and the extensiveness of this process of deterioration, in all of its demonic vulgarity and barbarism, undoubtedly shows the diminished degree of resistance to the conditions that produce destruction, shaking foundations and scorning eternal values.

Clearly our social and cultural situation lies ensnared in the nets of deconstructionism, of fragmentation, of what José Ortega y Gasset prophetically called "extremism as a way of life." And clearly such a situation categorically rejects what Richard Weaver posits as an axiomatic principle of human existence: "While culture is not a worship and should not be made a worship, it is a kind of orienting of the mind toward a mood, a reverence for the spirit on secular occasions." Disorientation in the shape of spiritual collapse and mutation thus informs our "secular occasions" and gives answer to the terrible question that William Butler Yeats posed not long after the Great War: "And what rough beast, its hour come round at last, / Slouches towards Bethlehem to be born?" We need more than ever, then, to think as moral realists as we contemplate a disorientation that is spiritually barren. We need to arm ourselves with spiritual weapons and with spiritual disciplines of *logos* and *praxis* as we continue our mission, our struggle, our witness.

The preservation of our sacred patrimony requires tenacious commitment, for the struggle to retain even the semblance of a civilized world of dignity, reason, and order is unending. This struggle is ultimately a spiritual struggle for first and last principles, for the great spiritual possessions bequeathed to us by Athens, Rome, and Jerusalem which constitute our "entailed inheritances" and sacred tradition. This patrimony is our mainmast and we need to steer carefully. But how can we preserve and protect the great traditions of our patrimony? This is a question we must ask ourselves as we determine our responsibilities in the midst of the irreverence, the chaos, and the decadence that besiege modern life and its institutions.

No inventory of the epochal changes that have affected society and culture can ignore the *furor impius* that pitilessly ravages our spiritual foundations, our patrimony, and leads us further into "the kingdom of enmity." Surely it is a spiritual crisis, at a time when our link with origins has been forfeited, that should engage our most active concern. We must be ever on guard against the corrosive elements which, in Eric Voegelin's words, constitute an "incubus on the life of the spirit and intellect." A spiritual neutrality cancels itself out once it disregards the unifying idea of transcendence, of transcending permanencies and hierarchies. If we are to continue to combat a "metastatic faith," on which, to invoke Shakespeare, "incertainties now crown themselves assur'd," then it is with an armed spirituality that the conservator of "important things" should wage this fight. We must not forget that any reorientation of character and mind is finally tied to moral standards of permitted and forbidden action, irrevocably connected with and continuing principles of belief, truth, order, right rule, tradition.

Inevitably the nature and the quality of modern life register the changes that have altered human meaning and destiny in our time. Our society and culture mirror the dissipations that attend the breakdown of standards of value defining an ordered way of life. These are precisely the dissipations that Irving Babbitt, back in the 1920s and 1930s, diagnosed as the symptoms of what he termed "the disillusion of decadence," "free temperamental outflow," "the quicksands of relativity." And clearly these dissipations have multiplied as Americans have indiscriminately surrendered to utopists' dreams and millenarian illusions. "This tendency to put on sympathy a burden it cannot bear," to recall Babbitt's prophetic admonition, "and at the same time to sacrifice a truly human hierarchy and scale of values to the principle of equality has been especially marked in the democratic movement, nowhere more so perhaps than in our American Democracy." His words contain a truth that conditions today verify to a troubling degree. Anyone who bothers to reflect on them will see their direct relevance to the moral malaise which afflicts us. Indeed, all the signs of the crisis of modernism are etched in Babbitt's words.

It is altogether apparent that we have chosen to ignore a moral thinker like Babbitt. Instead, we have chosen to listen to "terrible simplifiers" and to pursue "strange gods" who promise to fulfill all our fantasies. Even as the present situation makes a mockery of these fantasies, we persist in ignoring the realities of our situation. We choose to scorn the "permanent things" that orient a higher human meaning and a higher spiritual order. The history of modern American society is one in which the idols of romanticism and the lures of sentimentalism muddle thought and vision and now bring us to the last frontier of the secular process, in which the modern age transforms into the New Age, as its evangels boastfully call it. The struggle between the dynamic of change and the principle of continuity is unending. "Let us guard with vigilance what we have received," Saint Athanasius counsels.

In our headlong pursuit of new beginnings we glorify "inventors of evil things," as Saint Paul describes them. The "permanent things," as the culmination and body of tradition, are shunted aside. Principles of unity and harmony are renounced as, more and more, we create a vacuum of disinheritance. Nowhere is this profane process better seen than in the debasement of modern art, language, and literature, in short, in nonoriented and nonorganic tendencies impervious to the opposition of good and evil. The results speak for themselves, as Aleksandr Solzhenitsyn has written: "In the twentieth century the necessary equilibrium between tradition and the search for the new has been repeatedly upset by a falsely understood 'avant-gardism'—a raucous, impatient 'avant-gardism' at any cost."

We have an ever-increasing need of leaders who heed the "voice of tradition" and accept "guidance from tradition," to use here John Henry Newman's phrases, and who point the way to rediscovering and restoring the place of tradition in contemporary life. Their task is neither simple nor enviable in a period of history when distrust of the past, of anything and anyone testifying to a sacred patrimony, is pervasive. Any defense of the merits of the idea of conservatorship is subject to attack; and anyone who ventures to defend the twin disciplines of continuity and tradition in contemporary life must have unusual courage. The word tradition joins other words of value and virtue now consigned to the postmodern dustbin, as the rewriting, restructuring, and reordering of human existence proceed at a furious pace. Hell-bent on creating the "new man" of a "traditionless future," we permit little room for dissent. And yet, if intellectual nullity characterizes a pervasive condition in the academy, it is certainly not one that should silence or deter us from accepting the special mandate Czeslaw Milosz defines in these words:

> Those who are alive receive a mandate from those who are silent forever. They can fulfill their duties only by trying to reconstruct precisely things as they were and by wresting the past from fictions and legends.

Acceptance of this mandate signifies a willingness to wrestle with the problem of overcoming the fear of the tyranny of the past and "the pathology of traditions." Jaroslav Pelikan rightly tells us, in his *The Vindication of Tradition* (1984), that we perceive a "living tradition" through "its capacity to develop while still maintaining its identity and continuity." But since we live in antinomian times, when lines of continuity are erased, and when any perception of tradition is finally controlled and regulated by the ruling ideology of change, it is tough to make a case for tradition. Inescapably, then, we have to confront the daunting power of a *Zeitgeist* posthistorical and postmodern in temper. As such, the case for tradition must contend with an age that instinctively rejects limitations and blurs boundaries of right and wrong.

The steady loss of a religious perspective in the general consciousness of our age further deepens this difficulty. We have become so accustomed to living in chaos that we are unable to discern even the smallest hints of tradition. Minimalism and trivialization can hardly command us to consider ultimate problems. The problem of tradition in contemporary life is inseparable from the larger "problem of tradition and modernization . . . [as] a fundamental part of the religious situation of modern times," to cite Paul Valliere's words from his excellent entry on tradition in *The Encyclopedia of Religion* (volume 15, 1987). Unless we begin to identify the spiritual emptiness of modernism, we cannot begin to profess the values of tradition which the late Austin Warren, revered American man of letters, designates in relation not only to one's role in "society visible and invisible" but also to one's distinct awareness that all we are we owe; that we do not, and cannot, begin *ab ovo* and *de ovo* but are heirs to a great inheritance of tradition and wisdom, represented in the West by our joint indebtedness to the Greek philosophers, the Hebrew prophets, and the Christian saints.

Only when we have acknowledged the truths of Warren's words will we begin to understand the place of tradition in contemporary life. An age that venerates "the march of things" enforces a collectivity of solipsisms, confusions, equivocations. These combine to become our prison of self-delusion, from which it is hard to flee. An entire generation of Americans is now at ease in such a prison, which makes it harder to argue the case of tradition.

The seductions of what William James calls the "great empirical movement" promulgate a philosophy of flux and multiplicity. Undeniably, the degree to which respect for tradition prevails is closely tied to the moral disposition of the people of that nation. In the absence or the repudiation of tradition the law of universal flux prevails and transforms human character. It seems that nothing remains sacred any longer, that nothing has abiding value, that nothing has permanence of meaning, that nothing is worthy of being handed over from age to age, and from generation to generation. Thus, where the memory of human and communal values has been wiped out, the continuous "partnership in all science, all art, every virtue" that Burke upholds becomes inoperable. The main stream has been cut off and its life-giving values have been blunted forever. "It is in that stream," Sir Gilbert Murray insists, "that we find our unity, unity of origin in the past, unity of movement and imagination in the present; to that stream that we owe our common memories and our power of understanding one another, despite the confusion of tongues that has now fallen upon us. . . . "

To be sure, no tradition is unchanging, and yet no change can occur without the *traditio* that gives it flesh and blood. Tradition is not some rigid orthodoxy or reductive uniformity. "Tradition is the living faith of the dead, traditionalism is the dead faith of the living," Pelikan reminds us. It is a sacred, living tradition that has been replaced by a soulless and gnostic modernism which accommodates every blasphemous abrogation of our metaphysical moorings, of the idea of the holy, of those worthy signs of continuity and community.

How are we to save the tradition that humanizes life, that undergirds the graces of civilization, that universalizes the virtues which define the sacredness of life? This is a question that we also have to answer, or at least to clarify at a time of history antagonistic to covenantal and metaphysical precepts. How are we to grapple with those powerful forces of modernism that are in ascendance and that seek to extirpate any transmission of a "deposit"? To identify the dangers of an imperial modernism, and of what happens when traditional foundations and moral determinants are eclipsed, is a demanding task. (Yet, too, the case for tradition cannot be trusted to political theorists and their agendas, or to proselytizing exponents of modern techniques, or to fomenters of "political illusion.") First, and above all, what we need to know is that, ultimately, the deeper and greater threats to tradition are embodied in the wearing down of standards and in meretricious changes. Once the leveling process takes shape it is difficult to arrest, and the rhythm of disintegration solidifies. Resistance to this insidious, destabilizing process requires constant and unyielding vigilance.

Though total and final dissolution is not inevitable, it may well come when public institutions and political leaders unilaterally embrace the sovereignty of might and power, at which point mankind will incarnate the terrors of Thomas Hobbes's "war of all against all" and Joseph de Maistre's "nothing is where it belongs." As the teachings and authority of tradition undergo devaluation, the "traditions of the antitraditionalists" surface to replace time-proven and time-honored values, even as the expansive appetites of modernist ideology leave less room for tradition or for its civilizing restraints.

As a product of a new ontology, the contemporary world represents the supreme reduction of modernism. In this process we behold the growing dissolution of man's moral substance and also of order of soul. A crisis in tradition, in these circumstances, has enormous implications for the order of society. Simone Weil detects the nature of these implications in the context of contemporary social life when she writes: "Nowadays, every attempt to turn men into brutes finds powerful means at its disposal." No words better record the disintegrative tempo of twentieth-century life "In this valley of dying stars / In this hollow valley / This broken jaw of our lost kingdoms," to quote T. S. Eliot's lines evoking spiritual dispossession and deracination. If any sense of order, in the face of the growing terror of disorder, is to be maintained then the case for tradition becomes all the more crucial in contemporary life and demands unyielding attention. Once the faculty of attention is engaged, the quality of effort is bound to assert itself and to have genuine effect, as Jacob Burckhardt reminds us when he declares: "Every people is incomplete and strives for completion, and the higher it stands, the more it strives."

~ 🔥 🔥 ~

A Bibliographical Note
and Acknowledgments

"The Moral Imagination" was first published under the title "The Faith of Men of Letters" in *The University Bookman* 5 (1987): 10-15.

"The Quest for Transcendence" first appeared as the introduction to *In Continuity: The Last Essays of Austin Warren*, edited by George A. Panichas (Macon GA: Mercer University Press, 1996) ix-xxv.

The first part of "A Few Reasonable Words" was published as the introduction to *A Few Reasonable Words* by Henry Regnery (Wilmington DE: Intercollegiate Studies Institute, 1996) xi-xxv.

"Man of Letters" was first published under the title "Russell Kirk as Man of Letters" in *The Intercollegiate Review* (Fall 1994): 9-17.

The preface was first published under the titles "In Continuity" and "The Case for Tradition: A Prefatory Note" in *Modern Age: A Quarterly Review* (Winter 1984): 4-8, and (Spring 1994): 212-16, respectively.

The following writings also originally appeared in *Modern Age*: "Everything Is Disequilibrium" under the titles "The Crisis of Modernism: An Introduction" (Summer/Fall 1987): 197-202, and "On Spiritual Disorder" (Winter 1996): 195-98; "The Woodstock in Ourselves" (Spring 1995): 194-99; "Beyond a Certain Point" under the title "Oklahoma City: 'Beyond a Certain Point . . . ' " (Fall 1995): 2-6; "The Eclipse of Excellence" (Summer 1993): 290-95; "Abettors of Irreverence" under the title "Incensing the Impudent" (Fall 1977): 424-28; "Apologists for Mediocrity" under the titles "Prefatory Notes from Old Deerfield" (Winter 1988): 4-8, and "Arresting Antitheses in Higher Education" (Summer 1985): 194-99; "Agents of Reductionism" (Fall 1984): 310-13; "Avatars of Betrayal" under the title "Hero Worship in Retrospect" (Summer/Fall 1986): 200-204; "Teacher and Critic" under the titles "Irving Babbitt and the Widening of the Circle" (Spring 1987): 164-71, and "An Act of Reparation" (Summer 1980): 296-303; the second part of "A Few Reasonable Words" under the title "Golden Moments" (Fall 1994): 78-83; "Sapiential Voices" (Winter 1997): 267-76; "A Corrective to Darkening Counsel" under the title "John W. Aldridge: A Corrective to Darkening Counsel" (Fall 1993): 73-79; "The Discipline of Criticism" (Summer 1994): 381-85; "Character and Criticism"

(Summer 1997): 286-90; "The Need for Leadership" under the title "Reflections on Leadership" (Fall 1996): 307-11; "After Ideology" under the title "To See Again the Stars" (Fall 1992): 61-65; "The Wrestlings of Soul" under the title "The World of Dostoevsky" (Fall 1978): 346-57; "Moral Discovery" under the title "Joseph Conrad's *The Secret Agent* as a Moral Tale" (Spring 1997): 143-52; "Spiritual Heroism" under the title "Aleksandr Solzhenitsyn: Hero of the Spirit" (Winter 1994): 178-83; "Orientation toward Something Higher" under the title "Irving Babbitt and Richard Weaver" (Summer 1996): 267-76; "The Courage to Go On" under the title "Growing Wings to Overcome Gravity" (Spring 1992): 194-202; "In Steady Ascension" under the title "Czeslaw Milosz and the Way Through" (Spring 1993): 195-203. "Advocates of Debasement," the third part of "A Few Reasonable Words," and "Keepers of the Flame" appear here for the first time.

For a generous grant to defray the costs of producing this book, I am grateful to Earhart Foundation.

I want to thank Dr. Robert Champ and Miss Mary E. Slayton for their probing examination of the entire text of this book. Their suggestions and changes have, I know, benefited its readability. Miss Slayton also prepared the index with her characteristic thoroughness and acuteness.

For encouraging me to press on with the task of completing the manuscript for publication, I am pleased to record here my debt to Marc A. Jolley, the assistant publisher of Mercer University Press.

Part one

The Crisis of Modernism

"Turning and Turning in the Widening Gyre"

1. The Abyss of Negations

Everything Is Disequilibrium

We fast approach the close of the twentieth century, and inevitably we begin to take measure of its triumphs and its tragedies. This is no simple or happy task, for the twentieth century can hardly expect to be marked as one of high civilization or of spiritual greatness. To be sure, in terms of technological attainments and material growth it has been a truly remarkable century of progress. But progress is never the last word when one stops to evaluate the spirit of a whole epoch. Clearly this has been a century in which dark and dangerous events have dominated our days, as political revolutions, ideological warfare, and totalitarian rule have led to human oppression on an unprecedented scale. The Great War of 1914–1918, the Great Depression of the late twenties and thirties, World War II, and devastating conflicts like Vietnam have brought on a tidal wave of death and destruction. The Holocaust, Hiroshima, the Gulag Archipelago variously specify the depth and the extent of this century's catastrophism, particularly as it has afflicted the order of history and the soul of humanity.

That no one is secure and that nothing is sacred are hard object lessons that this century has taught us. Traditions, values, certitudes, moral virtues and constants have steadily capitulated to the temple and worship of Juggernaut. Both the religious idea and spiritual meaning have fallen victims to an age in which sociopolitical upheavals and radical doctrines have indiscriminately multiplied. Any yearning for the harmony of things is often blasted by a world seething with change and increasingly having the character of violence, disorder, impiety. In the inner life, as in the outer life, prodigious transformations have occurred. The form and the spheres of civilization, in turn, have been altered, even devalued, as the "measure of man" has transformed into the "abolition of man."

A careful look at the symptoms of contemporary life and civilization may call to mind a prophetic utterance Simone Weil delivered more than fifty years ago: "We are living in a world in which nothing is made to man's measure; there exists a monstrous discrepancy between man's body, man's mind, and the things which at the present time constitute the elements of human existence; everything is disequilibrium." Her words go to the heart of those conditions that characterize the crisis of contemporary society. Indeed, no statement better images the secular and empirical dynamics of a world in which foundations have tottered than when Simone Weil also declares: "[O]ur present situation more or less resembles that of a party of absolutely ignorant travelers who find themselves in a motorcar launched at full speed and driverless across broken country."

Our present situation is, of course, the crisis of modernism. And this modernism, over the course of time and in the general consciousness of our age, has been an inclusive and unceasing process of secularization, of profanation and by extension the degradation of anything worthy of being held in reverence. Modernism, in fact, has moved beyond a defiance of men's moral and spiritual roots to assume a context and character all its own, no longer in reference to what has happened in the past, no longer simply against tradition, but completely cut off from the past, trapped in its own vacuum, its nonentity, its nothingness. The crisis of modernism finally transforms into its very plight, when beginnings have no endings and endings have no beginnings. As a consequence, the modern world has reached its last crisis—"it has reached," as Vàclav Havel remarks, "the limit of potential, the point beyond which the abyss begins." Thus, modern society is now confronted by the pitiful circumstance of having to piece together out of unrelated fragments those certainties and truths that are required for any civilized community to survive. This survival is ineradicably and ultimately joined to the urgent need for a return to traditional values, for a renewal of faith, for a new courage and a new transcendence. "The higher the ends," Aleksandr Solzhenitsyn reminds us in *The First Circle* (1968), "the higher must be the means! . . . Morality shouldn't lose its force as it increases its scope!"

For such a revitalization to succeed it is necessary not only to reflect on the crisis of modernism and all that this crisis entails and dramatizes, but also, in T. S. Eliot's words, to "have the strength to force the moment to its crisis." The process of reflection requires the examination of matters of utmost importance and at the same time of utmost judgment in the active context of critical discrimination and decision. It is to be hoped that this reflection will also induce what the ancient Hebrew prophets termed the "searchings of heart" and an eventual return to "the old paths" from which modern man has strayed. Undoubtedly such a contemplation will require the moral concentration and spiritual self-inspection that is at once disturbing, sobering, and yet illuminating. It cannot be otherwise when one is called on to examine matters that relate to the human condition, to human destiny, and to universal, ultimate questions.

That it will be necessary to enact the virtue of courage—"for the sake of what is noble, for that is the aim of virtue," as Aristotle asserts—is an axiomatic corollary of any critical scrutiny of the constituents and complexities of the crisis of modernism. If such a scrutiny contributes in any substantive way to the critical process of elucidation and adjudication, then its basic aim will have been entirely worthwhile. If it also serves to reawaken and reaffirm belief in the reality of human dignity and in the higher spiritual nature of life, then its larger purposes will have been gratifyingly achieved. Indeed, it will be no less gratifying if this effort also helps to diminish in any way a general reluctance to pursue pressing religious and philosophical questions that are germane to the long-range development of moral, intellectual, and authentic culture.

The diagnostic, censorial elements inherent in any inspection of the crisis of modernism are, admittedly, hard and even daunting. For some they will perhaps evoke Robert Frost's sonnet "Once by the Pacific" (1926), which ends with these troubling words:

It looked as if a night of dark intent
Was coming, and not only a night, an age.
Someone had better be prepared for rage.
There would be more than ocean-water broken
Before God's last *Put out the Light* was spoken.

These are prophetic lines that will also echo equally prophetic lines in poems like Matthew Arnold's "Dover Beach" and William Butler Yeats's "Second Coming." And in that echo—that same "terrifying echo" that E. M. Forster, in his novel *A Passage to India* (1924), memorably speaks of as the "ou-boum" of meaninglessness that afflicts life and the universe—we hear and recognize the peculiarly modern voice of fearful concern and of anguished apprehension. Inevitably Frost's words point to the problematic fate of modern man often described as waiting without hope and without faith. This is precisely the waiting to which Martin Heidegger assigns that peculiar terror of "a double Not: the No-more of the gods that have fled and the Not-yet of the god that is coming."

Poets, prophets, and priests of the modern age have been unusually consentient in describing the individuating conditions of modern civilization, "the ache of modernism," as Thomas Hardy described it. Many of the visual and aural images that one finds crystallizing in so much of modern life and letters render, and even define, those qualities that, cumulatively, contain the drama of the crisis of modernism. This drama is not one that is ineradicably bleak and hopeless, though bleakness and hopelessness are pervasive aspects of contemporary humanity that cannot be easily eradicated, as some existentialist thinkers have been at pains to show. It is a drama of human predicament that makes the crisis of modernism so uniquely frightening and revealing. In the end, it is a dynamic crisis that moves threateningly from one pole to another, from the "brave new world" to "the end of the modern era," as it has been described.

"All is possible. All is in doubt." These stark declarative sentences, as we often hear them quoted in discussions of modern existence, trenchantly tell us something about our condition and man's place in the modern world. They are sentences that easily (even if perhaps too neatly) capture the double rhythm of modern life, its faith and its faithlessness. They contain words, in fact, that etch the undulant movements of modern history and embody man's promise of greatness (the glory that is at the center of man's vision of possibility) and also man's experience of littleness (the horror that lingers in man's perception of his spiritual emptiness).

A transcendental supportive value system is largely nonexistent in a world in which the search after new and strange gods depicts modern man's unending yearnings. "Every truth we may think complete will prove itself untruth at the moment of shipwreck," Karl Jaspers contends. No words perhaps better capture the indissoluble contradictions of being or better point to the higher context of the measure of worth, the divine examples, that modern man has gradually lost or rejected. Dispossession, disinheritance, disorientation constitute a formidable pattern of the crisis of modernism and the consequential process of the desacralization of life. Our modernism, if only to affix here its fatal signature of power, persists in building its "crystal palace" and solidifying its "empire of might," the overarching symbols of a world that, in Eric Voegelin's terminology, is caught up in a "tension of existence" that reveals "the disorder of society" as "a disorder in the soul of its component parts."

Conditions of life and belief have been so swiftly and drastically altered in the twentieth century that it is now possible to comprehend only the basic framework of the crisis of modernism. "Faith dies and unfaith blossoms like a flower," Sophocles observed many centuries ago. If our crisis is in the end a crisis of unfaith, our comprehension of its full effects cannot at this disruptive and directionless stage of history be total, both because we are still active players in the drama of our modernism, and also because we are inadequately equipped to see life steadily and see it whole. The culture and the society that we have molded in the past five hundred years of a modernism in transition, as it were, preclude an organic sense of things that produces or nurtures either spiritual vision or harmony. Today even the wish to transform the rage that Robert Frost in his poem cruelly identifies often lacks metaphysical grounding in and the support of first principles.

In a very large sense the ongoing crisis of modernism must also remind us of the advanced stage of the perennial antagonism between what, in the early years of the twentieth century, T. E. Hulme, the critic and philosopher, identified as the opposing forces of "romanticism" and "classicism." Hulme's description of the two antagonists remains cogent and apt:

> Here is the root of all romanticism: that man, the individual, is an infinite reservoir of possibilities; and if you can so rearrange society by the destruction of oppressive order then these possibilities will have a chance and you will get Progress.

> One can define the classical clearly as the exact opposite to this. Man is an extraordinarily fixed and limited animal whose nature is absolutely constant. It is only by tradition and organization that anything decent can be got out of him.

The debate between those who counsel limitations and those who affirm possibilities is the debate between old enemies going back to the beginnings of human civilization. That debate now goes on with even more perilous implications, even as we now increasingly find that the modern house we have built, as Irving Babbitt declared more than a century ago, is "an immense and glittering superstructure on insecure foundations." Clearly the antagonisms Hulme depicts are much sharper and far more strident. It is the extreme degree and magnitude of the effects of the crisis of modernism that should concern us.

Richard Weaver, American visionary of order, helps us fathom the full shock of modernism in all its significance when he writes in *Ideas Have Consequences* (1948):

> The darkling plain, swept by alarms, which threatens to be the world of our future, is an arena in which conflicting ideas, numerous after the accumulation of centuries, are freed from the discipline imposed by ultimate conceptions. The decline is to confusion; we are agitated by sensation and look with wonder upon the serene somnambulistic creations of souls which had the metaphysical anchorage.

Weaver's words return us to earlier apocalyptic warnings voiced by D. H. Lawrence in his novel *Women in Love* (1920): "There is a phase in every race . . . when the desire for destruction overcomes every other desire." At the same time Weaver's words force us to look ahead to our present time and condition, to discern there a massive "crisis of consciousness in all spheres" that takes us even beyond chaos and confusion, even beyond modernism, to what is at once stasis and metastasis—to that entropic stage that Professor Thomas Molnar singles out when he writes: "Nothing has reference any more; the microcosm has been detached from the macrocosm, literature from myth, art from symbolization, science (gnosis) from sacred knowledge, astrology, alchemy."

The modern mind, as it becomes painfully more evident, scorns the law of measure and expels the transcendent virtues of order which are the mark of wisdom. Distrusting tangible things, the "permanent things," it pursues in unrelenting ways a "positivistic empiricism" and a "scientific materialism," avowing and legislating what the late philosopher Michael Polanyi speaks of as the "idea of unlimited progress, intensified to perfectionism, [which] has combined with our sharpened skepticism to produce the perilous state of the modern mind." The spiritual and moral effects of this orientation—a "fictitious orientation," in Ortega y Gasset's words—pervade the conditions of modern life.

The drama of the crisis of modernism accentuates *hubris* in all aspects of life, literature, and thought. "Without humility, all the virtues are finite," Simone Weil warns. "Only humility makes them infinite." But such a warning is often dismissed as irrelevant by the slavish purveyors of change. Theirs is a mentality that harbors what the Russian Orthodox philosopher N. O. Lossky, in a neglected but profound book, *The World as an Organic Whole* (1928), speaks of as "the ontological content of the kingdom of enmity": "The ultimate source of all the imperfections in the kingdom of enmity is the false purpose it sets before itself—the purpose of becoming the Absolute." Those who choose to live in such a kingdom represent, as Lossky further observes, the "exclusive self-affirmation of a dissentient being directed against the Absolute and the kingdom of the Spirit [and] is accompanied by exclusive self-affirmation of an infinite multitude of its own parts against one another."

Lossky prompts us here to turn our attention to the dual process of disconnection and dissolution that identifies some of the most alarming conditions of modern existence. The dialectical lures and joys of discontinuity in particular manifest the supertemporal directions, if not predispositions, of those in positions of leadership and influence who contribute to and shape the ethos of modern life. Such leadership often assumes the guise of enlightenment and formulates public policies and programs that encourage progress and growth and that conduct men and women on the path to a bigger and better society. For those who foment the doctrine of unlimited change and expansion—"pistol-shot transformations," as they have been imaged—discontinuity signifies infinite opportunity, "the wave of the future" that merges with "the wave of new technologies." An inescapable consequence is that in much of modern life, according to Father Stanley L. Jaki, a "mastering of the realm of quantities" is accompanied by the disappearance of a sense of higher aims and values. Not the principle of unity but the laws of multiplicity are those that are propagated unceasingly. And everywhere we find unchecked enthusiasms for the opportunities thrown up by discontinuity hurled in the faces of those who seek to preserve the discipline and traditions of continuity as a frontline defense against what Joseph Conrad discerns as "moral anarchies and cynicisms and betrayals."

But surely it is not Conrad's fears that are recorded these days, insofar as his fears are hardly viewed as being in the mainstream of things. And no matter where one turns one is confronted with the new creed of discontinuity, which, it is boasted, can turn established truths on their heads. Evidence of the promulgation of this creed of change and opportunity increasingly occupies center stage. Here let us take as a representative example a recent inaugural address to the 234th session of the Royal Society of Arts, delivered in London by its chairman of the council. It is not hard to discover in his address precisely the kind of rhetoric that seeks to move men to action but that also renounces "an ethics of rhetoric."

"I confess to finding discontinuity exciting," the new chairman declares. "It opens up new possibilities. The old order has to change. Older conditions no longer seem to count for much. What used to be insurmountable roadblocks are now only obstacles, to be removed or got round." He goes on to conclude with words that verge boldly on a kind of quasi-theological animadversion especially appropriate to a technologico-Benthamite world: "Discontinuous change, for me, is a great opportunity for that new life which alone makes death tolerable." These preceding comments, as quoted, underscore the sharp relevance of Weaver's censure of the "downward tendency" of words of "false or 'engineered' charisma"—words that "sound like the very gospel of one's society, but [that] in fact . . . betray us; they get us to do what the adversary of the human being wants us to do."

Irreverence, mediocrity, reductionism, debasement, betrayal dramatize the eclipse of excellence in both the cultural and spiritual realm. Increasingly we become prisoners of a culture of negations as mind and soul are made captive of a *Zeitgeist* that leads to the eclipse of excellence in its social, cultural, moral, and religious forms: those very forms that make for humane civilization and that push things up to their first principles, to evoke the words of John Henry Newman. Not only the creators of art but also the social and cultural directors of contemporary sensibility submit to a downward slide when they cease, as Solzhenitsyn notes, "to hold dear the great cultural tradition of the foregoing centuries together with the spiritual foundations from which it grew . . . [thereby] contributing to a highly dangerous fall of the human spirit on earth, to a degeneration of mankind into some kind of lower state, closer to the animal world."

~ ❧ ❧ ~

Negations finally attain their ultimate and most negative form in the spirit of nihilism, which pervades so much of modern existence. An unusually brave and discerning commentator on this happening is Eugene (Father Seraphim) Rose, whose extraordinary book, *Nihilism: The Root of Revolution of the Modern Age* (1994), examines the fatal ingredients of nihilism from an Eastern Orthodox perspective. To speak of an Orthodox Christian perspective is to speak of *the* Orthodox patristic standard of spiritual life as it was defined by the Greek, or Eastern, Fathers, "the Fathers of the Church," by such spiritual giants as Athanasius, Basil the Great, Gregory of Nyssa, John Chrysostom, Gregory Palamas. Saint Basil, in a letter to the Evaisenians, encouraging them not to be misled by the dogmatic and political vagaries of the time, evokes precisely this Orthodox patristic standard when he writes about "A Church pure and untouched by the harshness of our times . . . a Church that has preserved the apostolic doctrine unadulterated and inviolate"—a Church, in short, that refuses to accommodate faith "according to changing events."

The exposition and commentation of this little tract, a tract for our time, revolve around his contention that "there is no longer any point of orientation." Father Seraphim (1934–1982) was to share this concern, it should be noted, with other exemplary religious commentators like Josef Pieper, Etienne Gilson, Jean Daniélou, Henri de Lubac, and Max Picard. Indeed, he regarded Pieper's *End of Time* (1954) as being "in no essential point at variance with Orthodox tradition." No less than these commentators, whom he read and admired, Father Seraphim saw that the "multiplication of false Christs and false Antichrists" in modern life led to the emergence of those he called "Nihilists" whose goal was to enact "the annihilation of Divine Revelation and the preparation of a new order in which there shall be no trace of the 'old' view of things, in which Man shall be the only god there is."

This tract delineates with a concision matched by brilliance the different stages of the nihilistic dialectic, both symptoms and consequences. And its author judges them in terms of what he calls "the clear light of the Orthodox Christian Truth." The Orthodox dimension of Father Seraphim's findings, and one that identifies the special and intrinsic strength and interest of *Nihilism*, is that modern man cannot begin to experience any spiritual renewal until he is first aware of the apostasy of his age. In this respect, Father Seraphim goes beyond a general recognition of the antinomian features of modern society by also directly and specifically indicting the mentality and faults of apostasy in the infernal forms of rebellious departures from and renunciations of the order and principles of faith. Liberalism, realism, vitalism, and the nihilism of destruction comprise for him the various stages and shapes of the spirit and theology of nihilism. In powerful and fearless words, not unworthy of language employed by Dostoevsky in his monumental novels, Father Seraphim graphically pinpoints a

> Nihilist universe, in which there is neither up nor down, right nor wrong, true nor false. . . . Where there was once God, there is now nothing; where there were once authority, order, certainty, faith, there are now anarchy, confusion, arbitrary and unprincipled action, doubt and despair. . . . A subtle intelligence lies behind these phenomena, and on an intricate plan which philosopher and revolutionary alike merely serve and do not command; we have to do with the work of Satan.

Actually, *Nihilism* is the only completed part of a massive work that Father Seraphim first conceived of writing in the early 1960s on "the spiritual condition of man today." He had made this decision just at the time that he was abandoning a career in the academic world, which he found to be an intellectual sham and spiritually barren, in order to follow a Christian vocation. "To be a 'philosopher'—not a 'professional' or 'academic' philosopher," he wrote prophetically in his journal at the end of 1960, "but a man for whom to live is to *think*—means to suffer greatly. . . . " The big book that Father Seraphim wanted to write was originally entitled *Pseudo-Religion and the Modern Age*, and subsequently became *The Kingdom of Man and the Kingdom of God*, a title, interestingly, which echoes the "Kingdom of Enmity," and the "Kingdom of Spirit" depicted in Lossky's *The World as an Organic Whole*. In this book he hoped to examine modernist errors from an Orthodox Christian viewpoint, or as Father Seraphim wrote in 1961: "It is in the Orthodox Christian East alone, then, that is to be found the whole standard wherewith to measure the denial of Christian Truth that is modernism." At this time, it should be remembered, he had recently been introduced to the Russian Orthodox Church but had not as yet entered "the heart of hearts" sacramentally.

Father Seraphim never finished *The Kingdom of Man and the Kingdom of God*, though he had compiled thousands of pages of material in the form of handwritten notes and outlines. Of the fourteen chapters planned for his magnum opus the only one that was typed in its completed form was the seventh chapter, on the philosophy of nihilism, now published as *Nihilism*. The book itself, once written, would have been a diagnosis of modernism in the context of the schism of the soul. "The true crisis is now," he wrote, "as it has ever been, within us. . . . " This crisis, he said, echoing here the Church Fathers, signaled the negation of faith as the "assent" of the soul. In both the nihilistic dialectic and the nihilistic program he discerned the progressive destruction of assent, a process he describes trenchantly in these words:

> In the Nihilist "new earth" all human energy is to be devoted to worldly concerns; the whole human environment and every object in it are to serve the cause of "production" and to remind men that their only happiness lies in this world; there is to be established, in fact, the absolute despotism of worldliness.

In reading *Nihilism* we are reminded of what happens to human life on both a personal and a collective level when the assent of the soul is transmogrified. Given that Father Seraphim never completed his proposed book, this fragment constitutes a prolegomenon of nihilism; it is a frank, uncompromising piece of writing; and for those who have eyes to see and minds to understand, it is a work of exceptional metaphysical value. It abounds with wisdom and insight of a deep spiritual character, and has an aphoristic power that augments arduous and steady reflection. There is not a sentence, not a paragraph, that will not give spiritual shock, that will not induce meditation even on the part of some readers who, now the slaves of "psychocentrism" and "subjectivism," will at first find its inherently Orthodox concepts and principles alien to the modern consciousness, but who, pulled by the purity and sincerity of Father Seraphim's religious-philosophical thought, will come to appreciate its *askesis* and respect its Christian truths. The tenor of this tract is urgent and prophetic, and recalls these words of Christ: "I have yet many things to say to you, but you cannot bear them now" (John 16:12). Style and content have here their anchor in the "enduring things," and communicate clarity, vigor, and, above all, a powerful simplicity and focus. An intuitive spiritual concern lies at the center of this tract, as Father Seraphim identifies the lawlessness, the disorder and dissolution, of modern civilization—those terrifying signs and repercussions of what Saint Paul depicts as "the secret forces of wickedness [that] are at work."

At the end of all nihilism, Father Seraphim warns, lies the abyss, realm of all errors, which signifies the death of God and the death of the soul. The nihilist, insofar as he has "faith in nothing," believes that ultimate questions can have no answers. For the nihilist there is no possibility of spiritual illumination. And for the nihilist mentality, in effect, there is no standard of truth since its gospel is the absolute absence of the absolute. Nothing has value, nothing has meaning, everything is subject to the laws of change and multiplicity. The end-stage of nihilism is the nihilism of destruction, which Father Seraphim contends is unique to the modern age because of its willed doctrine and program of destruction. Indeed, nihilism becomes a faith, to be more exact, which Father Seraphim sees in terms of exclusively "antitheistic" assumptions and aims:

> It is an attitude of dissatisfaction with self, with the world, with society, with God; it knows but one thing: *that it will not accept things as they are,* but must devote its energies either to changing them or fleeing from them.

The breakdown that Father Seraphim sees as being symptomatic of present-day conditions emerges directly from the rebelliousness and the defiance that are the benchmarks of the "kingdom of man in the modern age."

Nihilism manifests itself as an inclusive revolution that seeks to radicalize not only the existing sociopolitical order but also the spiritual and moral order of life. Father Seraphim sees nihilist rebellion as having entered deeply into the fibre of the age and from which nothing is exempt. It reduces and finally invalidates the spiritual meaning of life by systematically annihilating the foundations of all authority and tradition. Often this process begins with the promise of "reinterpretation" and "revaluation" and ends with utter destruction. "Unprincipled politics and morality," he writes, "Undisciplined artistic expression, indiscriminate 'religious experience'—all are the direct consequence of the application to once stable sciences and disciplines of the attitude of rebellion." Nihilism, then, is a relentless, unrepentant process, a total rebellion no less menacing in its aims than the waging of total war itself. Its goals are clearly defined, programmatic, unconditional: "A-humanity" and "sub-humanism" constitute the new conditions of human existence—of the "new order" and the "new man."

The nihilism of the modern age exists in each one of us, according to Father Seraphim, and to understand and to resist its effects one must have the revealed truth and faith, which are precisely two things attacked and destroyed by nihilism. To circumscribe the nature or the success of nihilism in modern times, he believed, one must first discern its satanic energies: "Nihilism is, most profoundly, a spiritual disorder, and it can be overcome only by spiritual means; and there has been no attempt whatever in the contemporary world to apply such means." These are brave words at a time when some liberal ideologues are occasionally rattled by the nihilist infections they themselves have nurtured. Clearly, the annihilation of religious and spiritual principles of order persists, while dissident protests are rejected. Aleksandr Solzhenitsyn's mockers in the press, for example, can still be seen doing their utmost to slander his demand that we "subordinate our interests to moral criteria" and return to the "religious idea." We seem to accommodate every nihilist impulse as it erupts. We choose to ascribe each new act of irreverence and irresponsibility to those external conditions that have not as yet been reformed by "terrible simplifiers" and "social engineers."

Perhaps it is not too much or too late to hope, even in the closing hours of the twentieth century, that Father Seraphim's portrayal of the powers of nihilism will encourage us *not* to sit and wait for the final catastrophe. Perhaps his words will call out to our suffering and patience in which the Divine resides and inspire us to take the path that lies "beyond nihilism." We can, of course, reject this call, but the results, as Father Seraphim warns, will be severe and lasting: "Nothing less than Hell is worthy of man, if he be not worthy of Heaven."

The harmonious confluence of the life of the spirit and the life of the mind characterizes an important dimension of Father Seraphim's contribution. And, surely, we must now number him among "the called and the chosen" of the twentieth century—those great spiritual witnesses who believe that the highest value is the sacred and that no temporal power or tyranny can destroy it: for example, Edith Stein, Simone Weil, Dietrich Bonhoeffer. But what particularly distinguishes Father Seraphim's lifework from the others is its brave and steadfast exposition of the Orthodox Christian perspective, one not always clearly perceived, or understood, or appreciated, in the West. Father Seraphim, it should be stressed, read widely and deeply in the writings of Russian Orthodox thinkers of the nineteenth and twentieth century for he saw them actively engaged with "the problem of religion." "It was their conviction," to recall Father Georges Florovsky's apt words, "that human life without faith is a perilous adventure which is bound to end in disaster. Man without God cannot remain truly human; he sinks and decomposes." For Father Seraphim this decomposition summed up the plight of modern existence and was the prelude to "the worship of nothingness" that he saw as the embodiment of the spiritual disorder at the very center of the crisis of modernism.

~ 🕊 🕊 ~

But negations need not signify the last stage of the human condition in our time. There is a human destiny that reaches beyond negations. The final emphasis is the possibility of moral and spiritual recovery. There is an upward way, or path, that can still be taken, and that can defeat the mechanisms of negation—of ruin. Ascent and transcendence are a dual moral process that can defeat the forces of negation; that can, in ways which sometimes remain unexplored, uncharted, and unploughed, prevail over the crisis of modernism even as it accelerates; that, in short, can provide criteria of redemption in a broken world. The need to recognize the full force of the negations for what they are must, to be sure, precede the need to refuse to surrender to or accept the conditions of negation, and, indeed, to struggle against them with courage of faith. Viable pathways do survive even in the chaos of contemporary life if one looks hard enough for them and is willing to climb towards higher meanings.

The "imperial overreach of the modern age," as it is termed, need not discourage or thwart moral effort and aspiration. We can still oppose the kind of stagnation that not only makes the crisis of modernism even more dangerous, but also makes us far more empty and assailable in our encounters with its negations. The way of negation culminates in the desolation, the lassitude, the resignation, the fatality that now bring us close to the edge of moral darkness and annihilation. Voegelin rightly equates the way of negation with a madness of spirit and with the madness we call modernism. There is, there must be, another, even if hidden, way that we can enter and that demands of us the kind of moral effort that leads to the way of affirmation, which is also the way through. Finding this way at a time when the might of negations is oppressive and afflictive is not easy. For negation is, in a sense, concomitant with the affliction which, inseparable and yet distinct from physical suffering, turns its victims into things, possesses and marks the soul with slavery, to cite Simone Weil's words. "Affliction contains the truth about our condition," she stresses. To discern this truth is tantamount to discerning the extremities of profane life.

It is necessary first to face the reality of our condition, our negation, our affliction, and then go beyond it. Moral discovery and moral restoration are not as inaccessible or unattainable as the powers and principalities of negation would have us think. For even in the midst of what Voegelin calls "the incredible spectaculum of modernity" there do exist, in their infinite mystery and nobility, possibilities of renewal that would enable us not only to erase the marks of our slavery but also to acquire spiritual vision and, like the blind man of Christ's miracle, again to "see men as trees, walking."

If negation is seen as a strong and significant part of contemporary life, there can also be seen, and affirmed, dignity of life and the value of human conscience. This point of view draws its main source of strength and inspiration, its critical lessons, from models of belief that have abiding validity and order. Grace and deliverance reside in these paradigms for those who are brave enough to pursue higher goals. This double emphasis falls on the need to affirm the greater possibilities of human existence and, in turn, on the belief that the general crisis of modernism one encounters in the new barbarism which engulfs and diminishes human meaning does not conclusively subvert or make obsolete what the ancients spoke of as the first principles of things. Standards of affirmation, which inevitably collide with the massive social disorder and spiritual affliction of the modern world, are in our time neither commanding in authority nor dominant in persuasion. Hence it is all the more necessary to keep them alive and vibrant, bestowing as they do the full reward of the long ascent, the supreme struggle, the nobler vision, the great transcendence. In and through these paradigms we experience the moral and spiritual transfiguration that comes from growing wings to overcome gravity.

The Woodstock in Ourselves

Events which most occupy our attention, and to which our national newspapers and magazines devote endless columns of print and pictures, and which are also the main subjects of discussion in the electronic media, have a way of telling us a great deal about ourselves and our civilization. Clearly, we reveal ourselves through what we choose to celebrate. We can hardly hide from the hard evidence that discloses the condition of the American soul and the republic. This evidence makes known not only our inner and outer condition, but also our desires and aspirations. August 1994 was to mark the twenty-fifth anniversary of Woodstock, a three-day celebration and reunion held simultaneously in Saugerties, New York, and featuring a megaconcert by some fifty rock bands and superstars screaming such songs as "Feeling All Right" and "A Little Help From My Friends"—performers and spectators seeking, of course, to make Woodstock II as "meaningful" as Woodstock I, though lacking now the issue of a Vietnam War. Almost 300,000 persons were in attendance during this event commemorating the original event in 1969, held in Bethel, New York, about fifty miles northeast of Saugerties. From all accounts, Woodstock 1994 was no less a spectacle than Woodstock 1969. Some commentators described this Woodstock as a "festival" when, as one announcer on stage declared, "The sun is in our hearts." Organizers of the event went so far as to claim that, "If there is anything that comes out of this, it's a reaffirmation of the human spirit."

Those who came to celebrate the new Woodstock were mostly young white men and women, of college and even high school age, the males shirtless, the females often topless, and sometimes with painted breasts. They were out en masse for a weekend party of drink, drugs, intimate physical contact, voyeurism, anything that, according to one participant, would "relieve the animal instinct." Even some nostalgic parents, veterans of Woodstock I, accompanied their sons and daughters, so as to present, one could presume, a united front against any standard that smacks of decorum, orthodoxy, civilizing reticences, even if this kind of unanimity meant acceptance of the new-old mud, trash, stench, and chaos. No doubt the mood of the festival was dampened a bit by the round of meetings of Alcoholics Anonymous and Narcotics Anonymous that went on. The consequences of license and irresponsibility are always hard to escape even in the midst of pagan rites epitomized by the picture of a young man with the words "Give Me Your Drugs" painted on his chest. Defiance and shamelessness, it is almost unnecessary to add here, characterized Woodstock 1994, with the music and songs enacting taboo impulses detailed thusly in one reporter's account ("Special to the *New York Times*"):

> murderous feelings, polymorphous sex—in music that kept shifting, from hard funk and rock to lounge-band vamps to Latin polyrhythms. For spectacle . . . a sexualized rock-and-roll circus, complete with acrobatics on a rope, topless simulated Lesbian coupling and a baton twirler with a flaming baton.

No further descriptive detail is really needed here. Enough has already been given in the preceding paragraphs to acquaint nonparticipants with bizarre happenings at Woodstock 1994. Indeed, these happenings personify tendencies and habits of what is now becoming accepted practice in American society and culture, on television and radio, in movies, in books and magazines, in athletic events, in classrooms, in city streets, and even in some religious sanctuaries. Woodstock II is merely emblematic, an overarching symbol, to use the literary term, of conditions that are rampant in the American scene at the end of the twentieth century and that show to us just how far we have drifted since Woodstock I. Its fantasticality is in fact now the stuff of contemporary fiction, with its endless violence and depravity, its freaks and misfits. What was most striking visually about Woodstock were the neopagan forms that reigned: libertinism, eroticism, cult acts in modern dress. Those who attended Woodstock, in short, were enacting the rejection of those norms, checks, conventions, and traditions that foster civilization. What we heard in the music rendered by bands like the "Nine Inch Nails," "Metallica," "Aerosmith," and what we saw in the actions of couples who danced or romped in pits of mud, was derision of first principles and of the permanent things. The New Age and Woodstock are ultimately synonymous in meaning: a total disregard of standards of life or belief or conduct that restrain emotions, appetite, behavior. In short, unlimited rights, not duties, embody the meaning of Woodstock and its discontents.

Woodstock represents still another adventure in consciousness for moderns, free from any inner check or law. Woodstock 1994, in this respect, augurs that final phase in the modern age when romanticism slips into nihilism; when an old morality gives way to a new morality fashioned by "terrible simplifiers" promising a terrestrial paradise. Indeed, unlike the paleopagans who worshipped strange gods by offering up to them gifts and prayers, the neopagans at Woodstock are mired in nothingness and personify nothingness. One young university student, drawn by "the power of the Woodstock name," put it in a nutshell when she confessed: "Most of us are looking for something we know we're not going to find here. But we know we've got to look." Even to look at some of the photographs of nearly nude and muddied bodies, with fists shaking, voices snarling, feet pounding, the picture is of a collective and common act of dissolution. The most recent Woodstock celebrators showed no visible awareness of being either in a terrestrial paradise or in a paradise of snakes. They seem to have been caught up in the wave of the future envisioned by Marxist-Leninist ideologues who now thrive in academe. These are precisely the ideologues who sire the kind of denizens who tyrannized Saugerties, New York.

There was a futuristic quality about Woodstock-*meta*-Woodstock—a modern postmodern quality defying rational explanation. What is especially interesting is that Woodstock II had been much covered in the press and television, and treated as simply another routine happening in the larger American experience. Except for a few dissident sermons from the pulpit, little direct criticism was focused on it, and few if any value judgments were ventured. No one in a position of leadership and influence seemed to want to say anything about what Woodstock really signifies, what it tells us about American civilization, what dark and menacing signs it sends to us about ourselves. Certainly no moral assessment of the Woodstock phenomenon was even attempted, as if to underline the utter absence of any courage of judgment. The *New York Times*, for example, devoted a short editorial to the event, but it ignored its larger, deeper, and disturbing ramifications. Here is the concluding paragraph from that editorial, "Woodstock, Not Quite Redux":

> The music is darker than that of Woodstock I, the dancing rougher, but so are the times. In the end, the 300,000 young people who slogged through Woodstock '94 got exactly what they came for: the reenactment of a ritual whose mythology they were raised on; the grueling endurance contest with nature, and the bragging rights that come along with having survived them.

We, of course, have often encountered the cavalier attitude and the permissive tone found in the editorial through these many, many years, as conditions have worsened. Indeed, the editorial's martial and athletic images can neither mask the liberal attitude nor hide from a discerning reader the fact that no amount of linguistic cleverness can finally remove from our concern the deeper meaning of Woodstock. What the muddled

editorial refused to recognize was that Woodstock II glorifies "the enemies of the permanent things"; that it elevates its symbolic elements to
art form, no matter how raucous and disordered these are; that it panders
to its mythic reveries and folklore without one iota of discrimination;
that, in the end, it accepts what Woodstock was and is, and the conditions and circumstances that breed Woodstocks. The editorial failed to tell
us that Woodstock, as festival and pilgrimage, immanentized a modern-
day tribalism, with its own special ceremonies, ritual, language, music,
garb; its false gospel of illusion, magic, sexuality, autotherapy; its liberating agenda of dissoluteness and disorder in the name of majoritarian democracy. The editorial failed even to hint that a Woodstock contains the
potential for wiping away all vestiges of the ethical and the moral life.

Back in 1945, the Swiss philosopher and writer Max Picard warned
that there is a "Hitler in ourselves," in the course of pointing out that
Nazism was a consequence of a prevailing spiritual malaise found in the
general crisis of modernism. Something of the same can be said of
Woodstock in more recent social and cultural history within which
modern man continually defines and shapes himself, his nature, his
special conditions and purposes. Woodstock, seen in this context,
represents a destructive process, not militarily as in the case of the Nazi
development, but materially and spiritually, affecting both the inner and
outer essence of human life. This is what makes the Woodstock phenomenon so menacing and destructive. It is the barbaric tendencies that
Woodstock conceals and that pose an incalculable threat to the order of
civilization, to humanity. Woodstock, as such, reminds us that this order
of civilization is always vulnerable to the whirl of the world, always
fragile and always open to attack by antinomian forces that lurk just
below the veneer of human existence. Diabolism, in its religious context,
identifies destructive forces and urges that invade the human heart and
soul and seek to destroy the unity of life and the moral sense. Woodstock, the *Times* editorial notwithstanding, is a form of contemporary
diabolism assaulting modern consciousness. Those who try to dismiss its
lethal symptoms refuse in effect to see man as a symbolizing animal, the
animal symbolicum the philosopher Ernst Cassirer so acutely examined in
his writings.

Through symbolic forms we gain clues to the nature of man and his
civilization. And man, as Cassirer insisted, lives in a symbolic universe,
of which language, myth, art, and religion are integral parts. Symbolic
thought and symbolic behavior, as such, are characteristic features of
human life and ultimately help to identify man's hopes, wants, ambitions,
doubts, fears, illusions, disillusions, as well as to help one perceive man's

metaphysical capacity and direction. We need to interpret carefully man's symbolic forms in order to understand man's condition and his destiny: to see what he is thinking, what he desires. We thus gain insight into man's conscious and unconscious life, as well as into human history and culture. Examined along these particular lines, Woodstock 1994 is a cultural dynamic that helps to explain important aspects of modern social life in all of its tensions. Woodstock is representative of rage, anger, cynicism, distrust, in short, absolute hatred of order and civilization. It is a primal convulsion in a late twentieth-century shape, defiant of all constraints. It expresses a yearning to break free of prejudice and prescription, and to rush headlong into a realm that some thinkers regard as an open society but one that, in reality, seethes with intemperance and decomposition. Liberal and radical ideologues routinely equate this yearning with the creative impulse and the vital instinct, and hence with the life force of possibility, chance, diversity.

In the actions at Woodstock we can spot the abnormity of an age which, as T. S. Eliot observes, "advances progressively backwards." Even the insistent habit of the young today to wear their baseball hats backwards is emblematic of the deconstruction of human life to its elemental force. ("We have entered a stylistic postmodern wilderness," the designer Bill Blass reminds us, "where there is little to guide us in how we dress for weddings, parties, funerals, work, or the opera.") Woodstock epitomizes the negation of the standards of a civilized society and the derision of the general sense. Its naturalism, primitivism, emotionalism are representative of all those tendencies in American life that contain the seeds of social and moral breakdown. Woodstock is thus far more than contemporary spectacle. It is still another reminder that paganism is never dead, that "the triumph of Rousseau" in the modern world is inescapable, that disintegration is always present as a sign of social and spiritual disorder. Above all, Woodstock celebrates the impiety which is at the very center of the creed of modernity and of the new principles replacing first principles in the New Age.

These days we hear much from our "enlightened" social scientists about the "Hitler Youth" movement and its important function in Nazi ideology. We are told that the immersion of German youth in a nationalistic romanticism and the superiority of Germanic ethnic vitality was prelude to "the making of a storm trooper." We are also told that the Nazi system of education was nothing more than a "school for barbarians" in which "adventure in power" and "realism of conquest" were main concerns. Even though not politically organized, and obviously lacking the coherent doctrine and discipline of Hitler's Youth, the

Woodstock Generation, then and now, exhibits attitudes and actions that are no less threatening to a civilized society. The uniforms may be different but some of the motives and gestures are confluent, particularly when one examines the outward elements of eros, irrationalism, violence, and frenzy embraced by a youth culture in search of a new dynamic and a new social order. In this respect the distance from the Third Reich to the New Age is not as far as we like to believe. In a century of disorder, the "Hitler in ourselves" inevitably assumes new guises. Today, Woodstock habits and practices harden in the curriculum of American secondary schools, colleges and universities, as a growing number of gauleiters grab control of education and proceed to terrorize classroom and text. "Whoever has the youth," to recall Adolf Hitler's words, "has the future." Woodstock is certainly not something to be dismissed as some inconsequential episode of "rock music, the generation's signature art form." In Woodstock we see the unfolding crisis of modernity in all of its horror.

Some commentators have even noted elements of modern religious drama in Woodstock. The inclination, however, is to approve these religious elements in terms of religion as a "Life Force," as an immanent and not a transcendent religion. What these commentators do not note is that in this crassly secular religion we see both the "flight from God" and the "eclipse of God." For what we witness at Woodstock is religion spilling over into, and reduced to, orgy, sentiment, reverie, magic, savagery. This is a contemporary form of "Dynamic Religion" that Henri Bergson sees as breaking free from tradition, custom, creed. Here we have, then, all the ingredients of a phenomenal naturalism which, in Irving Babbitt's words, "exalts the unconscious at the expense of moral choice and conscious deliberation." Woodstock thus also emphasizes that Judaeo-Christianity did not conclusively defeat paganism. And the celebrators at Woodstock can be seen as acting out heresy, as they proclaim a new era of the man-god in ways even more perverse and profane than Dostoevsky's Titans. Ultimately the antimoral dimension of Woodstock helps us to gauge the serious dangers it poses for Americans preparing to enter the twenty-first century. Woodstock portrays a reversion to magical and primal religion—a rudimentary religion of instinct that liberates one from all ethical and moral standards and that, in effect, advises one that nothing is dangerous, or wrong, or sinful—that any spontaneous urge, however flagrant, is acceptable. Values and virtues vanish in Woodstock, and in ourselves, as do all distinctions between the sacred and the profane, between the clean and the unclean, between inhibitions and prohibitions, between right and wrong, between order and disorder.

That Woodstock, as the epitome of inspirations in present-day America, should trouble our conscience, is something that is relegated to silence. We do not want to talk about matters that require moral reflection and judgment. We choose to view the spectacle of a Woodstock as yet another example of social diversity in action. Clearly a blunting of critical intelligence and of the faculty of discrimination has been accomplished by the evangels of egalitarianism and by hucksters who promote a subliterate society. We seem to be woefully unaware of the symbolization of a Woodstock and what it discloses about the life of the soul and the life of the republic in our time. We are pressed either to avoid distinctions and definitions or to reduce them to a common denominator and function. Attention to important things and meanings is another silenced faculty. "It is a humble and hackneyed truth," Ortega y Gasset reminds us, "that in order to see one must look and in order to look one must pay attention." In short, the critical faculty as a whole has been subordinated to that utopian collectivist system that, in Russell Kirk's words, sentences us to a "colorless mediocrity and monotony in the world, an emptiness of heart, a penury of the imagination."

In the meanwhile, as the tide of barbarism swells, the true meaning of Woodstock excites little moral concern or critique. It seems we persist in living in that state of blankness now widely prescribed by our intellectuals, educators, and leaders. Things that should ordinarily dismay us are seen as unimportant, trivial. We scoff at any act of veneration, and we exalt any sin. We become blind to symbolic truths and to the perils that lurk beneath appearances. Our moral response is perhaps the most serious casualty of the spirit of our time, making us impervious to our condition of shipwreck. Unable to respond critically or morally to a Woodstock, and to everything it stands for, we perpetuate the structure of life we have been furiously fashioning in this technologico-Benthamite century. Woodstock, in the end, creates our spiritual emptiness, our social disorientation, our moral obtuseness. Surely there is far more to Woodstock than just an introduction to "Woodstock's Children," who are perceived by one supercilious commentator in the following way: "For its young majority, Woodstock '94 signaled a sense of hope, that some Edenic magic could be passed on to a generation that looks forward only to pointless jobs and polluted terrain." Here, in a single sentence, is the tendency, as always, to romanticize and to politicize a disorder symbol like Woodstock. Nothing could be more fatal to the character of human civilization—or more favorable to "the abolition of man."

The phenomenon of Woodstock depicts in a most frightening way the huge distance needed to "ascend the ladder of virtues" and yet our willingness to wallow in the abyss of negations.

Beyond a Certain Point

The April 19, 1995, bombing of the Federal Building in Oklahoma City was an action showing extremism at its most dastardly point. It tells us a great deal about sociopolitical conditions in this country and about the existence of dangerous forces above and below ground—angry, hostile, aggressive, seditious in behavior and attitude. The direct consequences of this foul mood at Oklahoma City were fatal in terms of many innocent lives snuffed out in the explosion. The reasons for the bombing will continue to engage commentators, and many theories will continue to be advanced. For the president of the United States, the explosion was a direct result of an ugly political climate manipulated by "purveyors of hatred and division." He especially singled out "reckless speech" heard regularly on the nation's air waves. Indeed, perhaps alluding to Richard M. Weaver's *Ideas Have Consequences*, the president also said that "People should examine the consequences of what they say and the kinds of emotions they're trying to inflame." Liberal publicists in the press and on television, often agreeing with the president, pointed the finger not only at conservative talk-show hosts but also at the majority leader of the Senate and the House speaker.

It is symptomatic of the terrorism in Oklahoma City that assessing blame inevitably returns to political axioms. The political mandate, once again, becomes the exclusive concern in matters of national urgency. We turn everything into a political arena, where discussion of acute public issues is but another offshoot of political deliberation to be converted eventually into political advantage. From top to bottom we are obsessed with the political—as discussion, as action, as policy, or as solution. There is nothing in the present situation that is not assigned a dominant political value or given a distinct political identity. The economic problem, the philosophical problem, the religious problem are absorbed by the political problem. We avoid diverting our attention from the exclusively political. All is politics and politics is all: that is the upshot of our perception of what constitutes the life of the citizenry.

In assessing matters affecting general conditions of life, we do not stray from the political axis. For many Americans, the political mind becomes the captive mind; and nothing could be more crippling to the national character. In effect we assess thorny issues, however profound, without due discernment, remaining as we do, as in the wake of the Oklahoma City bombing, in a political mind-set. We remain, that is to say, in the realm of life and thought progressively fashioned by the "terrible simplifiers" who promise us the fulfillment of all our dreams and longings and illusions, but whose promises are laden with deceits that fan disillusionment and cynicism, from which emerge the seeds of rebellion against God and man. Their legacy dictates conditions of life and thought and value judgments. Reactions to the Oklahoma City bombing, in the end, reflect in most telling ways the reductionism of the American mind through imposed uniformity and orthodoxy of the life of the mind. This is what we have come to, so sadly and swiftly, in these last years of the twentieth century: that we have made the political element the exclusive nexus of cause and effect; that political agendas now shape the new morality and the new saviors; that the exclusiveness of the political overrules all other considerations and principles of action and understanding; that the final arbiters of opinion are the political exclusivists who have no special affection for or loyalty to first principles or for wisdom and prudence; who, in short, furiously worship at the altar of specious ideologies.

This is not to say, of course, that what political partisans may see in common as an inordinate increase in violence through, for example, the unchecked proliferation of weapons among the populace, does not have validity; or that poverty, homelessness, unemployment, inequality, and injustice do not incite civil unrest and upheaval. (Visual squalor, as one architectural critic thus instances, gives rise to social disorder, even as any look at our urban problems will ratify.) There are, to be sure, external circumstances and conditions that do require effective social and political prescriptions in one way or another. But it is extremism, which has many faces, to believe in the sovereignty of the political, or to insist that only political measures can settle vexing problems which affect the polity. Excessive reliance on political dynamics too often blinds us to moral principles and judgments. As political ideologies have intensified in recent years, we have systematically separated moral and spiritual criteria from their proper place in civic life and political discourse, in our conduct and attitude, in ourselves and in our nation.

Insofar as we persist in practicing a politics of separation from the "permanent things," we choose to ignore the deeper metaphysical essences that can help us more fully understand the wider ramifications of an event like the bombing in Oklahoma City. Such an understanding would enable us to transcend political categories and to assess more

realistically causes and effects. It would also tell us far more about our
spiritual condition, taking us beyond what is immediate, transparent, and
ultimately exterior. It would tell us much, in fact, about the ascendant
rhythm of political disconnection from metaphysical moorings—and, in
the total picture, the outcome of this disconnection. It would compel us
to contemplate sociopolitical exigencies in the metaphysical context of
Dostoevsky's belief that political causes of incendiarism are to be found
not in the roofs of houses, but in the minds of men. We should start, in
other words, assessing an awful event like that in Oklahoma City not
alone in its political manifestations but in its metaphysical resonances. On
a much larger and more inclusive scale, then, we need to see just how
moral malaise frequently concludes in acts of moral anarchy. Here
precisely we will find the real clues to political incendiarism—to the
underlying factors that ignite the hatred and viciousness embodied in the
bombing of a federal building. No amount of legislation to preclude such
terrorism will in the end resolve the problem unless we are willing to
study both the exterior and interior facets of the human world—unless,
that is, we are one with Emerson when he declares, "Let a man learn to
look for the permanent in the mutable and fleeting. . . . " That we have
ignored Emerson's advice to see things in their eternal scheme defines the
limits of our modernism; gives to it its one-dimensional semblance; and
finally places human meaning and aspiration at the mercy of the
exclusively political.

Reactions to the bombing in Oklahoma City underline the inability,
witnessed on a national scale, to judge our predicament and its causes in
their comprehensiveness. And insofar as we have, at every level of
American civilization, sought to erase religious and spiritual absolutes,
as these impinge on and help fathom human actions, we choose to deny
the transcendent. We have been so much formed by a new secular orthodoxy, and so eager to create a new age, that we have pushed ourselves
more and more into ideological dead ends. And as critical intelligence has
been fragmented, and as human sensibility itself has become uncentered
by the absence of any personal and communal standards, we have seen
the unchecked growth of cultural anarchy and a collective pattern of
nihilism. Our sacred patrimony, both logocentric and Eurocentric in its
traditions and acceptances, has been steadily dissolving, removed and
replaced by a bold presentism that denies the sacred. The religious idea
and discipline are now everywhere under assault, derided in the academy, in the newspapers, in books of fiction and nonfiction, in the enter-
tainment industry, in the electronics media, and even in some religious
institutions. The blasting of tradition goes on without letup, with impiety

surging everywhere. Sensationalism, violence, and moral depravity become the daily tutors of young and old alike, as human meaning and humane values are cheapened. Could D. H. Lawrence be right when he declares that "There is a phase in every race . . . when the desire for destruction overcomes every other desire"?

Our world today updates the world of Franz Kafka, with its grotesqueness, negations, allegations, alienation, absurdity; as Kafka himself wrote of the terrors of the human condition: "Beyond a certain point there is no return." The bombing in Oklahoma City underlines this "beyond a certain point" to which American society and culture has now arrived. It is troubling even to contemplate the degree of destructiveness that we have reached in these twilight years of the twentieth century. But when we carefully study the sociopolitical process that has led us to this juncture in our history—a process that typifies the transvaluation of values in its peculiarly American version—we should not be surprised in the least by what is transpiring before us, about us and upon us.

It seems all too painfully clear from the response to the bomb outrage in Oklahoma City that we refrain from going to the bottom of facts and motives. We choose, from the president on down, to make comfortable assumptions and to refuse to scrutinize our value system and beliefs. We seem to be snared by an easy secular faith in the exclusively political. Our unceasing dream of an American Eden blinds us to the wider dimensions of the grave problems that now wrack us and that culminate in the bomb outrage in Oklahoma City, which becomes a kind of objective correlative of our sins of omission and commission in a century that has been dragged down by evangels of relativism—in short, by forces and creeds that conclude in anarchy and nihilism. Indeed, in our analyses of the happenings in Oklahoma City, we have confessed freely to an extreme sense of the immediate. In effect we scorn the historical sense, the metaphysical truths, the long view, or as Confucius avers: "The man who does not take far views will have near troubles."

Our ironclad preoccupation with social action and reform seems to leave very little room for any other viable considerations. Placing, for instance, "morality ahead of politics" (in Václav Havel's words) is not politically acceptable. But in ignoring the moral element in interpreting our present plight we reveal, once again, indifference to the life and order of the soul. This indifference, as we embrace and practice it, contributes not only to disorder in the soul but also, inevitably, to disorder in society. Oklahoma City embodies the dire consequences of this twin disorder. "If our souls are disordered," Russell Kirk reminds us, "we fall into abnormality, unable to control our impulses. If our commonwealth is disordered, we fall into anarchy, every man's hand against every other man's." These are words that should, in fact, have been on the president's lips when he talked about events in Oklahoma City, but he and many others in positions of leadership and influence chose to go the way of ideology—and ideology, as Kirk also cautions us, "means servitude to political dogmas."

In every aspect of American civilization, then, what we see in abundance is a brazen dismantling of things sacred. This dismantling has been doing immense damage to the ways in which we gauge matters of importance, such as interpreting and understanding the conduct of a people and the character of a nation in direct relation to our "encounters with nothingness," as in Oklahoma City. Moral concern and habit steadily wane in our midst, and the results become evident in a general failure to discern fundamental wrongs in ourselves and in our country. As we proceed to discard moral and spiritual standards we also lower our expectations of personal and collective life. Clearly the need for standards is tantamount to the need for order; and to attain this joint need requires exemplars, paradigms, texts, acceptations, values, traditions. In the past, this need has been fulfilled by a venerable patrimony, as recorded and defined by our Judaeo-Christian ethos and sacred texts. Modern ideologies have been cruelly supplanting both the patrimony and the texts, thus creating a vacuum that lacks spiritual substance. "In the city," as the Statesman-Prophet of Holiness Isaiah declares, "is left desolation, and the gate is smitten with destruction." Such defilement, the Hebrew prophet goes on to say, takes place when men and women "have transgressed the laws, changed the ordinances, broken the everlasting covenant" (24:5, 12). No words better capture the enormous consequences of what happens when we refuse to measure social and political phenomena by higher moral standards; in short, when we allow ourselves to be ruled by what is called "the absolute despotism of worldliness."

Until we begin to perceive that spiritual disorder in the form of nihilist doctrines and anarchic acts can also be overcome by spiritual means, the possibility of both individual and national renewal necessarily evaporates. Oklahoma City emblematizes in the most murderous way what happens, and will no doubt continue to happen, when we refuse to return to the known but forgotten things, the moral law, to which the major Hebrew prophets recall us. When our leaders persist in seeing the great historical crises of contemporary life in purely political (and politically correct) terms, we become even more aware of how far American civilization has withdrawn from the basic texts and truths of our sacred patrimony. Any civilization, ancient or modern, which persists in traveling on the path of moral apathy and irresponsibility, dictates its own destruction.

No bomb outrage committed by *agents provocateurs* will be easily forgotten or forgiven as long as the voice of conscience is able to speak out. But at the same time, we cannot ignore what the initial response to the bombing has ultimately disclosed, in its representativeness, and as symptom and portent of spiritual lethargy at the higher levels of governance and the shaping of public opinion. The president's response, in particular, was to show how the political mind (and method) denies an "enduring scale of values" by seeking "to account for everything in terms of time and place," to quote here Irving Babbitt's phraseology. In his response, and others like it, we see more than just another example of the steady deterioration of public discourse. We discern, that is, habits and attitudes fearful of unearthing some of the deeper causes of disorder in American society and culture.

Oklahoma City—everything that preceded the disaster, the disaster itself, and its aftermath—has a dramatic way of reminding any thinking person that our vision of order must in the end be our burden of vision. It cannot be any other way if the soul and the community, God and man are to have vital connection. Not to recognize the primacy of this connection is to invite catastrophism ad infinitum. "Moral and social order, or a vast part of it," Russell Kirk states at the conclusion of *The Roots of American Order* (1974), "may be destroyed by a few decades of contemptuous neglect. Then hope is lost, for many generations: for order is a kind of organic growth, developing over many centuries; it cannot be created by public proclamation." Our political chiefs would do well to ponder Kirk's warning, if any retrieval of the truth of order is still possible at a time when the aberrations and antinomies of our situation indicate just how precariously the people and the leadership of this nation have wandered into no-man's-land, to suffer there the full and final negation that awaits "beyond a certain point."

The Eclipse of Excellence

Excellence, which can be defined as the state of excelling and of surpassing merit, is now still another lost word of the English language. And increasingly the special qualities that this word denotes are banned in a nation which imposes diversity and political correctness. Today it is dangerously incriminating for one to cite or endorse these words as spoken back in the seventeenth century by Bishop Joseph Butler, English theologian and moral philosopher: "Superior excellence of any kind . . . is the object of awe and reverence to all creatures." We are now rarely urged to follow paths to excellence, no more than we are expected to revere standards of excellence. Both the idea and the act of excellence are relegated to the élitism that "terrible simplifiers" seek to erase from life. In consequence, it is also a word that one hardly or ever encounters on a metaphysical level of discussion. If excellence is noticed at all, as in the world of athletes, of entertainers, and of college and university administrators, it generally has a commercial and empirical significance. Spiritual and noetic elements of excellence are simply not recognized in this Age of the New Barbarians.

Excellence predicates aspiration and transcendence, a quest for a higher quality of attainment and, in effect, going beyond the moment—overcoming gravity, so to speak. Excellence asserts a straining motion and movement upwards and has an inherently metaphysical value, captured in one of its Greek equivalents, *aretē*. Excellence presupposes intellectual, moral, and spiritual ascent; and ascent specifies growth and development by dint of effort and commitment. Excellence means meeting difficulties and overcoming obstacles in the context of the Socratic dictum that without labor nothing prospers. It is not some commodity to be readily bought and sold, or something to be broken down and parceled out—or that which is continually reshaped, redefined, reinterpreted, recycled.

Even those brave enough to broach the subject of excellence tend almost automatically to fuse the pursuit of excellence with the pursuit of equality. The question posed by the subtitle of John W. Gardner's book, *Excellence: Can We Be Equal and Excellent Too?* (1984), underlines a pervasive disposition to blur the absolutes of excellence in one-dimensional relation to social engineering. Clearly excellence needs ardent champions willing to defend the exclusivity of both the concept and the word, if excellence is to be saved from quantitative and sociopolitical machinations and reductionisms. Ancient and modern thinkers like Plato and Irving Babbitt, not Jeremy Bentham and John Dewey, should be our guides in how we gain excellence in the human personality and civilization. Excellence is ultimately the approximation of greatness, neither diluted by sentimental and secular considerations, nor defiled by even small surrenders to the lures of utopian schemes. Without excellence there can be no greatness in life. At that point when excellence as an absolute surrenders to the fiats of the social sciences and the whims of the behaviorists—and becomes politicized, ideologized, gnosticized— excellence is no longer a real and great virtue. And when this transformation occurs on an individual and also on a collective level, the trivializing process ensues. Thus we insist on pluralistic alternatives to excellence and in this insistence we elevate the power of equality by sanctioning any tendency that reduces things to a single common equation.

The displacement of the idea of excellence also marks the implacable attack on all absolutes in the modern world. This displacement is part of an insidious pattern of attrition in which a new faith proper to the New Age is coming to the fore. Today the prevailing focus on diversity, multiculturalism, and deconstructionism embodies not only the continuing erasure of excellence as an absolute, but also the ongoing destruction of the kingdom of the spirit. Demonic ideologies, as these have rapidly developed in modern times, and especially as these are embodied in Marxism-Leninism and its contemporary surrogates and dogmata *in extremis*, have systematically contributed to a general breakdown of civilization. Excellence as an absolute and standard inevitably disappears in such a situation. The quest for excellence, no less than the principles of excellence, is confused with commonality and the religion of the average. Indeed, what we keep on seeing is a vulgarization of excellence at all levels. The line of mediocrity that Alexis de Tocqueville, in his *Democracy in America* (1835–1839), described in these troubling words has no end: "Almost all salient characteristics are obliterated to make room for something average, less high and less low, less brilliant and less dim, than what the world had before."

In a sense the very process of excellence has now been reversed by bringing its discipline and meaning downward so as to make things easier. As such, excellence is absorbed by sociopolitical programs and eventually remolded for popular consumption and instant gratification. Education that, above all, should speak for the discipline and attainment of excellence now surrenders almost blindly to broad social agenda in public schools—from education on sex and AIDS to the distribution of condoms in classrooms to discussions of gay and lesbian families. Everywhere, and at all levels, aspirations are quantified as concepts of the inherent value of Western culture and traditions are methodically attacked and destroyed, particularly in American colleges and universities—even at Yale, where, according to a disenchanted dean, education becomes a "mutual massage between liberal students and professors," the slothful habits of which become contagious and pervasive. Inevitably the triumph of mass-man contravenes all appeals to intellectual and spiritual excellence in the name of a "new morality," which Ortega y Gasset, more than sixty years ago, prophetically discerned when he wrote: "When people talk of the 'new morality' they are only committing a new immorality and looking for the easiest way of introducing contraband goods."

But how can standards of excellence survive, one must ask, when in fact the cabinet of the president of the United States, in its very composition, must accommodate the idea of diversity and quota systems? Our obligations to excellence are thus dismissed in the highest echelons of political leadership, with all the disturbing ramifications and consequences. It seems that we choose not only to encourage uniformity but also to legislate it in the name of the politics of inclusion. Inevitably, then, along with the word *excellence*, the word *civilization*—insofar as these two words exemplify a process that is interactive and interdependent—seems to be departing from our lexicon, yet another victim of the law of numbers and the drive to reduce things to the common denominator of numbers. Excellence, it can be further claimed, is an intrinsic aspect of morality, or a moral code and law, which now decomposes into the amorality of an egalitarian society concocted by Whitmanesque fantasies. Civilization, in these circumstances, erodes as is evidenced in the decadent cultural situation in which we presently find ourselves mired and from which a future generation emerges in those grim contexts that Ortega perceives: "For it is evident that in the long run the new type of human being now dominant in the world was born out of these defects and insufficiencies." How all this affects our economic position, present and future, is an issue that one fears to contemplate. Excellence clearly presupposes the givens of a defining discipline and centrality, of an intellectual, moral, and spiritual aristocracy that utopists endlessly chasing after a new social order reject. That some religious leaders now join this chorus of rejection instances still another diminishment of excellence in its spiritual character. What has happened to the discipline of ritual, let alone the idea of the holy and the great traditions of faith and order, is another area one also fears to contemplate in contemporary forms of religion.

Belief in excellence, both hierarchical and hieratic, is a major casualty of the whole process of adulteration now going on from top to bottom. Excellence is certainly not a heart-word among us when we stop to view the types of personalities and situations that the electronics media celebrate ad infinitum; or the kinds of books that are published and glowingly reviewed in our national newspapers and journals; or the heroes and heroines that our cultural dictators portray in an Elvis Presley or in a Madonna and Jane Fonda. Even the annual presentation of the Academy Awards all too often instances a mere sideshow for the promotion of cult figures. And even Nobel prize winners in literature and MacArthur "genius" recipients must first satisfy the requirements of diversity and political relevance, not excellence.

Vulgarism, trivialization, mediocrity are idols we enshrine as we follow every road except the one to excellence. And this is the very same road, as the tough lessons of history teach us, that Russia after the 1917 revolution traveled, to its final peril and perdition. Communism, as Václav Havel has said, "was an attempt, on the basis of a few propositions masquerading as the only scientific truth, to organize all life according to a single model, and to subject it to central planning and control regardless of whether or not that was what life wanted." We easily forget, then, that the bankruptcy of the Soviet system was from the very beginning rooted in the expulsion of all "things that are more excellent," to recall Saint Paul's words.

To forget that standards of excellence and standards of discrimination are mutually necessary and reciprocal is to invite the devaluations and deconstructions that now steadily erode society and culture, as well as human character and conscience. To disengage moral excellence from individual and national life further underlines our failings. Interestingly, but not surprisingly, entries on "excellence" do not appear in our most famous encyclopedias, including even the *Dictionary of the History of Ideas*. We speak proudly, too, of epochal periods of history such as the Age of Chivalry or the Age of Aquarius. But we do not venture to invoke a quintessential Age of Excellence.

Obviously we prefer to assign excellence to some manipulative category rather than to accept its absolute and primary essences. Like loyalty or piety or honesty, excellence is treated as a secondary word, a secondary idea, not worthy of the highest attention or designation, as our modern champions of relativism persist in degrading excellence in an era of systems, institutions, mechanisms, and statistical averages. Too often, therefore, excellence becomes a purely politicized and nominal word: a word to be subordinated to the law of change and the deceptions of left-leaning innovators and revisionists. We refuse to acknowledge excellence as a transcendent and enduring word of value and virtue. In short, it is a word that "the enemies of the permanent things" scorn precisely because they can neither recognize nor satisfy any standards of measure.

The enormous disasters that accompany the crisis of modernism in which we find ourselves variously illustrate the fate of excellence in the contemporary world. We are conditioned from every social direction and by every agency of leadership and governance to kneel to obscene technological and utilitarian schemes concocted by calculating radicals and tradition-hating ideologues. They seek to determine our every pattern of existence and to goad us to travel the roads to worldly bigness. Their experiments all too often lead to mediocrity and false universals endemic to a pseudoliberalism that reigns in this land and that ordains a monolithic state of mind antagonistic to excellence in the best critical and creative sense. We exhibit, as Aleksandr Solzhenitsyn says, "a stubborn tendency to grow not higher but to the side, not toward the highest achievements of craftsmanship but toward their disintegration into a frantic and insidious 'novelty.' "

A word like "excellence" underlines discrimination of value and attenuation of contrasts. An age that preaches equality and the notion of rights, without limit or restraint or criterion, can be no defender or conservator of the idea of excellence. In the name of pluralism and egalitarianism, we are exhorted to hunt down and kill excellence in any form and at all levels of individual and national life. Toleration itself becomes toleration of the average that culminates in a mindless uniformity. And as we further deconstruct excellence we engender the common denominator. We brutalize by collectivizing the "visionary gleam," which is the stuff of the creative life of excellence. Nothing else leads more quickly or more fatally to the extinction of civilization itself. Ascent and transcendence, the two central foundations of excellence, are infrequently encouraged. Paradigms of excellence, with classical and biblical origins, are everywhere being expunged from human memory. Excellence, with its individuating order and categories, can hardly be in tune with the generic tendencies and habits of a postmodern world. The life of excellence thus becomes a victim of the "bad metaphysics" of "new dealers" (to use Edmund Burke's phrases) who take us down the road to disaster by discarding first principles, including the principle of excellence.

That excellence means an irreducible process whereby obstacles and difficulties are to be confronted and overcome is something foreign to those who wave the banner of illusion. Excellence as an impersonal, transcendent, disinterested faculty and value is therefore to be scorned by architects of the Great Society. The collapse of the idea of excellence, it can be said, has been commensurate with the downslide of ethical, moral, and spiritual standards. We no longer hold anyone to some standard of conduct or accomplishment. We no longer believe that anyone should be expected to rise to a standard. Standards of excellence are steadily and systematically deflated at all levels, especially in education, where the dislodgment of the core curriculum has reached the point of absurdity. Education that is subservient to the general will invites endless drifting and confusion in the forms of unsound humanitarianism and majoritarian standardization. It invites, in short, the "decadent imperialism" that Babbitt trenchantly diagnosed in his *Democracy and Leadership* (1924).

Today, teachers of excellence like Irving Babbitt, Richard Weaver, and Russell Kirk are generally ignored or derided as the American populace en masse surrenders to the siren song of the shams who mold public opinion and policy. At one time known as "People of Action," Americans are now being cajoled to become the "Children of the Rainbow" who have the capacity to appreciate everything and anything without distinguishing between good and bad, order and disorder, obligations and rights, the sacred and the profane. This perverse contraction is one of the most disquieting symptoms of what has happened to the idea of excellence planted in critical and selective principles of thought and judgment.

By destroying standards we destroy excellence. The grim manifestations of this destructive process are inescapable to judge by our preoccupation with the daily spectacle of the grotesque, the ugly, and the corrupt. Endless columns in the nation's newspapers, great and small, glorify the trivial and inane when, for example, they show obsessive concern with late-night television personalities and the war of the networks to capture larger audiences by installing "a signature star, the likes we have not seen at this network in years," to quote a president of CBS Broadcast Group. Book reviewers, defying all critical standards and decency, shamelessly and endlessly discuss the unexpurgated journals of the novelist Anaïs Nin, bearing the title *Incest* (1992), in which she carries on, *ad nauseam*, with her extramarital affairs with Henry Miller, with the actor and director Antonin Artaud, with her analyst René Allendy—and, yes, with her own father, the Spanish composer Joaquín Nin, about whom she writes that he was her "evil Double," "the lion, the jungle king, the most virile man I have known." In the meanwhile, investigative reporters, both in the press and on television, lavish extraordinary attention on aberrant episodes in the lives of the British Royal family and of Woody Allen and his longtime lady, Mia Farrow.

Violence, decadence, perversion, impiety—those most cruel and ugly emblems of the disorder of soul—constitute our major celebratory occasions, with hardly one reference allowed to the life of excellence. These occasions embody the very movement and history, as well as the temper and tone, of our time, beginning with World War I, which inaugurated "the first darkness" of the twentieth century, or to recall here the words of the then British Secretary of State for Foreign Affairs, Sir Edward Grey: "The lamps are going out all over Europe; we shall not see them lit again in our lifetime." Surely those were monstrous years, 1914–1918, unleashing unthinkable physical terrors and moral disorder that now relentlessly conspire to push us into a New Time, a New Life, a New Age—into still another darkness.

Alas we travel on many roads—but not on the "good path," and certainly not the path to excellence. To travel on such a path requires spiritual strenuousness in an age given over to sloppiness in all facets of life. Our paths are now the wide roads of speed with no better destination than acquiring material power and enjoying vivid thrills. There is no halt to either our Titanism or our dreams of building new superstructures in an era when, to apply Ralph Waldo Emerson's words, "Things are in the saddle, / And ride mankind." The path to excellence signifies purpose and effort; a measure of accomplishment, a course of action, a line of conduct, a way of life. It entails rigorous self-searching, self-discovery, and self-understanding. This path, with its sometimes steep climbs and sudden turns and twists, is the path to edification and true enlightenment.

Instead we choose, as our present condition makes so undeniably evident, to travel on the great modern roads of our master builders, as we simultaneously chase after strange gods who assail the super-excellence of the transcendental, the supernatural, the spiritual order. Our world is burdened with an army of the agents of disarray. In the pages immediately following, we identify them and their work: the abettors of irreverence, the apologists for mediocrity, the agents of reductionism, the advocates of debasement, the avatars of betrayal. This is a world in which gravity reigns heavily. It is also a world in which life cloaks itself in the eclipse of excellence.

2. The "Terrible Simplifiers"

Abettors of Irreverence

The yearning for an earthly paradise, like hope itself, springs eternal in the human breast. Of this yearning we have no end of examples. A peculiarly American version is to be found in Morris Dickstein's *Gates of Eden: American Culture in the Sixties* (1977; repr. 1997). As with all utopian aspirations, *Gates of Eden* needs to be approached correctively. It needs, that is, to be judged in the light of critical standards that it smugly replaces with excesses instinctive to the liberal bent: romanticism, enthusiasm, sentimentality, reducibility. To read *Gates of Eden* without a counteragent, as it were, is to sacrifice historical and ultimately moral perspective, to enhance the barbarism of which this book is a sign. *Gates of Eden* proffers an ethos that gains in respectability and that also helps to define a prevailing orthodoxy of enlightenment. Generally such a phenomenon goes unchallenged precisely because the liberal power centers today are ascendant and frequently unassailable. That opponents of liberal doctrines are increasingly treated as outlaws is now a daily fact of existence in our "great society."

Hopefully, the special concern and approach of *Gates of Eden*, a sympathetic delineation of American cultural developments and changes in the 1960s, should embolden any discriminating critic—who rejects the premises and opinions, the superiorities, that pass for thought in this book—to speak out. If resistance to the cultural indiscipline and sloppiness that *Gates of Eden* ultimately salutes means that one will find oneself consigned to the status of outlaw, then it should be a welcome fate to one who refuses to acquiesce to or join the kind of cultural gangsterism that pushes and shoves its way through the pages of this book and euphemistically equates with healthful "shifts of sensibility."

Professor Dickstein seeks to apply to his coverage of "the sixties experience" the principles and methodology of literary criticism. Any hope that he has of legitimizing his aims, through his appeal to the disinterested pursuit of criticism, must finally totter. For as one reads on in his book, the realization dawns that Dickstein's position as a literary critic is a masquerade. Indeed, his critical sympathies, choices, judgments, and emphases are as misleading as are their equivalents in present-day tinsel journalism and in the electronic media. Which is to say that *Gates of Eden* cannot be trusted. What makes this book suspect is that Dickstein endows the 1960s with an epochal quality yet to be ascertained. Like the contemporary writers whom he lavishly, if not slavishly, examines, Dickstein is a hostage of everything that goes under the name of social and political relevance. And, interestingly, though an avowed enemy of classicism, he yearns to give classical standing to writers whose worth remains untested and unproved. Perhaps it should be said straight out that the writers selected for such pious attention in *Gates of Eden* are talented upstarts of the third rank.

The problem with Dickstein's approach is that he neither perceives nor asserts centralizing critical standards. For him there are no clear-cut criteria differentiating between religious and political impulse; between social justice and social chaos; between Shakespeare and Allen Ginsberg, literature and the movies, Beethoven and rock: in short, between civilization and barbarism. His main critical standard is the standardization enforced by an unprincipled cultural pluralism. Slogans, not moral values, are what finally characterize and trivialize Dickstein's cultural orientation and biases. His view of culture is ultimately dependent on the laws of flux and change, on the spectacle of immediacy. With delighted irreverence he makes declarations like the following:

> The public appetite for sexual display has certainly not abated, and it's hard to imagine returning to the moralism and hypocrisy that preceded the sixties. One of the healthier things we learned in the sixties, and are unlikely to forget, was to be more skeptical of the pose of authority.

> Like so much of what emerged from the sixties, fiction today is a lesson in the use of liberation. Whatever their results . . . , they remain superior to a return to the old stringent modes, which conservative pundits are always ready to impose.

These statements are an index to the workings of Dickstein's mind and the inner terrain of his psyche, even as they epitomize the spirit of radicalism that the 1960s unleashed. For Dickstein, and for the gurus of revolution ranging from Ginsberg to C. Wright Mills to Paul Goodman to Herbert Marcuse to Norman O. Brown, liberation is an obsessional word in their vocabulary of "alternative action." But for the state of American culture the unconditional stress on liberation has meant chaos on every level of life and behavior, in the arts, in politics, in education, even in religion.

What makes *Gates of Eden* especially depressing reading is its blurring of values, its sanctimonious twists and turns of mind, its sanctification of persons and forces that will in the end be seen as being of inferior significance. Simply put, Dickstein's thesis and text dignify mediocrity; and mediocrity, as Admiral Hyman G. Rickover once publicly warned, "excuses itself as the normal and healthy state of mankind." Even when he stops (with pained regret) to point out shortcomings in their attainments, Dickstein tenaciously insists on parading before us the achievements of Bob Dylan, the Beatles, and the Rolling Stones; of Thomas Pynchon, John Barth, Donald Barthelme, Eldridge Cleaver, and James Alan McPherson.

Far from being an attempt to assess critically "American culture in the sixties," *Gates of Eden* disintegrates into an oppressive arrogance at one with and loyal to the often neurotic, at times paranoiac, and always destructive goal of the 1960s: the "demystification of authority." As such Dickstein's criticism is as spurious as the cultural bastardization that he so obviously admires and endorses. And as such the subject of his book must be approached as a contemporary form of diabolism. Yet perhaps we should be grateful to have *Gates of Eden* if only to identify the impelling nature of the destructive urge. It should help us to understand the considerable and dissimilating strength of the enemies of cultural stability and order. And it should warn us against cultural barbarians. For those who have had even the slightest illusion about the meaning of the 1960s, this book should serve as a strong antidote.

Throughout, Dickstein discloses a consistent and predictable belief in the Rousseauistic reformation of man and society: in the New Eden, the New Age, the New World, the New Man. "Utopian hopes may be disappointed but can rarely be forgotten," he writes, eulogistically, in his concluding paragraph. "The gates of Eden, which beckoned to a whole generation in many guises, still glimmer in the distance like Kafka's castle, unapproachable and unavoidable." This is surely another blatantly epitomizing hyperliberalism: the quintessence of the dreams and fantasies that will gradually be seen to have been so much at the center of the cultural manifestations of the 1960s. The critical process, pace Dickstein, is not the spinning of fairy tales. Nor is it a surrender to gut feelings, to a transmuting parochialism and volatility, which, in *Gates of Eden*, assume such a grandiose, false credence. Criticism is courage of judgment, and of judgment that rigorously separates good from bad, right from wrong, appearance from reality. The critical act transposes into a discretive act of rejection. When seen in this light, Dickstein's book is not so much a view of culture as it is an apology for anticulture. It revolves around temporal standards. It glorifies a phase of American culture that comprised an ugly and consuming sophism. It approves the wanton forms of the emotional state: self-assertiveness, self-gratification, self-seeking. In a word it lacks, it negates, the discipline of self-transcendence, which liberal ideologues perennially seek to displace. *Gates of Eden* affirms the generic marks and concomitants of this displacement.

Liberal affirmations must not be allowed to go unexamined, without some substantive return to models, norms, standards, rooted in the history and tradition that Dickstein and his cronies renounce. We need to be urgently reminded that the true critical function entails judgmental rejection in a corrective sense. The spirit of adventurous, radical innovation cannot be permitted to be self-regulating. At every step of the way it needs to be questioned, scrutinized, checked, in the absence of which positive critical austerities the results can be perilous. *Gates of Eden* is a dire example of the need for critical correctives; its literacy and cultural proclamations (liberally stamped by the *un*critical spirit of the 1960s) are not to be treated as autarchic entities belonging to some sacred realm. The pseudoreligious terminology that intersperses *Gates of Eden* instances a contemporary species of blasphemy.

That man is subject to limitations; that his world is finite and that his accomplishments belong, in turn, to a temporal order; that his destiny is tragic; that he must always struggle with and against his "imperial self"—these are some of the corrective catechisms that a *Gates of Eden* cannot hide, nor hide from, without distorting all human meaning. The fact is that at no time of history have we been more in need of spiritual and intellectual disciplinarians than at present. If Dickstein's book has any value at all, it is that of reminding us of *this* need.

In his excellently conceived and edited anthology, *The Superfluous Men: Conservative Critics of American Culture, 1900–1945* (1977), Robert M. Crunden provides us with a volume that can be very profitably used in detecting and correcting Dickstein's self-congratulatory critical stance. The so-called "superfluous men" who are represented in Professor Crunden's valuable anthology—Irving Babbitt, Ralph Adams Cram, Donald Davidson, Walter Lippmann, H. L. Mencken, Paul Elmer More, Albert Jay Nock, Frank L. Owsley, John Crowe Ransom, George Santayana, Allen Tate—are commentators whose writings and thought provide that corrective critical discipline that *Gates of Eden* desperately requires. As Crunden declares: "One can read these men and then return to the literature, the criticism, or the philosophy with a renewed understanding of the complexity of the American experience and the fragility of easy generalizations about it."

To read here the selections from their works is to understand just how shallow and wanting are Dickstein's postulates. But this weakness is not merely weakness of thought. It is also one of style. The stylistic pretensions, poses, platitudes, conceit, crudities, and flabbiness of Dickstein's presentation are thus brought into a sharper and controlling focus. The manliness of Babbitt's prose style, the elegance of Santayana's, the clarity of Davidson's, the meditative eloquence of More's, the pungency of Mencken's are qualities for which one looks in vain in Dickstein's writing (and indeed, in the writings of the novelists whom he singles out for honors, and for the honor of attention). In this respect there is a crucial additional lesson to be drawn: The diminishing attention given to the classical discipline (and temper) by the moderns is commensurate with the diminution of disciplined expression, both written and oral. For Dickstein and the novelists he espouses, liberation has meant, among other cultural disasters, a general softening of standards of composition, as well as a general decay of sensibility.

It has been said that style is vision and vision is style. What, one must ask, was the vision of the 1960s? To say, with Dickstein, that the vision was one of cultural progress is to ignore not only the growing absence of form but also of content. For the culture of the 1960s that Dickstein treats with such exaggerated, unmerited reverence lacked the true visionary essence that Santayana has in mind when he writes that "there will always be beauty, or a transport akin to the sense of beauty, in any high contemplative moment." If any contemplativeness is to be found in the 1960s it was the contemplation of the empirical and instantaneous—a disintegrative contemplation of the unseemly. Moods and nerves, impatience and impulsiveness, anger and action, and then more action and anger—the emblems of Dickstein's pantheon of the 1960s—do not lead to great cultural order. It is Albert Jay Nock who pertinently provides us with the cultural insight that *Gates of Eden* abjures that

> inaction is better than wrong action or premature right action, and effective right action can only follow right thinking. . . . Great and salutary social transformations, such as in the end do not cost more than they come to, are not affected by political shifts, by movements, by programs and platforms, least of all by violent revolutions, but by sound and disinterested thinking.

What one discovers within the gates of Eden is a whirlwind of expansionism: immersion in experiment; tendencies; fervor; spontaneousness in rhetoric and drama, in ambitions and possibilities, and not in principles and limitations. It is not, of course, that the constituents of "alternative action," as the phrase goes, are of no use, and it would be foolish to discount the operative value of their necessity in civilization. Rather it is a disciplining humility, reverence, and wisdom that liberal fabulists ignore or deride. This triune absence underlines those glaring disproportions that make *Gates of Eden* unsettling and, in fact, terrifying. One longs to find in Dickstein's cultural observations those qualities and dimensions of thought that culminate in a final recognition of universal principles and eternal laws. For this mediating corrective one must turn to a selection from Babbitt's writings, and to words that Dickstein fundamentally contests:

> What is wanted is not sympathy alone, nor again discipline and selection alone, but a disciplined and selective sympathy. Sympathy without selection becomes flabby, and a selection which is unsympathetic tends to grow disdainful.

In the long run what the "conservative critics" in Crunden's anthology help us to explore and assess in *Gates of Eden* is an inner spiritual confusion, that which Paul Elmer More crystallizes in these words: "Not here and now only, but always and everywhere, when men begin to reflect, their reaction towards the world without God and without purpose is dark with despair and bitter with resentment." The world of the 1960s was a world of cultural disarray, dissipation, fanaticism, escapism; a world in which union of the secularist and the neopagan moved man closer to nihilism. Eternal values surrendered to the multiplicity of impulses. Moral strenuousness gave way to brute instincts. Spiritual potentialities slipped easily into rights. Indiscriminations were labeled discriminations.

José Ortega y Gasset earmarked this process of moral and spiritual decay when he wrote in *The Revolt of the Masses* (1932; original, 1930): "With more means at its disposal, more knowledge, more techniques than ever, it turns out that the world today goes the same way as the worst of worlds that have been; it simply drifts." Liberal doctrinaires, then and now, term these words the prophecy of a fool. We have reached a point, they tell us, when the opening of the "gates of Eden" is at hand. All we need to do is reach out and grab whatever we want. But for those who can discern the true nature of the human condition, this is a promise accepted only by those who steadfastly refuse to confront the true meaning in these words of a Spanish proverb: Take what you want, says God, and pay for it!

Apologists for Mediocrity

The aims of education should be sacred to anyone who is concerned with the order of civilization. Ever frail and vulnerable, these aims have been dangerously undermined in more recent years. Clearly there is a crisis at all levels and spheres of education, even as the stream of diagnoses and prescriptions has been unending. My own longtime witness to the swiftly changing conditions of instruction permits me to speak here from the crucible of experience. Indeed, it seems only yesteryear that I first entered the classroom—I was barely into my twenties—and had in fact absolutely no courses in education, or even practice teaching, let alone certification. It appears that the authorities who had appointed me to teach humanities in a small high school in a town in eastern Massachusetts were willing to waive specified requirements in my case. That was a fortunate decision on their part for even then I had no intention whatsoever of subscribing to the fiats and nonsense emerging from departments and schools of education. The art of teaching, I have always believed, transcends and perhaps even contravenes the educational methodologies that are characteristic of and consonant with social engineering in its total process, whether in theory or in practice.

Although I possessed no education course credits, I did possess an inherent allegiance to the humanistic purposes and meaning of education. I suspect that it was this that, in my early years of apprenticeship, led me almost instinctively to subscribe to the motto that none of my students was permitted to forget: "Observe, without labor nothing prospers." The admonishing words belonged to Socrates, I was proud to point out, and *not* to John Dewey and his disciples. That motto, I recall, sparked the aspirations of my young charges, though many of my colleagues and superiors seemed altogether indifferent. And labor we did, teacher and pupils alike, even as I myself came in time to appreciate the sharp relevance of T. S. Eliot's words—they can be found in his 1950 lectures on education given at the University of Chicago, the text almost simultaneously printed in the now defunct journal *Measure*: "I have never worked in a coal mine, or a uranium mine, or in a herring trawler; but I know from experience that working in a bank from 9:15 to 5:30, and once in four weeks the whole of Saturday, with two weeks holiday a year, was a rest cure compared to teaching in a school."

All the excitement and ambition and challenge of my formative teaching years were brought back to me with full nostalgic force during a recent walking tour of Old Deerfield, Massachusetts, located in the Connecticut River valley. On an early Sunday evening, at the very end of May, an old friend, John Lee, and I walked "The Street" of this historic town. It was warm, and fragrant, and so quiet that one could almost hear the muffled cries of the Pocumtucks, ranking among the "Great Indians" and the original native owners of Deerfield, nearly annihilated in 1664 by the Mohawks. We gazed at some of the magnificently restored houses— the Old Manse, the Asa Stebbins House, the Allen House, as well as the Brick Church, and admired in particular the majestic old doorways. The whole scene took us back suddenly to a mid-eighteenth-century frontier settlement, once the farthest wilderness post of the American colonists.

Somehow, then, we had been almost magically transported back into an early time, in terms of our wonderment not only at the incredibly fused aesthetic and antiquarian qualities of Old Deerfield, but also at the surrounding vista of rich farm fields and wooden hills (with their re-splendent and overarching oaks, sycamores, maples, beeches, and hemlocks). The countryside was deeply etched by browns and greens and darkening blue colors and glorious hues, the dusk adding to the stillness and aura of the time of day and season when past and present coalesce mysteriously to evoke "a New England symphony," so to speak. A local poet captures the scene I am trying to convey here—the restrained rhythms of life with its inherent archetypal history and order and con-tinuity—when he writes:

> The old names are here,
> And the old forms
> Not alone of doorways, of houses,
> The light falls the way the light fell,
> And it is not clear
> In the elm shadows, if it be ourselves here,
> Or others who were before us.

And one thinks, too, of the inscription on an ancient gravestone in the Old Burying Ground: "Your eyes are upon me, and I am not."

Our walk also led us to exploring the beautifully sprawling grounds extending far back, deep down from "The Street," and containing the main buildings of Deerfield Academy, established in 1797 and originally devoted to "the instruction of Youth, and the promotion of piety." The motto of the academy is "Be worthy of your heritage," words that an increasingly pluralistic society, now identified with a multiplying *Untermensch*, hardly appreciates or honors anymore. One very impressive building particularly attracted my friend and myself, and that was the Frank L. Boyden Library (bearing the name of the Academy's legendary headmaster during the years 1902–1968, and the subject of John McPhee's enchanting biographical essay *The Headmaster* [1966]). It was the interior life of the library, another dimension of holy ground, that now arrested me most, exciting and heightening my vocational commitment and seeming to encapsulate all at once my long, long years as a teacher—a *paedagogus* as that remarkable early Father of the Church, Saint Clement of Alexandria, uses that no-longer-hallowed word.

Within the various reading rooms of the library one could see young students solitarily reading, writing, thinking—studying, for it was final examination week. I found the expressions on the lean, handsome faces of students especially revealing—expectant, anxious, questful, serious, fascinated, radiant—as they pursued their particular study, poring over books, turning pages quietly and sometimes almost exultantly, as if to say that idea had finally been understood, or that problem solved, or that issue placed in perspective. Here they were, these schoolboys, preparing themselves for the future in the spirit of that "reverent discipline" that for me best defines the mission of humane studies. And as I studied the faces of these students, now engaged in their great adventure in learning, and in what should be a great expedition of truth, I reflected on some of the fundamental educational questions that we have to confront: What is the ultimate purpose of education in a modern society? What standards of excellence are required if we are not to slide into the pits of mediocrity? What are the basic subject areas, the core curricula, that we need to implement if we are to be able to connect with a common body of knowledge as a repository of ethical values and moral virtues that identify first principles? What should we do to resist and contain the vast and ugly programmatic encroachments that, like creeping armies of darkness, produce huge educational wastelands? At what point, precisely, are we to demand, as we must, that the idea of education must ultimately embrace the idea of transcendence? And what criteria, finally, define and preserve, in continuity, all that which makes us worthy of our heritage?

Answers to these questions have been sadly elusive. Indeed, these questions have too often been subordinated to crudely empirical considerations, to quantitative patterns of thought, and to all those spurious strategies and collectivisms that displace our sacred patrimony. Who and what, I kept asking myself, should be our educational paradigms, as my friend and I departed in awe from the Academy's library, leaving behind us those aspiring adolescents to whom the future belongs and on whose strong shoulders the mantle of leadership will someday fall. Spiritual and visionary paradigms, one inescapably discovers, give way to a relentless, surging decadence in the entire realm of education. And an all-encompassing failure of nerve seems to besiege leaders of education, even as wanton curricular dismemberments at major institutions like Stanford University underline, symptomatically, the bureaucratic betrayal of educational principles. This betrayal is in essence the demonic triumph of all those modern gnosticisms that have come to embody the anthill of modern civilization.

In vain does one look today among our educational chieftains for the kind of wisdom that a Simone Weil imparts when she asserts that the central duty of those who teach the young (and in effect act as spiritual guides) is to establish as clearly as possible the correspondence between the attitude of the intelligence and the position of the soul. That all-important correspondence has been scorned in the modern age. In the entire debate over the direction that education is to take, if it is to go beyond the confines of immanentism and nominalism, I have yet to hear words from our "enlightened" educational reformers that echo this one noble sacramental sentence with which Simone Weil concludes her celebrated essay "Reflections on the Right Use of School Studies with a View to the Love of God": "Academic work is one of those fields containing a pearl so precious that it is worthwhile to sell all our possessions, keeping nothing for ourselves, in order to be able to acquire it."

My reference to Simone Weil in fact reminds me that we have in recent decades abandoned sacred texts, classical and biblical, in educational instruction and experience. We arbitrarily restrict ourselves to only a sense of the moment or to revisionist (and often impious) exercises that vulgarize ancient texts and writers. The movement away from and even the blatant hostility to any value of tradition has been swift and aggressive. The legacy of Western civilization, its teachings and traditions, is the single most disastrous victim of the disorientation that characterizes modern thought. In the process first principles of education are being steadily destroyed in the name of the idols of the marketplace, even as we seek to placate the "terrible simplifiers" who would build a citadel of egalitarianism in the educational establishment.

Thus, in the American university, my own discipline of English Studies now becomes more and more a trivialized and fragmented amalgam of Marxist-Leninist literary theory, gay studies, feminist literature, Third World literature, sports culture, film, fantasy and science fiction, and whatever literary fad that happens to come along. No critical centrality of life and thought, no "poetics of value," is venerated. At Duke University, for instance, one professor teaches an English course on writers and moviemakers of the American West, asking the same questions of Zane Grey and Louis L'Amour that scholars ask about Shakespeare; the movies include *Stagecoach, The Wild Bunch, E. T.,* and *Close Encounters of the Third Kind.* Another luminary at Duke uses Shakespeare to show how seventeenth-century English society mistreated women, the working class, and minorities; this critical emphasis is called the "New Historicism," which purports to show power relationships between elites and the oppressed and scorns making eternal judgments. And so it goes, the sabotage in Durham.

There is still one other emblematic instance of disorientation in the humanistic disciplines that needs to be cited: the presidential address of 1986, entitled "The Triumph of Theory, the Resistance to Reading, and the Question of the Material Base," delivered to the Modern Language Association of America, by J. Hillis Miller, Distinguished Professor of English and Comparative Literature at the University of California, Irvine, formerly at Johns Hopkins and Yale—and one of the founding theorists of deconstructionism. It is neither a critically honorable nor distinguished address and is in fact a symptom and portent of disorientation in the academy, what Edward Shils has correlated with "the antinomian world-view" that sprang up in the 1960s. Miller is speaking, at one point, of the shift to history—the history that Jacques Barzun rightly says has been transformed into retrospective sociology—and politics in English departments and goes on to state:

> By "theory" I mean the displacement in literary studies from a focus on the meaning of texts to a focus on the way meaning is conveyed. Put another way, theory is the use of language to talk about language. Put yet another way, theory is a focus on referentiality as a problem rather than as something that reliably and unambiguously relates a reader to the "real world" of history, or society, and of people acting within society on the stage of history.

Here, then, in Miller's words we have it all in a nutshell, not only the rampant deconstructionism in the academy, but also the gobbledygook of language and thought that tells us so much about our present situation, and especially about the atrocities of language and thought that I myself as a university teacher have striven these many years to teach my thousands of students to avoid at their peril. To read Miller's address ultimately reminds me, too, of those young students at Old Deerfield, with all their youthful intellectual enthusiasm, yearnings, and hopes—

and, alas, of their coming fate at the deceitful hands of J. Hillis Miller and the nationwide gang movement of "New Pragmatists."

The aims of education, as I said earlier, should be sacred, and to our frequent dismay we find that they are not. Irving Babbitt, at the turn of the century, wrote with courageous conviction regarding deteriorating educational standards in *Literature and the American College* (1908), as did several decades later such penetrating critics as Bernard Iddings Bell in *Crisis in Education* (1949), Gordon Keith Chalmers in *The Republic and the Person* (1952), and Russell Kirk in *Academic Freedom* (1955). The two last-named books, published by the indomitable Henry Regnery, marked my own first appearance as a reviewer and had an impact on me of enduring power in the increasing struggle with ideas and visions in our time. Though each of these four books was favorably received not one of them was given the attention it deserved and, surely, still deserves.

Our educational theorists, to judge by their ongoing reforms and policies, have chosen to attack and ultimately silence writings and ideas that challenge their schemes that result in educational confusion and in the "diminished mind"—and, ultimately, in what Eric Voegelin terms "the corruption of order." These theorists are those selfsame "gnostics of education" Richard Weaver indicts in the following words:

> In the discredit that they have cast upon the higher faculties, in the way they have cut the young off from knowledge of the excellencies achieved in the past, and in the way they have turned attention toward transient externals and away from the central problems of man, they have no equal as an agency of subversion.

Indeed, at this very moment, in the central library of a good-sized New England city, not a single copy of Richard M. Weaver's *Visions of Order* (1964) or even a single volume of Voegelin's magisterial *Order and History* (1956–1987) is to be found. Even in a small way this bibliographical phenomenon can remind us of how sapiential thinkers, who help us to see our educational problems in both a temporal and an eternal light, as well as to alert us to insidious gnostic fallacies, are silenced.

In modern education, as in so much of modern society and culture, the virtue of reverence has been surrendered. The consequences of this surrender are far-reaching and possibly irreversible. As Eugène Ionesco has warned: "Man without God, without the metaphysical, without transcendence, is lost." Any critique of our educational problems that fails to respond to the force of truth found in Ionesco's warning can hardly begin to be either authentic or viable.

~ ❦ ~

Not surprisingly, then, after almost thirty years of university teaching, "under fire" as it were, I am increasingly troubled by progressivist leaders in education who express their concerns about conditions in higher learning. I am especially troubled when these concerns emerge from attitudes that are largely egalitarian, sentimental, and utilitarian. I am also troubled when I see these particular concerns translate into education policy. And I find, too, that these concerns and policies convey very little illumination or understanding. Attendance at committee meetings, faculty assemblies, and educational conferences through these long years has heightened my impatience, and my anger, as I have listened to a lot of dribble from liberal academics and titled administrators. For me the alarming devaluation of substance in educational deliberations and philosophy underlines even more the absence of the insight and wisdom that should be at the heart of the educational process. This process constitutes, in essence, the absence of standards in humanistic education.

The idea and tradition of *humanitas* entail, in the true educational process, the twofold need of fostering the principles of what I call a "reverent discipline" and "courage of judgment." Many of my colleagues in the profession, however, abjure the principles that I designate as being crucial to pedagogy and indispensable to the educated person. Now, whether it is out of fear of punishment, or out of ignorance, or out of indifference, or out of sheer exhaustion, my colleagues too often accept or embrace the new education no less than the new morality. The generation of educators now approaching retirement age has largely given up resisting the appalling bureaucratization and technologizing of the educational process. And many younger members of the profession, who come directly out of the politicized and radicalized era of the 1960s and 1970s, are gradually coming into control, the destructive consequences of which we are now beginning to see frequently and irrevocably. Their conception of humanistic standards or of the pedagogical function in relation to "the moral and the ethical life" hardly begins to exist. They are the flower children who sat at the feet of Professor Herbert Marcuse and Dr. Timothy Leary. They are Dr. Spock's babies who ripened in the drug culture and were immured in what has been termed "protoplasmic activity."

I now see these purveyors of the New Age being generously promoted all around me as my colleagues, and the sight is sometimes disturbing. Often their ignorance is appalling. Their irreverence is maximal, their sense of decorum is minimal. Their influence can be deadly. They embody our social and educational *Zeitgeist*, disordered and soulless. They are the nihilists—"the new men and women"—of Ivan Turgenev's *Fathers and Sons* (1862) in a contemporary situation. "Look what your nihilists are doing! They are setting Petersburg on fire!" These words, the first to escape the lips of the first acquaintance Turgenev met on Nevsky Avenue immediately following the novelist's return to Saint Petersburg at the beginning of June 1862, have an urgent ring today as one surveys American higher education and as the debate rages over its plight. This debate, regardless of what our educational naturalists and behaviorists insist on telling us, is ultimately a moral debate and requires a moral solution. "When a man resolves a moral perplexity successfully," Eliseo Vivas reminds us, "he adds a cubit to his stature."

The nature of the crisis of higher education (and of education as a whole) and the need to confront it openly and honestly, in the context of what Vivas notes, have been reinforced in my mind after my reading of two letters in the *New York Times*, the first by Professor Jacques Barzun, under the caption "Keeping Higher Education Higher," and the second, a reply to Barzun's by Richard W. Lyman, president of the Rockefeller Foundation, 1980–1988, and president emeritus of Stanford University, under the caption "Demythologizing Those Golden Days of Yore." The two letters, in their arresting antitheses, summarize the crisis of higher education and also point to the perplexity of those who seek to resolve its problems. No two letters better show the sharp philosophical differences between educators who affirm quality as the sine qua non of the educational process and those who affirm quantity, between those who insist on discipline of standards in education and those who believe in the democratization of education.

In a deeper and larger sense, what we are viewing is an unending educational quarrel between those who subscribe to classical precepts and those who embrace the romantic attitude—between, that is, the law of measure and the law of numbers. In his first great book, *Literature and the American College*, Irving Babbitt clearly identified the two opposing factions in this quarrel: that which contends that higher education should be a training for wisdom and character and that which contends that education should be a "training for power and service." In essence, it can be said, the educational debate is ultimately between the moralist who insists on fundamentals and the educationist who embraces technique. To be sure, neither Barzun nor Lyman makes any specific reference to or takes a specific position on the moral elements of education. But their statements, in their antitheses, have the effect of reminding us that an educational philosophy that lacks moral dimension leads to breakdown in civilization and, in particular, to the decadence that seriously afflicts contemporary education.

Barzun needs hardly any introduction to readers. He is a highly distinguished teacher, critic, and writer. In the years between 1929 and 1975 he taught history at Columbia University, where he also served as dean of graduate faculties, 1955–1958, and dean of faculties and provost, 1958–1967. His concern with higher learning and also the art of teaching has always been deep and abiding. Nowhere are his dedication and sincerity more apparent, or paradigmatic, than in his *Teacher in America* (1945), in which book this memorable sentence appears: "Teaching is not a lost art, but the regard for it is a lost tradition." Barzun has never wavered in defending or seeking to preserve the treasures of this lost tradition. He has never hesitated to speak out on the constant need to oppose the forces and tendencies that imperil educational standards. His letter to the *Times* epitomizes his lifelong commitment to universal principles that are at the very center of *humanitas* and *paideia*. That is to say, Barzun never forgets, as do so many in the intellectual community, that the relations between education and society are not discrete or separate from a nation's cultural and spiritual life, that these relations have organic unity, historical continuity, moral integrality. The pursuit of excellence is for Barzun synonymous with the mission of the university; this pursuit transcends the exigencies and the opinions of a defined time of history and of place. In this respect Plato's belief that the education of moral and intellectual personality is a quintessential need and goal comes to mind, even as we should also realize that that ancient belief has become an alien in the world of modernism as we know it in all of its disorienting forms.

In his letter to the *Times*, Barzun emphatically states that "It is not *going* to college that matters, but studying when one gets there, wanting to study and liking it." This simple but central requirement has been increasingly dislodged and the results now underline widespread chaos in the academy, which Barzun forthrightly crystallizes:

> [A]dapting the curriculum downward, not to needs but to wants; tempting teachers to be popular by being easy (latter-day "evaluation" by students adding to the pressure of departments for high enrollments); students begging and cajoling (or cheating) for high grades—"I need an A, please, can't you—?"

The debasement of higher education, as Barzun goes on to observe, is characterized by a steady capitulation to lower standards, that is, to mediocrity, to "the barbarism of 'specialization' " (as Ortega y Gasset calls it), to the disorder and the provincialism of one's own time that pervade both the inner and the outer life of American society. "That," as Barzun declares, "good work, good students, and good teachers continue to exist is surely true. But there would not be the repeated surveys and critical reports if these once normal elements still predominated as they should." The "normal elements" that Barzun refers to here have become the victims of hyperdemocracy and of a liberalizing system and a permissive ethos that not only exempt everyone from any moral demands but also indiscriminately promise everyone a "new deal." No paragraph in Barzun's letter can more bravely present "unfashionable convictions" (to use a phrase of Bernard Iddings Bell) than the following:

> The public error has been to believe that higher education was to everybody's taste and within everybody's aptitudes. It is, in fact, cruel and unusual punishment to those who lack the native bent, the preparation, or both. It is also true that high intelligence, talent, and personal and social merit are found in many forms other than academic ability. They deserve training and recognition on their own ground.

These are politically provocative words to express publicly. And they did indeed provoke Dr. Richard W. Lyman, who before he became a university president and then a foundation executive, was an academician and, by training, a historian. His letter of reply to Barzun personifies in tone, temper, and dialectic what we have learned to expect from our ruling and enlightened smatterers (and what Barzun himself calls "the self-serving pieties of educational leaders"). His provocation is angrily and revealingly spelled out in the last sentence of his letter: "We should recognize the reactionary intent that underlines the drive to restrict the educational opportunities to the young." The adjectival force of "reactionary" can hardly be underestimated: it is precisely that loaded word that, when applied in the intellectual community, is meant to discredit a dissenting opinion. Lyman echoes in his letter the typically quantitative affirmations that educationists have been mouthing since the days of John Dewey:

> Clearly the arrival on campus of previously excluded "persons"—members of disadvantaged minorities, women in proportion to their share of the population, and those whose "parents' resources" are insufficient to pay for higher education—has not introduced the less-than-devoted student or the less-than-demanding faculty.

In higher education Lyman's words are now gospel. Standards of achievement are metamorphosed into pluralistic standards as the principle of control surrenders to unrestrained expansiveness, or as Irving Babbitt reminds us: "The new education requires an enormously elaborate and expensive apparatus. This elaborateness is encouraged by the prime emphasis of the utilitarian on the progress of humanity through the cooperation of a multitude of specialists, as well as by the prime emphasis of the sentimentalist on innate gifts and their right to gratification." Today we confront this new education in the enormous superstructure of higher learning. And as we see in Lyman's letter, especially in its notorious last sentence, anyone who questions this superstructure with its proliferating functionaries, specialists, and technicians—its so-called "experts"—risks being branded a "reactionary."

Nowhere in Lyman's letter will one find any deep philosophical awareness of educational standards that start with the premise that education is a perpetual striving, a disciplining of mind and, yes, of character. Lyman's arguments, or better, his sentiments, are representative and symptomatic of those in authority who would equate education with adaptability to the *volonté générale*. It is precisely the emphasis on adaptability that has made a hodgepodge of the curriculum in colleges and universities and has led to rampant egalitarianism and careerism. Unfortunately, too, educators who accept the new education—who "play the game," as it were—all too often reap the greatest gains in terms of awards, distinctions, promotions, grants. Barzun rightly complains about the whole phenomenon of inversion in education when he cites the kind of teacher who is chosen as exemplifying the art of teaching at its best: "When a man is honored and publicized as the 'Professor of the Year' because he 'implores' students to learn and holds them by 'clever gimmicks' . . . , something has happened not only in the university but in the public mind as well."

Obviously Lyman is aware of this unseemly phenomenon, or of the sham methods employed in teaching, or of the sham courses taught in colleges and universities—courses often so remedial and elementary in content as to belong to some subeducational institution staffed by paraprofessionals. I should like Lyman to leave his office on the Avenue of the Americas just briefly to visit my own university campus, to meet there the students who have never heard of the Hellespont or of Pontius Pilate. I should like to have Lyman attend my graduate seminar on a warm spring afternoon as I struggle to be heard over the cacophonous din of rock music blaring at the highest possible volume and encompassing a sprawling campus. But, then, I suspect he would be completely at home with his fellow administrators—chancellors and deputy chancellors, provosts, assistant provosts, and assistants to the assistant provosts, all of them very well paid, many of them complacent, and some of them mediocre, as they, too, spit out the same clichés, expedient tolerances, and optimistic banalities that Lyman does.

But whatever our educational managers tell us, they cannot in the end hide the truth of what Barzun terms the current "state of mind unsuited to teaching and learning." Far more preoccupied with power and politics than with the content of instruction, our educational hucksters govern a system in which quantity becomes quality to a dangerous degree; in which ultimates and universals are servants of progress and technicalism; and in which the reversal of the relation between means and ends dominates.

The crisis of American education is part of the wider "crisis of Western education," to use Christopher Dawson's expression. With the occasional exception of a protest and warning like Barzun's, there is little evidence that educators are willing to alter the ideological course that they have set and follow so relentlessly. Lyman's reply to Barzun is still another example of the refusal and unwillingness of those who make policy to accept any criticism or to listen to any appeals for any reorientation of higher learning in America. Clearly there are now too many and too powerful vested interests in the business of education to make possible any principled changes in a system which affirms nothing.

It may very well be that the late J. M. Lalley, for many years the sage literary editor of *Modern Age: A Quarterly Review*, is right: that the only solution to the problem of higher education would be to "chuck the entire system and simply award each child at birth a baccalaureate." When Mr. Lalley first made that suggestion to me, many years ago, I found it to be threatening, perhaps because I wanted to believe that it was still possible to renew the spiritual foundations of higher learning. With many of us, it seems, illusions die hard; at any rate, the real threat to the humanistic conception of education clearly comes not from the radical surgery proposed by Lalley but from those within the academy— from a faithless professoriate and even more from arrogant educational administrators who control and implement programs and policy. During commencement exercises a few years back, for example, the then president of the University of Connecticut, Dr. John A. DiBiaggio, insolently told graduating students that tradition can be a barrier to success; that a "preoccupation with tradition leads to insularity, not just in a fiscal sense, but even more importantly, in a philosophical or emotional sense." "It can," DiBiaggio went on to say, "take us trudging down a path to second best."

We should be grateful to DiBiaggio and, of course, to Lyman for disclosing to us so unashamedly the extent of the animus in high places against any continuity of values and ideals handed down by tradition in higher learning. I myself can still recall my own first brush with this animus when, back in 1952, I reviewed in a New England newspaper Gordon Keith Chalmers's remarkable defense of the necessity of moral absolutes in education, as well as his indictment of "disintegrated liberalism," *The Republic and the Person*. Local educationists, I learned not too long after my review of Chalmers's book appeared, vehemently complained about it to the literary editor of the newspaper. By writing that *The Republic and the Person* sought to save Americans "from educational malnutrition and educational slackness," I had antagonized a powerful vested interest, and the book editor, a kindly but timid man, politely warned me that henceforth I should not target the educational progressivists. I see no waning of their power after all these years, and when one dares to challenge them and their orthodoxies one arouses the wrath of a gang movement of considerable vindictive power.

In the postmodern world of higher learning in which we view the final phase of the triple collapse of the moral measure of life, of the humanistic foundations of education, and of sociocultural standards, the question we must ask of ourselves and of others is this: Who is going to save us from our apologists for mediocrity, the Lymans and the DiBiaggios?

Agents of Reductionism

In the light of the declining condition of serious American journals of thought and opinion in general, an account in the *New York Times* of August 3, 1984, concerning *Harper's* magazine should not go unnoticed.

"With its latest redesign and marketing approach," the *Times* report unabashedly begins, "*Harper's* magazine is turning from the armchair intellectual, an audience few advertisers would covet, to the affluent and well-educated businessman and woman." The report goes on to note that "a breezier, faster-paced format" has now been introduced because, according to the magazine's publisher, "business people's tight schedules force them to read in bits and snatches." "We are less a magazine for the English teacher," he is quoted as saying. "There aren't enough of them, and they don't make enough money." The report then continues: "Gone are the lengthy ruminations and dense essays that filled the 134-year-old monthly, and could take even an avid reader hours to pore through."

Lewis H. Lapham, the editor, is also cited as hoping the new format—short extracts of articles published in other magazines, snippets of speeches, collections of obscure facts and figures, and a few original full-length pieces—will make "for quicker, more enjoyable reading," and secure a niche for *Harper's* in the "thought magazine field." The hope of those who now run *Harper's*, we further learn, is that the redesign of format and approach will help increase the number of subscriptions, improve advertising sales and total circulation, and perhaps finally bring a profit. The account in the *Times* concludes by again quoting the publisher: "It [the old *Harper's*] used to sit around the house worthy, but unread. The new *Harper's* isn't homework anymore."

The above summary of the report in the *Times* makes for sad reading and reflection, especially on the part of those who still treasure the memory of journals like *The Bookman* (1895–1933), the *North American Review* (1818–1939), and *The Forum* (1886–1950). But, of course, few if any readers from the generation now being nourished by *People* and *Us* know anything about those journals. For readers who revere the critical function of intellectual journalism and continue to value the "communion" between the cultivated layman and the author, the fate of *Harper's* is especially distressing as still another adulterative symptom and portent of breakdown.

The statement that outlines the revamping of *Harper's* (and is quickly confirmed by a perusal of a very recent issue) fills us with misgiving. We are especially fearful about the larger evolving consequences of what a redesigned *Harper's* means to a serious, educated readership, however small and dwindling it is in America. We are, to say the least, fearfully concerned about the state of American life and letters when a serious, intellectual journal is wantonly reduced to a pastiche of miscellaneous extracts, snippets, and "breezier, faster-paced" writings, pleasantly packaged and effortlessly read and digested, so that it "isn't homework anymore."

Maximize readability even if it means minimizing the reading level—this is clearly the message being given to us. The reading of a text, in other words, should *not* be demanding or difficult; nor should it adhere to any critical controls, to a hierarchy of meaning or to a ruling system of logic. It should be as easy and attractive as watching the evening news on television, after the usual "happy hour." It should give us, emphatically and abundantly, facts and figures, *not* theories and ideas. It should not be concerned either with eternal verities or with the enforcement of standards of discrimination in theory and practice. F. R. Leavis's dictum that discrimination is life and indiscrimination is death, in these circumstances, is utterly obsolete: an irrelevance in the "thought magazine field" now being revamped for the benefit of present-day readers so that they will "see everywhere the same facts," to use one reductionist claim.

The emergence of a "new *Harper's*" helps to dramatize, above all, present literary and critical conditions in America. Or to put it another way, it helps show a consequential process of reduction that is absorbing the life of the mind and, in consequence, eroding and devaluing the intellectual life as a vigorous, intelligent, and indispensable aspect of American civilization. A brutal pragmatism and a cloying vulgarization, it is apparent, are in league in leveling concepts of excellence as these relate to life, literature, and thought. No matter how high-minded the publisher and the editor of *Harper's* may sound in their hopes and aims, their testimony speaks for itself: It cannot hide the fact that, in the end, their special revamping is another disquieting example of the spirit of reductionism that affects so much of American society and culture; of an empirical and programmatic oversimplification that, in scorning and abrogating the disciplines of tradition and continuity, takes the form of experimentation and innovation, of technique and marketability, of enlightenment and power, and seeks "to reduce the world to something resembling a chessboard," to use George Orwell's phraseology.

It is not merely that the symptomatic kind of revamping that characterizes *Harper's* ultimately panders to a "cheap contemporaneousness." A worse feature is that it panders to mediocrity, which is a national sickness now approaching the point of total moral disaster. The modes of reductionism have become our affliction of self-destruction as one examines what our ideological pluralists with their liberal-to-radical "axiomatic structure" (and monomanias) are bringing about. The fact remains that there is not one facet of our culture that has not been substantively altered by a destructive reductionism. There is nothing, it seems, that is held sacred or that merits continuance. "We shall change everything, or be damned!" is, by all evidence, the incendiary battle cry of those who "demystify" and "restructure" whatever does not accept the law of change and numbers. Yet their arguments and their logics are equally specious, especially when one considers the far-reaching implications of reductionism that diminish our spiritual and intellectual patrimony.

The reductionist yen, as we diagnose its symptoms and experience its consequences, mirrors in direct and overt ways the desire to evade moral demands, moral responsibility, moral struggle. We are an impatient and stiff-necked people who believe that, in a majoritarian democracy, absolutely no difficulty or disappointment is to be tolerated; that, as the old song goes, "Whatever Lola Wants, Lola Gets"; that the hedonistic philosophy of "Easy Come, Easy Go" is a national pastime, abetted by one and all—journalists, academics, clergymen, politicians. "Welfare is what modern man expects of society," Professor Gerhart Niemeyer wisely wrote in *Modern Age* more than twenty years ago. Difficulty and effort, it seems, are words that have now dropped out of the dictionary. One needs only listen to political candidates on the hustings to comprehend the extent and depth of the tyranny of the vital urge, as Bergson calls it, as it governs our land in the name of reductionism. ("Aristocratic nations," writes Tocqueville, "are by their nature too much inclined to restrict the scope of human perfectibility; democratic nations sometimes stretch it beyond reason.")

Welfare and effortlessness are at the heart of the reductionism that, for example, makes *Harper's* more appealing and more readable—and less thought-provoking. Instant mediocrity, it seems, must get the better of "lengthy ruminations"; language and literature must be cleansed of any problem, or challenge, and be made palatable to the multitudes. "The characteristic of the hour," Ortega y Gasset writes in *The Revolt of the*

Masses, "is that the commonplace mind, knowing itself to be commonplace, has the assurance to proclaim the rights of the commonplace and to impose them wherever it will."

At the very moment of this writing, in a library of a good-sized New England city, I am reminded of "the rights of the commonplace" being imposed as I see library workers about me busily "weeding" books from shelves in accordance with a new policy requiring a book to circulate a certain number of times in a given period or be discarded. That there will necessarily be eminent discards—Sophocles, Dante, John Bunyan, William Blake, John Milton, Edmund Burke, Henry James—obviously makes little or no difference to the agents of reductionism in command here. This same library, I discover, has constantly circulating copies of books gloriously celebrating "the joy of sex," but not a single book by a Richard Weaver or an Eric Voegelin.

The agents of reductionism are doing their dirty work not only in the pages of *Harper's*. They can be seen wherever one looks in a so-called "dynamic society," and the consequences of their sabotage are telling and frightening. They are there in literary scholarship in the guise of deconstructionism, as powerful and insidious a force of nihilism as seen in recent history. They are there in education in the form of the politics of revolution, recklessly dismantling the tradition of *humanitas*. (As one radical dismantler argues: "Departments of literature in higher education, then, are part of the ideological apparatus of the modern capitalist state.") They are there in religion in the demonic form of liberation theology, which advocates class struggle, and Marxist theologians, who not only blasphemously transform the celebration of the divine liturgy but also annul the very Word of God. They are there in the electronics media, day in and day out, in the polychromatic shapes of baseness and depravity, arrogantly fulfilling the ultimate reductionist principle that sensations alone constitute the field of phenomena. They are there in contemporary music, in art, and in the cinema, in the forms of raucous noise, ugly inkblots, and mindless dialogue. And everywhere these dissimulating agents of reductionism spread their gospel of indiscipline and debasement with an astonishing abandon that meets with ever-decreasing resistance.

Of course, those of us who, in these matters, must speak out as dissentient critics will no doubt be derided as mere representatives of the "conservatism of despair." The dismissal of Aleksandr Solzhenitsyn from any mention in the popular press and periodicals is both a warning and scandalous example of the power of the ideologues of mediocrity and of the results of their ambitious policy of "planning and popularization."

"The mediocre must have their chance": this is a plea of the agents of reductionism as they go about establishing their intellectual gulags in every facet of our society and conducting us to a utopian future in which "the things of the mind" will encounter no difficulties, no criteria, no moral imperatives—a future in which, as Aldous Huxley disclosed in *Brave New World* (1932), one will easily be able to take a holiday from reality by means of soma. American society, it seems, has been taking precisely such a holiday, *ad absurdum* and *ad nauseam*, as one views the reductionist process steadily eating away at the roots of society.

To be sure, apologists for reformism will continue to promote the sociopolitical gospel of expansionism and progress and to insist in particular that "the principle of distributive justice," as Friedrich Hayek calls it, will be realized as American society is drastically restructured and reordered. In the ensuing process of reductionism, then, requirements, restrictions, limitations, obligations, and duties, as endemic properties of moral choice and growth, are condemned as "threats to democracy." No call to greatness and no demand for standards of achievement will be heard or tolerated. Thus a repeatedly voiced contention that high school students ought to be able to read certain selected books that comprise a great tradition, or a literary canon, and ultimately help to define a discipline of letters, draws this reply from a "neoconservative socialist" like Daniel Bell: "I don't like the idea at all. It is spurious and would only produce *ersatz* culture." This reply should come as no surprise; we have repeatedly heard it from the advocates of a Great Society. Yet we are again reminded that at the heart of the process of reductionism lies the ceaseless drive for equality, not only socially and economically but also spiritually and intellectually.

Collectivist habits of thought abound everywhere as Americans continue to chase after the myth that they all have equal potential and can achieve simultaneously equality and excellence, once the "reconstruction of the material basis of civilization," as Robert L. Heilbroner puts it, has been achieved. Our "dream of the golden mountains" does not abate, and we indulge freely in that dream of "the vast majority," refusing to see any incongruity between illusion and reality. In the meanwhile we shamelessly forget the moral truth of Thoreau's belief that "We must first succeed alone, that we may enjoy our success together." Liberal sages no doubt will deride Thoreau's remark as an elitist affirmation that characterizes a "custodian of discourse" and that precludes our collective ability to adapt to a changing intercultural world, to a new global economy, to the dictates of technique and technology, to an enlightened self-interest, to ordered structures of empirical concepts. But for those brave enough to look closely and dispassionately at what is happening in our society, it will be evident that the promoters of reform, and adaptability, are in truth agents of reductionism leading us into a paradise of snakes.

Advocates of Debasement

How do our "terrible simplifiers" view great religious geniuses? What ideological assumptions and prejudices color their estimates of men and women who possess spiritual insight and wisdom and whose religious acceptances reject the ways of the world? What exactly are the promptings and methods that identify those who support the new morality and the secular faith of modern civilization? How are we to respond to critiques by powerful public personalities and media elites who carry such weight of importance and often determine public attitudes and standards of thought? How can we resist that posture of irreverence and infidelity which hardens in a society in which the idea of the sacred and divine gives way to nonreligious and antireligious forces?

These are hard questions that one must ask oneself in an age of ideology hostile to a religious worldview. Particularly within the academy, where radical and Marxizing forces have been gaining an unusual degree of power and influence, these questions are doubly pertinent. Clearly the ideological process, as an insidious and even perverse modern phenomenon, has increasingly politicized almost all aspects of society and culture, steadily encompassing both the spoken and the written word. As a result, we find that ideas are reduced to ideologies and moral absolutes and universals are relativized. Ideologies become, in Raymond Aron's words, a "modern philosophy of immanence," and perceive the human realm "without reference to the transcendental." In short, ideology seeks to supplant religion and insists that salvation is attained in political action. Indeed, as Russell Kirk avers in *Enemies of the Permanent Things* (1969), ideology becomes "intellectual servitude" and, in the process, we are inevitably left with philodoxers, purveyors of *doxai*, which is to say, of illusory opinions and vain wishes. And, as Kirk goes on to assert, these "humanitarian ideologues, good though their intentions may be, can bring about a dreadful decay of order."

Kirk's words are especially appropriate when one stops to consider the many writings of Dr. Robert Coles, that much honored and influential child psychiatrist, educator, and prolific author. His *Simone Weil: A Modern Pilgrimage* (1987) is a book that particularly raises more questions than it answers. The euphemistic "pilgrimage" in the subtitle is to be seen as having secondary importance, for it tells us far more about Coles's own social and political quest for meaning since the time in 1960 when he and his wife went south to work with children going through the trials of desegregation, or with youth involved in the civil rights movement. His participation in the civil rights and antipoverty movements, especially in the Student Nonviolent Coordinating Committee, should alert us to the humanitarian concerns of this activist, concerns that also inform and mold his ideological view of Simone Weil.

The Simone Weil of "a modern pilgrimage" comes out of the sixties and is stamped by the psychopathology of that era, to which some minds, it seems, still return nostalgically. Coles sees this period of American society and culture in a curiously spiritual light, as he does Simone Weil, and in both cases what he sees ultimately reveals a confused sentimentality. That is, his overall view is muddled and finally misleading. The real Simone Weil eludes him, or rather eludes his modern social gospel, which is a form of modern gnosticism. He presents a Simone Weil who fits his own version of Christian Socialism, and he misses entirely the Simone Weil who is the greatest Christian Platonist of the modern age. His Simone Weil is, in the end, to be seen in the mold of Dorothy Day and the Catholic Worker Movement to which Coles admits "a close personal and religious connection."[1] Too, his examination of Simone Weil lacks centrality precisely because of what he terms his own "troubled feelings" about her, accepting as he does her mystery but also acknowledging her enigma. Perhaps a better title for this book would be "Simone Weil: The Mystery and the Enigma." In this respect, the book has a somewhat clinical orientation that at times smacks of "a doctor looks at literature" syndrome.

Of course, Coles is entitled to his interpretation of Simone Weil, but that interpretation is faulty for it neglects the supernatural foundations of her thought and life. It is also flawed by the fact that he too easily echoes the données of the New Left in its vintage years. What we have in his version of Simone Weil is the vulgarization of a religious figure of unparalleled spiritual importance in the twentieth century. Coles's Simone Weil is placed in the contexts of the social gospel not only of the New Left but also of the New Theology. It is the same Simone Weil whom Staughton Lynd of antiwar fame ranks in "the first New Left" and sees "as one of an international group of seekers" (for example, Ignazio Silone, A. J. Muste, C. Wright Mills) who fervently advocate "participato-

---

[1]"Simone Weil: The Mystery of Her Life," *Yale Review* 73/2 (Winter 1984): 317.

ry democracy."[2] And this is a coarsened Simone Weil, shorn of the experiences of transcendence and transfiguration, the Simone Weil who is specially fit for consumption in "the secular city" and in the pseudospiritual explorations of the "God is Dead" group. Coles's book has the musty smell of "the gospel of Christian atheism" and of gnostic heresies moving "toward a new Christianity." He fails to extricate himself from the malaise of these movements and in the process he judges Simone Weil's vision by commonplace standards of political relevance and activism.

Here the Simone Weil who emerges is a strange concoction of the sentimental and empirical, the theoretical and practical, leading us to "the gates of Eden." Coles's own sociopolitical illusion, it needs to be said, makes a captive of Simone Weil and distorts the meaning of her religious pilgrimage in the modern world. He fails to give us a glimpse of a brave woman whose search is one of mystical ascent and illumination. Revealingly, Coles notes that Dr. Anna Freud helped him during many conversations "to think through the moral and psychological complexities that the life of Simone Weil presents to readers." He singles out, in affirmation, Anna Freud's perception of Simone Weil as a "marvelous scold." Symptomatically, Coles subordinates both Plato and Christ, preferring inferior guides in a pilgrimage that arrives nowhere as far as Simone Weil is concerned.

Clinical and diagnostic habits of analysis continuously permeate Coles's interpretations, which make Simone Weil appear as a strange, twisted, tortured, enigmatic figure. "Her psychology nourished her religious aspirations—at the terrible expense of her earthly life," Coles writes at one point in regard to her chosen method of self-starvation and untreated tuberculosis culminating in her death. His words define the tone of his book even when he allows for her metaphysical speculations and her spiritual quest. This tone gets in the way of a proper understanding of the soul of Simone Weil in particular and the needs of the soul in general. Nowhere is this tone as disconcerting and as deceptive in impeding a right understanding of Simone Weil than in this jaundiced statement: "One feels sure that this brave and yet scatterbrained person, as shrewdly sane as could be, and as wacky as could be, had a central dream: her moment of release, her giddy ascent, His welcome."

An entire chapter is devoted to Simone Weil's "Jewishness" in which he examines or theorizes on the causes of her deep antagonism to Jewish

---

[2]Staughton Lynd, "Marxism-Leninism and the Language of *Politics* Magazine: The First New Left . . . and the Third," in *Simone Weil: Interpretations of a Life*, ed. George Abbott White (Amherst: University of Massachusetts Press, 1981) 110-35.

tradition and her critical feelings concerning her own Jewish background. "Her thrusts at Jewry," he declares, "demean her and have made many of us who admire her cringe." These "thrusts" relate to Simone Weil's view of ancient Rome as "the Great Beast of atheism and materialism, adoring nothing but itself," and of Israel as "the Great Beast of religion." In this connection, she dismissed the Old Testament as "a tissue of horrors" with the exception of the Book of Job, most of the Psalms, the Song of Songs, the sapiential books, the second Isaiah and some of the Minor Prophets, and the books of Daniel and Tobias. Her denunciations of Judaism, it should not go unnoticed, were concurrent with the Holocaust. Though this dimension of Simone Weil bothers Coles, he comes up with no original or substantive answers or even reflections. "Had she succumbed to the self-hatred of the victim?" he asks in frustration, elsewhere stating that the Jews and the Romans "are her scapegoats, embodying all the fleshly impulses and desires of mere mortals." Too often, when venturing an explanation for her anti-Jewish fulminations, it is Coles who utters clichés from his own clinical experiences:

> Perhaps we are left to speculate that part of Weil's "problem" with her Jewishness was that she always wanted to endure suffering on her own terms, for radical stands *she* had chosen. The Germans forced her into a category, a position she had not chosen, and she refused to identify with others in the same position.

> Simone Weil pays no attention to those Jews who followed Jesus, the disciples and authors of the Gospels. Risking psychological reductionism, one wonders at times whether a few ancient Jewish fishermen didn't present a challenge to her—sibling rivals of sorts, triggering old competition and self-hate.

But Coles's observations here and elsewhere disclose critical superficiality and hackneyed judgments, sometimes bordering on ignorance. Somehow, one thinks, we have heard these things before from our behaviorists and naturalists, and it is we who must cringe and hope that Coles's is not the last word on Simone Weil and Judaism. Though he assures us that since 1966 he has "kept reading her, struggling with conflicting feelings and opinions of her," we are in this particular instance led to believe that his reflections on her life and writings lack any genuinely keen insight and fail to rise above an intellectual level of shallowness that does no service to the memory or spiritual anguish of Simone Weil's body and soul. Deeper and more penetrating discussions of her anti-Jewish attitudes are to be found in writings by Martin Buber, Leslie

A. Fiedler, or Hans Meyerhoff.[3] Coles indicates no awareness of the testimony of these authorities, preferring his own self-righteous psychological pontifications with all their innuendoes and misrepresentations. At Simone Weil's expense he seems to be trying to parade before us all his liberal sympathies and tolerances. But all this is utterly characteristic of a flawed book as Coles repeatedly interposes his species of self-importance and self-righteousness between Simone Weil and his readers. One's irritations mount, too, when one stops to think that in 1940 Simone Weil herself, the daughter of freethinking Jewish parents brought up "in complete agnosticism," confessed quite candidly concerning her official separation from Judaism that

> the concept of heredity may be applied to a race, but it is difficult to apply it to a religion. I myself, who professes no religion and never have, have certainly inherited nothing from the Jewish religion. Since I practically learned to read from Racine, Pascal, and other French writers of the 17th century, since my spirit was thus impregnated at an age when I had not heard talk of "Jews," I would say that if there is a religious tradition which I regard as my patrimony, it is the Catholic tradition.

Coles chooses to ignore such a confessional statement and instead chooses to convey partisan opinions and half-baked theories that discredit and condemn Simone Weil in relation to her anti-Jewish attitudes. These criticisms of Coles should not be taken as a defense of or apology for Simone Weil on the subject of Judaism. They are presented in order to stress that Coles's simplistic remarks are finally irresponsible and inoperative. Her Jewishness calls for rigorous, sustained, and assiduous reexamination, untainted by the liberal posturings that recur in Coles's book and that prompt him to make injudicious and noncritical formulations. What he is doing, in fact, is to fan even more the flames of a difficult and disturbing aspect of Simone Weil's Jewish problem, as it might be termed. This is especially inexcusable for a book that is part of "The Radcliffe Biography Series" depicting the lives of extraordinary women and that is undoubtedly aimed at an ingenuous student audience. As a general introduction to the life and mind of Simone Weil, Coles's book can have

---

[3]Martin Buber, "The Silent Question: On Henri Bergson and Simone Weil," in *At the Turning: Three Addresses on Judaism* (New York: Farrar, 1952); Leslie A. Fiedler, "Simone Weil: Prophet Out of Israel. A Saint of the Absurd," *Commentary* 11/1 (January 1951): 36-46; Hans Meyerhoff, "Contra Simone Weil," in *Arguments and Doctrines: A Reader of Jewish Thinking in the Aftermath of the Holocaust*, selected and with introductory essays by Arthur A. Cohen (New York: Harper, 1970).

deleterious consequences, to say the least. For impressionable students, and other readers, first coming to Simone Weil, his book can inflict permanent damage in the regrettable form of distortion and misguidance.

That Coles himself has over the years devoted extensive lectures on Simone Weil in his teaching at Harvard University, where he is a professor of psychiatry and medical humanities in the Medical School, makes this part of his book almost inexcusable. One, after all, tries to believe that university teachers of Coles's stature have a good effect on their students' moral attitudes and intellectual opinions. It is sad to think that the Harvard that gave us the Irving Babbitt of *The Masters of Modern French Criticism* (1912) can now only give us the Coles of *Simone Weil: A Modern Pilgrimage*. We live in lean times, indeed, when we think of how we have moved in steady pedagogical decline from a magisterial teacher like Babbitt to a portentous luminary like Coles (who has reaped as many rewards and honors as Babbitt has received scorn and ridicule). But, then, Coles is in every way attuned to and in almost perfect accord with the ongoing age of liberalism and the sham attitudes and opinions it shapes and legislates. He speaks its language, acts out and propagates its gospel of religion and progress, and helps define its orthodoxy of enlightenment, to which he now fashions the new Simone Weil as an integral part of "the First New Left," consisting of radicals in the years 1930–1945.

And so we read on, rather drearily, in Coles's book as we move from "Her Jewishness" to "Her Political Life." In this chapter Coles's tone becomes supercilious as he commences to applaud her political activism but also to censure the murkiness of some of her political ideas and theories. He fails, in effect, to comprehend her political vision in its spiritual and religious depth and reach. Here, as in this book as a whole, he neatly packages her political position, and the results are characteristically simplistic: "She was on the 'left' in the sense that she approached both political thought and political action with overriding compassion for the poor." And characteristically he views her most famous piece of writing, "The *Iliad*, Poem of Might" (French original published in 1940–1941), as a realistic and unromantic indictment of "the lust for power as a constant protagonist in the human drama." What Coles seems to see exclusively in this astonishing essay is the sociology of power in its immanent forms. This immanentism blinds him to the crucial climax of this essay and the final accents that Simone Weil seeks to impart in its last few pages, as when she asserts:

> The Gospels are the last and most marvelous expression of Greek genius, as the *Iliad* is its first expression. . . . certain expressions in the Gospels have a strangely familiar ring reminiscent of the

epic. The adolescent Trojan, sent against his will to Hades, reminds one of Christ when he told St. Peter: "Another shall gird thee and carry thee where thou wouldst not."

Likewise, in discussing *The Need for Roots* (1952), Simone Weil's most systematic study in political sociology and social ethics, Coles emphasizes the sociopolitical dimension of her great visionary tract and simultaneously downgrades or misconstrues her implicit spiritual foci. He neglects not only the ultimate significance of the distinctions she draws between the heavenly and the earthly needs of the soul, but also their imperishable connections, which in turn underline her constant and overarching spiritual preoccupation with the life and truth of Faith in the light of the reality of man's approach to God and of the idea of affliction that are the subject of her theologically oriented meditation on "The Love of God and Affliction," in which she writes at one point: "There is not, there cannot be, any human activity in whatever sphere, of which Christ's Cross is not the supreme and secret truth."

In general Coles deflects the spiritual thrust of Simone Weil's contemplations, their theology as well as their eschatology. "But hers was, to the end, a politics of hope," he declares. "She believed man was capable of responding to new social and cultural forms, to new economic policies, to a moral vision and a religious one which would transform the world." Here, incontrovertibly, it is the voice of Coles the millennialist speaking of and connecting Simone Weil with some tenuous temporal vision of "The Great Society." The problem with this book is that Coles sees and makes the wrong connections, even as this pronouncement early on in the book should warn off any reader who is interested in understanding the real meaning of Simone Weil's spiritual pilgrimage in a world in which modern man is rootless precisely because he has cut himself off from God:

> In her last few months of life, Simone Weil was feverishly at work writing; she saw few people and slept and ate little. As she wrote "The Need for the Soul," posthumously to be a major part of *The Need for Roots*, her imperialist ego had triumphed over the needs of her body.

In stressing as he does Simone Weil's "politics of hope" (in terms of her "political *life*" as opposed to her "political thought"), Coles actually alerts readers to the tendency in this book to subordinate transcendent spiritual meaning to the dictates of self-fulfillment and self-realization. He fails, thus, to consider the intrinsic importance of Simone Weil's basic belief that "If you do not believe in the remote, silent, secret omnipotence of a spirit, there remains the manifest omnipotence of matter." In a sense, he makes Simone Weil too much a part of the world, and as a result he severely limits not only his own critical credibility but also her spiritual vision when he throws off a judgment like this: "Unlike her dubious rhetoric when engaged in rewriting religious history, her politics was solid." This misjudgment underlines the kind of weakness that decreases the authority and value of the book as a whole. It also should alert a reader to the spiritual vacuity of the book, and particularly its slipshod attitude toward Simone Weil's ceaseless preoccupation with *Logos* rather than *chronos*. One gets the feeling increasingly that Coles really sees and treats Simone Weil as a special and suspect case, a freak of sorts, even when he perhaps wants to recognize her special worth: "Her preoccupation, if not obsession, with purity, with its strong sexual overtones, made her social and political thinking always susceptible to the prudishness in her personality."

It may well be that Coles is sincere in expressing his mixed feelings about Simone Weil, but it is also clear that he lacks the metaphysical capacity to explore or discover the spiritual nature of her "pilgrimage." Coles accepts the fact that "she is engaged in the dialectic of the moralist," not unlike a Kierkegaard, a Camus, a Gabriel Marcel, or a Sartre. But his musings (and demurrings) finally disclose an incipient failure to perceive fully and finally Simone Weil as both a "Witness of the Absolute" and "A Pilgrim of the Absolute." To be sure, Coles shows empathic respect for Simone Weil's social compassion (as exemplified by her own experiences recounted in her essay on "Factory Work") and moral principles (as exemplified by her long study "Reflections concerning the Causes of Liberty and Social Oppression"). But this is precisely the Simone Weil who also exemplifies the "possibility of a rational New Left" (again to quote Staughton Lynd). She is the Simone Weil who has "spiritual kin" with George Orwell and Dorothy Day, or as George Abbott White writes in an essay on "Simone Weil's Work Experiences: From Wigan Pier to Chrystie Street": "Where George Orwell and Dorothy Day countered the system of oppression, Simone Weil entered its jaws and spoke of necessity from the belly of the beast."[4]

Sentimental idealism and egalitarian yearning ultimately identify the ideological dialectic of Coles's book and makes it impossible for him to fathom the metaphysical purity of Simone Weil's religious vision. At every opportunity, it becomes evident, Coles deflates her spiritual essences. Even when he seeks to show her attachment to spiritual life his

---

[4]In *Simone Weil: Interpretations of a Life*, 178-79.

operative order of values betrays his pose. His stress is, inevitably, on Simone Weil's reformist zeal rather than on her spiritual essences. This stress is the vital center of the book and makes Coles's a misrepresentative interpretation. His language and tone when adverting to Simone Weil's mystical experiences, and primarily her view of Christ, reveal him to be a hostile critic. "Once Simone Weil met Christ," he writes, "her life began anew, a slave, now, to a particular master. I think it fair to say that she fell in love with Jesus; that he became her beloved; that she kept him in her mind and in her heart." Any attempt at reverence slides, as seen here, almost automatically into contempt.

For Coles, Simone Weil embodies "that mix of ruthless logic and wild illogic" that instance a side of her that is both "exhausting and comic." He is incapable of making a straight, open, undefiled statement like this one from Alfred Kazin's astute six-page essay on Simone Weil: "She was a fantastically dedicated participant in the most critical experiences of our time, who tried to live them directly in contact with the supernatural."[5] Coles's antipathies get the better of him as when he explains Simone Weil's love of the Catholic faith but not of the Church: "I think she never forgave the Church for conquering the Roman empire." He fails to go on, however, to place her total religious allegiance in terms of an earlier Christian Hellenism—an allegiance that, when cited and weighed, tells us a great deal about her Catholic and Apostolic faith as an amalgam of Hellenism, Platonism, and Christianity. It is far better to turn to the words of Simone Weil herself in order to ascertain the validity of her religious affirmation and also to extricate it from the dialectical biases and imbalances of Coles's interpretation: "I do not believe that I am outside the Church as far as it is the source of sacramental life; only insofar as it is a social body."

In the final analysis, this book fails to attain a true and just estimation of Simone Weil precisely because Coles does not comprehend the numinous qualities of "the supernatural power of the sacraments," as Simone Weil expresses it. Symptomatic of this arresting failure is the fact that he relies too much on the authority of Anna Freud and not at all on, say, the testimony of Evelyn Underhill, whose remarkable book *Mysticism* (1911) would have helped Coles penetrate the contemplative dimensions, the interiority, of Simone Weil's transcendental quest. Instead he chooses to tell readers that Simone Weil simply "is obsessed with the psychology of

---

[5]"The Gift," in his *The Inmost Leaf: A Selection of Essays* (New York: Harcourt, Brace, 1955) 211-12.

the Cross," though no words could be more disparaging except as they are written by someone who has absolutely no understanding of the sacred realm of the transcendental order. All too often Coles's appraisal of Simone Weil's supersensible essences and spiritual consciousness is mechanistic. Concentrating on her "imperial self," as it were, he completely misses the pull of her contemplative, mystical self, which is (to use here an excellent modern definition) "in essence the concentration of all the forces of the soul upon a supernatural object." In Simone Weil's political activism and primitive religious orientation Coles discerns "a statement of her radical Christianity" that has earned her the right to be called "the saint of the churchless."

The radicalness of Simone Weil's religious faith is not to be either underestimated or deprecated, and Coles is fully justified in assigning to this radicalness a primary importance and also in maintaining that it is a "radical grace" that comes to her. But the picture of her that he ultimately etches is of a believer at the threshold of a justified heresy. The Simone Weil that he presents is the Simone Weil whose heterodoxy and even profanations he approves of as being required in our time. As such, it is a blessed heretic and religious rebel necessary to a radical renewal of Christianity who comes through. And, as a number of commentators have pointed out, this is the Simone Weil of *Lettre à un religieux* who has a kinship with the Pascal of *Lettres provinciales*. Coles assists in the task of a heretic's "return to the Christian realm," to quote Dr. Walter Nigg's phrase.[6] At the same time, this aspect of Coles's view of Simone Weil places an inordinate and one-sided emphasis on her radical religious vision. Such a vision, however, can also lead, or mislead, a reader in conjuring up a Simone Weil as an outsider who belongs to the revolutionary gangs who took to the streets in 1968. This is a distorted image of her that Coles imparts, sometimes in spite of himself. In this respect, he accents the modernity of her pilgrimage in the limitary paradigms of social resistance, revolution, and change. It is a politicized Simone Weil who dominates Coles's book and who, as one writer representatively puts it, provides "both inspiration and useful warnings for those still working for peace and a world with fewer slaves."[7]

Not unexpectedly, then, Coles's final chapter is devoted to "Idolatry and the Intellectuals." Here he places Simone Weil in the same grouping

---

[6]Walter Nigg, *The Heretics*, ed. and trans. by Richard Winston and Clara Winston (New York: Alfred Knopf, 1962) 409.

[7]Joseph H. Summers, "Notes on Simone Weil's *Iliad*," in *Simone Weil: Interpretations of a Life*, 93.

of "anti-intellectuals" as James Agee, George Orwell, and William Carlos Williams, and he emphasizes her perception of the idolatrous tendency of intellectuals "to adore" institutional and doctrinal beliefs and habits of mind and to capitulate to seductive attractions. He also believes that she was trying to create "a theory of moral psychology." He singles out, for instance, her statement, "A Catholic directs his thought secondarily towards the truth, but primarily towards conformity with the Church's doctrine," as an example of her view of the idolatry that exists in human nature. "There was something stubbornly Protestant in her wish to stand alone before God, to wait for grace on her own," Coles observes. Her faith, in effect, as he goes on to stress, contains "a Protestant rather than Catholic existentialism." Thus, in one of the concluding statements of his book, Coles writes as follows:

> In the last years of her life she worried that all beliefs, even religious ones, risk idolatry. Her insistence upon "a convention ratified by God" is another example of the thoroughly personal knowledge of God that she sought, and one gathers, believed herself to have attained. She seemed persuaded that under the auspices of the Church such personal knowledge simply does not come about; on the contrary, parishioners turn idolatrous and mistake a ritual, a habit, and alas, a social custom (to go to church on Sunday, say) for such a convention.

No statement better embodies the tendentiousness of Coles's interpretation than the foregoing one. The entire élan of the book crystallizes here and serves to disclose its underlying strategy of diminishing the spiritual meaning of Simone Weil's pilgrimage and converting it into "a modern pilgrimage" in all its conundrums and absurdities. What we have, in the process, is a metastasis that ends in the vulgarization of Simone Weil through a process of reducing and demeaning her spiritual significance. That is why, too, Coles's Simone Weil is made to belong to the *people*, to all of *us*: "Hers was a modern pilgrimage; she entertained all our assumptions, presumptions, and anticipations—her journey was ours. She experienced, in the few years she knew among us, our buoyancy, our optimism, and soon enough our terrible discouragement and melancholy." And that is why Coles focuses on the modern and not on the eternal elements of her quest. In the end Coles presents to us the Simone Weil of the *inferno* rather than the *paradiso*; he simply cannot begin to comprehend or accept the ultimate measure of her ascent and transcendence.

Somehow Coles restricts her spiritual vision and meaning to the cloying standards of the world of *chronos* and not *kairos*—to the nominalism that finally judges all things by the temporal values of self-fulfillment and self-assertion. And these values, of course, are the values of what Edmund Burke calls the "antagonist world" and what Simone Weil herself calls "the empire of might"—a derelict, disinherited, fallen, blasphemous, impermanent world that never stops proclaiming the death of God and the death of the soul. Perhaps at no other time in human history is that world—"the modern world [that] seems capable only of the *low dream*," as T. S. Eliot phrases it[8]—more profane than it is today. Coles plants Simone Weil at the very heart of a centrifugal world and he never really permits her to move out of it, to go beyond it. This is inherently a demonic world in which Coles enacts the vulgarization of Simone Weil. This world is his critical vortex, and void, as it also becomes a prison world in which "a modern pilgrimage" is necessarily confined. Within its perimeters, to be sure, Simone Weil's angst is registered with much pathos and forlornness. But it also brings to mind these memorable words written by Simone Weil: "Decreation: To make something created pass into the uncreated. Destruction: To make something created pass into nothingness. A blameworthy substitute for decreation." Coles reverses the spiritual order and purgative value of her words as he subjects her to a finite process of destruction and nothingness. That vulgar process may satisfy a Reverend William Sloane Coffin and a Dr. Benjamin Spock, but verily it does violence to the constituents of Simone Weil's authentically spiritual quest.

In the end, it will be seen, Coles seeks to accommodate Simone Weil to the modern world—to a scientific, pragmatic, empirical world that has little or no patience for things sacred, or as Simone Weil herself observes: "To find a place in the budget for the eternal is not in the spirit of our age." In these special circumstances, then, contemporary readers and interpreters are prone, perhaps even conditioned, to create a politicized, a personalized, and ultimately a debased Simone Weil, who is reconstituted so as to reject the intrinsic truth of her deeper and transcendent belief that "The world is the closed door. It is a barrier. And at the same time it is the way through." Coles denies Simone Weil this transcendence; and he denies her the existence of bridges, of the Platonic *metaxu*, or intermediaries, between nature and supernature, between man and God, or as she describes the eternalizing process:

> The bridges of the Greeks. We have inherited them but we do
> not know how to use them. We thought they were intended to
> have houses built upon them. We have erected skyscrapers on

---

[8]"Dante," in *Selected Essays* (New York: Harcourt, Brace, and World, 1960) 223.

them to which we ceaselessly add stories. We no longer know that they are bridges, things made so that we may pass along them, and that by passing along them we go toward God.[9]

It needs to be constantly stressed that Simone Weil belongs to the great spiritual tradition which finds meaning in final causes. The final cause for Simone Weil is the attraction to God—the God she meditates on with astonishing devotion and reverence in "Concerning the Our Father":

> Humility consists of knowing that in this world the whole soul, not only what we term the ego in its totality, but also the supernatural part of the soul, which is God present in it, is subject to time and to the vicissitudes of change. There must be absolute acceptance of the possibility that everything material in us should be destroyed. But we must simultaneously accept and repudiate the possibility that the supernatural part of the soul should disappear.[10]

What escapes Coles most in his portrait of Simone Weil is the strength and the depth of her sacramental vision, especially as it was consummated in the last five years of her short life, leading T. S. Eliot to describe her a "a woman of genius, of a kind of genius akin to that of a saint." For her, "contact with God is the true sacrament."[11] "My heart, I hope, is transferred forever into the Holy Eucharist," she wrote a year before she died. For the most part Coles stands remote from, if not wary of and even antipathetic to, the Simone Weil who affirms the "eternal word." Yet, surely, it can be said that her search for God became emblazed in the shadow of the Cross. "Christ," she insisted, "likes us to prefer truth to him because, before being Christ, he is truth. If one turns aside from him to go toward the truth, one will not go far before falling into his arms." Coles shows only meager understanding of Simone Weil's journey toward this truth in Christ.[12] And in the end he is a disappointing and unreliable interpreter of her witness in all of its gravity and grace.

---

[9]See "Metaxu," in *The Simone Weil Reader*, ed. George A. Panichas (New York: David McKay, 1977) 363-65.

[10]See *The Simone Weil Reader*, 492-500.

[11]Quoted from T. S. Eliot's preface to *The Need for Roots: Prelude to a Declaration of Duties toward Mankind*, trans. Arthur Wills (New York: Putnam's, 1953).

[12]See my essay on "The Christ of Simone Weil," *Studies in Formative Spirituality* 4/2 (May 1983): 229-42, also in my *The Critic as Conservator: Essays in Literature, Society, and Culture* (Washington: Catholic University of America Press, 1992).

Avatars of Betrayal

One who reads and reflects on Professor Robert Nisbet's *Roosevelt and Stalin: The Failed Courtship* (1988)—and particularly one who has lived through the dark years in which the epochal actions and decisions that Nisbet assesses took place—cannot ignore the censorial judgments that the book presents. Even liberal diehards should be hard-pressed to rebut Nisbet's diagnosis of events and personalities that have made a permanent imprint on the process of modern civilization. In particular, we are also reminded of how the quality of political leadership affects universal history. Clearly, what Nisbet reveals is that an intrinsic rhythm of disintegration was to identify the consequences of the kind of working relation that Franklin Delano Roosevelt and Josef Stalin developed. No two leaders did more to restructure the postwar world than did Roosevelt and Stalin. As both witnesses to and legatees of the unusual relationship of these two men, who held in their hands the fate of humanity for a crucial period of time, we can hardly minimize the momentous outcome of that relationship. Its political repercussions, no less than its historical psychology and sociology, are nothing less than amazing.

One's evaluative response to *Roosevelt and Stalin: The Failed Courtship* should give some sort of index to one's willingness to aspire to a deeper awareness of political conditions that in the end assume transcendent moral meaning and validity. For many readers, Nisbet's book should excite remembrance of things past. And for those born after World War II, his book should help provide historical circumspection that encourages the kind of probative understanding (and humility) that the lessons of history impart to those who live in the postmodern climate in which an insidious revisionism and relativism combine to foment the ahistorical, nonhistorical, and antihistorical attitudes that pervade the intellectual community in its present deconstructionist phase. These attitudes, however, are blasted by the explosive power of Nisbet's case against Roosevelt and by his rigorously sustained argument that the president's "political courtship" of Stalin reached its height first at the conference at Teheran in 1943 and then at Yalta in 1945. "Teheran was in a sense Stalin's Munich," Nisbet writes, "as Munich was Hitler's Teheran." No statement better illustrates the enduring truth of the comment written somewhere that one thought fills immensity! For what happened in the compound of the Russian embassy in Teheran had immeasurable effects that Nisbet estimates with candor and discrimination.

I myself find Nisbet's arguments irreproachable, painfully so. The adverbial addendum at the end of the preceding sentence has for me a deeply personal significance, for as a child of the 1930s who had witnessed the impact of the Great Depression, which to Americans was as traumatic an experience as the Great War was to European man, Roosevelt was my hero, and one whom my imagination has not fully been able to replace. As a boy of fourteen years of age, I was among the thousands who awaited with infinite excitement Roosevelt's "whistle-stop" appearances in the 1944 campaign when his train was passing through the small industrial city in southwestern Massachusetts where I lived. Some school friends and I even made some crude placards endorsing him in his bid against Thomas E. Dewey for a fourth term. I can visualize fully the moment on a crisp autumn day when he emerged from his private car to address briefly a huge crowd awaiting him from below a railroad overpass. Though I do not recall his words, I do recall his luminous presence as I looked up in wonder at the white-haired man, now larger than life, ablaze with heroic stature and dignity, and as he in turn gazed down at and spoke to us—paternally, confidently, reassuringly.

Roosevelt exuded a kind of nobility that no other statesman has for me ever equalled. In him my hero worship reached its pinnacle. All those virtues that encompass the highest standards of statesmanship—certainty, constancy, sincerity, fortitude, magnanimity—acquired in his presence, on that occasion far away and long ago, a sacrosanctness that I have never forgotten. If ever I revered any leader as much, it was Roosevelt, who appeared to many of us a hero at what was truly an epiphanous time in history. Even the passage of decades fails to lessen the aural and visual inspirations of that day in a New England city on the bank of the Connecticut River when one came to greet the president of the United States. Somehow even the war itself seemed an insignificant historical fact compared to the greatness of that moment as it mysteriously possessed the innocence of my psyche. "The heroic cannot be the common, nor the common the heroic," as Emerson observed.

The Roosevelt myth was always to be powerful and inviolate. When I chanced to come across a campaign picture depicting FDR behind bars in a prison cell, bearing the caption "Where he belongs!" I was horrified. Roosevelt, it seems, was once to me what Charles Stewart Parnell, the "uncrowned King of Ireland," was to James Joyce. When he died, I wept bitter tears, thinking in despair that the world had lost its greatest beacon of hope. That spring afternoon when the startling announcement of his death came over the radio was, I vividly remember, fragrant and sunny, but for me it was cold and dreary. (Indeed, the only poem I ever wrote in my life was an elegy on the president's death on April 12, 1945.) His death marked the death of an era and I feared somehow for the safety of my world. My mother was much more practical in consoling me. "This, too, will pass," she said. "The world will go on, new leaders will come as they always have come." And, of course, Harry S. Truman did succeed FDR. In fact, in 1944, I also went to the railway depot to meet the Democratic vice presidential candidate who was then campaigning in Massachusetts. "What a friendly, dapper little man," I thought to myself as he shook my hand firmly and eagerly—dazzled as I was by political potentates. But "the man from Missouri," as I told myself, was no Roosevelt. Later it was my mother, again, who remarked that it was far better to have a Truman than a quixotic Henry A. Wallace as Roosevelt's successor. And history itself was to attest to the appropriateness of this remark.

In time the gradual demythicizing of Roosevelt and the examples of cruel history were to teach me truths that cut to the bone. By the mid-1950s, which saw the brutal Sovietization of large parts of the world, I had grudgingly come to realize that there was a distinct difference between greatness and mere power. But even that realization, in its disillusioning context, pained me sharply. To this very day there is not a photograph of FDR that does not stir profoundly my nostalgia, my adolescent dreams and hopes—those reveries that, I now well know, are filled treacherously with the romance of lies. But it is always difficult for enthusiasts like my former self, stamped deeply by early life experiences and the perennial dream of a "brave new world," to rid ourselves completely of enchanting myths and ideals, or to forget our heroes even when they have, as we must finally learn to our sorrow, feet of clay.

To this day no other human voice has the capacity to stir me as much, in its singularly inspirational quality and conveyed confidence, as did Roosevelt's. His "fireside chats" echo in the depths of my consciousness, and I can still envision myself expectantly huddled with neighbors and members of my family in front of a small radio listening to each word dropping mellifluously from Roosevelt's mouth. As a speaker he was for many of us a modern Chrysostom. Even now I can hear his voice from across the grave in Hyde Park speaking to me as no other American leader's voice has ever spoken to me. And I can still travel back, effortlessly and shamelessly, to the Roosevelt era, hoping to discover there some lost inspiration, some exhilarating moment frozen in time, some far-off "shining city" in which to see, to hear again, my great political hero. My early reverence for and my later disenchantment with Roosevelt, I have to confess, were never to be altogether commensurate in their emotional intensity. Hero worship, as Thomas Carlyle tells us, "becomes a fact inexpressibly precious. . . . The certainty of heroes when sent us; our faculty, our necessity, to reverence Heroes when sent; it shines like a polestar through smoke-clouds, dust-clouds, and all manner of down-rushing and conflagration."

These autobiographical retrospections are sparked by Nisbet's *Roosevelt and Stalin: The Failed Courtship*. I record them here in order to emphasize the persuasive power and urgency of Nisbet's book as it diagnoses and corrects the history of the relations between two wartime leaders, their grim meaning and results in our time and for all time. In the end, I find, no amount of hero worship can blind us to those truths and data that liberate us from the nets of romantic attitudes and illusions. For that which violates the rational sequence of cause and effect is always in need of attention. We need, above all, to recall the lasting results of what Roosevelt and Stalin brought about. We need, that is, to confront head-on issues that "terrible simplifiers" would have us ignore or observe through rose-colored glasses.

What makes Nisbet's *Roosevelt and Stalin: The Failed Courtship* so pertinent in its scrutiny of matters of first importance is that it not only pushes aside the veil of illusion that often belongs to romantic attitudes and habits, but also shatters the hagiographic liberal myths that have collected around Roosevelt's persona and policies. Nisbet's critique of Roosevelt's courtship of Stalin speaks for itself as we look backward and forward since the 1940s: "It was Teheran, not the later Yalta, that was the setting for the Cold War." Thus, to glance at events in Poland in recent decades is to return to the Teheran where FDR did little or nothing to block tyrannous Soviet plans for that unfortunate country.

An absolutely amazing mixture of megalomania, haughtiness, adventurism, illusion, naïveté, and ignorance, as Nisbet demonstrates, identified Roosevelt's attitude toward the Soviet leader. "I tell you I can personally handle Stalin better than either your Foreign Office or my State Department," Roosevelt unabashedly wrote to Churchill on March 18, 1942. That boast never subsided. Nor did his appeasement of Stalin. Clearly, in FDR there was no real awareness of what the Marxist Revolution and its extermination machine in Russia were all about. In their own special way Teheran and Yalta were to become symbols of betrayal in a world in which, as John Paul II cogently put it before he became Pope, "falsity and hypocrisy reign supreme, public opinion is manipulated, consciences are bludgeoned, apostasy is sometimes imposed by force, and there is organized persecution of faith." Unconscionably impervious to, if not incapable of, a metaphysical conception of the inward crisis of modernity, FDR affirmed the spirit of Rousseau in his view of the Communist East as fallow ground for the growth of political and economic reform.

It is a pity that Roosevelt could never have read Aleksandr Solzhenitsyn's novel *The First Circle* (1968). Solzhenitsyn's extraordinary portrayal of Stalin as he appears at the age of seventy in 1949—"Growing old like a dog. An old age without friends. An old age without love. An old age without faith. An old age without desire."—unmasks the satanic nature of Stalin as well as the evils of monolithic Stalinism. *The First Circle* would have enabled Roosevelt to enter that most frightening of metaphysical, or ideological, hells. There he would have encountered the "seminarist-careerist" who, as Vladislav Krasnov has noted in his book on *Solzhenitsyn and Dostoevsky* (1980), "chose a more ambitious path, the path of atheism and revolution, and eventually became the 'sole and infallible' pontiff of world Communism." For Stalin, as one dissident commentator has stated, the word "soul" itself connoted something anti-Soviet. An exemplar of "men who have forgotten God," Stalin was verily a man-god whom a vain and self-deceiving Roosevelt presumed he could mold into yet another New Dealer in a Soviet marshal's uniform!

In his dealings with Stalin, no less than in his general understanding of foreign affairs, Roosevelt disclosed alarming deficiencies that must inevitably diminish our view of him as a great man of politics and war. His behavior at Teheran and Yalta had an unfortunate aftermath. In this connection, it is surprising that Roosevelt's appeasement of Stalin is yet to be perceived on the same level as Neville Chamberlain's appeasement of Hitler. But, then, Roosevelt was a clever publicist and coordinator of myths, and also something of a medicine man, unlike Chamberlain, whose intellectual coldness and lack of demagogy have always worked against him and have stereotyped him as a dour, ineffectual leader.

The wartime encounters between a patrician American president and a revolutionary Russian dictator have continuing reverberations that liberal apologists cannot easily eradicate. To look at the map of the world is to be reminded precisely of what happened when Roosevelt and Stalin joined to transform the geography of twentieth-century society and in turn the geography of the world soul itself. For those who have the courage to judge sociopolitical happenings and geopolitical movements of history, spiritual and political interdependencies are inescapable. Only when modern man accepts this consummate fact of human existence can he acquire the vision and the wisdom belonging to those whom Irving

Babbitt calls the "keen-sighted few," that minority of excellence to which the ancient Hellenes gave the title *aristoi*.

Nisbet underlines the relevance of Jacob Burckhardt's belief that a leader with "crazy and heartfelt optimism as to human nature" simply has "no comprehension of the type of mind which cares only for power and thinks only in terms of power." The picture of Roosevelt and Stalin that Nisbet illuminates is of one who suffers from an abysmal confusion that, as the great Swiss historian of the nineteenth century observed with prophetic insight in his *Weltgeschichtliche Betrachtungen* (1905; *Force and Freedom: Reflections on History*, 1943), characterizes "good, splendid, liberal people who do not quite know the boundaries of right and wrong and where the duty of resistance and defense begins."

Roosevelt and Stalin: The Failed Courtship recreates events of unique historical significance, it penetrates human folly and dreams, it destroys historical fantasies, it returns us to a time that absorbs our time, it enables us to discern man in history and history in man. But beyond these critical distinctions, the book has transhistorical and transdisciplinary values that affect the right conduct of mind in detecting the ingredients of an adulterative romanticism in an age dominated by liberal ideology: the power of illusion, the lure of myth, the decline of spiritual principles, the worship of false gods, the unchecked growth of critical gnosticisms, the attraction of unreal quests, the promotion of personality.

Refuting tendencies that circumscribe the demonic element in life demands intellectual and spiritual ardor and respect for a transcendent moral order. Finally, in helping us to stare into chaos, Nisbet underlines abiding historical truths that a Burckhardt grasps when he expresses reverence for "the survival of the human spirit, which in the end presents itself to us as the life of one human being. That life, as it becomes self-conscious in and through history, cannot fail in time so to fascinate the gaze of the thinking man, and the study of it so to engage his power, that the ideas of fortune and misfortune inevitably fade."

Part two

Shepherds of the Peoples

"Affirming
the Enduring Order of Things"

Teacher and Critic

Irving Babbitt (1865–1933) never wavered in what he viewed as being his commanding office as a teacher and critic. During the more than forty years of his career he held firmly to a position, both avoiding and scorning "sudden conversions" and "pistol-shot transformations." He never fell into the traps of confusion and expediency; nor did he ever compromise his position either out of self-doubt or of self-interest. His critical position, as hard and tough as it was sincere and authentic, sanctioned neither retreat nor rerouting. From the start he chose to travel and to stay on one road. Like Archilochus's hedgehog, Babbitt knew one big thing, related everything to a single central vision, and affirmed a single, universal, organizing principle. Even as storms of controversy (and abuse) raged around him he did not give way. He was, in his special style, a battler; "never say die," in the best tradition of that worn phrase, could have easily been one of his slogans. To claim, as is the habit of some commentators, that Babbitt is monolithic as a critical thinker is to subtract from the real worth of his achievement. It is to perpetuate the myth that his enemies came to create about his being a reactionary. His position was, to be sure, foursquare, but it was also a position that excelled in character; he never betrayed his conscience, the truths of which, once he had discovered them, he possessed irretrievably.

This tenacity of character and principle is compellingly present in Babbitt's creed of humanism, or of the New Humanism as it is better known. Unfortunately, his position has generally been misunderstood and misrepresented. His enemies gave it too little credit and his sympathizers expected too much from it. Babbitt himself defined his creed clearly, augmented considerably by the simplicity of his delineation of his ideas and judgments. Unprofitable subtleties, conundrums, complexities, and paradoxes never interfered with or distorted Babbitt's presentation of his creed. Its other most notable quality is its centripetal force. His vision of order was impelled by his principle of control. In this respect, Babbitt's position was to militate against anything that leads one to fantasy or illusion. Limits, not expansion, was an informing word in his concepts.

It could be said that the restrictive essences of Babbitt's thought worked against its popular acceptance, in much the same way that the human capacity for reconstructive change, or what Babbitt termed a "metaphysic of the many," as preached by his famous contemporary, the philosopher John Dewey, spurred on an epidemic scale a refashioning of thought not only in philosophy but also in law, in education, in politics. A "maker of twentieth-century America," Dewey appealed to man's expansionist impulse. His radical optimism, in the contexts and with the specifics of an inclusive program of social action, was appropriate to a national mood and a liberal trend. Human possibilities unlimited: to this doctrine of change and growth, in the attainment of pragmatic "consummations," Dewey gave his first and last loyalty, as even this one sentence from his voluminous writings shows: "Democracy is the faith that the process of experience is more important than any special result attained, so that special results achieved are of ultimate value only as they are used to enrich and order the ongoing process." Any emphasis, then, on inner, or spiritual life, as watched over by a purgative and humbling "inner check," as made by Babbitt, could hardly compete with Dewey's view of life as an evolving social experience of "shared good."

Babbitt's humanistic doctrine is ultimately characterized not by ambition but by humility with its intrinsic sense of man's need for self-discipline and self-reliance. There is nothing either programmatic or enthusiastic about Babbitt's doctrine; indeed, it is austere and even solitary, lacking any grand temporal plans or metaphysical promises of redemption. It is doctrine completely shorn of personal or collective illusions and nonessentials; the dreams of infinitude, of a "Great Society" and of a "city of God" alike, are for Babbitt vague and unrealizable. One could say in this respect that Babbitt's doctrine is spiritual, as this word conjoins ethical and moral constituents, rather than religious in a supernatural sense. It revolves around conscience rather than grace. His innately Protestant sensibility is severely schooled by his classicist and Orientalist metaphysic in its assimilated forms and consecration to what Babbitt terms "the service of a high, impersonal reason." For Babbitt, reason is an indwelling and salutary force of mediation, legislating restraint and proportion—the middle way, the law of measure, that avoids the extremes of human consciousness, whether as an Augustinian curse *of* or as a Rousseauistic adventure in consciousness. Babbitt was a genuine ecumenist. His humanism was a finely wrought reconciliation of East and West, of Confucius and Aristotle, of Buddha and Christ.

Both his friendly and his enemy critics have failed to appreciate the simple and direct meaning of Babbitt's doctrine. For T. S. Eliot, it was inadequately religious, an alternative or ancillary doctrine that suppressed the divine or outrightly denied the revelation of the supernatural. For Edmund Wilson, it was insufferably reactionary, a doctrine containing "not really conclusions from evidence, but the mere unexamined prejudices of a bigoted Puritan heritage." For Eliot, Babbitt's teachings lacked Catholicity, and for Wilson they lacked Liberalism. The point is that Babbitt's teachings failed to pass the "ultimate" tests of orthodoxy or of enlightenment and, as a result, were never given a fair hearing. Babbitt himself would rightly dismiss the charges of his enemy critics as a hodgepodge of humanitarian, utilitarian, and sentimental opinions, which fail to adhere to some higher principle of unity, or standard, with which to measure mere manifoldness and change or a mere multiplicity of a scale of values. But that both his greatest pupil and even his greatest ally, Paul Elmer More, chose to deprecate the spiritual dimension of Babbitt's doctrine must be noted as an unfortunate phenomenon. Babbitt, after all, was not a theologian. He was, however, a humanistic teacher and prophetic critic of extraordinary ability, as time and history proved.

"On being human," to use the title of a volume of one of More's New Shelburne Essays, and on being human in an age discrediting the older dualism, underlined Babbitt's prophetic concern. This concern is at the very center of his mission; it is a total concern as it relates to an ongoing interaction of economic, political, philosophical, religious, and educational problems in the modern world. No two passages from Babbitt's texts better catch his significance as an ethical prophet of modernism than the following, the first written at the beginning of his career, the second at the end:

> The greatest of vices according to Buddha is the lazy yielding to the impulses of temperament (*pamāda*); the greatest virtue (*appamāda*) is the opposite of this, the awakening from the sloth and lethargy of the senses, the constant exercise of the active will. The last words of the dying Buddha to his disciples was an exhortation to practice this virtue unremittingly (*appāmadena sampādetha*).

> He [Buddha] has succeeded in compressing the wisdom of the ages into a sentence: "To refrain from all evil, to achieve the good, to purify one's heart, this is the teaching of the Awakened." The Buddhist commentary is interesting: When you repeat the words, they seem to mean nothing, but when you try to put them into practice, you find they mean everything.

~ 🐦 🐦 ~

Now whether or not Babbitt is, say, a philosopher, or an aesthetician, or a literary critic, or a moral agent, or a social commentator, or a conservative ideologue, or a guru is a debate that, at least among academic boulevardiers, is fated to go on. No less evident, though more alarming, is the violent tone that marks this debate, as violent today as it was in the 1920s and 1930s when the New Humanism enjoyed something of a vogue. Identifying the nature of Babbitt's work and thought—his mission—is not difficult. If one must insist, however, on pinning some kind of nametag on Babbitt before admitting him into some grove of academe, and certainly before considering the significance of his contribution, not one but several nametags can be presented. Generalist, diagnostician, teacher, thinker—in each of those categories Babbitt acquitted himself honestly, honorably, humbly. That, as his pupil Austin Warren writes, Babbitt can also be counted among the New England Saints, in the goodly company of a Bronson Alcott, an Edward Taylor, a Charles Eliot Norton, is a claim that transcends all others and makes them finally superfluous. For some, no doubt, Warren's claim may be extravagant, even as for Babbitt, who insisted on basing judgments on immediate data of consciousness, it may have been found embarrassing.

A mediating designation that identifies Babbitt, and one perhaps neither he nor his enemies would quibble over, is catechist, the office of catechist defined as being that of not only instructing and teaching but also examining. Indeed, Babbitt's teachings and writings (and the latter are the fruit of the former) disclose precisely his catechistic style and approach, as well as his work, which was his act of faith. Only when Babbitt is seen in this refining light will proper recognition of his achievement be possible. Only, that is, when he is seen as a teacher in the old, and catechistic, sense will he be revered in the way that a Ralph Waldo Emerson is revered. Clearly, in the case of Babbitt, any plea for critical reconsideration must also predicate what is even more important, an act of reparation.

The prospects for any full-scale reparation are not good in the present derelict phase of American culture. It is a phase in which postliberal driftings and shiftings are everywhere in abundance, and with an abundance of frightening consequences, which Babbitt himself prophesied. If we can boast with all our liberal optimism of being a nation of New Adams, we are hardly a nation of catechumens. The catecheses of Irving Babbitt are no more to the liking of most Americans than any message that stresses moral and spiritual restraint of any sort. "Outward bound," the bigger the better, not the "inner check," characterizes the yearnings of most Americans today. Early on in his life, Babbitt chose to resist this centrifugal quest, equating it with an imperialism as dangerous in its psychic as in its sociopolitical dimensions. It is sometimes said by some of Babbitt's Harvard pupils that at the close of his life he grew pessimistic as to the efficacy of his mission. Such a feeling would be natural to any sensitive and intelligent observer of the chaos of values embracing the whole of modern life.

No modern American thinker exposed himself to more attack than Babbitt. From T. V. Smith to, just the other day, in a virulent letter appearing in *The American Scholar*, Ernest Earnest, the attacks have continued with the kind of intolerance prompting Douglas Bush to protest against the unqualified charges aimed at Babbitt by "automatic liberals who," he notes, "can be as intolerant of nonconformity as automatic conservatives." "Nonconformity" may seem the wrong word to use to describe Babbitt's thought. But when one deliberates on the matter and considers the power of the reigning orthodoxy of enlightenment, then one can easily see that Babbitt's catechistical thought, positing as it does the idea of a minority culture, goes against the grain. The fact remains that many Americans are by now so addicted to the illusion of liberalism that they can hardly be patient when confronted with demands—and Babbitt never ceased making them—for affirming the moral constant and the moral imperative. No, it is not easy, in the peculiar circumstances surrounding Babbitt, to make an act of reparation.

Ideally, such an act, as a spiritual act of "gravity and grace" (to use here Simone Weil's apt phrase), could start on a modest scale. It could start by having more people read and ponder Babbitt's books, not many, really, seven to be exact, six of them published in his lifetime, one posthumously. (There is, too, another posthumous volume, his translation from the *Pāli* of *The Dhammapada*, with its remarkable introductory essay on "Buddha and the Occident.") Babbitt's writings incorporate, in a very masculine, sometimes racy and aphoristic style, his teachings, again underlining the catechistic quality of his work and thought. Of writings that are teachings, as in Babbitt's case, we have immense corrective need, particularly when these are filled with wisdom. Any return to and restudy of sapiential literature can have both therapeutic and antidotal value.

There are at least two major problems to be overcome in encouraging readers to return to Babbitt's works. First, from a pedagogical point of view, there are no longer any "required texts" at any educational level. And second, most persons, including and even especially those who have had a college or university education, have never read the right books, the right poets and novelists, and the right critics and thinkers. What we see in this phenomenon is the absence of a great tradition, sacrificed, obviously, to the changing climate of opinion that goes hand in hand with our cultural pluralism, and to a compulsory mediocrity. To judge by the way civilization is going we can have only modest expectations of any effort to revive Babbitt's relevance to the modern situation. But, as in any permanent doctrine that revolves around first principles, modest expectations must themselves be accompanied and judged by unequivocal standards. Any effort to renew connection with Babbitt's work, in part or in whole, should be counted as a worthy one. "To be understood by a few intelligent people," observes T. S. Eliot, "is all the influence a man requires."

In Babbitt we observe a judging mind hard at work, and it is precisely this process that marks him as a modern profoundly aware of the disequilibrium affecting every aspect of civilization since the Renaissance. He connected this disequilibrium with man's expansive desires and with naturalistic trends, particularly as embodied in Rousseau's thought. To combat these conditions of existence he chose an active ministry of life, what he called a positive and critical humanism. He was to be concerned, as he insisted, not so much with meditation, the culmination of true religion, as with mediation, or the law of measure governing man in his secular relations. He is finally to be seen, then, as a sapiential and prophetic critic: as one who seeks to teach the meaning of wisdom, stressing, above all, the priority of self-reform over social reform, and who warns of the dire consequences, for man and society, when standards, containing a center of judgment, are not to be maintained. In this critical role Babbitt was to raise questions of a humanistic rather than eschatological nature.

Babbitt's primary concern was with life and with the destiny of man rather than with faith and redemption. He himself admitted that he did side with naturalists in rejecting outside authority in favor of the immediate and the experiential. But for Babbitt, as a critic relying on psychological analysis supported by a growing body of evidence, his answers to questions regarding moral and ethical life were to be radically different, and different in a tempering way. That is, he believed that, with Rousseau, the naturalists asked the right questions but gave the wrong answers. In short, Babbitt sought to show the unsoundness of answers manufactured in the liberal and democratizing contexts of "relativity" and of "the progress and service of humanity." He found in their answers not only a reliance on a crass materialism but also a sham spirituality. He had, first and always, the unhappy and unpopular task of citing the extremes and excrescences of the epoch in which we are still living, at once proffering and defending the disciplining exercises of "the veto power."

The dialectical essences of this task are nowhere more advantageously disclosed than in *Democracy and Leadership*. First published in 1924, but long out of print, it has reappeared as an inexpensive and handsome Liberty Classic (1979). One must hope that this reprinting of a book so long confined to ignominy initiates an act of reparation. It gives one even the smallest hope that the battle that Babbitt waged was not in vain, that it is still being waged in the underground by a small band of beleaguered humanistic loyalists. As a compendium of ideas, values, and judgments, *Democracy and Leadership* is Babbitt's most spiritually strenuous work. In it, beginnings and endings, first principles and last principles, conjoin and cohere. If *Democracy and Leadership* can be said to be Babbitt's catechesis, it can also be said to be his *stromata*, the bedrock of his critical teachings. It is a brave and honest book, written by a saint who is as unyielding as a saint ought to be. It is not a book for small minds, or for spiritual loafers. It is, in a very vital way, a homiletic book of ethical and moral discourse that gives a positive basis to humility; a book to be read continuously, catechetically, pondered and meditated on, assimilated and synthesized—and, as Babbitt would want it, lived. It is a great book, a great critical vision, a "supreme act of analysis" that traces causes and effects and distinguishes between things which are at the center different.

Democracy and Leadership is in some ways a misnomer, for it is much more than just a study in social science and politics. All categories and conditions of human existence, in their interrelations and interdependence, are examined here with critical ferocity. Babbitt is dogged in pointing out errors (for example, relativity, humanitarianism, naturalism) that lead to indiscipline and to breakdown, whether in private life or in public. Throughout, his diagnosis concentrates precisely on those "facts" that Rousseau and his followers insisted on setting aside: the discarding of standards and the experience of the past; the growing evils of unlimited democracy and the eradication of the aristocratic principle; the excesses of the "idyllic imagination" as it supplants the "moral imagination"; the establishment of a "civil religion," with all of its secular and material aggrandizements, and the concomitant diminution of both a hierarchy of values and of the centripetal elements in life; the substitution of the doctrine of natural goodness for the older doctrine of man's sinfulness and fallibility; the confusion of mechanical and material progress with moral progress. The political situation, thus, is viewed, defined, and characterized in its ethical and moral contexts.

Babbitt is unfailing in stressing that the absence in life of a reverence for some unifying center, or oneness, has its ancillary counterpart in man's "expansive conceit" (instanced as diverse forms of "imperialism": aggressive intellect, as well as aggressive will to power—the *libido dominandi*—rejecting all forms of control). It is the decline of the inner life, of inner vision, as voice of conscience and as the possessor of spiritual truth, that Babbitt focuses on, inasmuch as public life meritably reflects inner life. It is in the end, he keeps reminding us, a matter of perceiving and affirming the idea of value as it restrains "the cheap and noisy tendencies of the passing hour." Once this transcending and inclusive humanistic idea of value is negated, in any degree or part, the whole fabric of life is rent. For Babbitt, in this respect, the modern political movement signals a battle between the spirit of Rousseau, espousing the "law of the members," and the spirit of Edmund Burke, affirming the "law of the spirit." Appropriately, Babbitt uses as an epigraph to *Democracy and Leadership* these words from Burke's *Letter to a Member of the National Assembly*:

> Society cannot exist unless a controlling power upon will and appetite be placed somewhere, and the less of it there is within, the more there must be without. It is ordained in the eternal constitution of things, that men of intemperate minds cannot be free.

In the modern movement of democracy Babbitt sees not a "democracy of elevation," as Russell Kirk expresses it, but rather an unbridled political expression of naturalism that frequently results in "decadent imperialism." There is not only an absence of standards but also a confusion or inversion of standards, as Babbitt shows in his final and most profound chapter, "Democracy and Standards." The consequences of such a situation are far-reaching and damaging. The majoritarian ethos, or what he terms a "divine average," is incapable of effecting standards of discrimination. The critical process of selection or rejection is sacrificed to a utilitarian-sentimental conception of life and to what he speaks of elsewhere as "eleutheromania." Yet what this conception fails to recognize, Babbitt stresses—and here he helps considerably to distinguish between the positions of the "true and false liberals"—is the constant need for ethical effort, in all its disciplining and integrating forms. And here, too, Babbitt reminds us of a truth that apostles of modernism shun: "Civilization is something that must be deliberately willed; it is not something that gushes up spontaneously from the depths of the unconscious." To resist the individualistic and centrifugal tendencies of a democracy that transposes into a dreamland, as elusive as it is illusory, Babbitt notes the additional need of restoring the moral struggle to the individual: the recovery in some form of "the civil war in the cave."

Substituting sentiment for conscience and expansive emotion for the inner life epitomizes for Babbitt the evils of an unlimited democracy that flouts the aristocratic principle, which he primarily associates with the "inner check," or the *frein vital*—with, in a word, *character.* "The unit to which all things must finally be referred," he maintains, "is not the State or humanity or any other abstraction, but the man of character. Compared with this ultimate human reality, every other reality is only a shadow in the mist." "One should, therefore, in the interests of democracy itself seek to substitute the doctrine of the right man for the doctrine of the rights of man." These are brave statements that we do not now even hear from a preacher in a pulpit, preferring as we do to hear about "the power of positive thinking," still another form of utilitarian-sentimental self-deception advanced by religious and political leaders alike. Indeed, the problem of leadership was for Babbitt the major moral problem in an age, to use Burke's phrase, of "sophisters, economists, and calculators," whose "empire of chimeras" Babbitt steadfastly reproved with an altogether understandable prophetic disdain.

Democracy and Leadership depicts the austere and rigorous workings not merely of a "conservative mind" but also a "universal mind," speaking directly, and with courage and judgment, to a specific problem—"to the distinction . . . between a sound and an unsound individualism." To be regretted, the thought will occur to some readers, is the paucity of a compassionate mind, the mind that is ever in intimate dialogue with the heart. Words like "sympathy," "love," "charity," "kindness," "pity," for instance, are not a visible part of Babbitt's vocabulary, in which we hear the blows of a hammer rather than that which, as Shakespeare tells us, "gives us more palm in beauty than we have." But Babbitt was a critic of integrity, he wore no masks, he had no pretensions or poses as "man and teacher," he refused to "put on sympathy a burden that it cannot bear," and he allowed nothing to muddle a clean inspection of facts.

The pitiless facts of human history and experience (regardless of any claims for the "goodness of heart" as a substitute for moral obligations), Babbitt maintained, were incontrovertible: "What man needs, if we are to believe the Lord's Prayer, is bread and wisdom. What man, at least Roman man, wanted, about the time that prayer was uttered, was bread and the circus." Accordingly, Babbitt chose to describe himself as a "moral realist," going on with empathic forthrightness to add: "If the moral realist seems hard to the idealist, this is because of his refusal to shift, in the name of sympathy or social justice or on any other ground, the struggle between good and evil from the individual to society." Indeed, he often pointed to some disturbing similarities between the dilemma of ancient Rome, with the collapse of the traditional controls and "the disciplinary virtues," and the dilemma confronting America: "We, too, seem to be reaching the acme of our power and are at the same time discarding the standards of the past. This emancipation has been accompanied by an extraordinary increase in luxury and self-indulgence." To treat this twin process of decay and debasement Babbitt offered what he called an "unamiable suggestion": "The democratic contention that everybody should have a chance is excellent provided it means that everybody is to have a chance to measure up to high standards."

However heavy the burden of his troubling responsibility was, Babbitt did not succumb to world weariness, and he did not repudiate the value of spiritual effort. To be sure, he viewed the future with apprehension. "The latter stages of the naturalistic dissolution of civilization with which we are menaced are," he wrote, "thanks to scientific 'progress,' likely to be marked by incidents of almost inconceivable horror." With the force of insight and with ethical and moral gravamen, he wrestled with fundamental life questions that relate to the fate of man in the modern world. What he chose to say about the ever-growing spiritual anarchy of this world, and about the need for a search for a remedy, continues to make Babbitt's work and thought disturbing and unpopular. What modern man has increasingly chosen to listen to is the doctrine of John Dewey, which, Eliseo Vivas reminds us, prevents the development of piety and fails to stress nobility and dignity. Undoubtedly, Babbitt was intensely aware of the braying voice of the world, but he bore his witness bravely, uncomplainingly. Nothing less could be expected of a prophet of the "madding hour," when, to quote Alexander Pope's couplet,

> . . . rose the seed of chaos, and of night,
> To blot out order, and extinguish light.

~ 🐦🐦 ~

The power and example of Babbitt's thinking continue to command the attention of thoughtful commentators on our times, as Professor Claes G. Ryn discloses in *Will, Imagination, and Reason: Irving Babbitt and the Problem of Reality* (1986). "It is the controversial assumption of this book that the work of Irving Babbitt, the Harvard literary scholar and cultural thinker, will always stand as a monument to American intellectual culture at its finest. Though frequently misunderstood and maligned, Babbitt is likely to live on after most of his critics have faded from memory." These words, which make up the first paragraph in Ryn's introduction, determine the tone and the orientation of all that follows in his important book. Their sincerity and courage are critical virtues that are neither practiced nor honored in the intellectual community as we know it today.

Ryn's main critical concern is with Babbitt's ideas in relation to moral and aesthetic responsibility, and he seeks to mold those ideas "into a systematic whole, thus developing a new approach to the problem of knowledge." Though in recent years Babbitt has been receiving attention from the academy as his books have been reissued and as books about his books have been written, what he stands for has yet to be fully grasped or affirmed. The reason for this is not difficult to detect by anyone who reads Ryn's book and considers its aims. Babbitt possessed unwavering standards as these affect and mold concepts of will, imagination, and reason and ultimately define "a comprehensive view of life." The fact remains that Babbitt's moral and aesthetic standards are not perceived as being viable in the modern world, are too severe and demanding for a society dominated by egalitarian, relativistic, and ahistorical forces. Clearly, Babbitt's views in their power and conviction require a total commitment of discipline and belief that goes counter to the vagaries of the modern temper. It is the singular strength of Ryn's book that it both recognizes Babbitt as a classic and enhances his meaning in our time.

As Ryn trenchantly shows, Babbitt grappled mightily with basic philosophical problems, but it must also never be forgotten that Babbitt is, first and foremost, a man of ideas—a man of letters, to be more exact. And a man of letters insofar as he speaks to the total human condition is a generalist, a universalist, whose mission and message are not confined to any one intellectual theory or epistemological synthesis. As Allen Tate writes in "The Man of Letters in the Modern World":

> The general intelligence is the intelligence of the man of letters: he must not be committed to the illiberal specializations that the nineteenth century has proliferated into the modern world: specializations in which means are divorced from ends, action from sensibility, matter from mind, society from the individual, religion from moral agency, love from lust, poetry from thought,

communion from experience, and mankind in the community from men in the crowd.[1]

Any attempt to systematize Babbitt's thought must in fact be viewed as a methodological endeavor to locate and define that thought in selective parameters. Babbitt was, to be sure, a moralist who, as he wrote of Matthew Arnold, is ever aware that "in addition to his ordinary self of passing impulse and desire . . . has a permanent self as a power of control." Babbitt was not a builder of systems, and he was not a systematist. We may choose to see his achievement in its systematic orientation and phases, but that view does not tell the whole story or capture the organic meaning of his writings. Even a cursory review of his writings underlines the need to see Babbitt as a positive and critical humanist who, like Arnold, achieves the union of imagination and reason. As Stuart P. Sherman wrote of Babbitt: "He had given you theses about literature, about life, which you would spend a lifetime in verifying."[2] In the end Babbitt must be seen as an epigone teacher-critic whose text comes from the "alphabet of the universal spirit" and whose piety is for the "fathers," for what Goethe calls "tradition" and "those revered values by which the remote is bound, the torn made whole."[3] Like Goethe, Babbitt is a thinker and a sage, but not a philosopher or an ideologue.

In his attacks on proliferating specialization in the intellectual disciplines, Babbitt was unwavering. It much behooves us, now that more scholars are "revisiting" Babbitt's writings, to protect him from those who would transform him into a specialized academic commodity. The scholar's responsibility today is to interpret the whole of Babbitt in ways that would make his ideas more assimilative in the American mind and that would reinterpret his writings so that their wisdom and insight would be more readily absorbed in critical discourse. The civilizing value of Babbitt's ideas needs to be communicated by his interpreters in relation to culture and society and to become, as it were, an intrinsic and dynamic part of our critical heritage.

Will, Imagination, and Reason, in concept and content, is not an easy book to read and its appeal will be confined to a limited audience. It is a book to be pondered, a quintessentially serious and profound book that

---

[1] In *Essays of Four Decades* (Chicago: Swallow Press, 1968) 13.

[2] In *Irving Babbitt: Man and Teacher*, ed. Frederick Manchester and Odell Shepard (New York: Putnam's, 1941) 90.

[3] Quoted in E. R. Curtius's essay on "The Fundamental Features of Goethe's World," his *Essays on European Literature*, trans. Michael Kowal (Princeton NJ: Princeton University Press, 1973) 82.

stands in a great European intellectual tradition strongly opposed to a mathematically oriented naturalism and positivism and that bears the marks of the Swedish philosopher Folke Leander (1910–1981), Ryn's Swedish mentor—the "Optimus Doctor" to whom the book is dedicated.[4] The dedicatory inscription is altogether appropriate, especially because *Will, Imagination, and Reason* is based on Leander's own skeletal outlines, suggestions, and analyses of Babbitt's central ideas. Illness did not permit Leander to go beyond preliminary explorations of Babbitt's thought. By 1981 Ryn had written the first manuscript draft of this book, reworking, developing, and integrating Leander's original materials into a larger whole.

During the years since Leander's death, as Ryn tells us in a prefatory reminiscence, the manuscript was revised and rewritten and now stands on its own, the early drafts indistinguishable from his own thought and writing, though allegiant to the original, collaborative goal of exploring "the relationship between Babbitt's ethical and aesthetic ideas and the implications of that relationship for how we understand reality and the knowledge of reality." That goal is admirably achieved in *Will, Imagination, and Reason*. No scholar in the future will now be hampered by an inadequate assessment of Babbitt's thought and ideas. If the immediate circle of readers of Ryn's book remains small, it is also a grateful and influential circle that will in turn serve to create a widening circle of readers and, hopefully, catechists.

What Ryn indicates, above all, is that Babbitt possessed philosophical and spiritual qualities that ennobled his ideas and distinguished them from those who, like John Dewey and his followers, failed to observe the ethical element in man's moral and theoretical nature that transcends change. This book helps to show us that a genuine man of ideas exposes those forms of moral sloppiness that constitute a decadent romanticism and lead us deeper into what Babbitt termed "zones of illusion." It should also help us to extend and deepen our understanding of how Babbitt fuses intellectual breadth and philosophical depth, as well as ethical and moral functions. This synthesis is especially needful in a modern world in which moral standards and traditions are victims of the *élan vital* that Babbitt associates with man's expansive desires, which impede due restraint and proportion within individual and national life.

---

[4]See Claes G. Ryn, *"Non Videri Sed Esse*: Folke Leander (1910–1981)," *Modern Age* 27/1 (Winter 1983): 56-60.

Babbitt's authenticity as a man of letters, as well as his pedagogical and critical ardor, needs to be doubly stressed when false men of letters are cheaply manufactured in the intellectual community. In Babbitt, in the larger man and deeper nature, we have the real thing; he establishes standards that separate what is genuine from what is spurious. It is this Babbitt who needs most to reside in American life and letters if his values and virtues are to have visible impact on the crisis of modernism that grinds on at a furious and even fateful pace. To view the contemporary shapers of the liberal order—to view, that is, their mediocrity and superciliousness, but also their false and yet acclaimed power and influence in all facets of culture and society—makes Babbitt's thought invaluable as a corrective force in the inner and outer life of the commonwealth.

Everything in our national life and thought today defies the moral prescriptions of Babbitt's teachings and writings; defies what Ryn crystallizes in these words: "Great art has a higher function, that is, a higher purpose, in the economy of the spirit." The application of the "inner check" that Babbitt and Paul Elmer More counseled as an ought is rejected by a society that eleutheromania has turned on its head. It will be difficult to turn things around, the difficulty itself being compounded by the worship of the new gods of megatechnics. The current deconstructionist craze that possesses higher education is symptomatic of the obstacles facing those few who champion Babbitt's goals for attaining "centrality of vision." The conditions of American life that Babbitt prophetically diagnosed in *Democracy and Leadership* have steadily declined, so much that the law of numbers that Babbitt feared has now metamorphosed into the law of decadence, which D. H. Lawrence once described as a "greasy slipping into decay." If the America of the twenties and thirties was antagonistic to Babbitt, the America of the present day is inevitably even more antagonistic. This sad fact must be kept in mind when reading Ryn's book. And it must be kept in mind particularly in the creation of strategies for the recrudescence of Babbitt's worth to contemporary civilization.

Ryn's book emboldens us to persevere in our ambitions, and in our strategies, to reintegrate Babbitt's importance. At the same time we cannot be overly optimistic as to the outcome of our labors as we witness the ever-dizzying flux of modern life—the crass habits of mind and character, the lapse in conscience and conduct that ossify and signal the disorder and the nihilism assaulting all levels of human existence. Ryn's efforts (and those of his friends and allies) must be viewed in the context that T. S. Eliot recognizes when he declares that "we fight rather to keep something alive than in the expectation that anything will triumph."[5] Babbitt himself would not want us to be misled by any illusions concerning the possibility of a grand triumph; and he would not want us to misjudge irreducible realities of existence that he connects with the "immediate data of consciousness."

Ryn asserts that Babbitt's books "present *thought* about experience." His commentary enables one to pinpoint and evaluate more definitely Babbitt's humanistic concepts and distinctions. Though Babbitt did not systematically think through the subject of conceptual knowledge, as Ryn discloses, he nonetheless perceived the unsettling phenomenon in modern life of the man of science who becomes a "mere rationalist" and distorts experience for practical ends and thus ignores the place of the part in the experiential whole. Ryn is sometimes wary of Babbitt's inattention to the epistemological basis of his own ideas, but this wariness tends to obscure the fact that Babbitt was a man of letters and not a trained philosopher. It is a criticism that ascribes to Babbitt a particular function that he himself never pretended to possess. "I am merely a critic," he replied to those of his followers who sought to make of him something more than he was. We cannot, and should not, expect a man of letters to be more than what he is, though it should be said, in all fairness to Ryn's thesis, that Babbitt in his response to pragmatism was closer to an epistemology than he realized. Ryn's interpretations remind us why Babbitt's importance to us has never been fully ascertained, and that is because he had particular theories about ethical wisdom and universal values. Ryn makes an observation that cannot be disclaimed: "But until such theories become aware of and can defend their own epistemological foundation, they must lack confidence in philosophical debates and ultimately fail in the task of persuasion." Clearly this task belongs not to the man of letters but to his commentators, and it is a task in which Ryn excels.

Perhaps the greatest interior value of *Will, Imagination, and Reason* is that it leads one to grasp the permanent significance of Babbitt's perception of the facts of moral life and order. This perception, however, was that of a man of letters who did not presume to develop what Babbitt himself termed "a complete and closed system." Ryn remarks that "if he [Babbitt] had gone on to philosophize about the epistemological status of his own thought, the result would have been an explicitly systematic approach and a logic of philosophy." Babbitt's "scant interest in questions

---

[5]"Francis Herbert Bradley," in *Selected Essays* (New York: Harcourt, Brace & World, 1960) 399.

of philosophical logic" is, for Ryn, cause for regret and calls for the kind of complements, refinements, or revisions that Ryn provides with precision and authority. It is not so much a modified as a strengthened Babbitt who emerges from Ryn's study. The augmentation, as it is developed in this book, is that of a friendly critic seeking to assess Babbitt's thought and its relevance to the crisis of modern civilization.

Will, Imagination, and Reason impressively demonstrates that Babbitt had the capacity to be an "enlightener" and "enlarger." Regrettably, the special critical purpose and approach of Ryn's book do not also more fully reveal a Babbitt who transcended his doctrine precisely because he was a man of letters. Hence, to say as does Ryn that Babbitt's collected writings can be described as a "twentieth-century phenomenology of the mind" needlessly complicates the contribution of a man of letters. To be sure, Ryn is persuasive in showing that "Ideas are given new emphases, until a virtual transformation has been effected"; that "In every act of interpretation thought continues"; that "Weaknesses and strengths are discovered in the old formulations." But the philosophical and theoretical foci and truths of his book, as forceful as they are, tend to subordinate Babbitt's generalism. Doubtlessly the philosophical concepts that Ryn rearticulates and reformulates help to weed out mistakes and confusions. And doubtlessly his belief that "Human knowledge is a perpetual straining towards greater clarity and precision" attains an eloquent concreteness. Ryn's interpretations are invariably illuminating, but their hermeneutical nature deprives Babbitt of the humanistic constituents that shaped and stamped his teaching and writing in their sinuous reciprocity and unity. In a curious way, we are reminded here, Babbitt's significance becomes perhaps too much a province of the very academy that has always found his ideas threatening. In one way, then, Ryn adds to this paradox, though he does so in a positive way insofar as the moral concerns of his book establish a conclusive and overarching critical commitment of the first order.

Babbitt, as Ryn emphasizes, regarded ethical action as the final answer to questions of reality. And this action constituted a moral effort—individual moral effort and the exercise of the "higher will," or "power of control." Moral goodness was for Babbitt the end of life since it is in goodness that one finds happiness and peace. Ryn's discussion of Babbitt's conception of the inner check rescues this aspect of Babbitt's thinking from confusion and misunderstanding, as well as from the behaviorists and naturalistic psychologists, "the chief enemies of human nature." In short, for Babbitt ethical will has primacy over intellect, or as Ryn states: "Moral standards are in a sense the conjoint creations of the imagination and the intellect. But the final acceptance or rejection of particular norms thus formulated is an activity of the higher will."

Though this book revolves around Babbitt's epistemologically relevant ideas, it also is a book about Ryn's own ideas as these correct, supplement, and heighten Babbitt's. For instance, Ryn draws attention to certain weaknesses and inconsistencies in Babbitt's relationship to modern aesthetics, and singles out for criticism Babbitt's insufficient appreciation of Benedetto Croce's important contribution to the notion of the creative imagination. Many of Croce's ideas, Ryn iterates, are similar to Babbitt's but are expressed with philosophical precision and systematic development that the American critic lacks. Ryn seeks, hence, to synthesize to advantage the ideas of Babbitt the dualist and those of Croce the monist—"to forge their respective strengths into a systematic whole, thus developing a new approach to the problem of knowledge." "Ideas contain potentialities for development," he goes on to say, "in sometimes unexpected directions."

Particularly helpful is Ryn's discussion of Babbitt's view of the role of the imagination as a source of wisdom and as a source of dangerous illusion. The "higher will" can, in this connection, be described as an "inner check," an expression of a kind of moral "uneasiness" (as Ryn expressively puts it)—that is, an instance of "the transcendent God breaking into consciousness. . . . It affords man opportunity to reconstitute his intentions." Ryn clarifies Babbitt's view of the moral function of art, the "moral imagination," which "imitates the universal" and gives us "an elevated sense of order, proportion and reality." In contrast, the "idyllic imagination" of Rousseau contributes to a distortion of our understanding of reality. Unlike Croce, as Ryn points out, Babbitt was to develop an insight about which professional philosophers (and, one could add, professional critics) know little or nothing: that "through the moral imagination man has an *intuitive* perception of the universal."

Ryn's judicious reading of Babbitt enables him to pinpoint a major cause of decline in Western society: "At the core of the decline he [Babbitt] sees a corruption of the imagination and with it moral character." It is certainly a pity that within the academy we do not have a larger number of critics who can read Babbitt and arrive at the discriminating judgments that Ryn conveys with a sense of urgency. (But, as Babbitt himself indicated, we should be grateful for the "keen-sighted few" among us!) The sociopolitical consequences of "the idyllic imagination," Ryn stresses, are *there* in any reluctance to have one's (un)real vision of the world tested—to see it in terms of historical reality or to subject a vision or idea to the analysis of reason: "Training of the moral imagination is thus inseparable from the training of moral character." The need to distinguish between falsehood and truth in the imagination never ceases, and only when we acknowledge this central principle with Babbitt, and with Ryn, will we be able to grasp the eternal validity of first principles.

The examination of aesthetic and philosophic problems in Ryn's book is filled with challenge, though at the same time its pervasive theoretical concerns with aesthetics and philosophy in relation to Babbitt necessarily produce abstract considerations that must alert us to the aptness of F. R. Leavis's warning (in a famous exchange in 1937 with René Wellek) that literary criticism and philosophy are "quite distinct and different kinds of discipline."[6] Ryn's theoretical considerations have the effect at times of blurring Babbitt's identity as a literary critic and even dim the lucidity and the cogency of his critical expositions. Sometimes lost in Ryn's book is Babbitt's inimitable voice as a teacher, a great teacher—greater than a critic, as it is sometimes said. This voice is heard in an essay like "English and the Discipline of Ideas" (1920). The Babbitt of this essay is the Babbitt we need to hear more than ever; it is the Babbitt we forget at our peril, the Babbitt who is more fundamentally akin to *paideia* than to *episteme*.

In this essay we hear the voice of the teacher and we gauge its tone, its rhythm, its toughness, and its intrinsic humaneness. That voice must not be forgotten or transformed, even as it must be restored to its true critical primacy as it speaks to the problem of "literature and the American college" and of "democracy and leadership." If we are to derive the most value from Babbitt's public ministry of forty years, we must listen to what he has to say about American society and culture. And what he has to say attains its poignant representations in this essay:

> The issue . . . which must be faced squarely, is whether our education, especially our higher education, is to be qualitative and intensive or quantitative and extensive. Those who are filled with concern for the lot of humanity as a whole, especially for the less fortunate portions of it, are wont nowadays to call themselves idealists. We should at least recognize that ideals in this sense are not the same as standards and that they are often indeed the opposite of standards.

> If we are told that it is not democratic to produce the superior man, we should reply with Aristotle that the remedy for democ-

---

[6]See "Literary Criticism and Philosophy," in his *The Common Pursuit* (London: Chatto & Windus, 1952) 211-22.

racy is not more democracy, but that, on the contrary, if we wish a democracy that is to endure we should temper it with its opposite—with the idea of quality and selection. True democracy consists not in lowering the standard but in giving everybody, so far as possible, a chance of measuring up to the standard.[7]

The Babbittian voice found in the preceding extracts is the voice that must take precedence over any other voice that is assigned to him. These extracts best reflect his mind, his manner, and above all his "plain style." They have the same effect and advantage of containing sound sense under the weight of words, a quality that Babbitt shared with an earlier man of letters, moralist, and critic, Samuel Johnson. Like Dr. Johnson's, Babbitt's writing takes the terse, vigorous tone of his talking as it emanates from the rostrum in the lecture hall and as it inevitably relates to "the vacuity of life." And that style conveys, unmistakably, the concreteness, the masculine directness, the transparency, and the sagacity that are characteristic of Babbitt as a man of letters always aware of his main critical responsibilities. Babbitt's words, as F. O. Matthiessen reminds us, "always bring us back to the phrase from Arnold he liked to quote: 'the imperious lonely thinking power.' He demonstrated in his own practice the cardinal importance for any civilization of a man's retaining his hold 'on the truths of the inner life.' In a period of prophets and confessors he refused to be either. He fulfilled the function of the critic, bleak though his isolation often was."[8]

The concrete reality of moral heroism in Babbitt the man of letters is registered in the civilized voice of the critic of literature, politics, and religion. Babbitt was a moralist through and through, believing as Arnold did that the struggle between the higher and the lower self is the essence of human life, and can be understood dialectically in the light of "the imaginative reason." When studied in terms of its criticophilosophical and historicotextual essences, *Will, Imagination, and Reason* should encourage readers to conclude that if Americans could be made to listen to Babbitt's voice in its civilized and prophetic tone, our social and cultural situation would be manifestly better. It may very well be that Babbitt's influence today is not greater because there are certain overemphases in his so-called doctrine that becloud his true worth and hinder the unfolding of the true Babbitt. We must listen to his voice in its consistency

[7] *Irving Babbitt: Representative Writings*, ed. George A. Panichas (Lincoln: University of Nebraska Press, 1981) 64, 65.

[8] F. O. Matthiessen, *The Responsibilities of the Critic: Essays and Reviews*, selected by John Rackliffe (New York: Oxford University Press, 1952) 165.

and continuity before we venture to reevaluate the texts it speaks with cogency and lucidity. And until we do so Babbitt will continue to be perceived as something of an enigma in American intellectual and cultural history.

No American man of letters has equalled or surpassed either the maturity or the gravity of Babbitt's judgments, not even an Emerson, for precisely the reasons that More posits when he writes:

> He [Emerson] is preëminently the poet of religion and philosophy for the young; whereas men as they grow older are inclined to turn from him, in their more serious needs, to those sages who have supplemented insight with a firmer grasp of the whole of human nature.[9]

The comparative connections that Ryn finds between Babbitt and Croce underscore and turn our attention to the sweep of Babbitt's vision. Other men of letters have made singular contributions in the American scene, but not with the kind of straightness and openness that Babbitt displayed. He did not have the impishness of a John Jay Chapman or the crankiness of an Edmund Wilson. He did not have to flee from his native shores as did his greatest student, T. S. Eliot, in order to mold his vision and find his faith. He did not give in to the ambivalences and the ambiguities of a Lionel Trilling. He was a man of letters who, robustly and tenaciously, personified Man Thinking, and he has not yet had a true successor.

For most Americans, Babbitt's greatness remains too great to fathom or bear, even as his integral Americanness continues for the most part to perplex or irritate his countrymen. His writings have yet to become a bona fide part of the American literary canon in the academy that now sanctifies "prophets of extremity" like Foucault and Derrida who breed the "purely insurrectionist attitude" (to apply Babbitt's own prophetic phrase).

Babbitt's Americanness is distinguished not only on a personal level of responsibility—his solidity of character and his burden of conscience as these identify his moral discriminations—but also on a spiritual and intellectual level—his sense of vocation and his moral earnestness in diagnosing the American experience, its conditions, tensions, needs. Not to be overlooked is his steadiness of purpose and his paradigmatic fortitude, for even as he observed pernicious negatives, this schoolmaster of a nation and good men did not capitulate to negations. He exemplifies

---

[9]Paul Elmer More, *A New England Group and Others*, Shelburne Essays 11th ser. (vol. 11) (Boston/New York: Houghton Mifflin, 1967 [1921]) 94.

"the making of the American mind" in the very framework of universal history itself as a part of noetic life. Anyone who examines, say, an essay like "The Critic and American Life" will appreciate precisely those values and universals that Babbitt seeks to bring to bear on the quality of general critical intelligence in its American ambience. The whole circle of his ideas, surely, is present in these two sentences from that essay: "The serious critic is more concerned with achieving a correct scale of values and so seeing things proportionately than with self-expression. His essential virtue is poise."[10]

Increasingly the humanistic standards of discipline, decorum, and duty that Babbitt espoused, the moral law of cause and effect that he esteemed, and the courage of judgment that he exemplified are fatalities of disorder and decadence. Babbitt's Americanness remains essentially homeless in an age in which an arrogant orthodoxy of enlightenment not only proscribes first principles but also demands that, as Eliot puts it, "we conceal from ourselves the unpleasant knowledge of the real values by which we live." We must continue, therefore, to work for Irving Babbitt's final homecoming if we are to climb out of the abyss of negations, and if we are also to escape from the clutches of the "terrible simplifiers."

---

[10]*On Being Creative and Other Essays* (Boston/New York: Houghton Mifflin, 1932) 204.

The Moral Imagination

When virtues of insight and wisdom are complemented by eloquence and humility in a work of criticism, there is always reason to celebrate. And when the critic's choice is Thomas Stearns Eliot (1888–1965)—"our last great poet," as Dr. F. R. Leavis has affixed Eliot's imaginative genius— there is added cause for celebration. Much nonsense has been written about Eliot, critically and biographically, and there is no need here to summarize or quote from its abundance. That kind of reference would merely acknowledge the negative, a condition that, particularly with the advent of the deconstructionists, holds too much sway. In fact, we need to be saved from precisely such an aberrant and soulless attitude as much as Eliot needs to be saved from it.

First published in 1971, and then revised and enlarged in 1984, Dr. Russell Kirk's *Eliot and His Age: T. S. Eliot's Moral Imagination in the Twentieth Century* not only occasions celebration but also foments the kind of critical salvation indicated in the preceding sentence. As such, it is a gift for one to have this book, to be able to read and reread it, to reflect on it, to learn from it, and to derive from it generous and civilizing lessons relating to "T. S. Eliot's moral imagination in the twentieth century." At no other time has there been greater need than there is now to be exposed to the criterial qualities that identify the moral imagination, which has been progressively deconstructed in the modern world, indiscriminately generating a "culture of narcissism" and all the horrors that go with it. Edmund Burke speaks of such a world as "the antagonistic world of madness, discord, vice, confusion, and unavailing sorrow." No other modern poet, as Kirk so convincingly shows, comprehended more fully the power and scourge of this antagonist world than T. S. Eliot.

Eliot and His Age is a big and thorough book that examines the totality of Eliot's vision. Kirk blends in his commentary all those elements that are the root substance of a poet's vision—the creative and the critical, the literary and the social, the political and the economic, the religious and the philosophical. If all these elements are to be elucidated, the critic who fulfills his true responsibility must possess the historical sense and also establish connections proportionately. The possession of these critical properties helps to define the exclusiveness of the critic's function and to make that function pertinent to the meaning of civilization and the destiny of man. The critic, no less than the creator, who views the world as an organic whole, enables us to understand the world in all its manifestations. He enables us, as Eliot once observed, "to see beneath both beauty and ugliness; to see the boredom, and the horror and the glory." Such a critic is more than a critic; he is a man of letters who, as Ralph Waldo Emerson wrote, "has drawn the white lot in life."

In a little-known essay that appeared toward the end of World War II, "The Man of Letters and the Future of Europe," Eliot emphasizes that a man of letters is concerned with the cultural map and exercises "constant surveillance." A man of letters has his first and permanent loyalty to literary art, as Eliot stresses, but he has other major interests as well, and these involve the moral state of the world. Or to quote here Russell Kirk himself, echoing Burke, with reference to what constitutes the estate of the moral imagination as it in turn is supremely recognized by Eliot: "The moral imagination aspires to apprehending of right order in the soul and right order in the commonwealth."

In that rare instance when the poet as man of letters meets the critic as man of letters we have an encounter of uncommon advantage. That is what happens in *Eliot and His Age* as the spirit of critical inquiry soars in a memorable pattern of ascent. Illuminations, judgments, explorations, discoveries circumscribe each page as men of letters meet in critical discourse as it is shaped by the moral sense. We are not hectored here by the pedantries and claptrap that easily identify the sham criticism that is written large in the academy and that eats away at the foundations of *paideia*. Rather, we are reminded of the central function of the man of letters in the modern world, and that what he must first do is what he has always done: to "recreate for his age the image of man . . . [and] propagate standards by which other men may test the image, and distinguish the false from the true," to use Allen Tate's salient injunction. This injunction, it is sad to say, has been contravened by alien bands of critics—gang movements of the worst character and conduct—that have charged recklessly beyond the frontiers of criticism and have aspired to a decadence and nihilism of the most dangerous kind. Such has been the arrogance and impiety of these anticritics that the critical function has been severely abrogated. The results are dismal to an incalculable degree as we survey our literary and cultural scene, to find there the increasing absence of the man of letters. Intellectual and spiritual blight boldly proclaims the proliferation of the hollow men in the realm of what Eliot terms "leadership and letters."

At the very end of the lecture with the words just quoted as his title—delivered on November 3, 1948, as the "War Memorial Address" at Milton Academy—Eliot declares: "There will always be situations in which one man, or a few men, will render a service to their society simply by standing alone in an unpopular opinion and telling their countrymen that they are wrong, with no hope of accomplishing anything except witnessing to the truth as they see it." These words, clearly propelled by Eliot's great mentor, the New England sage and saint, Irving Babbitt, give the essence of the faith of the man of letters. And as Kirk shows with critical acumen, Eliot bravely fulfilled the role of man of letters. Those who subscribe to or propagate the idea that Eliot was effete, passive, defeatist—"like a beautifully carved skeleton—no blood, no guts, no marrow, no flesh," to quote Frieda Lawrence's cruel jab—are vigorously rebutted in *Eliot and His Age*. In this respect, Kirk echoes Leavis's estimation: "I see Eliot's creative career as a sustained, heroic, and indefatigably resourceful quest of a profound sincerity of the most difficult kind. The heroism is that of genius." This heroism informs Eliot's achievement as a poet, dramatist, critic—and, yes, a believer, a religious man.

Eliot possessed creative courage, but he also possessed, as Kirk demonstrates better than any other commentator, a consummate spiritual courage. This confluence of creative and spiritual courage finally permits Eliot to attain his greatest visionary moment in his composition of *Four Quartets*—a poem that distinguishes him as an upholder of the moral imagination, as well as a modern continuer of Virgil and Dante. ("His was the true Dantescan voice," Ezra Pound insisted, "not honoured enough. . . . ") The thirty pages that Kirk devotes to *Four Quartets* provide the most illuminating interpretations of that work that can be found anywhere. No student of Eliot can afford to omit this discussion and will, it is certain, be helped to discover the same discovery in all four poems that Kirk describes: "The central discovery, the meaning, is this: through the transcendent consciousness, it is possible to know God, and through Him to know immortality."

Equally illuminating is Kirk's discussion of Eliot's social criticism as found in scattered essays, in books like *After Strange Gods* (1934) and *The Idea of a Christian Society* (1939), and in the commentaries that Eliot, as editor, contributed periodically to *The Criterion*, the quarterly magazine he edited between 1922 and 1939. Eliot's *Criterion*, Kirk insists, contained "the ethical voice," or as Eliot himself asserted: "For myself, a right political philosophy came more and more to imply a right theology—and right economics to depend upon right ethics. . . . " Far from being a reactionary as some of his adversaries charge ad nauseam, Eliot sought during his editorship to attain some semblance of a vision of order in a world swiftly drifting into "the second darkness," as E. M. Forster was to image the post-Munich events. In "Burnt Norton" (1936), first of his *Four Quartets*, Eliot shows the abject conditions of this drifting with terrifying honesty:

> Here is a place of disaffection
> Time before and time after
> In a dim light: neither daylight
> Investing form with lucid stillness
> Turning shadow into transient beauty
> With slow rotation suggesting permanence
> Nor darkness to purify the soul
> Emptying the sensual with deprivation
> Cleansing affection from the temporal.
> Neither plenitude nor vacancy. Only a flicker
> Over the strained time-ridden faces
> Distracted from distraction by distraction
> Filled with fancies and empty of meaning
> Tumid apathy with no concentration. . . .

The Criterion, which never had more than 900 subscribers and ceased operation in January 1939, left ostensibly an uncertain legacy, unlike Leavis's *Scrutiny*, a critical quarterly published between 1932 and 1953 that exerted wide influence and adumbrated standards of discrimination that in time became canonic in character and program, especially in English literary and educational circles. Julian Symons, the English poet, novelist, and biographer, expressed a representative judgment in 1938 when he complained that the "moral scale of values by which [*The Criterion*] judges literature and life is one that no longer has much meaning." (Earlier, in 1935, Symons's friend George Orwell, in an even more incensed manner, said of *The Criterion* "that for pure snootiness it beats anything I have ever seen.") Kirk's view of *The Criterion*, of its value and contribution, is far more judicious and historically perceptive, insofar as he places the magazine in the total picture of Eliot's achievement. In the process he shows a deep and sensitive understanding of the permanent importance of "small and obscure reviews" like *The Criterion* that "must be depended upon to maintain a continuity of culture, under painful circumstances." Long accustomed as we are to insidious attacks on the ideas and beliefs of "the conservative mind," we must remain grateful to Kirk for his revaluation of *The Criterion* and of its worth:

> The times having been what they were, it is surprising not
> that *The Criterion* perished, but that it lived so long. Eliot knew

this; also he knew that though he had addressed a small Remnant, in subtle ways his review may have quickened the minds of people whom he never would meet, but who might make their mark during the next thirty years or longer.

When Russell Kirk founded his own quarterly, *Modern Age*, in 1957, Eliot's *The Criterion* served as an exemplum and an inspiration in the struggle to preserve cultural and social tradition, "our common patrimony of culture," as Eliot expresses it—in the struggle to preserve, as he wrote prophetically in *Notes towards the Definition of Culture*, "the essentials of our culture" against those bent on "destroying our ancient edifices to make ready the ground upon which the barbarian nomads of the future will encamp in their mechanised caravans." Eliot's critique of liberalism was bold and direct and remains as yet unanswered.

That Kirk chooses to pay serious attention to Eliot's verse drama is also to be commended. Many critics have been unsympathetic to Eliot's plays or uneven in their treatment of them, pointing mainly to their structural faults and flaccidity. Back in 1951, for instance, Philip Rahv confessed that in writing for the theater, Eliot "has made me more skeptical than ever of the ability of poets to master dramatic form while maintaining a high level of poetic expression incorporating the movements of modern speech." Indeed, Leavis singles out *The Cocktail Party* for special censure when he castigates it for "an implicit snobbery" and goes on to cite Eliot's "superiority of religious and theological knowledge" as evidence of the play's "ignorance of the possibilities of life; ignorance of the effect the play must have on a kind of reader or spectator of whose existence the author appears to be unaware. . . . "

Of course, Kirk is familiar with the thrust of the censure of Eliot's plays, but he does not allow this to cloud his perception of the plays in Eliot's *oeuvre* and to measure their larger, ethical, and religious significance. "Eliot's imagination," he states, "working through the drama, made possible emancipation from the prison of a moment in time and from the obsessions of the ego." Leavis's adverse view of the plays, as Kirk makes clear, is immersed in the widening gyre of a moral empiricism and is therefore inadequately aware of the place of theology, and specifically Christian theology, in Eliot's vision. To separate theological constituents from an active relation to an artist's imagination diminishes his meaning, Kirk rightly reminds us, and nails his vision to a one-dimensional humanism. Critics who deprecate Eliot's theological essences dismiss precisely those essences that shape the theological imagination of a Dante, a Cervantes, a Milton, a Dostoevsky. Here it should perhaps be remembered that, no less than Dostoevsky in the nineteenth century, Eliot lived through a period of dissolution in Christian culture and experienced it as a personal tragedy. His writings, in their unity, are his witness to the crisis of modernism.

Wherever one turns in *Eliot and His Age* one finds paradigms of critical thought and integrity. The book never falters in its central purpose of assessing Eliot's "piercing visions," which Kirk regards as "the clearest light" that has endured in the general darkness of the twentieth century. "If we apprehend Eliot . . . we apprehend the intellectual and moral struggles of our time." Thus writes Kirk early on in his book. It is no small achievement that he empowers his reader to gain precisely this double apprehension. Kirk's book has a profound cumulative effect on the reader as it insightfully penetrates Eliot's vision in its moral and sociopolitical dimensions and as it evaluatively interrelates his achievements as philosophical poet, dramatist, literary critic, social essayist. To this daunting task Kirk brings those civilizing qualities and disciplines that also identify him as a man of letters. Unfailingly he demonstrates the critical instinct that Henry James stipulates: "I have to the last point the instinct and the sense for fusions and interrelations, for framing and encircling . . . every part of my stuff in every other. . . . "

Throughout, Kirk's tone is balanced, his attitude is humane, his judgment is sound. And throughout, his writing is rich and subtle, controlled and concentrated, dignified and honest, not unleavened as occasion demands by subtlety and allusiveness, by wry humor and an engaging authorial presence. Clarity of expression and precision of thought in this book are those felicitous elements of style that amply corroborate Austin Warren's aphorism: "Style is not disjunct from substance; it is considered substance rendered expression." Examples of Kirk's stylistic gifts strikingly multiply as one peruses the pages of *Eliot and His Age* and of which the following passage, viewing Eliot's *Prufrock and Other Observations* (1917) against the backdrop of the Great War, is excellently illustrative:

> J. Alfred Prufrock, strolling mean streets in Boston at teatime, oppressed by small timidities and a vast ennui, unable to love or to escape from the stuffy closet of self, never saw the Somme; but he knew his own Hell. Prufrock, too, would be an aspect of the new antagonist world. After 1917, many a man like a pair of ragged claws would scuttle about the world; and the Prufrocks would be such a man's prey. No longer would Matthew [Arnold] and Waldo [Emerson] slice teatime's cake of custom. Not out of the War, but out of a bank's cellar beneath a London street, emerged the poetic vision that was to take the measure of the century.

If *The Conservative Mind* can be judged as Kirk's most important book in which he speaks as a discerning political philosopher and historian, *Eliot and His Age* is his greatest book in which the man of letters speaks with that Burkean voice that belongs to the "epoch of concentration," to use Matthew Arnold's phrase. No less than Eliot himself, Kirk discloses in this book a constant "reverence for some centre of oneness," to use Babbitt's phrase. Ultimately it is the numinous quality of reverence that distinguishes the man of letters from the atomistic critic and that defines and undergirds his faith, "the substance of things hoped for, the evidence of things not seen." Ultimately, too, this quality guides the man of letters to respond to a poet who, as the ancient Hellenists taught, should be admired because through his genius he makes men better in their cities.

Critics in the mass tend to ignore and even disdain the moral dimension of the archetypal triad of thought, words, and creativity. We now see in our midst a swarm of critical gnosticisms, impieties, cynicisms—that selfsame situation in which, as Thomas Carlyle observed in 1840, Chaos sits as umpire and spiritual paralysis prevails. Unlike a Carlyle who regarded the man of letters as "a very singular phenomenon," "our most important modern person," there are today many in the intellectual community who categorically reject Carlyle's high esteem of the man of letters. In T. S. Eliot, and in Russell Kirk, we find a living and courageous continuity of the great tradition of the man of letters. And in the Age of Eliot we experience a restorative communion with the Hero as Man of Letters, he who "is the soul of all" and whose faith makes us whole.

The Quest for Transcendence

The essays composed in the 1970s and early 1980s are the last that Austin Warren (1899–1986) wrote in a long and distinguished career as an American man of letters. Disabling illnesses in the years immediately preceding his death, however, prevented him from fulfilling his plan to publish in his lifetime a book containing his late literary criticism. He had hoped to join this book to his two earlier books of practical criticism, *Rage for Order: Essays in Criticism* (1948) and *Connections* (1970). As in the essays assembled in his other books, his final writings were published first in various quarterly reviews and, in a few instances, as contributions to other books. With the recent publication of *In Continuity: The Last Essays of Austin Warren* (1996), his plan for a critical trilogy has now been realized.

In his critical writings Warren never failed to disclose sincerity and integrity of purpose. Partisan and polemical approaches he found unacceptable. Equally unacceptable were ideological preconceptions, which he condemned as leading to critical conformity. Throughout his career as a professor of English in leading universities, he came also to disdain more and more what he perceived as the decadent tendencies of the academy. He himself remained steadfast in his refusal to belong to any one academic coterie or critical camp, insisting that he be his own man and not part of what Henry James once decried as the "associational process." Intellectually and spiritually, Warren sought to maintain his independence even in and despite the isolation that allegiance to critical principles can often impose.

Any cursory glance at Warren's critical essays will show an absence of anger, or haughtiness, or impatience, or pride, or vindictiveness. A wonderful openness of spirit, of a friendly and unaffected general intelligence, of a steady even-temperedness identify the main sources of his critical powers and efforts and also account for his good influence. But at the very same time these irenic and magnanimous qualities, which no doubt also conduce a particular temperament, must not be seen as harboring or inciting an excessive prudence, or safeness, or timidity. Rather they were the qualities of a critic who not only discerned his own rage for order but also confessed his constant need for an inner check. He had no fear at all of both confronting and voicing those felt truths that emerge from the rigors of a critic's quest for value:

> But to write and publish at all can be considered an act of aggression; and the more modest, tentative, and exploratory a man is, the more (appearing in public, there to conduct his self-education) he finds it necessary to don some armor—of belligerence or extreme courtesy, or both.

As a university teacher of literature, of "culture" or the humanities, from 1920 to 1968, and as a writer of books ("not as a means of professional advancement" but rather as "an indispensable instrument of self-definition and intellectual clarification"), Warren aspired most to the virtues of measure and humility. These are precisely the virtues that were to nourish his critical achievement, as well as to endow it with the insight and wisdom that Warren's famous Harvard teacher, "my old master," Irving Babbitt, affixed as the highest goals of the critic. Indeed, it can be said that, among the major modern teachers in our time, Warren was an exemplary servant of the critical spirit, possessing what other critics so often lacked, freedom from sectarian vehemence, and the gift of fusing the dignity of literature and the dignity of critical thinking.

Warren belongs to that critical line of classical humanism that begins with Matthew Arnold and continues with Babbitt, Paul Elmer More, and T. S. Eliot, whose critical ideas and texts he assimilated and ramified. From Arnold he no doubt acquired a deep appreciation of disinterestedness and flexibility as the chief ingredients of expounding one's critical concerns and sympathies in their breadth and depth. In particular, he embraced Arnold's own confidence in the humanities, the liberal and humane arts that Warren stalwartly honored in his teaching and criticism.

From Babbitt he learned his greatest spiritual lessons—"that in my classical humanism (with its Eastern equivalent in the humanism of Confucius) and my Catholic-oriented religion (with its Eastern equivalent in Buddhism), I was heir to great, to perennial traditions." To be sure, Warren did transcend the dogmatic and didactic bias that characterized Babbitt's contributions to the republic of arts and letters. But from Babbitt he derived his greatest critical lesson, a profound understanding of the interpretation of values, which Babbitt summed up on the first page of *Democracy and Leadership* and which Warren was fond of quoting:

> When studied with any degree of thoroughness, the economic problem will be found to run into the political problem, the political problem in turn into the philosophical problem, and the philosophical problem itself to be almost indissolubly bound up at last with the religious problem.

No other words better confirm for Warren the internal values that the critic as man of letters should subscribe to. If, as Warren averred, he came in time to feel closer to Eliot than to Babbitt and More, "finding him more literary, more 'aesthetic,' than either," it was Babbitt who transmitted to him first principles of criticism that were to remain irreversible in influence and importance. Stuart P. Sherman's words of tribute to Babbitt—"He had given you theses about literature, about life, which you would spend a lifetime in verifying"—found genuine enactment in Warren's life and thought.

From his great masters of modern criticism Warren learned well lessons that stayed him and gave him the inspiration that he needed to climb the critical ladder. He was their catechumen without at the same time being a mere enthusiast or slavish sectary. From the beginning his critical writings disclosed that the critical principles, the lessons, that Warren had learned also gave him a creative critical courage. The true "cost of discipleship," as Dietrich Bonhoeffer reminds us, dictates a transcendent discipline and a greater heroism. Criticism, too, must have its "costly grace," if the work of a critic is to develop viable and authentic distinctions.

Never failing to show his "loyalty to earlier admirations," Warren went on to define his own critical perspective and make his own critical connections, which came to underline his critical independence, if not uniqueness. His intellectual eclecticism, in this respect, was always a disciplined one; and reverence, he emphatically disclosed, must ultimately translate into something higher, as the critic makes his ascent, "transcending by including." He firmly believed that the "critic needs both reverence and courage of judgment." At the same time he emphasized that "the critic must judge for himself, and then be possessed of the final courage to utter his judgment."

In Warren we view the critic as seeker who ascends to become "the man of letters in the modern world," to use here the title of Allen Tate's 1952 essay. Warren frequently returned to this essay, and it is not difficult to understand his admiration for it when one considers Tate's fervent depiction of the man of letters in strenuous contention with a world of increasing fragmentation.

Warren's critical writings, in their parts and in their whole, embody uncompromising resistance to and rejection of all those fragmentations that give rise to "a vulgar contemporaneity" and erode "the values and the virtues of 'Culture' and 'Tradition.'" Indeed, Warren affirms the role of the modern man of letters who understands the full meaning and demands of his critical responsibility to communicate "a few reasonable words," to invoke here Goethe's phrase.

The cornerstone of Warren's achievement, what defined his critical perspective, stamped its essential character, mobilized its conscience, in short, what gave it both moral energy and spiritual vision, was his generalism. "As a literary critic," he asserts, "I have no 'method,' no specialty, but am what is called, in another discipline, a 'general practitioner.' " His admirations and loyalties, the sum of what he owed to his mentors, ancestors, and kinsmen, in whom he discerned a deep metaphysical heroism that infused their calling and vocation, provided him with paradigms that he sought to preserve and yet also advance in a modern world of rapid, at times even reckless change, when what Joseph Conrad termed "the endangered stability of things" becomes an acute and pervasive problem.

At the heart of this change, affecting as it did culture and society, Warren found an increasing and imperious presence of the specialized attitude leading inevitably to the very destruction of the world as an organic whole. He confronted this attitude in his essays, in his books, which he shaped with precisely that "spiritual discipline" that he associated with the task of "confronting disorder in one's self and in the world . . . [and] of facing existentially, as a total human being living in time, the responsibility of vision and choice." For Warren this responsibility was to center in the critic's responsibility as a generalist "who seeks to reclaim the ancient, the primitive, freedom of scope."

Warren's generalism was neither unfocused nor uncentered. It had an inherent order of discipline that gave his criticism authoritative identity and guidance. "The final necessity for the critic," Warren states, "is, ideally, space and time for withdrawal, for critical distancing; absorption, withdrawal, often repeated, are constantly procedures of criticism." His writings were to emerge from these procedures that not only the creative artist but also the creative critic honors and that can yield to each the highest degree of accomplishment. Warren's writings in their totality—whether in the form of a review, or a review essay, or an essay, or prefatory comments, or, finally, a book—emerged from a sustained, inclusive process of critical thought wrought by painstaking contemplation.

From his earliest theological writings in the 1920s and 1930s in two Swedenborgian periodicals, *The New-Church Messenger* and the *New-Church Review*, the devotional element in Warren's writings was pronounced. There is, in fact, something toughly ascetic about his essays in the search for a purity of exposition and a sincerity of commentation. One cannot fail to discern in them the critic as seeker who rises above himself through complete adherence to his critical vocation. His essays inevitably register a transcendent search for order:

> If there be a *universe*, and not a chaos or a pluralism, then a man must set himself resolutely in search of its order, and must construct, for himself at least, a tentative hierarchy of values in that smaller world (presumably representative of the larger cosmos) in which he lives and functions.

Criticism, for Warren, thus signifies a "serious call"; the critic's task is to reconcile self-definition and self-discipline in ways that bring directly to mind Ralph Waldo Emerson's declaration that "each man and woman is born with an aptitude to do something impossible to any other." Criticism, Warren also showed, was no mere academic activity; "the business of criticism" was clearly a phrase that he rejected as intimating a crassly secular pursuit. In the ascending character of their composition and structure his writings have the quality of interiority that eludes many modern critics. For Warren the creative imagination and "the experience of literature" affirm the life of the soul. This affirmation, written and unwritten, was to give his voice its special tone and his thought its special quality.

In his achievement we discern an astonishing confluence of the art of criticism and the witness of criticism. In effect each piece of writing was for Warren a spiritual exercise which demands the utmost effort of concentration and meditation and which, in James's words, exalts a critic "who has knelt through his long vigil and who has the piety of his office." A celebratory seriousness, it can be said, was to emerge from such an effort. Few modern critics were to excel Warren in his open celebration of great ideas, great writers, great souls. Literary greatness for him meant spiritual greatness, that is, the kind of greatness that gives us guidance and helps to orient us towards the good, or, as Plato puts it, to make us "grow wings to overcome gravity."

~ 🌶 🌶 ~

As a critic Warren was to be intensely aware of his spiritual responsibilities, finding and determining the value of a work of art which testifies to some spiritual reality a writer himself may not have consciously discerned; and also defining as fully and honestly as he can the poet's spiritual cosmos in terms of the literary structure which corresponds to it. This is not to claim, of course, that Warren was essentially a religious critic, for he eschewed any exclusive category that limited his understanding and elucidation of literary texts. For the religious faculty Warren had much feeling; in temper and sympathy he was of an integral religious disposition without at the same time being possessed by fixed views that restricted critical exploration and discoveries. He had too much reverence for literary texts, for the mystery of the word, to allow them to be used for proselytizing purposes. He was a critic rather than an evangel of the religious imagination. How does the critic reconcile valuation and celebration? That was the challenge that Warren grappled with in his writings. The poets, novelists, critics, and thinkers who evinced his admiration were those who struggled with "ultimate religious questions about ultimate values." Their spiritual quests became, in a deep sense, his own, as he so acutely demonstrated in his two companion books of "culture history"—the "disguised autobiography" of a "latter-day Transcendentalist," as Warren's friend Glauco Cambon observed— *New England Saints* (1956) and *The New England Conscience* (1966).

From beginning to end Warren remained a Christian humanist who sought to reconcile, in word and work, the tensive values of human existence. His own critical view of inner and outer tensions made him unusually aware of the interplay of the tensions of existence in their undiminishing power. "I belong, like Tillich," he admitted, "with those whose lot it is to live 'on the boundary,' with those who are 'torn between.' " His critical interpretations emerged from a thoroughly disciplined and exacting consciousness of the constant encounter of the physical and the metaphysical.

If he saw himself as a Christian humanist continuing in the footsteps of the Christian Platonists of Alexandria and the Cambridge Platonists of the English seventeenth century, of Anglican Bishops Jeremy Taylor (1613–1667) and Charles Gore (1853–1932), and of Baron Friedrich von Hügel (1852–1925)—whose writings he did not cease to study—he also saw himself as a Christian realist sensitively attuned to the human condition in all its problematic facets. He shunned illusion and reverie in any guise, intellectual or spiritual. He remained suspicious of all institutional forms, especially in religion and education, "for I am at ease only on the periphery of both," he insisted. And yet in that periphery he found the critical latitude to be his own man and to effect a mediation between his skepticism concerning the nature of institutions and also his "steady faith in the importance of continuity."

Warren wanted connection, not separation; *sophrosynē*, not rashness; order, not chaos. But above and beyond these wants he was a critic who practiced the courage of discrimination that transcends bias in spirit and in aim. Living in an age of cruel disarray, he particularly sought for the renewal of the virtue of order as a form of moral life within both the individual and the community. With "Mr. Pope"—"the moral poet of all civilization," Lord Byron wrote—he could fully fathom the meaning of the words, "Order is Heav'n's first law." His critical heroes, his saints, were those capable of teaching one "attention, concentration, the scrupulous analysis of one's own mental and affective state." For Warren criticism was in effect an exercise in self-courage and self-discipline. The critic cannot be passive or complacent or shrinking in his recognition and defense of fundamentals:

> It indeed takes courage to face, in one's own silent thought, in one's speech, in one's letters and in one's published writings, this ceaseless and fatiguing discrimination—never to allow oneself to slip into easy compliance with the currently accepted compromised standards of one's neighborhood, one's university (academics are not noted for their courage), one's inherited nation, one's church or religion. There can be no relaxation of the critical spirit, no unbending of the bow; and no sphere is exempt from its operation. . . .

Reconciliation is a sacred thread in Warren's Christian humanism. The act of reconciliation, embodying for him a tempering and ordering of human tensions, brings one closer to harmony and proportion. To Warren the reconciliation of religion and culture was of especial importance, and he was assiduous in explaining and defining his perception of the checks or balances he deemed essential to the process of union. "Christian Humanism is the combination of religion and culture, of learning and spirituality," he wrote. "This proper balance—I better say— is ideal, difficult, and precarious." Spiritual religion, he went on to argue, is the more fundamental of the two, but he also insisted that culture served as a check on religion. Without religion culture can become, for the gentleman, urbane, but superficial; and if it is "the culture of the professors" it simply becomes "intelligence without commitment or moral responsibility." Without culture religion can become fanatical, bigoted, obscure: "Religion stands in need simultaneously of some restraint by culture and some relief from it." Warren's Christian humanism defined his critical humanism, its beliefs and criteria, with the characteristic precision and honesty that identified his perspective as a whole. An exemplar of what he reverentially named a "literary priesthood," he abjured the "tradition of infidelity," as C. S. Lewis saliently described it, which many other modern critics eagerly embraced.

Warren composed nothing without showing or demanding care, conviction, seriousness. No literary pomp, no pretense, no falsity could betray his method of writing. "It is impossible to name his style without naming his character: they are one thing," is a statement that could be said of Warren as it was said of Emerson by John Jay Chapman, another, if forgotten, New England Saint. The power of words was to fill Warren with the fear and trembling that inhere in the responsibilities of the critic. No less than the manifest accent of his own New England speech—crisp, austere, precise, lucid, measured, unhurried—his written language attains its equivalent discipline of style, enduring in construction, absolute in meaning, unstinting in integrity. Indeed, his style emerged not so much from his critical thought but from his character and conscience. Ultimately Warren's is that transcendent style of which Alfred North Whitehead speaks as the ultimate morality of mind.

A lifelong member of the academic community, Warren was not always at ease with academics and the orthodoxies and conformities they tend to create and expect of each other. "But then," he wrote to one of his epistolary friends, "all my life I have found the company of literary people, especially poets and poet-critics, much more congenial than the company of academics; for literary people have convictions, views, and tastes—in other words, life, while (as you bitterly know) academic people have none of these, and so are 'dead.'" A gentle, courteous man, Warren did not wantonly initiate conflicts or animosities with his colleagues in the professoriate. Decorum and civility were virtues he practiced patiently and scrupulously. Adversarial situations he found contrary to his sense of *douceur*. Of academics, as of authors of whose work he disapproved, or from whom he strongly dissented, he chiefly practiced what he called "the rhetoric of silence." Clearly he had his own work to do, his own character and talents to explore, his own values to impart as teacher and critic: "Integrity is the best—and almost the only gift—we can hope to transmit to the young."

The quest for transcendence requires a greater courage on the part of the teacher as critic "in multiplying sharp distinctions" and putting these "distinctions into the service of the character and will," to quote here words from Babbitt, whom Warren honored as "an enlightener and an enlarger." The academic marketplace was not for him. The teacher, no less than the critic, must try to go "beyond personalism" and attain a form of "decreation," as Simone Weil, whose writings Warren studied and admired, uses that word. "With the man of integrity," he wrote in his journals, "his whole being takes incarnation in his every act, his every paragraph. He is always representative." In this connection, too, Warren recognized a peculiarly cleft quality in himself that unveiled in his avoidance of polemics and confrontation. "Mine is an irenic spirit, and talent. . . . In me, from the start, have existed an artist (or at least an aesthete) along with a moralist (sternnest in self-judgment)," he confessed. This self-dichotomy he never entirely resolved, choosing as he did to err, if necessary, on the side of kindness and magnanimity.

Himself a native New Englander, Warren could speak as forthrightly to others, to his students and readers, as did his "New England Saints," "my spiritual ancestors and kinsmen," "to whom reality was the spiritual life, whose spiritual integrity was their calling and vocation"—Archbishop Fénelon, the Reverend Edward Taylor, Charles Eliot Norton, Irving Babbitt, John Brooks Wheelwright. He wore the mantle of prudence with distinction. Yet he could also speak with thorny simplicity and directness when axiomatic truths were in question. He always had a reservoir of fundamental goodness, kindliness, unselfishness; he possessed, too, a quick and warm sense of humor. Behind his manly candor there was redemptive decision, and behind his rectitude, deep affectionateness and compassion. Nowhere are all these human qualities better illustrated, or illuminated, than in the following paragraph from a letter to a younger academic, and friend, with whom he had had an acrimonious exchange:

> I deeply regret that ill-advised and bad-spirited letter I wrote you (an evil spirit entered me and spoke through me). But I cannot *wholly* regret it, for it served as a warning to me and as the occasion for searching self-examination, which, though painful, had, as you suggest, its own form of purgation. *But*, I wounded you who stood in no need of further wounding, *from a friend, too*, so I ask your forgiveness.

The moral sense of responsibility shapes Warren's prose and heightens his critical substance. An abstinent quality appears in the leanness of his prose and in the sinewy force of his critical thinking: "Civilization as we understand it may fail; let us, at least, not fail it." "Civilization is the art of the complete consciousness, in the individual and in society." In his words and thought we hear "the call" to moral responsibility. No excess, no undue softness, no crooked line, no sentimentalism, no false aplomb enfeeble the vigor and centrality of his writing. His composition is also his construction, each as much a keystone as the other, both built to be permanent, the one empowering the other, each depending on the other and each holding the other as a companion in common pursuit of order and understanding. Yet in the very sturdiness of his verbal constructs and judgments there are also some wonderfully subtle and supple, even poetic, notes, never reaching too high or too low, demanding patient attention, trust, lest one lose sight of the whole circumference of the critical presentation.

The symmetry of Warren's language and thought; the potency and resonance of his creative intelligence, the felicity and judiciousness of his probings: these are the major properties undergirding and overarching his critical achievement, which at the maximum point of its value and insight is inclusively moral, conveying as it does, as it must, honesty of concern and purpose. In whatever subject he chose to write about—and the conceptual grasp and sweep of his literary interest in lives and letters was rich and comprehensive—he depicts his humanism, forging it with *Serenitas Conscientiae* in the hard face of the crisis of modernism, with its fragmentations, its impieties, its "Terrible Presences"—"Where do they come from? Those whom we so much dread," to recall a line from W. H. Auden.

~ 🦉 🦉 ~

In 1970 Warren moved to Providence, Rhode Island, where he lived during the remaining sixteen years of his life in retirement. After thirty years of university teaching in Iowa and Michigan he gladly returned to his ancestral New England. The New England that he knew and loved, it should be added, was not the New England of Mary E. Wilkins Freeman, and of rural life in eastern Massachusetts, as some of Warren's early commentators assumed, but rather the New England of Boston, and of Massachusetts north of Boston—Waltham, Stow, Littleton, Lincoln, Fitchburg, Ashburnham—as well as Connecticut, from Middletown to Willimantic. Indeed, Hebron was the Connecticut village in which he and his Wesleyan University friend Benjamin Bissell established St. Peter's School of Liberal Humane Studies, an intellectual and cultural community patterned after Little Gidding and Alcott's Concord School of Philosophy. This "creative enterprise"—in the years 1923–1931—marked, as Warren wrote, "my first critical effort at finding my vocation."

His house in Providence, located at 90 Oriole Avenue, close to Brown University, which awarded Warren an honorary Litt.D. in 1974, quintessentialized both order in place and order in time. Ancient, stately, and commodious, it was a house in which intellect and spirit, dignity and serenity, wisdom and insight cohered with a beautiful quiescence that his many visitors—pupils, friends, auditors, colleagues—found restorative. For Warren this house aided the double rhythm of reflection and composition that he saw as being indispensable in his determination to effect connections and continuities as a literary critic and man of letters. The loving support of his wife Antonia, a former medical doctor and woman of broad intellectual and humanistic interests and independent judgment, as well as a gifted writer of short stories, helped immensely to create and sustain those domestic, everyday conditions that play their due role in the unrelenting procession of one's works and days.

His Providence years gave him much happiness and free time to devote himself uninterruptedly to a life of meditation and to "the truths of the inner life." His last writings were the extraordinary offshoots of this happiness and this meditation, and they reflect unflagging concern with the intellectual life and the spiritual life. Indeed, Warren's Providence years were a period of rededication, with Warren as emeritus teacher and humanist critic continuing his quest for value: "We have to do our work, our thing, *ohne Hast, ohne Rast*. . . . "

The same sensitive but robust quality that stamped his earlier writings stamps his last writings. At the same time a more contemplative temper distinguishes these last writings. In them we observe what More calls "a steady growth in Grace." There is no pretension here, no pontificating, no oracular bent. To the end humility remained a constant virtue in Warren's work and thought. He was ever aware of the tensive task of combining the eagle and the dove, never an easy or a necessarily successful task for any critic. Confronting the neoclassical with the baroque, the aesthetic with the moralist, was for him a battle that he kept on fighting.

For Warren this battle was a form of invisible warfare, one in which the critic fights to regain a spiritual center and to achieve conditions of criticism that go beyond purely evaluative interpretation and also beyond the contraries of thesis and antithesis and the indigenous strife they foster. To raise criticism to a higher metaphysical level by recovering the ancient precept that the visionary artist is also a teacher, a "shepherd of the peoples," who can help make men and women better in their cities by overcoming the hubris that destroys the city was an aim that encompasses Warren's aspirations. This aim is central to identifying his critical humanism. It also signals axiomatic qualities that further identify Warren as a Christian humanist who builds bridges between faith and knowledge. Here, also, his long-lasting admiration of Saint Clement of Alexandria, one of the Old Fathers of the Church who struggled to integrate Christian beliefs and ancient Greek principles of *paideia*, has a distinctive relevance. Clement's statement, "When a man is reminded of the better, of necessity he repents the worse," has a distinct echo in Warren's critical purposes.

In his last writings there is no parade of high morality, though moral effort is decidedly one of his impelling criteria. The critical orientation of these writings is toward the Good, the True, and the Beautiful. His critical perceptions convey confidence, encouragement, affirmation, spiritual joy and buoyancy. Yet these last writings do not belong, either necessarily or qualitatively, to a late or even final phase of Warren's achievement. Rather they disclose a line of continuity in his humanistic interests and thought, not monolithic but pliant. Proportion was the final object, Warren believed; his search for order was simultaneously his search for proportion. He instinctively admired "the human voice in its middle register." The even and poised quality of his critical explorations and thought, already evident in early books like *Alexander Pope as Critic and Humanist* (1929), *The Elder Henry James* (1934), and *Richard Crashaw: A Study in Baroque Sensibility* (1939), prevails in his last essays. If the state of contemplation now radiates their intelligence and grace, a feeling of confidence empowers their content and facilitates the serenity and the assurance that emerge from a combined sense of control and moral discovery. Inevitably the right word and the right accent conflate to give rise to Warren's apprehension of right order.

Warren's realization of his vocation as a man of letters in the modern world perhaps reaches an apex in these essays. In them we find the critic who is at last at peace with himself and the world; who knows fully the value of his values; who communicates these with surety, perseverance, urbanity—and with what might best be called an unselfconscious humility that lies at the heart of his critical calling. Warren imposes no arbitrary standards in these essays but instead allows his standards to record the fullness of his acceptances and affirmations. In these essays, above all, we hear the voice of a humanist teacher and a friendly critic and not of a literary magistrate. The tone is honorific, celebratory, confessional, always respectful of T. S. Eliot's admonition, in *East Coker*, that "the only wisdom we can hope to acquire / Is the wisdom of humility: humility is endless."

Some of the essays are the fit occasion to express "gratitude" to a writer like Lewis Carroll, whose books Warren cherished, or to pay "homage" and "tribute" to great poet-critics like Allen Tate and T. S. Eliot and spiritual heroes and saints like William Law, to all of whom he was naturally attracted for their paradigms of honesty and faith, and for a legacy that continues "to challenge and to bless." Other essays contain his "pondering" of a writer like Walter Pater, who has a unique ability to teach one "attention, concentration, the scrupulous analysis of one's own mental and affective states." Still other essays are written in the form of what Warren speaks of as a "revisitation" of major poets like Robert Herrick, Robert Frost, and W. H. Auden, who have long meant much to him. In his old age, then, he was to reexamine, rethink, rejudge, and reflect on their achievement, as well as on their character, and often in the context of what Warren calls a "psychograph," in which "the proportion of stylistic analysis to biographical, or biographical to ideological, will be found to vary from essay to essay," chiefly for the purpose of delineating the "spiritual cosmos" of the particular writer he is reconsidering. And still other essays are written in the form of "personal and private visions" in which Warren concerns himself with ultimate spiritual values and conditions—the love of art, the love of knowledge, the love of man, the love of God.

Behind these last essays is a formidable man of mature thought, a *spoudaios*, who gratefully avers that his "religious faith and faith in writing, and writing have kept me going"—"with the steadiness of his first zeal," to use here Emerson's phrase. The last twenty years of his life were to see seismic changes in the cultural and spiritual life of the country. "I regret that we live in such a barbarous age, which grows steadily more barbarous," he wrote in a letter dated July 31, 1976. It was a situation which, understandably, made him apprehensive of the state of the humanities. In the midst of this anxiety he could hardly escape the "bleak and black state of depression" that so often affects refined and introspective writers and fills them with feelings of lassitude and doubt. Still he labored on with the characteristic patience and devotion of "a contemplative worker who had faith in his 'inner working.'" "And through whatever masks we speak," he wrote, "it is a living soul in search of verbal incarnation which is sent into the world. . . . "

Doubtlessly Warren did experience much personal satisfaction during his retired years in Providence, free from the burdens of his "oral teaching" as a university professor—a New England "apostle to the midwest," as he described himself. But at the same time he felt keenly his own isolation in a society and culture increasingly hostile to the humanistic spirit to which he remained faithful and to which his last essays testify so eloquently. Yet his inner resources were "the fruit of the Spirit." And with those selfsame New England martyrs and saints he so deeply revered and with whose aspirations he equated many of his own, he refused to give in to the Kingdom of Enmity. Had he not, after all, been the pupil of one whose whole life was an act of courage and the memory of whom was deeply rooted in his heart and soul? Of that recollected person, Warren was to write: "To mention his name once more, Babbitt, in his noble isolation, so fortified my youth that his example still strengthens [me] in my isolation."

In the happiness of his Providence years Warren conquered his isolation, even as in his isolation he molded the spiritual happiness that sustained the equanimity and the wisdom that grace his last writings and that define their critical spectrum. One cannot read any one of these writings without being aware somehow of Warren's rising above inner and outer ambivalences in the process of "becoming what one is." A critical transcendence, even resolution, characterizes the tone and the ethos of these writings, their steadiness of purpose, their quality of insight, their energy of intuitive intelligence. His mastery of English prose, and of his own prose style (with its aphoristic vigor and distinction always in arresting evidence), punctuates his undiminishing reverence for and responsibility to the *logos*. The sapiential thrust of these writings deepens their critical outlook, gives them significance not of the little day but of the longer time. A perfectionist not only in the aesthetic but also in the spiritual sense, Warren sought to bind the two in order to consummate their totality of value—the value of valuing, in short.

Invariably Warren reveals a life in search not of administrative principles of criticism but of sensibility of principles, of humane values and their proper place in the great triune of life, literature, and thought. To the end a quiet but persevering fortitude was to guide him in his "thinking, striving, and writing"; and to the end he persevered in his allegiance to the supreme task of "pushing things up to their first principles," to use here the words of another of his strong admirations, John Henry Newman. Never one to exalt himself or his work, he had originally captioned the manuscript containing his last writings simply as "Literary Essays of 1970–1980's." The task remains for his readers, indeed, his votaries, to assess their intrinsic worth and the critical nature of their completeness and fullness. This task, however, must first begin with the recognition of an interior visionary quality that makes these more than simply literary essays. And in them he speaks more than as simply a literary critic.

Warren's critical vision can perhaps best be described as a syncretistic vision that discerns at once things visible and invisible; and that knits together the gifts and excellences of the teacher of literature, of the scholar who has been assigned the fact, and the critic, the value, and, finally, of the teacher as critic who reaches towards the center and participates "in that archetypal balance which is not compromise but tension and balance." The attainment of this mediation illumines his critical essays as these render his search for principles of order. "We need definition of ends and standards," he declares. "We need to have literature correlated with the other arts, and with metaphysics, and with life. And, in needing these, we are but avowing our need of the critic." All these needs, it can be said, are met and integrated in his last writings.

Constant and consistent, as his last essays attest to, are both his concern for "first and last things" and his pursuit of "an honest facing and ordering for my own inner voices." His criticism here, as always, proceeds dialectically, in continuity. "Whether theoretical or practical," writes Warren, "the best criticism is, however, nearer the catechetical than to the expository. The best criticism is that of the critic asking himself questions he finds hard to answer, and giving the most honest (even if tentative or uncertain or negative) answers he can." It is the *honnête homme*—widely read, philosophic in temperament and attitude, and ever aware of the whole intellectual and spiritual life of society—who speaks to us in these essays.

In this "age of criticism" there have been too few good and wise men to whose texts we can turn for inspiration and guidance. "The wise man," Warren reminds us, "looks down at the earth with one eye and up to heaven with the other; yet his vision is single." We now see a severe contraction of the frontiers of criticism as literary theorists and ideologues increasingly set out to regiment moral, intellectual and cultural life. Doctrinaire, destructive attitudes much distort the literary and critical situation in our time, and thus much reduce both the critical sense and the larger interests of humanity. Against such usurpers and usurpations Austin Warren took his stand, striving no less bravely than Emerson's "great men" "to exact good faith, reality and a purpose; and first, last, midst, and without end, to honor every truth by use."

A Few Reasonable Words

Henry Regnery (1912–1996) earned a distinguished and lasting place in the annals of American publishing. As a longtime independent publisher—he founded the Henry Regnery Company in 1947—he sought to make available to the reading public the works of great writers that might otherwise not have appeared in print. For him the power of words and the responsibility of writers were absolutely interdependent, and the books that appeared under his imprint amply illustrated the truth of this criterion. The books he published were essentially, though not exclusively, conservative in orientation, and focused largely on acute philosophical, educational, literary, religious, sociopolitical, economic, and cultural issues, especially as these related to the modern era in the years directly following World War II. Some of the European and American authors whose writings he published were those of religious thinkers like Max Picard, Romano Guardini, and Gabriel Marcel; of educational commentators like Robert M. Hutchins and Mortimer Smith; of literary artists like Ezra Pound, Wyndham Lewis, and Roy Campbell; of sociopolitical critics like Montgomery Belgion, Raymond Aron, and Ernst Jünger; and of literary and cultural critics like Eliseo Vivas and Richard M. Weaver. It is worth adding here that Regnery's *Memoirs of a Dissident Publisher* (1979) endures as a valuable autobiographical document in the history of publishing and also of conservative thought.

It was the publication, in 1953, of Russell Kirk's *The Conservative Mind* that perhaps marked the highest degree of vision on the part of the Henry Regnery Company. No other book in modern intellectual and political history has had more impact on the destiny of the conservative movement in the United States or more affected the direction of the conservative political imagination. "Kirk not only offered convincing evidence that conservatism was an honorable and intellectually respectable position, but that it was an integral part of the American tradition." Thus writes Regnery in a long essay on Russell Kirk's achievement and significance included in *A Few Reasonable Words* (1996), a volume of selected essays composed and published by Regnery during the past three decades. This essay includes a detailed and often fascinating narration of the publishing history of *The Conservative Mind*, as recited by the publisher himself. The essay contains incisive commentary on other books subsequently written by Kirk, also published by the Henry Regnery Company. Regnery concludes his essay on Kirk with these words:

> In a disorderly age he has tirelessly and eloquently made clear the necessity and sources of order; against the false prophets who proclaim that all values are relative and derive from will and desire, he shows their immutability; and to those who believe that man is capable of all things, he teaches humility and that the beginning of wisdom is respect for creation and the order of being.

These preceding words give to us the measure of the major and intrinsic concerns of the essays that Regnery devotes to other American conservative figures found in the first two sections of *A Few Reasonable Words* and whose works he also published. As in the Kirk essay, the separate essays on Albert J. Nock and on Richard M. Weaver, as well as a joint essay examining particular books by James Jackson Kilpatrick, Felix Morley, and James Burnham, seen in the special context of an "emerging conservatism" in the 1950s, Regnery exhibits the kind of critical seriousness and percipience exemplifying the other essays in his book. In the essays that immediately follow, he gives witness not only as a publisher of books of high civilizational value, and which testify incontestably to his standards of discrimination, but also as a writer who possesses literary talent and critical axioms, and who addresses himself to the same urgent problems of the modern world that the books he published also addressed. Indeed, what makes this book especially stimulating is to have on view here the fertile, disciplined working of a mind concerned, critically and judgmentally, with the world of books and ideas, with the men who create books and shape ideas, and with epochal events in modern history which impinge on our common humanity and which, in the end, incite the books and the ideas that speak of the modern human condition. It is this fundamental, overarching concern which gives Regnery's book its unity of outlook and helps define its aims and values.

The essays in *A Few Reasonable Words*, it can be said, chart Regnery's intellectual journey in the modern world, and invite the reader to take part in that journey. A reader who accepts this invitation will be the richer for it; indeed, a younger generation of readers will find in these essays, individually and collectively, a trustworthy guide who, above all, ably describes the temper of the period following World War II and of events during and after the war that "represented the final triumph of liberalism." The lead essay in this book, "The Age of Liberalism," should be required reading for younger readers shaped and conditioned by the sham promises of new and fair deals, let alone the new morality and the new age that "terrible simplifiers" have long been laboring to establish in place of first causes and first principles. Regnery's keen historical sense, no less than his moral sense, cannot but have a restorative effect on readers endlessly exposed to the liberal tales of a terrestrial paradise. In an age in which specious ideologies thrive, an encounter with Regnery's dissident views is bound to give needed shock to the mind.

For Regnery the search for historical truth must be a disinterested endeavor, even when this search becomes yet another lost cause. "Whether writing or publishing the historical truth brings any immediate practical results or not," he writes, "if we believe in anything, we must believe that the truth is worthwhile for its own sake. If a free society is to survive, is to have any meaning, men must be made accountable for their activity, we must know what our leaders did, said, and agreed to in our name." These words, in fact, faithfully express Regnery's aim as a publisher of books, as well as a writer of essays, questioning decisions made by political leaders, like Franklin D. Roosevelt and Winston Churchill, that helped shape the peace after 1945. And both as the publisher of books like Charles C. Tansill's *Back Door to War* (1952) and George N. Crocker's *Roosevelt's Road to Russia* (1959), and as the writer of a two-part essay, the longest in his book, "Historical Revisionism and World War II," Regnery presented the case for historical revisionism with courage of conviction and dissent. In an era when ideology and political correctitude control and manipulate the academy, the world of newspapers, publishers, and reviewing practices, and increasingly the electronics media, Regnery's example of dissent has much corrective value.

"A Few Reasonable Words," the words in the title given to this book, catch the spirit of Regnery's preoccupations, and of the subject and themes the essays as a whole center on throughout. It is a title entirely appropriate for a writer who deliberately avoids ideological extremes, who counsels clear and disciplined thought, who speaks in sensible terms and tones, always forcefully but also always restrainedly. The title of Regnery's book crystallizes the moral measure of an author who presents to his reader a selection from the various essays he has written over the years, possessing as he does both a keen historical and an active moral sense. In this respect, a reader would do well to ponder especially Regnery's short essay, originally given as a commencement address in 1960, "The Responsibility of the Educated." In title and content, this essay augments and sharpens the main title and direction of the book, and ultimately points to Regnery as a man of prudence and of probity, those quiet virtues underpinning the entire book itself.

Reasonable words and responsible acts are for Regnery mutually necessary: are, in fact, what a world in disarray desperately requires if a humane civilization in a modern setting is not to dissolve altogether. "The Responsibility of the Educated" is an essay that provides a reader with a cogent purview of Regnery's basic position, of the values and principles that he affirms and that he counsels as an antidote to our present troubles. Here he speaks out with much feeling and candor, in the vital context of "What I Believe." It is an essay that essentializes his position and beliefs. In it we hear the conjoining voice of Regnery as a determined publisher, committed writer, and concerned American citizen alerting his listeners to instances of poor leadership and, in turn, poor decisions that have incalculable consequences in the life of a nation and also the course of history. Citing the dismal story and aftermath of the Yalta, Teheran, and Potsdam conferences (and of the great personages taking part in them), Regnery goes on to lament the fact that the educated, then and now, have not fulfilled their responsibility in speaking out against vacillating governmental policies and political programs and agendas that lack moral roots and convictions. Above all, Regnery stresses that our national leaders have not lived up to the standards of the Founding Fathers who knew that

> history was a struggle for power, for existence, for advantage, that life itself is struggle, and that to see it otherwise is rank self-deception. But they also knew that the task of civilization is to bring, insofar as it is possible, order and justice out of the chaos of the struggle for existence. They knew that man is imperfect, that human institutions are equally imperfect, and that to expect perfection from the one was as futile and deceptive as to demand perfection from the other.

The last two sections of the book reveal a distinct literary dimension, as Regnery concentrates on gifted individuals who comprise his representative men, so to speak: in short, men whose ideas, values, and standards he esteems and recommends to readers. The essays in these sections give an added dimension to those that precede in the form of reminiscences, tributes, and critical appraisals. Regnery thus adds to the sociopolitical and historical aspects of the earlier essays a more evocative tone and a more sapiential thrust. Through his representative men he seeks primarily to convey paradigms of character, of thought, of attitude that reinforce and refine his inclusive emphasis on the intellectual and moral uses of responsibility. A spirit of affirmation prevails here, and the men whose lives and attainments he respects and salutes often serve as a counterpoise to some of the conditions and circumstances he has delineated in the earlier essays and sections. One will readily discern, too, how these men acted as inspiring guides and good influencers in Regnery's own life and work, helping him to appreciate more fully and deeply higher concepts of character and culture, of culture and society, and of art and thought. These representative men, it can be said, instilled in Regnery loyalty to first principles, now often dislodged or abandoned by our intellectual and political leaders.

That Regnery was a man of measure—of restraint, reserve, reticence—is clearly observed in the essays as a whole, both in style and in content. Romantic excesses and indulgences, which he doubtlessly connected with a vulgar liberalism, repelled him. For Regnery, Goethe's belief that in limitations one first shows himself the master was a central and impelling belief. Indeed, the crisis of modernism, as Regnery's essays demonstrate, often stems from a rejection of the law of limitations—a rejection fanned in turn by the insistence that everything is possible. The dispassionate note that one encounters in Regnery's writings must not, however, be seen as overruling any expression of emotion or strong sympathy. Two essays, in particular, the autobiographical essay on "Hermann Schnitzler," originally written as a testimony of gratitude, and an appreciation of "Richard Strauss," which views the German composer as a classic of our time, illustrate, respectively, Regnery's capacity for human affection and intense aesthetic rapport. The first of these essays confirms the undying truth of an ancient Greek poet's declaration that a man counts it a great joy if he but have the shadow of a friend. The second salutes an outstanding modern composer of symphonic poems and operas, and celebrates a life that "came about as close to complete success and fulfillment as is permitted to man, flawed and imperfect creature that he is." The essay on Schnitzler, it should be noted, shows Regnery's literary sensitivity at its best; and that on Strauss, his lifelong musical interests. Clearly, Regnery wrote these essays with considerable personal joy, which is certain to touch and transform a reader.

The men whose lives Regnery honored in memory are, as he made plain, also men of our time who were able to resist, in civilized and creative ways, the modern spirit of doubt, change, disillusionment, destruction, decadence. In their examples he asks us to find the strength and the courage we need to contend with the sickness of the modern world. No less compelling, in this respect, is Regnery's short but trenchant tribute to the Swiss-German philosopher and metaphysician Max Picard. It was Hermann Schnitzler who first introduced Regnery to Picard's writings, of which the Regnery Company eventually published, in English translation, *Hitler in Our Selves* (1947), *The Flight from God* (1951), and *The World of Silence* (1952). The beautiful and wise soul which Regnery recognized in Picard (whom he visited on several occasions, which he vividly re-creates in his tribute) conflates with Picard's writings and ideas.

Regnery's own decision to become a full-time publisher owed much to his wish to publish Picard's *Hitler in Our Selves*, a book which helps explain the catastrophe that overtook European civilization, and which diagnoses its breakdown. Though essentially concerned with Nazism as a German phenomenon, this remarkable, prophetic book sees Hitlerism as a terrifying portent and symptom of the general crisis of modern man, especially the spiritual chaos into which modern civilization has fallen, with its attendant discontinuity, fragmentation, destructiveness, apostasy, and the despotism of worldliness. Regnery writes that, by publishing Picard's books, he was giving Americans "the opportunity to come under the influence of an extraordinary man who has something to offer we very much need." Clearly, Picard's books have lasting relevance in the present time, when there is no longer any point of orientation and when the Hitler in ourselves now transmutes into the nihilism in ourselves. If Regnery's circumspect comments do nothing more than alert a reader to even one of Max Picard's books, they will have done a good deed.

The men, both Americans and Europeans, whom Regnery admires and celebrates, are men who had a common calling, a common vocation: to tell us truths about our modern world, about ourselves, and about our origins. Regnery saw their writings and thought not only as gifts to a modern world in dire need of moral direction and renewal, but also as a fervent defense of civilized values. In a long and percipient essay on the results of their "creative friendship," for example, Regnery elucidates in detail how T. S. Eliot, Ezra Pound, and Wyndham Lewis in the first half of the twentieth century responded to what the latter spoke of as "the threat of extinction to the cultural tradition of the West." It is exactly this threat at an ever-increasing scale that concerns Regnery and that shapes the thrust of his essays in their parts and in their whole, in general and in particular. That this threat has also become even more pronounced and pervasive in the years since the end of World War II is, in fact, what especially troubles and preoccupies Regnery in this book and what gives to it a far greater sense of urgency and timeliness. In no way, however, does the possibility of the annihilation of our sacred patrimony, and thus the final victory of those whom Russell Kirk aptly identifies as "enemies of the permanent things," daunt Regnery. Despite the debasement and deterioration that he saw in our midst, he did not succumb to despair, he refused to surrender to the kingdom of enmity. His faith in the order and the dignity of human life, his brave affirmation of the higher meaning of existence, did not desert him whatever the threats of the "antagonist world," to recall Edmund Burke's phrase.

For Regnery the union of what can best be termed the critical spirit and the creative spirit was essential to a civilized society, and to the idea of order. Such a union deters sloppiness, chaos, excess, debasement. It was the luminous presence of this union, however transient it was, that Regnery observed in his book on *Creative Chicago* (1993), particularly as found in the achievement of Louis Henri Sullivan, one of America's greatest architectural geniuses. When this union thrives, vision finds its fulfillment in what Sullivan calls "the beneficence of power"—of power and responsibility, one could add. And when such a union falters, the losses to civilization can be disastrous, even fatal. In *A Few Reasonable Words* Regnery particularly examines figures of achievement and significance in the light of how each assumes the responsibility of vision and choice. Yet he is profoundly and invariably aware of the hard, tensive realities that grip life, and does not fail to warn of what takes place when the critical and the creative spirit is sundered, and how the rhythm of disorder, in one's self and in the world, besets the human situation. Still, it is characteristic of Regnery's attitude and outlook that the negative is subordinated to his accent on human effort, on aspiration, on ascent. In this connection, Simone Weil, whose celebrated essay on "The *Iliad*, or, The Poem of Force," Regnery read with deep admiration when it was first translated into English by Mary McCarthy and published in Dwight McDonald's magazine *Politics* in November 1945, provides the appropriate note here: "The world is the closed door. It is a barrier. And at the same time it is the way through."

The essays in this book bear witness to Regnery's constancy of faith and purpose. And those whose writings and ideas he illuminates in his essays exemplify the dynamics of this constancy. Thus, with George F. Kennan, American statesman and sage, and the subject of the penultimate essay in this book, Regnery (quoting from Kennan's *Around the Cragged Hill: A Personal and Political Philosophy* [1993]), registers his own "'basic *preferences* . . . for the small over the great, . . . for the qualitative over the quantitative, for the discriminate over the indiscriminate, and for the varied over the uniform, in most major aspects of social life.'" And with Kennan he also agrees that, "'if we are to have hope of emerging successfully from the great bewilderments of this age, weight must be laid predominantly upon the spiritual, moral, and intellectual shaping of the individual.'" That which elicits Regnery's greatest attention and respect, as *A Few Reasonable Words* reveals again and again, is the example of a writer and his work ever striving, often in the face of powerful ideological opposition, to achieve the fulfillment of vision and thus to portray the human spirit at its highest point of excellence. Particularly alarming to Regnery is the suppression of life-values in the interest of ideology, in short, of unprincipled politics and morality emerging in the garb of the "New Order" and the "New Man."

Appropriately, *A Few Reasonable Words* concludes with an essay on Aleksandr Solzhenitsyn, who possesses the inner courage and creative faith that Regnery admired in a dissident writer who, refusing to capitulate to totalitarian rule, insists that we need "to subordinate our interests to moral criteria." Indeed, the essay on Solzhenitsyn returns us to the first essay in the book, "The Liberal Age," by reminding us of the power of the liberal left and of its disdain for a writer like Solzhenitsyn who has a prophetic calling to which he remains absolutely loyal as he shatters the illusions of the apologists for a bankrupt Marxism-Leninism, as well as of the "terrible simplifiers" who endlessly strive to create a new heaven and a new earth. Solzhenitsyn, as Regnery contends, has always presented a "problem" to the liberal mind, desperate in its effort to replace man's vision of God with the vision of man without God. In Solzhenitsyn, he sees the might of the word in the struggle between good and evil. In him, too, he sees the example of a writer who accepts not only the moral responsibility of his calling, but also the full consequences of that acceptance.

Of the fourteen essays included in *A Few Reasonable Words* eleven of them were originally written for publication in *Modern Age: A Quarterly Review*, between the years 1971 and 1995. With Russell Kirk, it will be remembered, Regnery was instrumental in the founding of *Modern Age* in 1957, and he steadfastly maintained interest in its purposes and direction. In his *The Sword of Imagination: Memoirs of a Half-Century of Literary Conflict* (1995), Kirk memorably recalls the challenges and the difficulties of an undertaking aspiring to inform and persuade: "Certain Modernist excesses incited . . . [us] to found a periodical comparable to the vanished *Bookman* and the *American Review* that might publish reflections on the permanent things and offer some intellectual resistance to a reckless neoterism. . . . *Modern Age* was intended to become, in considerable part, an American protest against the illusions of Modernity; and so it has remained." Regnery's book must be read, then, in the light of what Kirk had to say about the mission and ethos of *Modern Age*. His essays, in the form of both articles and reviews, validate the importance of a quarterly review in the intellectual community, and particularly at a time when *les clercs* have disowned their charge. In their content, above all, Regnery's essays further illustrate, by enlarging and enriching, the worth of a journal of opinion, of dissent to be more exact, in providing a focus of ideas and a center of resistance for those disturbed by the drift of modern civilization in the last half of the twentieth century.

A Few Reasonable Words depicts the generous range and depth, as well as the resoluteness and integrity, of a man of thought. In the essays here, written in a crisp, direct, unadorned style, without any affectation or pretension, an appreciative reader will discover those exceptional qualities, or endowments, that are intimately associated with morality of mind: in short, the insight and the sapience, the critical intelligence and the courage of judgment that characterize the keen-sighted few who, like Regnery, make possible the survival of humane values of civilization. We live in a time of history when morality of mind, let alone moral virtues, is not held in high regard; and when the trivial and the tawdry are the predominant tendencies in the social and cultural life of a nation and its people. To our peril, we stubbornly refuse to recognize the transcendent power of morality which José Ortega y Gasset invokes in words that have, in our time, increasingly fallen into silence: "For morality is always and essentially a feeling of subordination and submission to something, a consciousness of obligation and service." In word and in work, in principle and in practice, Henry Regnery staunchly affirmed and enacted the truth of this living morality. The essays assembled in *A Few Reasonable Words* reaffirm and reenact the reality, the continuity, and, yes, the nobility of this truth.

~ ❦ ~

The condition of American civilization long occupied Henry Regnery's attention, as his *Creative Chicago: From* The Chap-Book *to the University* vividly demonstrates. This is a beautiful book—visually, conceptually, intellectually—a pleasure to read and to ponder. It poses important questions regarding the city and culture, even as it depicts inevitable tensions affecting life and letters in a megalopolis. As the title itself indicates, the main and immediate concern is the cultural situation of the city of Chicago, "From *The Chap-Book* to the University." What a reader will notice most in this book is the pervasive tone and ethos that emerge from and mirror authorial sincerity.

Neither specialist nor academic, Regnery was a man of thought in search of civilizing values that shape American opinion and character. What he has to say specifically about visionary men and women, and generally about "the creative spirit in a prairie setting," has relevance to his larger concern with the human condition. His story is about a particular city in a particular region of the country and covers a particular period, a little over a hundred years, from about 1840 to 1950. In recounting this story he demonstrates enviable ability to remain within the limits of his subject and aims and to present his story with clarity and concision. There is no pretentiousness here, no vague gropings or flights, no impractical claims or pronouncements. Honesty and temperateness are virtues that Regnery honored and that, in turn, honor him and his work.

The interweaving concern of the various "papers" that make up this book, as Regnery employs that generic word, is with the question, Why has Chicago, with all of its pioneering spirit, geographical advantages, and material assets, failed to become a literary center? Or, to rephrase the question, Why has this great city with such great creative energy failed to achieve its promise of greatness? Regnery does not make it his job to give hard-and-fast answers to the questions he raises; he does not force judgments on or presume to speak for his reader. Rather he gives his report from Chicago, so to speak, staying close to the historical record, without adornment or illusion. Veracity shapes the focus of his presentation. His report is the result of careful assimilation and concentrated thought.

These papers, composed over a period of time for different occasions and audiences, return to, reconnect with, and reconfirm their author's central concern. It is clear that Regnery, in the context of his own experience of the Chicago scene, had been wrestling with the issues his book examines. This long and taut wrestle had led him to see things with unusual lucidity and sagacity. Here there are no forced critical premises and gestures, no "yes . . . but" vagaries, no formulaic thesis, antithesis, synthesis. His book generously allows the reader to encounter "creative Chicago" in all of its enigma, with all of its accents, colors, variations, and with all of its excitement and disappointments.

It is the pursuit of excellence that dominated Regnery's attention and gained his respect. He was, of course, always aware of human failure and he knew that failure cannot be easily escaped, that it is a significant and common part of human fate. Again and again, his report from Chicago registers the presence and consequences of failure. But this report ultimately moves away from the shadow of adversity. Regnery's pursuit of excellence in terms of the exemplars and paradigms that illumine the pages of his book was always in steady ascent. On occasion one will hear a sigh of resignation as the author records losses, as when a leading literary magazine like *The Dial*, originally founded in 1880 by Francis F. Browne, left Chicago for New York in 1918. This was a magazine that maintained high standards of criticism, encouraged authors, shepherded creativity, and had strong influences on literature. "Browne, obviously," writes Regnery, "was no moral relativist; the difference between good and bad existed and was discoverable."

The transfer of *The Dial* to New York, as Regnery sadly notes, quoting Browne's son, was the result of "the spirit of the time and the place of his labors—the all-pervading materialism to which intellectual concerns were chiefly claptrap and high purposes moonshine." But neither disappointments nor defeats daunt Regnery. In Francis Browne, Regnery perceives the power of a "saving remnant." As long as Browne's example endures, as long as we have before us his sense of commitment, his determination to bring culture to the prairies, his editorial leadership and principles, the pursuit of excellence, in Chicago and elsewhere, remains alive.

We need to remember the greatness of what we have lost or not recognized fully. This is Regnery's message to the reader as he relates the accomplishments of Chicago writers, editors, book publishers, educators, and an architect. "Even the most crass among its citizenry," Regnery asserts, "would concede that a great city like Chicago cannot live by trade alone." As such, *Creative Chicago* is the story of a heroism intellectual and spiritual in scope and influence, one which soars beyond the demands of the marketplace, of popularity, of quantity and measurement. This is a book of reminders that, with quiet dignity, with strength and courage, prods us to remember past examples of greatness. To remember and to revere these examples elevates the human spirit by bringing it closer to the life of value. The twin act of remembrance and reverence has both individual and communal beneficence as *Creative Chicago* testifies, confirming as it does these apt words of the late Richard M. Weaver, an old friend and early ally in the front line of the battle for Western culture: "Cultural life depends upon remembrance of acknowledged values, and for this reason any sign of a prejudice against memory is a signal of danger."

More than anything else this book helps us to remember that enormous determination and sacrifice are needed to shape and sustain cultural life. Regnery pays tribute to those creators whose accomplishments enhance the cultural situation. What he has to say about Harriet Monroe, a Chicago woman and "friend of poets" who in 1912 founded *Poetry: A Magazine of Verse*, which coincided with the "Chicago Renaissance" and survives to this day as one of Chicago's most respected literary institutions, reflects the ethos of *Creative Chicago* as well as its critical impulse. When Regnery quotes these words from Harriet Monroe's posthumously published autobiography, *A Poet's Life* (1938), they are words that also tell us much about Regnery himself and his own contribution to cultural life in Chicago and in the total American scene:

"Is it not enough for us that life is magnificent, and now and then offers golden moments which shake out the soul like a banner in the wind." Harriet Monroe's statement could easily serve as an epigraph to *Creative Chicago*. For, in the end, this is a book about "golden moments" in a city's cultural history. Regnery commends these in the reverent spirit of "remember and be glad."

To be sure, Regnery was a realist who distinguished between vision and fulfillment, who understood the cruel import of T. S. Eliot's warning that "Between the idea and the reality falls the shadow." And shadows do indeed fall upon golden moments, as Henry Blake Fuller (1857–1929), "the first Chicago novelist to win national recognition as a literary figure," was to attest. This "unwilling Chicagoan" resented the fate that condemned him to spend his life in Chicago, and to William Dean Howells's urging that he write another Chicago novel, he tartly replied, "Who wants to read about this repellent town?" For the author of such realistic novels of Chicago as *The Cliff-Dwellers* (1893) and *With the Procession* (1895) the problem in writing about Chicago was perhaps not so much the city itself but rather the limitations of his personality. Regnery's critical comments on Fuller are evenhanded in their discernment:

> There can be little doubt that he developed a degree of attachment to his native city and pride in the long association of his family with its history. He was a product of Chicago, as the character and specific quality of his work make clear, and with his high literary standards and unfailing critical judgment made his own contribution to its cultural life. At a time when Chicago was best known for its stockyards, it was Henry Fuller, as a young man in his thirties, who astonished the eastern reviewers by the quality of his writing.

The sympathetic and at times touching discussion of Hamlin Garland is equally discerning. Here, Regnery judiciously centers on Garland's life and work in order to elucidate not only his achievement but also his Chicago connections, as these directly affected his career as a novelist. The section on Garland, one of the early realists of American literature, is designated as "an appreciation" of his short stories and autobiographical "Middle Border" series of narratives. Born in 1860 in LaCrosse, Wisconsin, Garland did not actually settle in Chicago until 1893, attracted as he first was by the prospect of Chicago becoming a great literary and cultural center. But in 1915 a disillusioned Garland moved to New York. "For twenty-three winters," he confessed, "I had endured the harsh winds of Chicago, and fought against its ugliness, now I was free of it." During his Chicago years, we learn, the two new Chicago publishers to whom he had entrusted his *Prairie Songs* (1893), a new edition of *Main-Travelled Roads* (1891), and *Prairie Folks* (1892), foundered, with all the financial and professional consequences that Garland inevitably suffered. But he did his best, as Regnery shows, to build up the aesthetic and literary side of the city's life, most notably with his founding in 1908 of the Cliff Dwellers Club for artists and writers. Garland became its first president, but the high standards he set for its meetings—no alcoholic drinks, no small talk, no business lunches—led to his dismissal. Garland's Chicago experience is still another of that city's golden moments coming to an end.

No account of the city of Chicago can be complete without mention of the University of Chicago, founded in 1891, with William Rainey Harper as its president—a "providential man" who charted the way. (An American Hebraic scholar, Harper was the author of, among others, *Religion and the Higher Life* [1904], even the title of which, in the present educational climate, would weigh heavily against appointment to a college or university presidency.) Regnery's discussion of Robert Maynard Hutchins, a "worthy successor" who served as president (1929–1945) and chancellor (1945–1951) of the University of Chicago, is both penetrating and evocative, and there is no doubt that he holds Hutchins in high esteem, as he should. For in Hutchins we have an educational leader who is an educational thinker before being merely a university administrator. That is, Hutchins was allegiant to standards of humane education and sought to use his office and influence "to give American education a degree of organization and purpose . . . it did not have." The need for "general education" he felt to be a crucial one, so as to avert mediocrity and aimlessness. "If education is rightly understood, it will be understood as the cultivation of the intellect," Hutchins insisted. His books *No Friendly Voice* (1936) and *The Higher Learning in America* (1936), as Regnery notes, are still relevant even in this twilight hour of political correctness and the dread afflictions it brings to the realm of American education.

To read Regnery on Hutchins is to be reminded of how deep American education has now sunk into what another thoughtful educational thinker, Arthur Bestor, later described as our "educational wastelands." Sadder, still, Regnery's commentary also reminds us that, by any standard of comparison, we do not have university or college presidents who can even begin to measure up to Hutchins; that our present-day educational chiefs are at best managerial technicians who indiscriminately accept and even abet the decadence in higher learning that the late Russell Kirk long and courageously diagnosed. The savage demolition of the liberal arts and of anything with Eurocentric roots has now reached epidemic dimensions. Undoubtedly Hutchins is now a forgotten name, which contemporary educators would be hard pressed to identify, or if they could they would do so with loathing. In his time, in any case, Hutchins's tenure at the University of Chicago marked another golden moment in that city's history. Of very few university presidents in our era will one be able write, as Regnery writes of Hutchins, these words of tribute:

> For all the turmoil and violent changes occurring during Hutchins's administration of the University of Chicago—the Great Depression, the Second World War and its aftermath—he never lost faith in the goal of higher education which, as he never tired of pointing out, is "the training of the mind." There was an unmistakable aura of nobility about Robert Maynard Hutchins that is a reflection of the faith he never surrendered in the higher purpose of education.

One of the greatest architectural geniuses in America, Louis Henri Sullivan, is the subject of the final paper, which revolves around his compelling book, an account of his life, *The Autobiography of an Idea* (1924). Born in Boston in 1856, he spent most of his life in Chicago, where he died in 1924. Not only as an architect but also as an innovative designer, writer, teacher, and thinker, he was to have an extraordinary influence. He first arrived in Chicago in 1873, just two years after the devastating conflagration of 1871. His heart, he wrote, "was stirred, his courage was tenfolded in this raw city by the Great Lake in the West." With the exception of 1874–1875, which he spent studying at the Ecole des Beaux Arts in Paris, he lived and worked in Chicago until his death in 1924. From 1881 until 1895 he was a partner in the firm of Adler and Sullivan, where, to recall, Frank Lloyd Wright spent six years as an apprentice.

Sullivan is closely identified with early skyscraper design, and his collaboration with Dankmar Adler includes, among other landmarks, the Auditorium Building, Chicago, as well as the Guaranty Building, Buffalo, and the Wainwright Building, St. Louis, Missouri. Architecture, he believed, should not only fulfill a social and structural function but also have a civilizing purpose. He rejected mechanical theories of art; imagination, beauty, uplift, aspiration, responsibility composed, for Sullivan, the principles, indeed the morality, of his creed as an architect. "Nothing more clearly reflects the status and tendencies of a people than its buildings," he asserted. "They are the emanation of a people; they visualize for us the soul of our people." There is clearly a Wordsworthian element in Sullivan's thinking, as Regnery reminds us when he observes that Sullivan's genius and concept "fulfilled his definition of architecture as Art that would . . . uplift the eyes of the world."

The pages on Sullivan are the most impressive in *Creative Chicago*. Sullivan's attainment crystallizes those "golden moments" when creativity and civilization meet and merge in the highest way, when man, in Sullivan's words, does things "in the beneficence of power." "This belief in man's power and his responsibility to use it 'beneficently' . . . became central to the development of Louis Sullivan's thought and is the subject of his book," Regnery states. His autobiography ends in fact with the Chicago World's Fair of 1893, with which Sullivan's own career largely ended. Indeed, after 1900, his only commissions were eight banks in small, Midwestern towns. Sullivan lived his last years in loneliness, poverty, alienation. By 1920 he had no office and had to live in a single room in a seedy Chicago hotel, dependent on his friends' generosity.

For Sullivan the 1893 Columbian Exposition was a bitter disappointment; his own contribution, the Transportation Building, was painted in various colors, setting it apart from the all-white buildings in a classical style, as a kind of conscious protest. He saw the Exposition not as a "symbol" of Chicago's "basic significance as offspring of the prairie, the lake, and the portage," but rather as the triumph of the spirit of "hustle": "Make it big, make it stunning, knock 'em down." In Chicago's World's Fair he had witnessed precisely the rise of what E. M. Forster, in his novel *Howards End* (1910), later called the "architecture of hurry." Indeed, in the collapse of Sullivan's career we see how golden moments give way to goblins, as Forster describes them, "walking quietly over the universe from end to end. Panic and emptiness!"

Regnery's description of Sullivan's last years conveys that sense of panic and emptiness that announces both the shattering of a brilliant career and the halting of cultural advancement. Though Regnery avoids abstract speculation and answers to equally abstract questions, his book induces a reader to reflect on the larger questions connected with the state of culture and of the conditions and circumstances that affect it. For no less than a creative Chicago, a creative civilization has its problematic side and experiences mysterious regressions that have a long-term impact. Golden moments, as Regnery shows, are fleeting, but their interludes are luminous as the human spirit leaps ahead and emboldens men and women to resist chaos and darkness. Regnery chooses here to accent the splendor and the heroism that mold human greatness. He refuses to accede to, even as he fully understands, the view of a Theodore Dreiser, about whose Chicago experiences he has some very thoughtful things to say, that Chicago, far from being an archetypal city, was simply "a good place to make money."

Creative Chicago attests to the truth of William Blake's belief that "All deities reside in the human breast." Justifiably, then, Regnery leaves it to Louis Henri Sullivan to express with courage of faith that which affirms and celebrates human possibility:

> One life surely is enough if lived and fulfilled. . . . [But] we have yet to learn the true significance of man; to realize the destruction we have wrought; to come to a consciousness of our moral instability. . . . [M]an is godlike enough did he but know it—did he but choose, did he but remove his wrappings and his blinders, and say goodbye to his superstitions and his fears.

~ 🌶 🌶 ~

Measure is that which perfects all things. Viewed in this context, measure signifies principle, prudence, proportion, standard, and as such opposes what is extreme, chaotic, radical. Thus, to describe one as a man of measure is to attribute to one a quality or merit that is consistently revealed in one's life and work. The twentieth century has been notoriously inhospitable to the virtue of measure in general and to the man of measure in particular. Extremism and extremists have embodied the furies of this century in the episodic form of wars, disorder, catastrophes, and in the human form of dictators, destroyers, demonists. The man of measure, no less than his brave compatriot, the man of character, has been pitilessly ignored, or oppressed, or scorned. His tempered voice struggles to be heard, but is often muffled by shrill and insistent voices that counsel unreason and unrestraint. The terrible twentieth century, as it has been called, has been manifestly a century of abandon, evident in both personal and collective life and behavior, as rational terror has joined with irrational terror to extinguish intellectual, moral, and spiritual truths, and ultimately to create a circle of violence from which escape is difficult, and in which protest and dissent are throttled. Social historians have as yet to assemble a complete catalogue of this century's sins and errors; nonetheless, a rhythm of barbarity, pronounced and constant, identifies the overarching spirit of an age that will crush whatever resists its brutal dictates.

Henry Regnery was a discerning witness to the tumultuous historical, sociopolitical, and geopolitical forces and conditions assailing the life of measure throughout this century. He saw dramatic change, trouble, and confusion on both national and international levels, and he steadfastly gave his testimony, without fear of recrimination. His voice never wavered in its espousal, and also in its defense, of the virtue of measure as an indispensable need for twentieth-century man in the face of powerful and divisive ideologies that defy human limits and divine laws, and rebel against God and man. In the twin evil of this defiance and this rebellion, Regnery viewed the diminishment of ethical and moral axioms; of the historical sense; of civilizational values—and, in short, of "the permanent things." With courage of judgment, and with calm consistency, he registered his objections to the enemies of civilization in a century in which he himself lived and worked and tried to understand, always with the hope of remedying, or at least containing, its transgressions. His voice, his tone, his temper were always measured: nor did he ever lose faith, regardless of the power of adversity or of adversary, in the enduring value and virtue of measure with which to resist movements that bring destruction to civilization.

The survival of a humane civilization was a central concern of Regnery's work and thought. Whether he was glancing at the general state of modern life, or commenting on important social, cultural, intellectual, and literary issues, or looking at the lives and achievements of men of principle, or simply estimating the import of a particular book he saw as exemplifying intellectual or social and political excellence, he was astute and insightful. His candor, his concern, and his criteria coalesced to give integrity to his thought and help imbue his critical and intellectual role as quintessentially a man of measure. Pretense, punditry, affectation, bombast, egoism he silenced in his writings and judgments. And his writings took on an urgent tone as he looked at the multiplying dangers which beset the inner and outer life in modern times, which he often traced to their origin in the age of liberalism that has become synonymous with the magnification of ideology. Regnery gave careful thought to his fears and concerns, which he articulated with transcendent probity and dignity. In him we observe the union of the man of measure with man thinking.

Critical seriousness and critical intelligence consistently informed his opinions, however dissident or unpopular they happened to be in their distinctly conservative orientation. Indeed, Regnery was to reveal key aspects of the conservative mind at its maximum point of sympathy and relevance. He was deeply involved in the modern drama of human destiny, and he was deeply devoted to those higher moral and spiritual values that redeem the human condition, and humane values, from being totally collectivized and reified in a technologico-Benthamite world. By no means, however, did Regnery propose to command the obedience of his contemporaries. Rather, he insisted that they embrace and maintain a sense of responsibility, which in the end shapes both individual and national character. Where and when he saw the erosion of responsibility he also saw the erosion of character, a dual process that he regarded as leading to mediocrity and barbarism. Regnery, it can be said, spoke both out of a moral sense and out of a sense of loyalty to human tradition and civilizational order. He never underestimated the disruptive and destructive power of specious ideologies. For him the consequences of irresponsible thought and action were inescapable, and he confronted and gauged these consequences as they besiege and alter the world. In this connection, he did not fail to cite wrongs or to assign blame on the part of "terrible simplifiers" who strive to fashion the world according to their own one-dimensional illusions. Regnery exposed these simplifiers as deceivers and their utopian dreams as filled with deceits. Unlike many modern intellectual and political leaders, he was not afraid to censure inept decisions and actions that weaken the roots of order.

Basically a generalist, he examined some of the bigger questions and looked towards the bigger patterns. For him the critical function was instinctively Arnoldian in goal and scope: to recognize, to understand, and to propagate the best that is known and thought in the world. As such, the writer has a larger and wider purpose in the totality of ideas, values, and thought as these determine the complex fate of civilization. For Regnery there was a fundamental necessity to speak out on matters of selective importance to the quality of life, literature, and thought, particularly when the stuff of quality is being reduced and plundered, and the moral fabric of civilization is falling apart.

He belonged to the old critical tradition that an Irving Babbitt honored precisely because he, too, was to honor the disciplines of tradition that shape and sustain character and culture, intelligence and sensibility. And as one who esteemed universals and moral order, he rebuked those who breach universals and moral order, and in the process annul civilization. In vulgar liberalism, above all, he detected the particular personalities and movements that undermine civilizational values and principles. With admirable clarity he censured their sham methods and doctrines—and their faults and hazards. But what was most to characterize his beliefs and opinions was the poise and the worthiness of the way in which he spoke out, unequivocally, as a man of measure. The modesty, humility, loyalty, and wisdom which mark the man of measure identically marked Regnery's long labors, in which there are lessons for all of us.

Loyalty is a virtue that Regnery revealed consistently as he recalled and saluted old friends and teachers and writers he encountered during his long career. How they illumined his life, enlarged and enriched his view of the world, opened doors and windows of his mind and heart were emphases that he registered with gratitude and openness. These were often the selfsame persons who taught him how to cope with the world, to accept gladly its blessings, and to wrestle with its sorrows and paradoxes. They were, in a word, exemplars who provided him with wonderful and generative paradigms of hope and aspiration; and who summoned him to nourish and refine his human understanding and sympathy, and to travel undauntedly on the high road to excellence. Above all, they exemplified for him a transcendent vision of human existence and meaning, as well as the need to overcome the force of gravity that cloys and drags down the life of belief and the creative human spirit. Regnery was profoundly aware of this oppressive force, and he never flinched from exploring and assessing the endless affliction it brings both to individuals and to society as a whole. But the hard and sometimes dark realities of life did not intimidate him to retreat into the realm of abstraction. For him there was always the promise of greatness in the midst of human affliction. Indeed, even when the dream of destructiveness shrouds the human scene, he was to display remarkable perseverance as he confronted the world into which man has been thrown, and which man must strive to make better. Although he fully perceived the negative, and contended with it, negations did not break his belief in the life and idea of value. He possessed a living principle and a dynamic faith that enabled him to enact his acceptions and his affirmations.

The century now drawing to a close has been one in which epochal changes have taken place and have drastically altered the character of life. Regnery reflected on the outcome of the changes, and he helped us to gauge their impact on our lives and our society. What he found and said gives us a deeper understanding of our condition and our time. The destructive impulse, he concluded, unceasingly assaults the very foundations of a humane civilization and of our sacred patrimony. Destructiveness, of course, assumes concrete shapes and forms, visibilized in the ruins of peoples and their cities and nations—in the terrors of totalitarianism, in social and political strife, in ruthless and tyrannical leadership, in antinomian behavior and attitude, in concentration camps and gulags, incendiarism and death. The destructive impulse, he stressed, is also to be found in the ruin of those first principles and unwritten laws which so many ages have venerated. Metaphysical violence, no less than physical violence, he reminded us, is equally devastating in terms of human destruction—objectified in the moral malaise, enmity, and anarchy that lead to debasement of the spiritual nature of man. This destructive impulse is thus the enemy in ourselves, insidious, diabolic, corrosive, and it is in our inner selves where the most real and lasting damage occurs and from which recovery is not easy.

Neither the empire of violence nor the kingdom of hostility that spawn the crises and the tragedy of the modern world were to weaken. Yet they never threatened his allegiance to a humane world, or to his view of the world as an organic whole, or his standards of discrimination, or his deep respect for the moral life and the ethical life. To the regnant spirit of denial he unhesitatingly opposed the spirit of affirmation. He did not despair, he did not give in to disaffection, he did not resign himself to human woe, destruction, ruin, loss, decay. Bravely and unfailingly, Henry Regnery sought to call attention to the truth of Ralph Waldo Emerson's words: "It will always be so. Every principle is a war-note. Whoever attempts to carry out the rule of right and love and freedom must take his life in hand."

Man of Letters

It was Thomas Carlyle (1795–1881), the Scots essayist and historian whose guiding genius, Emerson said, was his moral sense, who gave emphatic praise to "The Hero as Man of Letters," one of the lectures later included in his book *On Heroes, Hero-Worship, and the Heroic in History* (1841). The man of letters, he declared, is "our most important modern person," a "heroic seeker" of the light who belongs to "that Priesthood of the Writers of Books" containing "the Thought of man; the true thaumaturgic value." A man of letters like Samuel Johnson taught "a Moral Prudence" and "stood by the old formulas," Carlyle thus maintained. "Formulas fashion themselves as Paths do, as beaten Highways, leading men towards some sacred or high object." Indeed, Carlyle himself was to exemplify his own conception of men of letters who "plant themselves in the everlasting truth of things" and proclaim that "life must be pitched on a higher plane." For him the eighteenth century, in particular, embodied "a Sceptical world" stamped by "spiritual paralysis" and "the disorganised condition of society"—a world in which skepticism contributed both intellectually and morally to "a chronic atrophy and disease of the whole soul." At the very center of this world in crisis, Carlyle insisted, "the battle of Belief against Unbelief is the never-ending battle."

No less heroically than his Scots forefather in his time, Russell Amos Kirk (1918–1994), the American essayist and historian of politics, honored the office of man of letters in our time. To him this office was his calling, and he devoted himself to it with all of his strength—selflessly, reverently, honestly. His life, his writing, his teaching illustrated, both in their union and in their unity, those special qualities that unmistakenly identify a man of letters and set him apart from the literati and intelligentsia of his generation. Some aspirants to the office of man of letters may have the critical intelligence and sensitivity that a literary scholar must have to succeed. Those assets, by themselves, are not enough, however. Kirk, as even a quick glance at the range of his interests and writings will confirm, did own these particular assets, but he also went far beyond them, enriched and enlarged them, deepened them. He invested them, that is, with character—with a moral and spiritual character—precisely that added element that is so often elusive and that cannot be readily obtained since it has an intrinsic worth that is beyond price. In the end this is a quality that, to possess, gives distinction denied to others. To Russell Kirk it was given in the form of a divine spark, so to speak, so that his calling ascended to a higher calling. For what we finally see in the fullness of his achievement is the way in which a man of letters bears witness.

To say that the man of letters bears witness is to say also that he seeks "to point the way to first principles"—those universals, values, traditions, virtues, and standards that create both order of the soul and order of the commonwealth. In Kirk the man of letters attains his substantive definition, character, worth: intellect and spirit join forces, with a common concern and a common front. Function and responsibility are anchored in the moral imperative. The mission of the man of letters thus revolves around basic beliefs: that principles of order abide, that justice is more than human, that art is the servant of enduring standards. The man of letters, as such, is both conservative and conservator, "a guardian of old truths and old rights" who defends the discipline of continuity and the idea of permanence against the lures of progression, experimentation, innovation, in which he discerns the makings of a twin disorder—"disorder in private existence, and disorder in social existence." For Kirk, Edmund Burke's declaration that we are all subject to "the contract of eternal society" informs the faith of a man of letters in the modern world who is simultaneously a man of vision, or as Kirk writes:

> From revelation, from custom and common sense, and from intuitive powers of men possessed by genius, we know that there exist law for man and law for thing. Normality is the goal of human striving; abnormity is the descent toward a condition less than human, surrender to vice.

In Kirk we view the man of letters allegiant, above all, to his moral obligations and to his belief that "humane letters give to the imagination and the reason a moral bent." To be sure, a man of letters has a generalist orientation, is concerned with the human condition, with human destiny, with the totality of problems that relate to the process of civilization. But that orientation and that concern have a higher focus, ethical and moral in nature, mirrored in what Kirk terms "normative truths"; John Henry Newman pinpoints its essential impulse when he speaks of the constant need to push things up to their first principles. As such the man of letters has the task of teaching others that there are abiding standards by which we measure our ambitions and achievements but from which we also too often fall away. Kirk never failed to alert us to this falling away from the center, and for him as a man of letters this was a fundamental need, a "sacred function." What finally distinguishes the man of letters from "the eager little knot of intellectuals hot after novelties" is precisely a willingness to judge matters in terms of authority, tradition, and the illative sense. In this triad resides the "moral bent" that Kirk affirms and that he sees as missing in the modern consciousness. Above all, the man of letters is guardian of the Word, and his "normative duty" is to maintain the law of continuity and to save the "permanent things" from totalist ideology. How to give heart, then, to the forces of "the Great Tradition" in human life and morality, is a question that Kirk sought to answer in his long career as a man of letters:

> The prophets of Israel, the words of Christ and his disciples, the writings of the fathers of the Church, the treatises of the School-men, the discourses of the great divines of Reformation and Counter-Reformation—these are the springs of American metaphysics and American morality, as they are of European metaphysics and morality.

To save American civilization from falling into a slough was a lifelong concern of Kirk as man of letters. The grim fate of Soviet Russia since 1917 never disappeared from his mind and writings. Indeed, his various sociopolitical writings and views emerged from his perception of the sins enacted by Marxism-Leninism during his own lifetime. His responses to the negations that he associated with ideology, it needs to be said, were not so much those of a political thinker or theorist but of a man of letters who viewed the *conditio humana* at all levels and who saw unending interconnections and interrelationships between literature, politics, economics, philosophy, and, especially, religion. With Eric Voegelin, whom Kirk much admired, he insisted that "politics, like science, like art, arises out of belief in a transcendent religion; and when faith decays, politics degenerates." This process of degeneration he portrays with utmost critical acuteness and severity in his work and pinpoints in its irreligious tendencies and opinions. The religious side of Kirk's achievement comes from his deep understanding of the disorder of soul that he finds mirroring the disorder of society itself. Kirk never failed to see the world as an organic whole. Put simply but emphatically, Kirk is not a political but a transcendental man of letters, one who, even as he is an active witness to the crisis of modernism, rises above it, refusing to be consumed by its corruptions and catastrophisms, but at the same time always and utterly aware of their effects on the life of the soul and the life of society.

Both as a dedicated man of letters and as a firm upholder of humane letters, Kirk sought to steer clear of "the errors of ideology." He chose to defend "prudential politics as opposed to ideological politics," which he connected with fanaticism, with utopian schemes, and with revolutionary tactics that strive to transform human society and human nature. Religion and metaphysics, he insisted, were the prime targets of ideology, which he defined as "the politics of unreason" and which he viewed as the major enemy of tradition, custom, convention, prescription, old constitutions, in short, the traditions of civility and our cultural patrimony. Kirk cites Marxist-Leninist ideology, in particular, as an example of what ultimately destroys the situations and themes that inspire humane letters. In ideology, Kirk perceived a dogmatic political theory, or doctrine, striving to substitute secular forms and doctrines for religious goals and doctrines and that ultimately creates "a series of terrestrial hells." In ideology, then, Kirk sees not only the death of the imagination, particularly the moral imagination, but also the ruin of all those living values which give birth to the man of letters and to which he swears his allegiance. Ideology signifies, as such, the triumph of what Burke calls "the antagonist world"—a world of disorder that inevitably erodes the study of humane letters and, in effect, the office of the man of letters himself. The true man of letters, as Kirk so amply and aptly demonstrated in a career spanning four decades, has a latitudinarian, long-range view of the world in the sense that, as Confucius remarks, "the man who does not take far views will have near troubles." A man of letters, in short, stands at the opposite pole of the "terrible simplifiers": ideological reformers who seek, at any cost, to establish "the Terrestrial Paradise."

With the "keen-sighted few" who belong to the great tradition of English-speaking men of letters—Irving Babbitt, Paul Elmer More, T. S. Eliot, Richard M. Weaver—and also of European men of letters like Voegelin, Werner Jaeger, Josef Pieper, Max Picard, Kirk unfailingly sought to teach wisdom rather than illusory opinions and vain wishes. (Not surprisingly he was an admirer of Joseph Conrad's novels, especially *Under Western Eyes, The Secret Agent,* and *Nostromo,* which he saw as having absolutely no illusions about ideological schemes that lead to the dead ends of anarchism, nihilism, liberalism, imperialism.) This intellectual tradition emphasized transcendent reality, the supreme leap in being, the discipline of continuity and of moral order, the "inner check" and principles of order that the New Humanists affirmed, as distinguished from the lures and frills, the vagaries of the "open society," zealously espoused by the social scientists and social engineers, and by modern progressivists and utopians. The latter, whom Kirk classified as "philodoxers," lovers of opinion or arid doctrine, help to create precisely that spiritual disorder that brings on both individual and collective abnormity. Kirk knew that only with the acceptance of defined limits and of standards does the man of letters have anything of value and good influence to impart. In spite of the pressing demands of stringent criticism and the habits of critical diagnosis, Kirk was ever sanguine. Though he admitted that "The world belongs to the vulgar—including the vulgar intellectuals," he also found grounds for hope: "Yet here or there endures a wise man of the stamp of Pascal or Samuel Johnson, abiding in a tradition, still employing the power of the Word to scourge the follies of the time."

If Kirk possessed the historical sense, he also possessed the religious sense, which shapes and sharpens his critical judgments and discriminations. He was never to waver in his belief that "the flight from God" destroys humane letters. This belief gave centrality to his writings, to their perspective and significance. Whatever Kirk wrote was centered in his awareness of the divine otherness that radiates the whole of human existence. And this it was that separated his writings, his thought, his life, from a "sham otherness" and from the decadent productions we have come increasingly to associate with "the treason of the intellectuals" in the modern age. Kirk added manifestly, in his time and through his many and various writings, to "the literature of vision." He refused to accede to that spirit of the time requiring us to "be utterly demythologized, disenchanted, desacralized, and deconsecrated." He fought hard against the mentality of the "secular city." Humility was for Kirk, as it was for T. S. Eliot, one of the highest of the "permanent things"; without it the "moral imagination" could not survive. The "tragic sense of life," Kirk further stressed, deepens one's perception of life free of illusion, of sentiment, a quality that he singles out in the writings of Ralph Ellison and of George Orwell. No sentence, in fact, better captures Kirk's critical acuteness than this:

> Orwell's was that radicalism which is very angry with society because society has failed to provide men with the norms of simple life—family, decency, and continuity, the sort of radicalism which does not mean to disintegrate the world, but restore it.

Kirk asked the question that any dedicated modern man of letters should ask of his contemporaries: Can humane civilization survive in that modern wasteland which an Orwell and an Aldous Huxley prophetically portray? Throughout his life and career Kirk sought for answers to this "accursed question." The chaos and decadence he saw all around him reinforced his awareness of ascendant evil in society and culture. But he never despaired as he gave his witness in essay after essay, book after book; his was not so much a career as it was a moral mission to redeem the time. To the very end he insisted that "the purpose of literature is not simple amusement, but rather the guarding and advancement of the permanent things." No one fought harder or more nobly than Kirk for this purpose; and no one understood more fully the multidimensions of this purpose, literary and political, social and cultural. The clarity and coherence of Kirk's judgments are always evident; his powers of discernment are invariably strong and subtle. "Man thinking" comes alive in Kirk as a man of letters who knows how to evaluate things in their true meaning and importance, to rescue them from ideological claptrap. How Kirk rescues Woodrow Wilson from "revisionist liberals" and sees him as an essentially "prudent conservative reformer, desirous of keeping America what she has been," is a trenchant example of Kirk's critical acuteness:

> He may be recorded as the last of our literary statesmen, bringing to the presidential office the humane and juridical disciplines. He did not merely drift with events: he perceived some of the deeper issues of this century better than anyone else among successful politicians. . . . He was the sort of leader who makes possible the existence of democratic republics.

To read Kirk on "Woodrow Wilson and the Antagonist World" is to be reminded of what a man of letters in the modern world should be and do, or as Allen Tate best describes his function and process: "He must do first what he has always done: he must recreate for his age the image of man, and he must propagate standards by which other men may test that image, and distinguish the false from the true." It is good to remember Tate's words when estimating Kirk's worth as a man of letters. In an age so blatantly contemptuous of standards, Kirk never flinched from searching for and applying them in the name of order itself. Thus in clarifying the nature of Wilson's "failure"—"His failure was the failure of the nation's political imagination in those years, a normative failure"— Kirk emphasizes the absence of prudence, prescription, and prejudice. He never failed to make connections, to show interrelations, to gauge causes and effects, ends and means. Unfailingly, he accepted Irving Babbitt's dictum, uttered in the very first paragraph of *Democracy and Leadership*— for Kirk "one of the few truly important works of political thought to be written by an American in the twentieth century—or, for that matter, during the past two centuries":

> When studied with any degree of thoroughness, the economic problem will be found to run into the political problem, the political problem in turn into the philosophical problem, and the

philosophical problem itself to be almost indissolubly bound up at last with the religious problem.

The critical problems, the defining concerns and responsibilities, of which Babbitt speaks in this arresting sentence are precisely those that occupied Kirk in his body of writings. Clearly he was to extend the frontiers of criticism in ways that purely literary and academic critics have been unable to do. And clearly Kirk was possessed by the larger problem and the larger concern, even as he was speaking to the larger audience, to man at large. His thought reached beyond an institutional complex, beyond a specified area of endeavor, beyond immediate issues. The world as an organic whole was his constant concern, and he sought to guard the organic character of life from the incontinences and reductionisms that modernism has created with a vengeance. With Burke he believed that "Good order is the foundation of good things." The man of letters as a guardian of our "entailed inheritance" attains in Kirk a primacy of importance. He had learned well the lessons Burke articulated: "A spirit of innovation is generally the result of a selfish temper and confined view. People will not look forward to posterity, who never looked backward to their ancestors." The conflict between the forces of integration and those of disintegration signified for Kirk our crisis of modernism. In his scrutiny of this conflict he brought to bear "the two principles of conservation and correction" that Burke affirms. These two principles are requisite to Kirk in his function as a man of letters.

The man of letters attains a preeminent stature, both literary and moral, in Kirk. His writings, in their full variety and meaning, magnify the very term "man of letters." Indeed, this term achieves, with Kirk, far more significance and authority than the secondary status to which T. S. Eliot, albeit respectfully, assigns men of letters (as distinguished from men of genius) whose main function it is to preserve the continuity of a great tradition of literature. To be sure, Kirk served this particular cause faithfully. But, as any examination of his writings finally shows, Kirk propels the man of letters to a much higher level, the lasting importance of his work being commensurate with that of writers of genius who embody the moral imagination. In this respect, Kirk opposes the nominalism that neoteric critics and teachers, especially behaviorists, social scientists, and Marxists, embrace. He insists that "Only by a return to the true sources of wisdom—which in part are the visions of genius— can the critic of society find standards by which to measure our present discontents and to propose remedies." Invariably he exposes the dissipations that accompany "vulgarized pragmatism." Religion and prescriptive morality are primary aspects of his commentaries on a civil social order that culminates in a technologico-Benthamite society. To repeat, as a man of letters Kirk addresses himself to the total human situation; literary, historical, and political texts, hence, are only parts of the whole. A man of letters, Kirk makes clear, must have perspective, but he must also have vision, which, according to Swift, is "the art of seeing things invisible."

What gives Kirk's work its special, revelatory powers is his genius for understanding things visible and invisible, in direct relation to the "permanent things"; in his writings all these things attain transcendent reconciliation. The metaphysical quality that illuminates Kirk's achievement makes it possible for us to fathom what Gabriel Marcel calls the "mystery of being." No other modern man of letters helps us more than Kirk to experience both communication and transcendence as meaning and possibility; the outer life and the inner life, in short, are not profanely divided in Kirk's writing. In reckoning their connections and also their confluence Kirk avoided the vagaries of the relative and the abstract. Anyone who studies the elements of style in Kirk's writings will quickly recognize a concrete, stable temper and tone—solidity, balance, composure, robustness. He is, undeniably, a master of English language and style, as these paragraphs on "John Randolph of Roanoke" (1773–1833), American statesman and orator, vividly remind us in their simplicity, clarity, economy, and poignancy:

> Randolph of Roanoke died in a Philadelphia inn, strange and wonderful to the last. There is no statue in his memory. The fierce lover of permanence was buried in the woods of Roanoke. But in 1879, his body was exhumed and taken to Hollywood Cemetery, in Richmond. The roots of a great tree, penetrating through his coffin, had twined through the dead man's long black hair and filled his skull. So, doubtless, he would have wished to lie forever. Yet modern America, ill at ease in the presence of things immutable, will not permit even the bones of genius to rest secure.
>
> Against the lust for change, Randolph had fought with all his talents. And though he lost, he fell with a brilliancy that was almost consolation for disaster.

Kirk's style, it can be said, is guided unceasingly by the principle of prudence, "the soul's stern sacristan," as one poet expresses it. Not surprisingly, prudence is a heart-word in his lexicon.

As a man of letters Kirk is also a teacher who strives mightily to train the intellect and also to shape the soul. The educational process for Kirk in effect involves a double discipline leading to "order in the soul of the person, the direction of will and appetite by reason . . . [and] order in the commonwealth, through the understanding of justice, freedom and the public good." The primary function of education is to rouse the moral imagination, to impart a moral heritage—"to teach that the virtues and the vices are real, and the individual is not free to toy with the sins as he may choose." The "ideology of Democratism," Kirk further insisted, has dissolving effects on all levels of society and culture, which Edmund Burke had prophetically recognized back in the eighteenth century and whose words Kirk never stopped pondering, or forgot, in his lifetime:

> All the superadded ideas, furnished from the wardrobe of a moral imagination, which the heart owns, and the understanding ratifies, as necessary to cover the defects of our naked shivering nature, and to raise it to dignity in our estimation, are to be exploded as a ridiculous, absurd, and antiquated fashion.

Kirk never surrendered his sacred texts, "those grand and decorous principles and manners," to recall Burke's phrase, that build and define modern Western civilization. To the end he gave his loyalty to loyalty. "Only through prescription and tradition," Kirk wrote, "only by habitual acceptance of just and sound authority, only by conformity to norms, can men acquire knowledge of the permanent things."

Kirk never weakened in his resistance to the "adulterated metaphysics" (to quote Burke again) of modern times. His writings, though by no means having a particular system of thought or doctrine to convey, in their discrete parts and in their organic whole, can be viewed as essays of resistance to the profane spirit of the time—to the forces of nihilism that increasingly besiege humane letters and life. That resistance continued to the very end of his life's work; he opposed the "enemies of the permanent things" at every step of the way, across a wide front, under fire—"And, through the heat of conflict, keeps the law," to recall here Wordsworth's "happy Warrior." In their "dogmas of negation" he perceived dangers that, not to be resisted, prove fatal. Kirk's example reminds us that the man of letters must also be a brave man of character who does not succumb to the blandishments of "sophisters, economists, and calculators." With patience and singleness of vision, he confronted the "antagonist world," diagnosing and judging it according to moral criteria. In the ideology of a "new morality," Kirk viewed the ultimate point of corruption, of human degradation and nothingness. It is with special and characteristic approbation that he chooses to quote these words of Gustave Thibon (b. 1903), the French religious philosopher: "The decline of moral habit produces, in its first stage, a rigid and exalted moralism; and in its second, an immoralism raised to the level of doctrine; sooner or later, it invariably gives birth to the lowest level of morality."

Kirk graced the office of the man of letters with dignity and with style, the ultimate morality of a mind, just and clear. In word and work, in his ministry, so to speak, he manifested above all the great gift of perception, which is essentially a diagnosis. But perhaps the greatest of all gifts apportioned to him was what Saint Paul speaks of as "the discerning of spirits." Kirk possessed the discriminating sense, the ability, that is, to make exact distinctions after observation and reflection. This ability is itself a sign of one who has thought and measured; and of one whose critiques emerge from an intrinsically heroic recognition that the "need for roots" and the "roots of order" are indissoluble. His censorial inspection of modern conditions and circumstances was always conduct-ed in the spirit of affirmation, in the firm belief that adversity "frequently opens the way for the impulse toward virtue." Even when Kirk is most caustic he is not, as Carlyle wrote of another great Scotsman, Robert Burns, "a mourning man"—"A large fund of Hope dwells in him." He is always guiding us out of the wasteland of modern existence to the way of affirmation—an "encourager unto all good labours," as well as "encourager of letters and the arts."

There are no entries for "man of letters" in the major encyclopedias. Rather perfunctorily, *Webster's Third New International Dictionary* defines "man of letters" as "1 : a learned man : scholar 2 : a literary man : AUTHOR, LITTÉRATEUR." Any future estimate of Russell Kirk's achievement should considerably expand our view of what "man of letters" signifies. These same marks of greatness that one finds in the poet, the novelist, the seer, as Kirk's example shows with abundance, can be equally present in the man of letters. He had the extraordinary ability to make us see things in ways we never did before. Thus, he helped change forever Americans' understanding of the conservative mind and of the moral imagination. Only an independent, creative man of thought can bring about this epochal happening, particularly in a time of history hateful of what Burke calls "the ancient permanent sense of mankind." To the office of the man of letters, then, Kirk brings a critical comprehensiveness anchored in wisdom and insight. But beyond this, he gave to his high calling an integrity that the man of vision must possess absolutely if this contribu-tion is to have viability. It is, in fact, a transcendent visionary quality fusing the temporal order and the spiritual order that he depicts in his writings and thought.

As a man of letters Kirk was far more than one who possesses much learning and complete intellectual command. He was to address himself to the total human situation, and to "speak to the condition," to use the Quaker phrase, with a seriousness and sacredness of purpose found only in great visionary writers of prose and poetry, those who in the end belong to a great tradition and strive to preserve humankind from injury, violence, or infraction—for example, a Samuel Johnson, an Edmund Burke, a Walter Scott, a Nathaniel Hawthorne, a Joseph Conrad, a T. S. Eliot. In Kirk the modern American man of letters achieves the quintessence of his calling, his witness. To the office of the man of letters, above all, he gave the added sapiential dimension of one who, in the ancient Greek context, is both a *spoudaios*, a man of character, of excellence, of moral importance, and a *hierophylax*, a keeper of holy things. It is no small achievement that, through his long and heroic labors, Russell Kirk raised the man of letters to true greatness in rank and dignity.

A Bibliographical Note. From a general perspective, I have composed this essay on the basis of my study of Russell Kirk's major writings as these have been published since the appearance of *The Conservative Mind* in 1953. My particular view here of Kirk as a man of letters emerges from my frequentation of his many essays as these have been collected in separate volumes through the years. Of his various collections, *Enemies of the Permanent Things: Observations of Abnormity in Literature and Politics*, first published by Arlington House in 1969, and reissued in a revised edition by Sherwood Sugden and Company Publishers in 1984, best depicts Kirk as a man of letters and brings out, maximally, his representative ideas and criticism. For me, *Enemies of the Permanent Things* remains the keystone of his books of essays insofar as it contains the central principles of his critical exposition and thought.

The Wise Men Know What Wicked Things Are Written on the Sky (1987), *The Politics of Prudence* (1993), and, though to a lesser extent, *America's British Culture* (1993) also figure prominently in my overall estimation. These books continue and develop the literary, social, and cultural lines of concern identified earlier in *Enemies of the Permanent Things*, clearly a book indispensable to a proper understanding of Kirk's contribution to the republic of letters. Not to go unnoticed is Kirk's *Eliot and His Age: T. S. Eliot's Moral Imagination in the Twentieth Century* (1972, 1984), which examines Eliot as the "greatest man of letters in his time."

Especially helpful to me have been three essays by T. S. Eliot: "The Classics and the Man of Letters" (1942), in his posthumous collection *To Criticize the Critic and Other Writings* (New York, 1965); "The Man of Letters and the Future of Europe," in the *Sewanee Review* (Summer 1945);

and "Leadership and Letters," in the *Milton Bulletin* (Milton, Massachusetts) 12/1 (February 1949), originally given as the "War Memorial Address at Milton Academy, November 3, 1948."

I want, too, to mention Allen Tate's "The Man of Letters in the Modern World" (the Phi Beta Kappa address, University of Minnesota, May 1, 1952), found in his *Essays of Four Decades* (Chicago, 1968). For a book-length study of men who shaped literary opinion in England during the Victorian, Edwardian, and contemporary eras, one should consult John Gross's *The Rise and Fall of the Man of Letters: A Study of the Idiosyncratic and the Humane in Modern Literature* (London, 1969).

Both the phrase and the subject of "man of letters" have long interested me; the final essay in my book *The Reverent Discipline: Essays in Literary Criticism and Culture* (1974), entitled "Austin Warren: Man of Letters," views Warren as being essentially a New England man of letters, in accordance with my belief that "great criticism demands a great humanity: a great critic must also be a great humanist." In addition to Thomas Carlyle's discussion of "The Hero as Man of Letters: Johnson, Rousseau, Burns," in *On Heroes, Hero-Worship, and the Heroic in History*, I have also found of much value Ralph Waldo Emerson's "The Man of Letters," included in his *Lectures and Biographical Sketches* (1895). Here Emerson addresses those in pursuit of a career in letters; his words, as quoted in the following sentences, could easily serve as an epigraph to Russell Kirk's achievement: "I offer perpetual congratulation to the scholar; he has drawn the white lot in life. The very disadvantages of his condition point at his superiorities. He is too good for the world; he is in advance of his race; his function is prophetic."

Sapiential Voices

Of wisdom, human and divine, there is always need. In an age of negations this need is far more acute, even as the sources of wisdom are manifestly diminished by the swift growth of secularization. Indeed, in the religious realm itself, in which the sapiential voice has traditionally been heard, that voice has been unusually silent—or silenced. Clearly, wisdom speaks to the interior, spiritual self, but that self has been relegated to abstraction or irrelevance in the modern age. The self that we see prized today is a sensate, external self that is a servant, even a prisoner of the temporal world. And, invariably, that world dismisses wisdom from the lexicon of life and conduct. Likewise, teachers and thinkers "filled with the spirit of wisdom" are dismissed by principalities and powers that legislate divers ideological systems, particularly liberalism and socialism. "Terrible simplifiers," not men and women of wisdom, regulate the rhythm of sociopolitical life under the banner of democracy, which in reality, as the Swedish historian and philosopher Tage Lindbom (b. 1909) attempts to show, is "the myth of democracy," words he uses as the title of his book.

In both purpose and achievement Lindbom's book explodes this myth. Eloquence of argument, force of belief, wise and reasonable disquisition identify the strengths of *The Myth of Democracy* (1996), and also its remarkable discriminations and judgments. For contemporary readers it has urgent interest, especially if the present outlook of Western secularism is to be perceived in all of its threatening symptoms. At a time, too, when those who shape opinion and define attitudes of taste and thought possess imperial power and influence, we need to ponder the writings of brave dissenters like Lindbom challenging a regnant modernism that insists on "human supremacy as our ultimate aim." These dissenters are, as Lindbom writes, "Men of tradition [who] are now in a serious situation." This "situation" is further exacerbated by the phenomenon of contemporary man usurping the place of God. Lindbom critiques this phenomenon in its historical process and consequences; that is to say, he traces in convincing ways the process of secularization.

Thus Lindbom points to some of the major inaugurators of this process: Roger Bacon, in the thirteenth century, who believed that through mathematics it will become possible to secure knowledge equal to divine truth; William of Ockham, in the fourteenth century, whose nominalism was a hard blow against the conception of creation as a total unity; René Descartes, whose *Discours de la Méthode* (1637) was a fundamental document of modern scientific positivism; John Locke, whose *Essay Concerning Human Understanding* (1690) brought sensualism to its philosophical perfection. In short, what we see transpiring in secularization in the Western world is the reduction of Man to rationalism and sensualism, and the rise of a spirit of doubt and denial eroding belief in the transcendent and divine Reality. This erosion, of course, prepared the way for radical historical movements and happenings, and for a revolutionary change in man's view of himself, of the world, of God. The French Revolution of 1789, hence, was to condemn the old traditional order and proclaim a new worldview, in effect molding the modernism that discredits the belief that divine power is at the center of creation and that there is a perennial cosmic equilibrium that provides man with principles of order. Lindbom aptly sums up the revolutionary transformation that occurs in human history and destiny in these words: "For the modernist, history is the story of rapid change in which all things are relative; and these he considers as permanently necessary conditions, necessary in order to open new and expanding fields for human activity."

What we often speak of as the crisis of modernism is one in which the image of the City of God fades as the foundations of the City of Man are erected. Lindbom sees the City of Man, modernism, and democracy as a " 'trinitarian' Gestalt" aggressively emerging in the years following World War II, with the extinction of the last remnants of order in the West. In this connection he singles out Martin Heidegger (1889–1976) as "the Philosopher of the City of Man" denying not only the existence of any higher powers or higher values, but also dualities like spirit and matter, good and evil. For Lindbom, Heidegger's mechanistic worldview provides an ample and representative statement of "the new outlook," in other words a new and raw secularization increasingly characterized by the belief that truth is the world of phenomena, of sensation and perception, and that any acceptance of the "permanent things" is insupportable and irrelevant. "Western secularization is at the threshold of its fulfillment," Lindbom declares, "and Martin Heidegger provides the philosophical formulations for this decomposition." Heidegger's horizontalist philosophy, he contends, removes all points of reference from the human consciousness, and at the same time it provides a consciousness of chaos and disorder, of man's rootlessness and homelessness.

Heidegger's atheistic existentialism glorifies the self that man in the modern world seeks in his individual self, which, to recall here Marjorie Grene's apt comment in her book *Dreadful Freedom* (1948), "he must forge for himself out of such senseless circumstances, such meaningless limitations, as are given him."

Heidegger's place in modern philosophical thought epitomizes for Lindbom the negations that are at the core of the crisis of modernism, and of the consequences that emerge from a view of human existence founded on the belief that, as Lindbom cogently expresses it, "there are no firm points in our existence; all is flux." Lindbom, in this book, is measuring the results, historically and morally, of a philosophy like Heidegger's, proclaiming as it does "a one-dimensional existence and, consequently, total subjectivism in a continuous stream." Perhaps the most alarming feature of this consequence in modern thinking is the grim spiritual deorientation that ensues: the repudiation of "eternal laws"; the growing disorder and the disharmony in life as men and women surrender more and more to the profane dialectics of a modern cosmology (as it is conceived by a Sartre or a Heidegger), which proceeds to create a world of "dead souls."

For Lindbom the new world order, ahistorical, or posthistorical, in character and temper, has no stable point of reference, no genuine metaphysical ground of being, no commonly accepted universal values and verities. "In its pseudometaphysical Gestalt, democracy is the City of Man; in its existential Gestalt, it is modernism." Democracy becomes static and nonhistorical, a myth without reverence for the future or the past. Jean-Jacques Rousseau, Lindbom believes, has thus won his victory; his myth of sovereign Man expresses what constitutes the true power in the world and also discloses the two "archetypes" of liberty and equality. Liberty, Lindbom asserts, echoing here Eric Voegelin, is an energy, or dynamic, that invariably seeks to free itself from the structures and systems of order, to create a "life without prejudice"—and the consequences are telling, as "the myth of liberty becomes anarchy." This democratic myth, Lindbom argues, has to have another foundation stone to guarantee its triumph and to display its own order: equality, but this is quantitative equality, to be more precise, that belongs to the utopian dream world, but that also dominates the polity, redefines and restructures moral systems, and translates power, in meaning and application, into something that is numerical and statistical, evidenced in the Popular Will, in the mass-man and mass-mind Ortega y Gasset has portrayed with prophetic insight.

A major strength of Lindbom's critique is that it helps remind us how a false metaphysics proclaims its own ideological systems and its own gods, as well as its own intellectual monisms. The prime casualty of this process is the Kingdom of the Spirit, now replaced by the Kingdom of Man in which, especially as conceived by Karl Marx, all life has its basis in biological and sensory reality. Whether in the form of liberalism, socialism, or Marxism-Leninism the "self-idolization by man is Luciferism, pure and simple." And because of progressive secularization, and what emerges from it, the West has been trapped in Luciferism, the full consequences of which we have been confronting throughout the twentieth century. Lindbom prompts us to take inventory of these consequences, not only in the socioeconomic sphere, but also in art and letters, now being pushed to their Luciferian limits, with distinctions between good and evil, beauty and decadence being annulled. Anti-art, antinovel, antimusic are the solipsistic effects of a wanton secularization. "When the divine is totally denied," Lindbom stresses, "the ineluctable consequence is that there is nothing else to take its place but the spirit of negation, the satanic."

Of Lindbom's significance to us, Professor Claes G. Ryn, in his exceptionally full and astute introduction, writes: "He incisively confronts dimensions of problems with which Western intellectuals are increasingly unable or unwilling to deal with but which require close attention." *The Myth of Democracy* puts us in contact with the philosophical mind and the moral and spiritual vision of that great tradition that, in this century, includes a Nikolai Berdyaev, a Romano Guardini, a Gabriel Marcel, a Max Picard. And no less than these great men of wisdom, Lindbom helps us to discern the tragic fate of civilization in its "flight from God." The specificities of this fate in terms of contemporary disorders, devolutions, confusions, and misdirections are found in Father Francis Canavan's *The Pluralist Game: Pluralism, Liberalism, and the Moral Conscience* (1995). The thesis of this distinguished collection of essays is that we have no alternative but that of seeking for "a better intellectual and moral foundation for polity."

Lindbom's sapiential reflections on secularization, and, in turn, on "the degradation of the democratic dogma" which the historian Henry Adams had focused on in his time, help us to penetrate the peculiar rhythm of this degradation as it is specified in *The Pluralist Game*. Father Canavan, a political philosopher and teacher, illustrates the alliance between liberalism and secular monism, an alliance that Lindbom diagnoses in its metaphysical contexts. Father Canavan enables us to pinpoint what this alliance brings about in secular pluralist society in its contemporary American version. Above all, he demonstrates that even in a pluralist society there must be a public morality; that the law itself, as the conscience of the community, has a worthy function in the realm of public morals and can proclaim a public moral standard, especially in a time of moral liberalization, when rationalistic and utilitarian suppositions dominate the "public square." Father Canavan holds resolutely to an axiomatic position, in short, to a moral standard, increasingly imperiled in American pluralist society:

> All that attacks or corrupts life and all that weakens the institutions that shelter and foster life, is evil. Only when modern men regain this vision can we stem the tide of opinion that is now undermining Christian morality and is therefore sweeping away the legal structures inspired by that morality.

As Father Canavan counts up the costs of secularization at all levels of American life, it is not hard for a reader to see how Enlightenment views give way to the demonic distortions that Lindbom warns against. In the "segregation of religion from the nation's public," especially as seen in the light of Supreme Court decisions on religion, he discerns the establishment of "the religion of secular humanism." Father Canavan stresses that our pluralism, as it has evolved, has reached a point when there are now millions of Americans who are left "with the feeling that they are now strangers in their own land." He also notes that the neutral state that we have inherited is the liberal state, that liberal government is neutral government, and that the ultimate liberal ideal is one of "normlessness." This specious neutrality, as it is unmistakably made clear both in *The Myth of Democracy* and in *The Pluralist Game*, ends in the final and absolute repudiation of any assumption of truth and any idea of value. Father Canavan's book identifies the shapes and forms of the secular process of disintegration and destruction that Lindbom calls "the bitter harvest of Luciferism." "[T]oday's pluralist society," Father Canavan writes, "is not merely the result of the loss of faith by multitudes in the past. It is also an advanced stage on the way to a post-Christian secular culture."

What Father Canavan has to say about life norms becoming more secular and post-Christian as we move into the twenty-first century should be of great importance at this stage of the American experience. In particular he warns that churches seeking to accommodate the new morality risk their true religious mission and character. The pervasive tendency to accept artificial contraception, pornography, premarital sexual intercourse, remarriage after divorce, and legalization of abortion, he stresses, underscores the decline in the institutional life of the Church in

America. "The pluralistic society, therefore," Father Canavan declares, "stands upon no moral principles but is unified only by procedural principle of an official neutrality that treats all beliefs equally." This "pluralistic game," in effect, has no common standards, no absolute values, thus carrying with it the inevitable consequence that pluralism will degenerate into mere individualism, that is to say, a curious mixture of libertarianism and egalitarianism that is at once vacuous and yet destructive, and concludes in the dissolution of norms, or as Father Canavan notes: "We lack . . . an ordering principle [that is, a common moral principle] because we are so devoted to liberty and equality as the supreme norms of a democratic society that we will not admit their subordination to any higher norms."

No less than Lindbom, Father Canavan is deeply preoccupied with the problem of liberty in a democratic society. And for both commentators liberty, when lacking some inner check, or restraint, leads to the excesses now found in the attitude that rights transcend obligations, moral laws, moral virtues. The belief that there is an irresolvable conflict between individual rights and public morality is central to the liberal ideology and its unceasing effort to establish what Father Canavan terms "a purely procedural and substantively neutral model of society." This belief now fashions the new morality of the Western world in general and of American society and culture in particular. *The Myth of Democracy* scrutinizes the metaphysical dimensions of "the Luciferian process"; *The Pluralist Game* measures this process in its distinctly American constituents, as a case study, so to speak. It is a real privilege to have in hand two books which complement each other in powerful ways, and help one to see the nexus of causes and effects. That which, finally and firmly, unites these two books is a common concern with the moral virtue of order in the soul and in the commonwealth. How liberty plays a fateful role in the order of human existence has an overarching part in this concern. Tage Lindbom and Father Francis Canavan never forget these words of Edmund Burke: "But the liberty, the only liberty I mean, is a liberty connected with order, that not only exists with order and virtue, but which cannot exist at all without them."

A Corrective
to Darkening Counsel

The daunting perversities of the present-day literary barbarians—deconstructionists, new historicists, academic ideologues, smatterers—must not be allowed to blind us to the fact that the true function of criticism is the judgment of vision. Nor must we allow the contemporary cultural situation which panders to the yearnings of mass-man and to the sonorous doctrine of egalitarianism to dismiss the need for select standards of discrimination that induce excellence. A decline in critical responsibility and standards, as we should know from the eternal records of history, is inevitably accompanied by those moral shifts that often culminate in disorder. Indeed, in the very function of criticism we view principles of order in their practice and application. Our greatest artists often remind us that their own "rage for order" is ultimately their "search for order." Clearly the discipline of criticism has its autonomy and hierarchic role and place—its ordering criteria and values. It has, in short, a significant part to play in the ethical formation of the character of a society and culture.

The Arnoldian ring of such a claim will no doubt annoy those who now denigrate the imperative of critical responsibility and any tendency to weigh and measure the literary imagination in terms of universal criteria. It is all too evident that the critical function today, and for some years now, has been steadily annexed by the dogmatists of social engineering who want to gag the exemplars of the critical spirit whom Paul Elmer More salutes as "discriminators between the false and the true, the deformed and the normal; preachers of harmony and proportion and order; prophets of the religion of taste." A great deal, of course, has been said and written about contemporary critics who seek to dislodge any existing form of literary tradition that is rooted in a classical and biblical canon, or that emphasizes centrality and an underlying unity of literary study, or that has a moral and logocentric orientation. Here it is enough to say that what we are seeing in the current species of literary hucksterism is a continuation of the new-old barbarism violently hostile to the "permanent things."

Its gospel is the word "power," its creed is the belief in the relative, its enemy is moral law, its ritual is irreverence. And its major absolute is one of reductionism—the transvaluation of all values, as it were. What we thus view all around us is the defilement of the critical spirit that accompanies the desacralization of human meaning and destiny in the modern and postmodern world. Ours is the age of impiety that encompasses all facets of life, literature, and thought. There are a very few living critics and men of letters brave enough to challenge the depth and extent of the crass reductionism which particularly affects the literary imagination—that minimalizes and ultimately trivializes the imaginative fictions, which in turn reflect the general breakdown of civilization in which nothing has value and nothing is sacred. Contemporary artists, critics, and teachers defiantly enact precisely this process of defilement of the great treasures and legacy committed to our charge.

Among those brave few struggling, in Edmund Burke's words, "to preserve the structure from profanation and ruin," is the critic John W. Aldridge (b. 1922). No one who looks at his half dozen or more published volumes of critical essays, beginning with *After the Lost Generation* (1951), can come away from them without saluting their integrity and the courage of judgment which Professor Aldridge shows especially in his assessment of American novelists who have appeared since the end of World War II. With profound constancy and consistency throughout the past four decades, Aldridge has given his witness as a practicing critic. He has done so with exceptional honesty and sensitivity, preeminently loyal as he has been to the maintenance of high literary and critical standards and to the allied need of ferreting out literary pretentiousness, quackery, sloppiness, of the kind that produces the solipsisms and entropies that now pervade the creative and critical realm. His has been an exemplary and fierce independence of critical exploration and interpretation, of moral strenuousness, which has distinguished him from the hucksterism that, in the academy above all, has contributed to literary and cultural decline. His has always been a courageous dissident voice raised against the dictates of the orthodoxy of enlightenment.

For Aldridge literature and criticism, both in teaching and in practice, are neither a game nor the property of an academic gang movement. In his criticism we discern first, last, and always a presiding moral sense, moral impulse, moral responsibility. Seriousness and severity characterize his critical diagnosis of the state of American fiction and also of the cultural situation as a whole, insofar as he does not separate one from the other. Their conditions are interactive and interrelated, as he invariably shows in his acute analyses. For him the republic of arts and letters has humane and civilizational significance, not to be compromised or diminished by pseudoart or pseudocriticism. He is not afraid to invoke first principles when they are needed and essential, or to expose faults and fallacies as they appear. He knows the terrible consequences of remaining silent and therefore chooses to speak out on fundamental issues regardless of how much and whom it hurts. Loyalty to standards is transcendent in Aldridge's critiques of literature and society. He does not fudge. He does not flatter or trifle. He does not sentimentalize. Critical honesty and critical responsibility merge as absolutes, and absolutely, in his critical work.

For Aldridge the critical function has civilizational value as well as moral pertinence. He knows and shows that the critic can play a quintessential role in life and literature by defining and conserving values and virtues that help enhance and elevate the creative imagination, pushing things up to their first principles, to repeat John Henry Newman's apt words. Aldridge is that kind of critic, as Norman Mailer has observed, who can teach a writer something about craft and meaning. The critical discipline and the creative act have an inclusive connection, as Aldridge's own creedal statement regarding his critical vocation insists upon in these words:

> I have never considered criticism in any sense a minor or inferior literary form, and one of my ambitions has been to write criticism in such a way that it can be seen to have the qualities of style, structure, and dramatic development which are normally associated with fiction.

If there is one phenomenon in the American literary and cultural situation that Aldridge has unceasingly confronted and bared in his critical writings it is mediocrity—its symptoms, portents, stains, dangers. Above all he has shown how mediocrity engulfs a literary world absolved from critical standards. His work helps to remind us that the process of literary devaluation which he examines is perilously tied to the state of criticism itself, and specifically to the attack on literature now being systematically carried out in the academy, in the departments and by professors of English who have obsessively embraced a "prophet of extremity" like Michel Foucault (1926–1984), whose positivist philosophical ideas have influenced a whole generation of American academics like the new historicist Stephen Greenblatt, who pays this tribute to the French philosopher: "Foucault was a model for a certain kind of intellectual daring and courage." The "daring," of course, is found in the shameless effort to destroy meaning by liberating all things, all humane values, from what Foucault terms "transcendental narcissism," and thus to enjoin disunity and discontinuity.

In the end, the literary barbarians who now wield immense power in the academy propose to "erase" every idea of transcendence, which in turn also inspires the virtue of reverence. It is one of the biggest disasters of modern times that the opaque but treacherous theories of a Foucault, a Roland Barthes ("Incoherence seems to me preferable to a distorting order"), and a Jacques Derrida enchant American academics and critics to an incredible degree, if one is to judge by the magnitude of the disorder that prevails in the universities, in the curriculum, and in the teaching (by "cursing") of literature. There can be no more frightening phenomenon than that of American educators, critics, and intellectual leaders fanatically adopting bankrupt empirocritical doctrines while at the same time arrogantly dismissing the "canonic" thought of English-speaking critics like Matthew Arnold, Irving Babbitt, T. S. Eliot, Lionel Trilling. This phenomenon is not just a paradox but also madness, and its ramifications have no limit. When Aldridge asserts, then, that "We have suffered a paralysis or eclipse of imagination before the nightmare of history in this age," it is not too difficult to see in that nightmare some of the radical factors contributing to it as we have proceeded, almost methodically, from "the death of God" to "the death of literature." In any civilization in which the urge to deny "elsewhere," to erase sacred canons, and to destroy meaning and established truths is dominant the paralysis of which Aldridge speaks is inevitable.

In *Talents and Technicians* (1992) he reminds us that sham art thrives when the conditions of criticism are no longer rooted in a time-related value system and in a metaphysical framework. That the deregulation of critical standards leads to the devaluation of creative vision is the major operative emphasis in Aldridge's position. When, too, an entire culture subscribes to secular and material doctrines that culminate in the "abolition of man," the mystery and sacredness of life dissolve. In effect, the tensions that exist in moral and ethical problems, and that are of major concern to the artist who renders them, disappear. And the novelist, Aldridge stresses, by surrendering to the technic spirit of our time, can no longer invest what he is rendering with dramatic or revelatory significance. Art as edification and instruction gives way to vapidity, to neutralization, to technique, to thematic absurdity, and to pseudocharacterization. In contemporary writers like Raymond Carver, Amy Hempel, Donald Barthelme, he sees an absence of the critical spirit and a confluent and curiously comfortable estrangement from their culture, from the life of memory, of the community, of tradition, which prohibits them from conveying any fictive truths speaking to the human condition. Life without meaning is the main reference point of such minimalist fiction which gradually succumbs to nihilism itself.

Indeed, what Aldridge is in the end protesting against is the rise of both a critical and a creative nihilism in the new generation of American writers. His are reports from the literary battlefront, severe in their honesty, undeviating in their critical principles, unsparing in their probity. Aldridge is intensely aware of the critic's absolute need to scrutinize cause and effect, at all cultural levels, no less than he is of the artist's need to honor aims and duties. Mediocrity is for him the enemy, and he is utterly unafraid to fight its apologists and those conditions in the cultural and literary situations that produce such an enemy. He rightly laments the decline of the critical spirit in the nation's great newspapers and periodicals. Publicists who write in the name of criticism contribute considerably to the collapse of standards and the enshrinement of inferior fiction writers. An entire network of merchants promoting books and building reputations, without any real concern for excellence or any real perception of what constitutes creative vision, emerges without meeting substantial resistance. Creative writing programs in the universities further embolden the process of the democratization and the diminishment of the literary imagination. In consequence, a strategy of technique replaces a central concern with content, as the "new minimalists" like Jay McInerney and Bret Easton Ellis thrive in their "assembly-line fiction":

> They appear on the whole to have only moderate intellectual culture [Aldridge observes]. They evidently possess very little critical or satirical perspective on contemporary life, slight knowledge of the past, and apparently no sense that they belong to a literary tradition that might prove nourishing if they were able and willing to learn from it.

Clearly the contemporary successors of Thomas Pynchon, Don DeLillo, William Gaddis, and Joseph Heller are now taking fiction into areas removed "from that private arena of personal loneliness, agony, humiliation, or remorse, where fiction in the past has always found its most vital materials." In *Talents and Technicians* Aldridge forces us to view American fiction in the downward age; the symptoms, direction, and scale of this descent are no less alarming than "the dehumanization of art" and the "error of perspective" that Ortega y Gasset perceived in the early decades of the twentieth century. Aldridge's theory of fiction, as it might be called, when joined to his writings as a critical practitioner, shows him to be the complete critic of American life and letters. His critical essays, it can be said, flesh out his critical theories. One does not meet in them the kind of critical machinations and conundrums that pervade present-day criticism. He is deeply concerned with literature on cultural and disciplinary grounds—with literature as a "discipline of ideas," to recall Babbitt's phrase.

Classics and Contemporaries (1992) richly demonstrates those remarkable qualities of "the art of criticism" in style and content. Aldridge's critical ethos prevails, and will endure, even in the midst of that spectacle of criticism that Henry James detailed in a sentence that describes conditions of criticism today as much as those one hundred years ago: "The vulgarity, the crudity, the stupidity which this cherished combination of the offhand review and of our wonderful system of publicity have put into circulation on so vast a scale may be represented, in such a mood, as an unprecedented invention for darkening counsel." It can be said that Aldridge's literary criticism serves as a corrective to the darkening counsel that inheres in the American version of the *nouvelle critique*. To read the essays in *Classics and Contemporaries* is to be reminded of the presently neglected or suppressed elements of sanity and intelligence and sincerity among critics who now act more as storm troopers than humane expositors and elucidators of literary texts. Indeed, to read Aldridge these days helps save one from being caught in the dialectical traps of "the politics of theory" and "the ideology of the text" that are set by, say, an American Marxist critic and theorist like Frederic Jameson (b. 1934).

What is literary greatness? What do imaginative fictions reveal about the modern age? What are the excelling qualities of sensibility, of vision that we encounter? What brings these qualities to fruition? What are the critical standards by which we define the Americanness of this sensibility and judge the Americanness of this vision? What conditions most characterize the moral issues relating to the crisis of modernism, that is, of a world in moral flux and disarray? What does modern literature tell us about civilization, how "thought, words and creativity" (to use F. R. Leavis's phrase) shape civilization? These are some of the central questions, especially the last one, that Aldridge confronts directly and boldly. He does not seek, in his evaluative critical judgments, to burden us with "transcending" transatlantic methodologies, or with championing a constant "revision" of literary history, or with presenting "versions of a Marxist hermeneutic." It is with unspeakable relief and reward that we read Aldridge's critical interpretations, in their crisp and clear command of language unencumbered by the linguistic savageries and conceptual degeneracies which the American professoriate manufactures and legislates ad nauseam.

Thus, whether Aldridge is discussing Henry James and T. S. Eliot as early classic modernists, or Edmund Wilson, Henry Miller, or Malcolm Cowley as classics of the twenties, or J. P. Marquand and James Farrell as products of the thirties, or James Gould Cozzens and Robert Penn Warren as men of the forties, or Donald Barthelme, William Gaddis, John Barth, Norman Mailer, and Saul Bellow as our contemporaries, he unyieldingly honors those "responsibilities of the critic" that F. O. Matthiessen (1902–1950) outlines in these enduring words:

> But for his own work the critic has to be both involved in his age and detached from it. This double quality of experiencing our own time to the full and yet being able to weigh it in relation to other times is what the critic must strive for, if he is to be able to discern and demand the works of art that we need most. The most mature function of the critic lies finally in that demand.

Aldridge aims, as a critic, to speak to "a readership of educated people" who are willing to read and discuss "books and ideas in a cultural atmosphere, however thinning, in which books and ideas . . . [have] some living relation to the daily conduct of life." There can be no more noble or honorable aim that distinguishes and enhances the critic's vocation. For Aldridge, hence, there can be no separation of criticism from creativity; and to the principle of this inseparability he gives his unflinching loyalty. His writings become for us both restorative and reconciling lessons in criticism that simultaneously sharpen the life of the mind, discipline character, illumine conscience. The more we choose to reject the intrinsic moral dimension of these lessons—the more our civilization flounders. To counteract, then, the negations—the "darkening counsel"—which assault so much of art and criticism, of society and culture as a whole, it behooves us to listen to the voice of a critic like Aldridge. For what he has to say to the creator, to the critic, to the reader—to all those who are concerned with the condition of our civilization—can have a good influence.

Those who believe, with Arnold, that "civilization is the humanization of man in society," will find in Aldridge's writings a defense of those principles of art that help create order and protect civilized life at its vulnerable points. The function of language certainly belongs to this frontline defense, as Aldridge frequently emphasizes. He sees in language, and specifically in what D. H. Lawrence calls "art-speech," absolutes of meaning and use that stem the pull of gravity to which some writers too easily succumb. Ernest Hemingway's control of language in

The Sun Also Rises is a representative "lesson in heroism," Aldridge argues, which erects a barricade

> against the nihilism that threatens to engulf his characters, the nihilism that is always seeking to enter and flood the human consciousness. . . . [H]e gave us as well our only means of defense against it—the order of artistic and moral form embodied in a language that will not, in spite of everything, give up its hold on the basic sanities, will not give up and let out the shriek of panic, the cry of panic, that the situation logically calls for.

The novelist, Aldridge further insists, has a responsibility to honor and preserve the idea of value, to which the fate of language itself is closely tied. The conflict between freedom and order, as he shows in his discussion of Marquand, contains an intuitive moral sense that no novelist can reject if he believes that something has meaning, has value—that something matters:

> If Marquand cannot be identified with the modernist movement in most of the usual ways, it is obvious that he was deeply identified with it in one vital respect. He shared with many of his contemporaries and classic predecessors an essential mistrust of the ideal of unrestrained liberty, for he recognized that while the moral codes and obligations of the past were unjustly inhibitory, they were also necessary to human life and gave meaning and purpose to life. Specifically, they directed individual energies into channels that were ultimately beneficial to both the individual and the community. They were, in fact, the structural embodiments of those values that the culture as a whole deemed most critical to its existence.

Aldridge endows the office of the critic with a concentrated seriousness and dignity and with a humane and moral thrust missing from most current discussions of literature. Ideology and not evaluation dictates not only critical judgment but also a view of the world, of life, of humanity and sense, or as he puts it in the course of paying tribute to William Gaddis's ability to reflect chaos "in a fiction that is not itself artistically chaotic because it is imbued with the conserving and correcting power of his imagination":

> Certain assumptions about the fundamental coherence and value of human existence have somehow been lost. There is simply no discoverable rational structure in anything; hence, nobody makes sense either to himself or in his efforts to communicate with others. The spoken language with its endlessly reiterated ambiguities, its steady dissolution into streams of utterance signi-

fying nothing, stands as the index of the berserk sensibility of the modern corporate state.

Above all, Aldridge's writings testify to the faculty of discernment, that which enables the critic to discern between the "perverse things" and the "enduring things." To come across and then to reflect on the following passage, as found in his brilliant reading of "Robert Penn Warren's Legend of the South," instances those critical powers of judgment that lead to the recognition of the terrible plight of the literary situation in our time:

> We now seem to believe that the only really tenable view for the novelist is the nihilistic view in which events without meaning are seen to occur in a world without standards, and neither author nor characters presume to suggest what standards there may once have been or ought to be. The fictional situation we tend to find most artistically serious and relevant to life is one involving the continuous search for identity among people who have no realization of either the presence of the past or the possibility of the future, and so exist in a state of paralysis or dreary preoccupation with the merely sensational, with violence enacted without motive, sex enacted without passion or love— hence, from which all human meaning has disappeared.

Perhaps the highest value of Aldridge's critical achievement is that of heightening our awareness of how art and criticism have progressively become the victims of a contemporary nihilism and of the enormous costs of this process of debasement. Many artists and critics writing today revel in this process, or else choose to pass by it in silence, failing to give their witness, and in effect constricting the truth of the imagination and the demands of critical responsibility. Stalwartly refusing to drift with the tide of this nihilism, John W. Aldridge exemplifies the critical spirit at a maximum point of moral attention, which is the soul of criticism.

The Discipline of Criticism

Among our younger critics, Professor Stephen Gurney (b. 1949), exemplifies the qualities that John W. Aldridge considers essential to the discipline of criticism. Gurney's most recent book, *British Poetry of the Nineteenth Century* (1993), is an eminent example of the critic's moral sense of responsibility. Concerning the basic aim of his book, Gurney thus declares: "My purpose, here, is to achieve both a breadth of historical awareness—which will enable the reader to grasp a poet's relationship to his precursors, his peers, and the intellectual climate of his age—and to provide a knowledge of that poet's life and achievement that is more than merely perfunctory." He goes on to emphasize that "the study of the past has an intrinsic value inasmuch as it enables us to rise above the restrictive or reductive vantage point of our present moment."

Both Gurney's critical aim and his critical emphasis are admirably accomplished in this unusually discerning study. It takes moral courage to defend, as he does, the role of history in the examination of English letters at a time when specious empirocritical theories exert oppressive power in teaching and criticism. The decline of humane literary and critical values, of the historical dimension, and certainly of moral imperatives is now more than a mere threat to the order of things. Even the English language now faces diminution in the social and educational realms, something which should frighten anyone who holds that, once the native language of a nation dissipates, then the commonweal of that nation declines.

Gurney addresses these problems in his book; he gives his witness, to be more exact. Here he speaks for all those who are committed to those humane principles and moral values that shape the glory of the English language and literature. Clearly, Gurney refused to ally himself with forces and tendencies that inevitably perpetuate "the treason of the intellectuals." His moral allegiance to the purposes that he pursues, as well as his unhesitating affirmation of the "permanent things," is stamped in every paragraph and page of this book. Those who share his concerns—who fear for the fate of arts and letters in our time—will find not only sustenance but also their voice in this book. They will join Gurney in his struggle to be heard. To be heard as such is, of course, not an easy or simple matter at a time when the electronics media, the literary supplements, the general periodicals, the publishers, and the academy as a whole manipulate minds and opinion according to the agenda of political correctness. In challenging these agenda, Gurney also insists on regaining those moral values that nourish great ideas, great literature, great criticism, great civilization.

In his examination of "The Romantic Ethos" and "The Victorian Ethos," Gurney vindicates enduring standards and supports the sense of history against the sense of the moment. His own literary admirations and enthusiasms are strong and forthright and manifestly harbor a romantic bias, or at least a romantic disposition. Even his prose style in its palpitant rhythms, its outpouring, its flow of inspiration has a demonstrable but contained romantic gleam. In particular, he displays critical ease and sympathy with the romantic poets, especially John Keats. But though he identifies with the romantic sensibility, which the philosopher T. E. Hulme once characterized as "spilt religion," Gurney does not embrace or glorify it or its evangels. Gurney is a distinguished example of a critic who has mastered his passions and added to his insight. Perhaps because he himself possesses an incipient romanticism, he is also finally aware of the traps of romanticism, its lures, raptures, effusions, subjectivism. His criticism, in honoring the need of an "inner check" which counsels centrality, restraint, decorum, exposes the fatal flaws of what Babbitt terms "free temperamental overflow."

In this book we have a critic who confronts the romantic temptation and all that which conduces, in Babbitt's words, "a disquieting vagueness and lack of grip in dealing with particulars." This confrontation, in Gurney's case, instances moral effort through which he attains a transcendent moral criticism and invests the office of the critic with character and conscience. No less than the moral imagination, it can be said, moral criticism has the power to make men and women better citizens in their community, as the ancient Hellenes viewed the main function of the poet. In his aspirations and ascendancies Gurney reveals himself to be the true critic who is ever conscious of first causes and first principles. One who reads and reflects on this book will recognize a critical process that mirrors metaphysical growth and depth and that brings to fruition the wisdom and the insight that belongs to the soul of criticism.

In exploring the romantic energies of genius, Gurney also explores his own critical energies and gives them substance and form—gives them, in short, discipline and order. He struggles with these energies, measures their value, goes beyond them, transcends them. As noted, his personal sympathy with the romantic writers is often clearly evident, but Gurney's critical judgments go beyond sympathy and beyond personality. He does not allow himself to be captured by either a romantic or a critical idealism. His criticism does not submit to centrifugal elements; he is, whatever his sympathies, profoundly aware of the solipsisms, emotionalism, and turbulences of the romantic personality. As a critic, then, he chooses to affirm Bossuet's belief that "good sense is the master of human life" and Goethe's warning that "anything that emancipates the spirit without a corresponding growth in self-mastery is pernicious." His final loyalty is to a discipline of criticism undeflected by excessive sympathy or sentiment. Gurney's critique of the great geniuses of romanticism is an inclusive one that proceeds from Spinoza's memorable admonition, "With regard to human affairs, not to laugh, not to cry, not to become indignant, but to understand." And Gurney does indeed understand the antinomian pattern of romanticism and transforms his understanding into the critical act of judgment.

His criticism essentializes not only a generalism but also specificity, concentration, focus; it is both catholic and critical. His critical strengths also become his critical virtues that enable him to balance analytical percipience with spiritual and religious discernment. In Gurney one finds a generous amalgam of the best English-speaking critics: the ethical strenuousness of Irving Babbitt; the religious humanism of Paul Elmer More; the cultural concern of a Lionel Trilling; the moral toughness of an F. R. Leavis. These critics are now gone, but Gurney preserves their excellence.

Ideology in its most blatant and insidious forms now replaces the common pursuit of criticism, as critical responsibility surrenders increasingly to a critical nihilism. Here Gurney delineates earlier forms of this nihilistic attitude that evolved among the poets he examines, as poetic sensibility shifted in the middle of the eighteenth century and dissent from the mainstream of neoclassical taste began to occur. In the poets of the 1890s—Ernest Dowson, Lionel Johnson, Arthur Symons—he pinpoints symptoms of decadence in the cultivation of pessimism, beautiful in expression, yet demoralizing in effect. Unfailingly he shows the adverse consequences to poetic vision when moral principles are violated or scorned.

Above all, Gurney's criticism reveres the life of value, the religious idea, and spiritual transcendence. The great divide between imaginative vision and a community of common belief is as disastrous for Gurney as it was earlier for T. S. Eliot. His discussion of Francis Thompson's "Hound of Heaven" is a fine example of how at least one poet of the 1890s "shatters the artificial hothouses of aesthete or decadent and makes us aware that one of the principal but hidden motives behind the conflicted range of human endeavor is the flight from God." In his view of Thompson's ode as a derivation of Christian humanism Gurney instances the critical perspicuity that emerges from an awareness of and respect for civilizing powers of tradition and continuity. This awareness, rooted in order and history, enables Gurney to formulate this apt literary and critical generalization: "In its combination of baroque grandeur and Romantic spontaneity, Thompson's ode rises above the ethos of the nineties and takes its place among the great odes in the English poetic tradition, from Milton and Crashaw to Wordsworth and Shelley."

Gurney's estimations are consistently detailed and illuminating; one must admire his deep sense of critical responsibility and moral probity. Inherently a generous and sympathetic critic, he is also one who ultimately conveys disinterested judgments. We see this in his chapter on William Blake, whose gnostic poetic vision he approaches in its enigmatic aspects, as is indicated in this sentence that goes to the heart of the Blake problem: "Blake's attempt to legitimize his radical mythos of creative freedom by assimilating it to the Judaeo-Christian tradition only exacerbates the unwieldy incoherence of his vision." Gurney's abjudications are also carefully crafted, often with aphoristic power, as found, for example, in what he says about William Wordsworth: "This is the authentic Wordsworthian note: a spirit of meditation so intense that it passes beyond the material forms which summon it into being."

His critical formulations, in effect, enable us to view a poet's persona and imaginative power in their totality, as when he sums up Lord Byron's character and purpose: "Byron is chiefly concerned with his own emancipation and his own uniqueness." What, too, he has to say about one of Byron's great poems graphically underlines the trenchancy of Gurney's critical commentary: "*Don Juan* is fatalism with a smile—but behind the façade, one can detect a nihilistic undercurrent that skirts the border of despair." No less trenchant is what Gurney has to say about Shelley: "Shelley's dilemma is that of the mystic who cannot bring himself to believe in the truth of revealed religion."

It is especially helpful that Gurney defines and critically inspects the ethos of a particular period in relation to the state of poetry. For him the word "ethos" has a metaphysical connotation and a moral element that contemporary critics instinctively abjure. Insofar, then, as Gurney embraces and applies principles, standards, and universals, ethos signifies a living reality. "A society that forgets its spiritual patrimony," he reminds us, "in the pursuit of fashionable causes risks moral bankruptcy and political chaos." Accordingly, his approach to the poetry of the

Victorian Age revolves around what he sees as "a loss of a stable system of values and beliefs that could give meaning and purpose to the human enterprise." Armed as he is with an acute recognition of the consequences of spiritual loss in the life of a people and of the imagination, Gurney delineates the thematic concerns and aesthetic problems that the Victorian poets faced and that make their achievement so "familiarly modern." Thus in Tennyson's poems he finds that the keynote is disquietude; and in Arnold's poems he weighs the tensions and burdens of self-division. In Gerard Manley Hopkins, on the other hand, Gurney emphasizes "a kind of no-nonsense supernatural realism that enabled the poet to see both art and beauty from the perspective of that ultimate source from which they derive and toward which they point."

It is one of the most notable strengths of Gurney's critical interpretations that he looks at things not in their parts but in their whole, not in their isolation but in their interrelation. In short, he looks at the world as an organic whole. Connections and continuities are intrinsic and impelling constituents in Gurney's critical examination of a great poetic tradition.

His firm grasp of our classical and biblical patrimony is representatively present in his excellent assessment of A. E. Housman and Thomas Hardy, transitional poets who, Gurney rightly admits, are difficult to fit into his survey. In these two poets he observes a deep pessimism, yet one that is, "paradoxically, dependent on religious traditions they interrogate or reject." The treatment of Hardy is especially good in demonstrating the essential tensions in that poet's verse between what Hardy called "the ache of modernism" and the "appetite for joy." Focusing on Hardy's poem entitled "The Darkling Thrush" ("a lyric that pays conscious homage to Hardy's poetic forebears even as it anticipates the challenge of a new uncertain age"), Gurney shows how, in spite of disenchantment and empirical evidence, Hardy is still able to glimpse "the inklings of a critical order immune to time and process." Only a critic who, like Gurney, venerates the idea of continuity and understands the concept of tradition and its claim upon us, to recall here Josef Pieper's words, can venture to express such a transcendent judgment—one refreshingly distant from the relativism of contemporary criticism.

No account can do full justice to Gurney's book; only if one studies diligently its carefully organized content—the chapters and the subjects that unfold with astonishing penetration and authority—will one be able to fathom and experience the book's critical worth and moral essences. Nineteenth-century poetry, movements, figures, ideas, all come to life for the reader in their historical contexts, literary meaning, and cultural relevances. Ultimately this broad critical survey becomes a journey of discovery. And the guide here is a magnanimous and keen-sighted critic who can be trusted; his concern, sincerity, and assuredness will never fail to inspire. What Gurney finally attains and, indeed, celebrates is the reconciliation of literature and history, criticism and order, intellect and spirit. To the office of the critic he restores the task of this reconciliation at a time when purveyors of ugly ideologies mold a literature and criticism of disorientation. We must count it providential that as long as a critical voice like Gurney's is able to speak to our condition the possibilities for a humane civilization are not dead.

Character and Criticism

Milton Hindus, in *Irving Babbitt, Literature, and the Democratic Culture* (1994), shows how a keen understanding of Irving Babbitt's writings makes one an even better critic. One can only hope, even if such hope is small at the present precipitous stage of American civilization, that present-day students and teachers of humane letters are exposed not only to Babbitt's ideas and beliefs, but also to his gifted interpreters. Babbitt is an American man of letters who exerts good influence and has enduring value for those who, like Professor Hindus, read him seriously and who examine his achievement intelligently. That is all, really, that Babbitt himself would have asked from his readers and auditors. In him, in his work, measure and humility were virtues that illuminated his views of life, literature, and thought. Hindus's essays, as collected and presented in this book, convey these virtues and also assimilate them. Though his essays, in the main, are about Babbitt, they are ultimately essays that keenly display Hindus's own autonomy and integrity as a critic. They remind us that the critical spirit, when and if it truly absorbs the greatness and excellence given generously by a major critic like Babbitt, can attain both latitude and depth—and enduring beneficence. The need for exemplars is today more urgent than ever, if we are not to become captives of the destructive habits that afflict American intellectual life in general and the critical function in particular. "No one more faithfully continues Babbitt's task than Milton Hindus," writes Russell Kirk in the introduction.

Half of the essays here are about Babbitt, but Babbitt's ethical precepts are the shaping spirit of the other half of Hindus's essays on literature and democratic culture found here. That Babbitt's ideas have lasting value, and that his influence survives in spite of the nihilisms that stalk the academy, are amply and thankfully evident in Hindus's book. To be sure, Babbitt's ideas and influences are hardly welcomed in the American intellectual community, or in the general periodicals, or in the world of higher learning (about which Babbitt wrote with deep insight in a book still in print and worth study and reflection, *Literature and the American College*). But that, in the past two decades, a growing number of books by and about Babbitt have been published and command respect, underscores the perseverance and the vigor of a minority critical movement in the United States. This movement, or remnant, points to the need to oppose the intellectual and critical totalitarianism that now takes us even further down "the road to serfdom."

Here, then, Hindus testifies to those properties of the critical pursuit that Babbitt was to honor and exemplify in his teachings and writings: moral responsibility, seriousness, discrimination, discipline, order. For Hindus, no less than for Babbitt, the critical function is inescapably tied to the ethical character of man and the character of civilization—and to the political, economic, philosophical, educational, and religious interrelationships that necessarily define and mold character in its whole and in its parts, and at all levels of civilized life. And for Hindus, no less than Babbitt, the final test of the critic is that of distinguishing between the wisdom of the age, with its flux, transience, corruption, and the wisdom of the ages, as it emerges from historical experience in the individuating forms of "tradition as history" and "tradition as heritage."

The essays directly elucidating Babbitt's achievement are invariably helpful to a reader, and make unmistakably clear why his work speaks to our condition. Throughout Hindus emphasizes Babbitt's central concern, the problem of conduct as it is inextricably tied to convictions and principles. For Babbitt, what distinguishes man from thing is the human capacity to exert interior discipline and, in effect, to implement the classical qualities of decorum, proportion, restraint, and measure as these are translated into the "inner check." The disciplinary element inherent in these qualities, as Hindus stresses, is what guards against the anarchic freedom and the license of the emotions that Jean-Jacques Rousseau glorified and that modernism enshrines *ad absurdum*. Babbitt, in short, affirmed the confluence of standards of the inner self and standards of the commonwealth.

In his essays on Babbitt, as Russell Kirk notes, "Milton Hindus opens our eyes to a great conservative man of letters." Thus, whether Hindus is assessing Babbitt's *Rousseau and Romanticism*, *The Masters of Modern French Criticism*, *Democracy and Leadership*, or Babbitt's translation of *The Dhammapada*, he provides one with generous critical directions that one does not meet in contemporary critical movements that breed confusion and disorder. Centrality, not dissipation, is the benchmark of Babbitt's contribution and meaning, and in underscoring *this* fact Hindus registers minority dissent that has the capacity to restore to the critical function its basic purpose to distinguish and to pass judgment upon literary works, separating true art from false art. Refusal to recognize the validity of this view of criticism, Hindus reminds us in his essays, leads to the mediocrity that now assumes forms of decadence, as any glance at both imaginative literature and literary criticism will confirm.

It is especially appropriate, given conditions and circumstances of the present time, that Hindus quotes this prophetic sentence from *Rousseau and Romanticism*: "But though strictly considered, life is but a web of illusion and a dream within a dream, it is a dream that needs to be managed with the utmost discretion, if it is not to turn into a nightmare." Evangels of the new social order, of the new age and the new morality, have steadily, and arrogantly, chosen to live in a modern dreamworld with its unchecked ideologies, chimeras, fantasies, reveries, utopias that plunge us deeper and deeper in a vacuum of disinheritance and in that "dark night of the mind," of which Richard Weaver speaks. The dream, the nightmare, is never absent; it captivates mind, body, and soul; and it becomes the mainstay of our technicism in all of its manifestations and empty optimisms. It is a dream, as Babbitt would say, that categorically separates one from "the immediate data of consciousness." The "terrible simplifiers" who infest the American mind and soul, and who dictate taste and sensibility, unfailingly sanctify this dream, cruelly rent from the realities that Babbitt wants us neither to ignore nor yet to despair of, but to grapple with strenuously and positively.

Reading Hindus on Babbitt prompts the thought here that no American statesman, teacher, or philosopher—no American holding a position of leadership—should consider himself, or herself, truly educated, and yes, truly enlightened, who has not studied *Democracy and Leadership*. Such a reading could even inaugurate, correctively, the beginning of the "inner check" that both leaders and polity sorely need if the nightmare that Babbitt warns against is not to become absolute, the irreversible "abolition of man."

Hindus's essays not directly relating to Babbitt nevertheless deal with subjects that long preoccupied the latter as teacher and critic: American society, culture, politics, education, literature. For the reader these essays are much rewarding in terms of critical commentary and judgment. Indeed, there is in these particular essays a double critical, and catechetical, value, as the reader derives from Hindus's explorations and scrutinies insight into contemporary problems, and also the additional benefit of Babbitt's steady influence. There is also an inclusive and defining solidity of critical thinking here that that coalesces with an older critic's effect on his critical inheritor. A line of continuity emerges in enriching and enlightening ways, reminding us of the truth of Babbitt's contention that "there is always the unity at the heart of change." Indeed, we are equally reminded here that when there is no continuity, no centrality, no abiding principle, no ethos, the result is disconnection and, in effect, the destructiveness that now passes for critical thought in the academy.

Hindus does not choose to ignore the paradigms of an older criticism, that is, a great predecessor's enduring worth. He is a critical practitioner who knows the full and continuing value of the virtue of loyalty that a regnant "orthodoxy of enlightenment" outlaws and persecutes, to the peril of American society and culture. He does not seek, in other words, to declare his independence at the cost of rootlessness. The critic's loyalty to an American father of criticism transforms into a transcendent sense of responsibility, forged as it is in the ongoing crisis of modernism. In this respect Hindus's critical metaphysic has the kind of ontological validity and relevance that resides in the need for "roots of order"—and also in "visions of order."

Following Babbitt, Hindus speaks for what Stephen Tonsor calls a "conservative creative minority," in short, for a point of view that, however unpopular, refuses to bow down before "men deep in Utopian Speculations," a phrase that Hindus quotes from the *Federalist Papers*, which he associates with the qualities of wisdom, moderation, humility. In remarking on "the future of democracy in the United States" Hindus stresses: "We are in no particular need of reform again, or reconstruction, or dreams of perfection designed to make the mechanism of government more responsive to a restless desire for change." And in examining "literature and the democratic culture," he affirms the need of standards in order both to judge and to save literature from sophistic and gnostic deformations.

In looking at the autobiographies of three American presidents— Martin Van Buren's (as published in volume 2 of *The Proceedings of the American Historical Association* for the year 1918); Ronald Reagan's *Where's the Rest of Me?* (1965); and George Bush's *Looking Forward* (1987)—Hindus singles out the qualities of responsibility, restraint, and humility which he finds missing from the "more imperious, charismatic personages who have occupied the presidency." It is refreshing, in this respect, to find here a critic who ultimately views criticism as the pursuit of virtue—a view that contemporary critics disdain. Hindus focuses on transcendent standards of character in his critiques of these autobiographies in particular, and of art in general; he refuses to be fooled by sham values, and claims, as well as by pseudocriticism. To emphasize standards of character, as does Hindus, requires fortitude, especially in a time of history when character and the moral virtues are deemed meaningless and valueless. For Hindus the office of a critic has a higher purpose: it fulfills a major and crucial need that Babbitt speaks of in these words: "It is the critic's business to grapple with the age in which he lives and give it what he sees it needs."

Hindus is a brave exception to an inordinate number of American critics who remain imprisoned in a sheer relativism that falls into anarchy. "America ... seems to be subject to the strong pull of its fantastic and overheated imagination," Hindus warns, "which suggests that nothing is impossible, that history is bunk and can be safely ignored, and that there are no limits to human potential. When such a fantasy threatens to part us from the ground of reality, strong cables are necessary to hold it down." The failure to heed this warning has grave consequences, which are everywhere apparent in American civilization. Of course, our leaders at all levels believe they are cognizant of these consequences, especially in the world of education. But their solutions are those of "social perfectionists" whose faith in the religion of illusion is unbending. "Deformed ideologies," to quote Eric Voegelin's phrase, increasingly fuel this religion, and put huge obstacles in the way of those who will not embrace it. Still, the future does not, cannot, belong to new "sophisters, economists, and calculators." For as long as there are critics who possess "force of character," the legacy of Irving Babbitt, to which Milton Hindus gives witness, preserves "the living principle."

Part three

To See Again the Stars

"And the fire and the rose are one"

The Need for Leadership

"In the long run democracy will be judged," writes Irving Babbitt in *Democracy and Leadership*, "no less than other forms of government, by the quality of its leaders, a quality that will depend in turn on the quality of their vision." Babbitt's words should remind us that the need for leadership, always urgent, remains ever more urgent in our time. We have now reached a stage in history when the sociopolitical crisis of leadership goes hand-in-hand with what might be called the spiritual crisis of nihilism: that ultimate negation of moral principles of order and belief. In many ways this twin crisis is the offshoot of what Jacob Burckhardt was to speak of, with particular reference to the French Revolution, as the "authorization to perpetual revision." In American society and culture, especially since the end of World War II, but going on throughout the twentieth century, we have seen an incessant revision of standards of leadership, as well as of American civilization itself, as leadership at all levels of national life has taken on specious forms.

Increasingly we have discarded standards of leadership that make for greatness and for that vision without which a civilization perishes. It is all too evident that many Americans do not relate confidently to the qualities that typify a great leader, one who, in Burckhardt's words, "is the man of exceptional intellectual or moral power whose activity is directed to a general aim, that is, a whole nation, a whole civilization, humanity itself." These are noble words, to be sure, and portray the noble aims of those who have "greatness of soul." Burckhardt, of course, does not permit idealism to overshadow hard facts, hard realities, and he cautions us by emphasizing that the idea of greatness, both as benefactor and as beneficence, has intrinsic ambiguity, if not relativeness. "Greatness is all that we are not," he emphasizes, if only to warn us that to find exemplary leadership is often problematic. We must always be prepared for disappointment and disillusionment in our search for a leader, given the human condition. Here, in any case, it is well to recall the admonition that we must have absolute standards and modest expectations. In the present time, when the lures of mediocrity inform human aspirations, as well as concepts of leadership, the desiderata that Burckhardt associates with great leaders merit close attention. Growing wings to overcome gravity, to evoke Plato's wondrous image, is, or should be, a continual goal. Human culture and character advance, creatively and critically, only insofar as ascent is our purpose and effort. "Who shall ascend the hill of the Lord?" is an eternal question that the Psalmist asks of Man.

We must not allow ourselves to be misled by "terrible simplifiers" who would reduce human life and achievement to the lowest common denominator, even as we now see and experience the baleful results of this phenomenon in all facets of contemporary life. At the point when we no longer proclaim qualitative standards, subordinating them to sociopolitical agenda and expediency, we sink into the trough of mediocrity. If we are to avoid the awful costs of such a descendancy, we must, however unpopular and vulnerable our position may be, insist that standards of achievement, of life, of discrimination, should determine our range of awareness. If, too, we are not to be subsumed by the anthill of modern life, we must maintain at a maximal point a keen awareness of excellence, of criteria, of obligations—of greatness. Above all we must insist on those qualities of leadership that measure not so much practical success but rather the capacity for growth of insight and wisdom in terms of the moral life and the ethical life. To adopt a policy of silence or of neglect with regard to the higher metaphysical attributes of leadership, or to convert these attributes into exclusively egalitarian demands, and fallacies, trivializes the meaning of leadership. When and where standards are ignored, scorned, or silenced, the consequences are injurious to civilization, to the polity, to governance. A morally impoverished society will produce morally impoverished leaders. Either we strive to strengthen leadership or we proceed to trivialize the very nature of its responsibility, if not its *raison d'être*.

In whom do we now recognize and salute qualities? Who are representative of great leadership? What accounts for the growing diminution of standards of leadership, of "men of light and leading" who, for Edmund Burke, combine "a disposition to preserve, and an ability to improve"? One who dares to answer these questions in the light of current practices and habits is bound to notice both a general drifting of leadership and a shifting of standards. The process of reductionism and debasement, once begun, is difficult to arrest, particularly in a technologico-Benthamite society that respects neither moral determinants nor moral deterrents. Such a nullifying process is registered in the ways in which men and women today judge the nature, the mission and ethos, of leadership, and of leaders who are unfriendly to the venerable triad of reason, Scripture, and tradition. With the growing absence of standards and discipline of leadership one can also observe a commensurate absence of leaders capable of guiding the citizenry to a higher moral and in turn sociopolitical ground. As such, leadership itself is annexed by the marketplace; it becomes its handmaiden and accomplice, complying with the prevailing climate of opinion and adapting itself to the whirl of the world. The idea of and the needs for leadership are thus reduced to a quantitative state, to a kind of emptiness, even entropy.

A tyranny of "quantitative reductionism," as Father Stanley Jaki uses that term, afflicts an entire society and culture and conduces decay at all levels of life. Leadership itself, both as a concept and as need, undergoes transmutation once the forces of reductionism take hold. The transcendent purpose and meaning of leadership are made relative as standards and expectations are minimized or scuttled. Clearly, the eclipse of the idea of excellence is directly reflected in the eclipse of the quality of leaders—and, too, of a people's perception of representatives of leadership. This perception increasingly becomes a decadent one that cruelly excludes those canons of leadership that identify Ortega y Gasset's "select man" of magnanimous words and work. Today our "representative men" inevitably mirror the consequences of "authorization to perpetual revisionism," hostile to centrality, principle, discrimination, as well as to both the historical and the moral sense that provide the prudence and the virtue that restrict the force of barbarism. "Barbarism," Ortega reminds us, "is the absence of norms and of any possible appeal based on them."

Leadership that succumbs to the "absence of norms" in effect admits to a failure of nerve, the results of which are everywhere in evidence, as sham leaders come forth to fill the void. Still, the search for leadership does go on, but at lesser, surrogate levels. In a society in which qualities of leadership have receded and leaders exert no deep appeal to the heart, mind, and soul of the citizenry, the consequential vacuum must be filled to compensate for the absence or even the breakdown of leadership. When we fail to identify with the idea of leadership embodying prescriptive standards of virtue, character, conscience, of taste and sensibility—and of leaders who elevate us to a higher ground, and who, no less than great visionary poets, make men and women better citizens in their cities—we begin to accept inferior qualities, inferior leaders, inferior aspirations, inferior choices. Joseph Conrad, in his novel *Nostromo*, memorably renders this rhythm of disintegration among leaders who have "but a feeble and imperfect consciousness of the worth and force of the inner life." Particularly in a democracy in which responsibility and freedom must strenuously interact, when the quality of leadership deteriorates there is a comparable deterioration in the actions of the led. It is precisely in the course of this deterioration that we

can discern how the demand for and pursuit of leadership are prostitut-
ed, that is to say, exposed or subjected to a destructive agency or impulse
devoted to an unworthy or corrupt cause.

The results of this prostitution are all too visible and alarming, as
fundamental qualities of leadership are subject more and more to
revision, to deconstruction, to use here a word that enjoys much favor in
the intellectual community. We reach the point, then, of trivializing the
idea, and the ideal, of leadership, and proceed to manufacture multiple
substitutes seemingly satisfying the human longing for leadership. That,
too, public, and particularly political, leaders not only accommodate but
also enact a general loss of standards further weakens the idea of
leadership and heightens the atmosphere of cynicism and contempt in the
"public square." In a sense, the prostitution of the idea of leadership
melds with the pursuit of leadership in nondiscriminating ways and
forms, opportunely abetted by social scientists and behaviorists, and by
commercial and journalistic interests. The sharp decline, too, of the
religious idea, even on the part of the religious themselves, adds
significantly to the process of prostitution. Ultimately the crumbling of
moral climate and spiritual terrain eventuates the crumbling of "the
partnership between principle and process . . . the first fact of life and of
our work," to recall one of Lao Tzu's famous sayings.

Any diminution of the moral sense and the discriminating faculty is
bound to be pernicious to one's capacity for the recognition, analysis, and
measurement of leadership and of its representatives in all areas of
human endeavor. And any detrition of standards of leadership must be
accompanied by a confluent detrition of the character of leadership and
in turn of our estimation of leader-types. Pseudoleadership and pseudo-
leaders characterize current conditions as more and more citizens confuse
leadership with the cult of personality and the world of celebrities.
Immoral and amoral conditions breed immoral and amoral tendencies.
And the leveling or the absence of standards influences one's view of
leaders and of the qualities that they project and that, ostensibly, satisfy
one's hopes and desires. Our choice of leaders underscores the anoma-
lous and, above all, the antinomian features of American life and
character in the modern age. Doubtlessly, the scarcity of visionary
political and intellectual leadership affects in drastic ways human
judgment and selection. Choices are symptomatic of the corrosive
tendencies of American civilization and polity as these are impelled by
our obsession with change, usually to the detriment of the "permanent
things," it need hardly be said. Indeed, what most characterizes the
conditions of our situation is a pattern, if not a pathology, of disorder.

This pattern of disorder determines our conceptions of leadership, and of the leaders we choose. Insight, wisdom, authority, faith, and fortitude are neither the virtues nor the values for which we necessarily seek or honor in leaders. We make standards subservient to a pluralistic and fragmented society, to Jacobin impulses and doctrines. Those whom we esteem and reward and follow often accede to the disorder-pattern besetting the life of the republic and the life of the soul; such leaders mirror public and private insolvency at the brink of chaos. They project precisely the traits and propensities of those who comprise the "anonymous mass" and who suffer from the malady that Walter Lippmann, in *The Public Philosophy* (1955), pinpoints in these words: "There is a profound disorientation in their experience, a radical disconnection between the notions of their minds and the needs of their souls." Athletes, television stars, and entertainers, Hollywood actors and actresses, smatterers, rock and rap singers and musical groups, publicists, along with pseudo-artists, -academics, and -critics (*la trahison des clercs*) who command enormous attention and acclaim: they encompass the new secularist elite to whom we look for leadership; they set the standards, style, and taste of postmodern, postmanagerial society; they become our sentinels of art and letters as they write a new lexicon of thrills and titillation.

What, then, can we say about the prospects of leadership? How can we expect great leadership to emerge from a disjointed culture, "rotten and rotting others"? Can we possibly produce genuine leaders in a society that accommodates or follows "the enemies of the permanent things"? Those who choose to answer these questions buoyantly ignore our present predicament. Nowhere is this predicament better epitomized than in the educational realm in which the canon lies in ruins and arrogant ideologues formulate with an iron fist entire areas of teaching, administration, texts, and policies. "All education today serves to prepare the individual for the world of disjointedness," to recall here Max Picard's observation. In this situation there is neither past nor future; the dogma of presentism thrives everywhere and makes it difficult for any true nourishment or birth of leadership. Hence we must measure realistically and sternly the prospects of leadership against existing realities.

And yet we also cannot be content with an attitude of "So be it!" or even to practice the despair in virile acceptance some existentialists preach. The possibility of ascent, however perilous it may be, is never extinct, as history has confirmed even in the worst of times and climes. Maintaining, in Eric Voegelin's words, "conscious opposition of the well-ordered soul to the disorder of the society around it" is a major need. Recognizing, too, that political skill is not political wisdom and that political maneuvering is not political leadership, is another major need. Indeed, we have to understand the limits of political leadership itself, neither romanticizing nor exaggerating its possibilities. We can only hope, as T. S. Eliot asserted not long after the end of World War II, that "there will always be situations in which one man, or a few men, will render a service to their society simply by standing alone in an unpopular opinion and telling their countrymen that they are wrong, with no hope of accomplishing anything except witnessing to the truth as they see it."

In a profane age in which paradigms of leadership are not abundant, it is especially important to look first within the inner life of memory and continuity for those values and verities that the outer life has declared inoperative. No tyranny, collective or individual, can outlaw or eradicate that capacity for critical reflection. Of the need to reflect on the qualities and the state of leadership there can be no end. This is doubly true at a time when the subject of leadership seems to be the exclusive property of clever journalists, television celebrities, best-selling authors, political pundits, and pollsters who glibly spell out the function and constituents of leadership, with very little regard for its moral dimension and responsibilities.

It is worth noting that the twentieth century has variously excited significant reflections on the phenomenon of violence. For instance, *Reflections on Violence* (1908), by the French social theorist and "metaphysician of socialism," Georges Sorel, argues the case for an "ethics of violence" and praises the role of violence as an agent of progress and amelioration. And from an opposing vantage point there is the celebrated essay entitled "The *Iliad*, Poem of Might," by the Christian Hellenist metaphysician of "the invisible church," Simone Weil, who sees violence as an example of demonic might that "makes a thing of man, for it makes him a corpse." Such reflections on violence should definitely claim our consideration if we are to locate and resist its principalities and powers. But no less legitimate and no less necessary, we also have to reflect on the nature of leadership, and of leadership that can help us soar beyond the walls of violence within which life is often trapped. Surely the nexus between violence and leadership can hardly be escaped.

We need to restore moral value to leadership, and thus free it not only from its purely sociological and political contexts, but also from its empirical configurations. Leadership is yet another word that has been emptied of its hierarchical order and has experienced the same dismal fate of other words of absolute value—loyalty, nobility, virtue, goodness, generosity, honor. No less than these words, leadership relates to the struggle between good and evil. We need to save the meaning of leadership from the kind of devaluation that tears down the structure of language and, in effect, the structure of truth. When leadership is robbed of its metaphysical value, when it is detached from universal referents and standards, then leadership is stripped of its dignity. And when the idea of leadership falls into the realm of the vacuous, it honors no moral imperative and is absorbed by degraded conditions and oblique purposes. As a result we make leadership an equivocal commodity—purchaseable, temporalized, manipulated, condemned to unending alteration. The true measure of leadership, in these circumstances, is supplanted by *ersatz* forms and types ordained by the ruling spirit of the time.

In the order of human existence in society and history the problem of leadership is, and has always been, one that involves human destiny. More than at any time in history, and especially now as we are about to enter a new century, we have every reason to heed Edmund Burke's warning: "We must have leaders. If none will undertake to lead us right, we shall find guides who will contrive to conduct us to shame and ruin."

After Ideology

If modernism has been seen as the triumph of the machine, if it is synonymous with change and progress in general, it has not had an equivalent success in the life of the soul. More than ever the inner, invisible life discloses radical discontent and disconnection. Material achievement and spiritual well-being are not necessarily confluent; the City of Man and the City of God do not necessarily coexist. Spiritual disinheritance and dispossession mark the modern human condition in spite of all palpable advances. Disorder and alienation manifest the collapse of millenarian experiments rooted in ideological schemes and programs. All the claims of a New Deal and of a Great Society, that in effect we have entered the gates of Eden, ring hollow.

In *After Ideology* (1990), a timely and eloquent book, Professor David Walsh demonstrates that no examination of the crisis of modernism can be complete without discerning at its epicenter the crisis of the human soul. The failure to make such a distinction further solidifies our spiritual *stasis*, that is, makes us even more the prisoners of our nothingness. Such a failure, then, perpetuates an existential sickness unto death—the kind of spiritual exhaustion that impedes a search for moral and sociopolitical order.

Revolutionary nihilism, Walsh shows, is inevitably the consequence of secular, gnostic, and liberal ideologies that assault biblical and classical traditions and principles. How can modern man recover from the impact of this soul-killing process? This is one of the central questions in *After Ideology*. But it is also the singular strength of this book to move beyond questions, even beyond diagnosis, by pointing the way. Walsh provides here a moral and spiritual compass, a gift that no reader can turn down. In him we have at least one university teacher and political scientist who sensitively comprehends the needs of the soul in relation to the needs of temporal life, and who, at the same time is not afraid to speak out on this need of needs. Nor is he afraid to use great and sacred words like transcendence and faith, which he pinpoints as indispensable to the process of spiritual recovery that modern political systems have systematically sought to crush in an age of ideology. The disintegration of the communist nations of Eastern Europe dramatizes the excesses of ideological barbarism in modern times. Willfully, however, the American intelligentsia chooses to be blind to these excesses with their impersonal idols of liberalism and social action that a John Dewey worked to enshrine in American culture and society. In our time Dewey's successors have gone beyond him with abandoned prodigality.

At a time, too, when even religious leaders in their outlook and preaching give cause for sorrow, Walsh discloses in impressive ways how one can overcome the closure and violence of the secular world. Throughout, he carefully distinguishes between spiritual lassitude and spiritual death, and the book as a whole holds a life-giving and faith-building message of hope. It is precisely this hope that inspires Walsh's religiophilosophical thesis that descent into the abyss of negations can also become the ascent from it. His sense of reverence is ever confluent with his courage of judgment in page after page of meditative deliberations, rich in their critical content and even richer in their metaphysical lift. Here, in these pages, we have the testimony of a scholar-teacher who refuses to bow down to the chronolatry, to the profaneness and blasphemy of the modern world. And that refusal, too, occasions hope. Walsh reminds us that not all teachers have surrendered to the sundry demonisms that afflict the realm of education; that there are teachers who give their witness with conviction and also with exceptional authority that emerges as insight and wisdom. Accustomed, if not compelled and even conditioned, as we have been to hearing the heavy and deafening language of impiety in the intellectual community, we may at first even find *After Ideology* startlingly unorthodox in its premise and ethos.

As one ponders Walsh's elucidations and contemplations—all of these the inevitable offshoots of honest and hard thought—the royal doors of penitence, as it were, open. In its own humble ways this book facilitates a joyous entrance. Yet it must also be stressed that *After Ideology* is neither a theological tract nor a devotional manual (though the theological and devotional motifs are strong and fervent in this book). This is a serious and disciplined work of scholarship rooted in Christian affirmation. It brings to mind the kind of writings made famous by those remarkable thinkers who, after 1917, made possible the Russian religious renaissance of the twentieth century—Nicholas Berdyaev, Sergius Bulgakov, Konstantin Mochulski, S. L. Frank, N. O. Lossky, Georges Florovsky, and others. *After Ideology* points to a resurgence of Christian faith and culture in the contemporary period no less significant than the writings of the great postrevolutionary Russian Orthodox exiles. With them Walsh boldly continues to define a common theme: the revalidation of philosophy and Christian teaching in the modern world. In one sense Walsh is himself a believer-teacher who is in exile in his own nation; he stands unalterably opposed to the decadence of American culture and also to its spiritual renunciations.

Walsh is writing from another country, so to speak. What he has to say in *After Ideology*—the religious positions he posits and affirms; the inherently Christian ethos he expounds—clearly marks him as an outsider. His book indicts and contravenes everything that the American intelligentsia prescribes and everything that characterizes American polity. A fearless intellectual honesty and an equally fearless spiritual viewpoint inform the composition of this book from beginning to end. Neither Christian dogma nor apologetics, however, characterize the purpose of the book. Rather, the author is a scholar and thinker who pleads for order in soul and in society, who wants to recover the transcendent foundation of order, and who believes that a philosophic Christianity is, or should be, the ground of such a search and recovery. The bankruptcy of modernism makes such a religious search all the more urgent. Insofar as we now live in an age in which ideological systems anchored in a secular humanity have been found woefully wanting and inoperative, as well as morally corrupt, and leave in their wake anarchy and nihilism, the need for a postmodern viewpoint that is both viable and pertinent is even more urgent. And central to this need is the rediscovery of philosophy and revelation that is joined to a confirmation of transcendent reality of order.

For Walsh, the process of restoration is ultimately an either/or process—either order or disorder, belief or denial, Christ or the Devil; in short, either the Kingdom of the Spirit or the Kingdom of Enmity. Walsh views this process—it is in essence a form of spiritual warfare—in the larger historical framework of Renaissance thought, introducing as it did a revised and often antinomian version of Christianity in which the human being became a secular messiah and all distinctions between the sacred and the profane became increasingly blurred. This conflict as it has continued and advanced in more recent times has presented us with a radical transfiguration of man as the man-god. This transfiguration, Walsh rightly shows, has been a failed and false one: the progeny of failed and false ideologies emblematized in social, political, cultural, and economic breakdowns, of which the former Soviet Union is now a monstrous objective correlative.

We have thus reached the omega point when we must confront the whole problem of human destiny as it screams for spiritual relief in the bitter aftermath of a modern world in which ideologies *in extremis* have prevailed. Walsh views the present period of history, then, as one in which the lure of ideologies has brought us to the extremity of total disorientation. What comes after ideology? What must we do to emerge from not only the ruins of modernism but also the twilight of ideology? For Walsh these questions are teleological in nature, and they can be nothing less in a world in which nihilism and chaos are the all-too-evident consequences of monolithic ideological dismantlings that reject the tenets of a humane civilization. The bankruptcy of the liberal-revolutionary process of secular and gnostic ideologies creates a vacuum that is dangerous and unacceptable. Walsh views such a vacuum as one that heightens spiritual closure and the total enfeeblement of the value of order. To save us from such a fateful situation that has its end in no-end—in public unconsciousness, abject lostness, unchecked disorder, unending despair—is, for Walsh, the greatest challenge now facing us. Only with the advent of spiritual recovery, of an attained luminosity, he maintains, can we escape from the tyranny of ideological movements in their sundry modern guises.

To recover the philosophic and Christian symbolizations of order Walsh calls on four great writers for guidance and inspiration. Dostoevsky, Camus, Solzhenitsyn, and Voegelin are modern shepherds of being who, Walsh believes, can help rescue us from the furnace of doubt and guide us to repentance and regeneration. In their writings, as in their lives, we view the full drama of the crisis of modernism, and we participate in all of its forms of metaphysical revolt and alienation, but also of spiritual recovery.

The selection of these four exemplars is certainly valid, though it is also one of the drawbacks of *After Ideology* that the criteria for Walsh's selection could be more rigorously explicated. In addition, he fails to examine in more detail the larger subject of the end of ideology in our time; in this connection, he ignores the important work done by Karl Mannheim, Raymond Aron, Edward Shils. There are, then, some regrettable *lacunae* in *After Ideology*. The reader, as a result, will on occasion have to infer the rationale for Walsh's selection of exemplars in the search for transcendental moral order, as well as fill in some of the details of the intellectual history of ideology. In any case, the organizational and structural infelicities of the book, in which there are six long chapters, each containing a varying number of subheadings, can sometimes overtax the reader's patience and concentration.

Ordinarily problems such as these can be irremediably damaging. Fortunately this is not true in the case of Walsh's book, for in it we are in close contact with a resilient mind, authentic concern, judgmental authority. Critical integrity and an abundance of insight in the end dispel any quibbling or doubt. Here one sees a cumulative critical discrimination at work and one is the richer for its results. *After Ideology* adroitly challenges one's attention and thought; impels one to reevaluate conditions and circumstances affecting civilizational order in contemporary life. The true meditative value of this book is to be found in how it affects one's view of moral and spiritual issues of the first importance—issues that our evangels of enlightenment would prefer to deconstruct or silence. Walsh consistently resists the large encompassing moral apathy and spiritual indifference that are in themselves the legacy of a modernism that has not been adequately questioned or inspected. In its critical integrity *After Ideology* commands our respect; its diagnostic focus, prophetic findings, and prescriptive powers are heightened by its religious commitments and acceptances. Walsh's own holding to a religious position is in itself as paradigmatic as that of his four exemplars of spiritual concern and transfiguration.

In its total exposition and commentary—the critiques of selected texts from Dostoevsky, Camus, Solzhenitsyn, Voegelin are judicious and sensitive in illustrating their cathartic spiritual meaning and ascent—*After Ideology* stresses a quintessential fact of human existence arrogantly dismissed by the liberal intelligentsia: that political order is first and last dependent on the order within the human soul. This is the crux of Walsh's position, and he develops it forcefully in the great moral line of an Irving Babbitt, who urged modern man to convert the idea of value into the life of value, and a Simone Weil, who beckoned modern man to become a geometrician in the apprenticeship of virtue. Walsh's warning that modern liberal democracy, when lacking moral and spiritual foundation, invites disintegration, has especial relevance for Americans. And indeed today we see the violent spectacle of this disintegration in every facet of our national life. Clearly anthropocentrism is an implicit ideological dimension of contemporary society and must be perceived as such if a new awareness is to prevail. For Walsh the four writers he presents to us as paradigms of spiritual release from the abyss of negations instance victory over ideology and all its dominions.

After Ideology is an encouraging book; in particular, from the Camus who believed in the necessity of some kind of rule and some kind of order it takes its positive cue of steady resistance both to the spirit of negation and to the monolithic secularization of the West. To be sure, the Americanization of the mind, as Gottfried Dietze memorably describes it, is itself a disturbing and far-reaching phenomenon that should perhaps make Walsh more cautious about the scope of his religious contentions and conceptualizations. The American situation, as we are so often dramatically reminded, has gone from secular to neutralist to pagan extremes, jeopardizing the very possibilities that Walsh proclaims. But Walsh is also a Christian realist who fully registers the cruel mathematics of this situation, which at times approaches a totalitarian conclusion, made especially and inevitably obvious by the self-dissolution of liberalism. What is finally the most arresting aspect of *After Ideology*, what makes this book speak to our condition, is its thoroughly reasoned delineation of a modern world in which spiritual attrition has run its dreary course. In this postmodern stage of our civilization, thus, we live in a *meta*crisis (with all of its disordered symbolizations) in which liberal assumptions and demoniac ideological approaches reveal their utter depravity. And it is precisely at this precarious point, Walsh insists, that we must begin to gauge our plight if we are to see again the stars.

The great writers whom Walsh uses to probe the experience of spiritual descent and ascent are not only prophets of destiny but also prophets of redemption. Their experience, worthy of our emulation, harbors hope for all of us. The fact, too, that they are writers and thinkers, not saints or holy men, further strengthens the relevance of their spiritual example and direction. Their search for postmodern truths helps to remind us that all constitutional order must finally rest on moral and religious foundations. No other time than the present provides us, then, with a better opportunity for genuine spiritual reorientation. It can be said in this respect that Walsh's book contains some basic lessons in metaphysics that are as assiduously argued as those of Ortega y Gasset in an earlier era. Even this comparative reference should say something about the depth of thought in *After Ideology*.

Two exemplary acts of metaphysical courage make *After Ideology* a truly distinguished contribution in these troubling and confusing times: the moral courage to see economic, educational, political, and philosophical problems tied to the religious problem; and the spiritual courage to reaffirm the values of our civilization as these have been interpreted and nurtured by the ancient Greek visionaries, the Hebrew prophets, and the Christian saints and martyrs.

The Wrestlings of Soul

We not only read a novel, we enter into its created world. We identify a novelist by his world, that is, the world that specifically conveys the body of his vision. We relate the novelist's world to a particular place and time in history, to a particular human condition, and above all to particular physical entities. The novelist's world becomes both a process of discovery and a journey of revelation. His fictional world makes us more aware of the map of our human world. What the novelist does finally, if he is really successful, is to dramatize for us the inner and the outer aspects of the world which we call our home, our universe, our *topos*. Since too often we know, or think we know, that we possess and control the world we live in, we perhaps take it too much for granted. Which means that we do not always see, and see into, our world as fully or incisively as we can or should.

The world in all of its forms and shapes, its sunshine and shadows, its sunsets and dawns, which the novelist paints in a work of art, gives, or should give, the reader a shock of recognition. It should help him to comprehend more vividly the world's infinite mystery, wonder, beauty, as well as its paradox, its enigma, in short, its inspiration and its unfathomability. It is a world with landmarks and touchstones. On its roads and pathways, in its crowded streets, as in its open spaces, we travel, meeting ourselves and others, touching the known and the unknown. Its topography is our most visible connection with the seething immensity of life, as saints, mystics, prophets, philosophers, poets, and painters have testified to from the earliest times. The world comprises a ceaseless double rhythm of creation and of death, of cohesion and of dissolution; it is the *alpha* and the *omega*; our whatness, our temptation, our judgment, our beginning and our ending—the final apocalypse. "The world is the closed door," again to recall Simone Weil. "It is a barrier. And at the same time, it is the way through."

The world, as I have tried to describe its encompassing perimeters, fills immensity. Man, it is often said, cannot jump over his own shadow. The poet—and by "poet" I mean a writer of imaginative works in verse or prose—leaps over the universe. He can, in William Blake's words, "See a world in a grain of sand." The poet gives us his visions, or sense perceptions, of the spectacle of the world. I use the word spectacle in order to stress the poet's dramatic sense, as well as his imaginative grasp of the human scene in its wondrous totality, and specifically its spirit of place. The poet gives voice to the world. He conveys its most essential qualities of body, of weight, of color. The world is the poet's center of gravity, a geographical point of actions in convergence.

Undoubtedly, one poet's world will differ from another's. The primitive world of Homer is our own world from moment to moment. The medieval world of Dante, on the other hand, is a world which we step into. Homer's is an immediate physical world as it is felt and seen. Dante's is a prophetic world in which we view the journey of the soul, self-lost, self-sought, self-found. The *Iliad* tells us about the destruction of the city of man, the greatest of griefs that can afflict man. The *Divine Comedy* tells us about the attainment of the city of God, the greatest of spiritual joys that can be given. One of the supreme glories of the poet, as both Homer and Dante confirm, is to be able to present the kingdoms of the world in a captured moment of time—the world now and the world to come.

The poet as novelist includes and portrays in his work a particularizing world, a visible landscape, which serves as the stage of what happens in the story that is being told. Of course, this landscape may ultimately indicate something more than what is merely physical in appearance and atmosphere. Indeed, it may have the deepest and widest of implications, connecting story and action and people (or things) with happenings, with significances, of an internalizing nature, of a most profound psychology. The great novelist is one who includes and renders the world's physical properties in order, as Henry James believes, to make us catch a glimpse of a great space, the complete and profound mystery of the soul and of the conscience of man. In great art the world attains its true and most relevant meaning in these transcending and transcendent dimensions. These dimensions of great fiction are moral—"they deal [as James also believes] with something more than mere accidents and conventionalities, the surface occurrences of life." We must make our judgments of discrimination in order to distinguish moral vision from sham vision. Our hesitation to do so merely leads to drifting consequences, for ourselves and for our world.

At the risk, then, of being labeled a traditionalist, I shall reassert, and reaffirm, T. S. Eliot's dismissal of a novelist as useless if he neglects or lacks a "moral preoccupation," which is the ability to perceive evil and good. At the risk, too, of being labeled a moralist, I think it necessary to apply Eliot's criterion to the ways in which the novelist handles his fictive world. If the world into which the novelist invites us, in which he even traps us, does not have its impelling moral interest, it neither contains nor communicates the seriousness and the profundity that Eliot associates with moral preoccupation.

If we are to avoid the awful consequences of nonoriented and disoriented thought in our comprehension of modern literature, and if we are to penetrate more meaningfully into the artist's world, it is necessary to restrict our attention to the world of the novelist that has its source in the moral imagination, that qualitative imagination which is aware of the difference, the eternal struggle, between good and evil. This requirement is especially pertinent to our tough-minded generation whose moral interest in art is in eclipse. It is hardly necessary for me to note that the supersecular appetites of our age lead increasingly to moral immobility, a condition that spreads dangerously to all areas of personal conduct and collective life. Hence we need to be severely selective in our reading and reckoning of novelists and to make our selection on the basis of the validity of a work of art in terms of the human awareness and the moral interest it promotes.

It is nowhere enough merely to see in a novel a particular world in its intensity of self-consciousness, but rather, and above all, to gain a deeper moral knowledge of our world. How a novelist's world develops in us a real moral understanding; how it shapes first our perception and then our conception of our own world, helping us thus to fathom its meaning and to approach more closely to spiritual reality through physical phenomena; how, in short, the novelist, through the world he creates, can acquaint us with the idea of moral value and character: these should shape our concerns as well as the standards that we should be applying rigorously to imaginative art, if it is to escape inanity and chaos. What I am saying here—the criteria I am trying to define and to defend in relation to separating and saving what is of value from what is of little value—comes down finally to this critical principle: If we believe that the human world is significant because of its moral significance, the art that is morally rooted can help us better understand the conditions of our existence.

For the true novelist the burden of vision and responsibility is imperative and unavoidable. Consequently, in his fictional world we are thrown into a world of good and evil; a world in which moral struggle, loneliness, and choice, accompanied by pain and misery and terror, become a transcending and a transforming experience. This experience of moral crisis can be a prelude to moral awareness. Art that provides for this heightening experience belongs to that ancient and higher tradition of wisdom that returns us to the world of the Bible, of Sophocles, of Virgil, of Dante, of Milton.

The world that the modern poet-novelist creates discloses the extent and the depth of his capacity to be, in Aleksandr Solzhenitsyn's words, a "discerner of spirit." In this redemptive role he helps us to grow wings to overcome gravity. A novelist who is a "discerner of spirit" contends with and dramatizes ultimate questions, the "everlastingly accursed questions" as they are called. Such a novelist reveals in the world he portrays a special dimension of moral insight, a special mission, a special aspect of the human situation. He thus reveals the uniqueness of this poetic vision and, inevitably and finally, its identifying moral meaning. To be sure, poetic value is something different from moral value. Yet the two, when they do converge, have a reciprocal effect on our life-outlook and life-values. The novelist's vision-world engages our rapt, intransitive attention, as Eliseo Vivas describes it. (And the fact remains that we become what we contemplate.) It also enables us to locate a center of values.

In dramatizing his moral concern, the novelist helps us to envision "man in the modern world," perhaps even "the end of the modern world." The fictional world of Franz Kafka, for example, expresses an existential morality. That is, his world contains a permanent hope-defying paradox against which man, both as victim and assailant, struggles. Kafka's is a nightmare world: an airless, grotesque, dark, suffocating city-world in which it is always three o'clock in the morning. It is a world filled with the intolerable tension of man's predicament. "If one is not being pursued by the world or carried off by the world, one is running after it," Austin Warren says of "kosmos Kafka." In it one suffers through a never-ending waiting for grace; one is always trying to reach something that, at the same time, is always withdrawing, insofar as that something—call it God—is not there, not yet. To the question, Will a savior ever appear to us? Kafka replies that, yes, a savior will come. "But he will arrive the day after his arrival, he will not come on the last of the days, but on the day after the last." It is true that Kafka's world depicts man in search of salvation, but his search, with its relentless but elusive moral expectations, has no *telos*. "There is a goal but no way" Kafka writes: "what we call the way is only wavering." We discover in Kafka's world how moral angst subsumes moral fantasy and becomes a permanent human condition.

On the other hand, in D. H. Lawrence's fictional world we have a naturalistic morality, revolving around the legitimacy and the holiness of the human passions in which he finds man's infinite possibility and final redemption. His assertion that the true artist "always substitutes a finer morality for the grosser" helps us to gauge Lawrence's moral perspective and purpose. He refines his moral vision from a natural, a sacred and a primordial, world in which the sun and moon, the "birds, beasts and flowers," the "city's gold phosphorescence," and even the scars on the landscape assume moral implications. Lawrence's is a paradisal world in which the passions themselves are embarked on a paradisal quest. The very last sentence of *The Rainbow* (1915) crystallizes Lawrence's vision of a reborn world: "She saw in the rainbow the earth's new architecture, the old, brittle, corruption of houses and factories swept away, the world built up in a living fabric of Truth, fitting to the overarching heaven."

In contrast to Kafka's moral concern, which is existential and metaphysical, Lawrence's is physical and intuitive. This intuitiveness makes him aware of the vulnerability of a "finer morality" that he offers and affirms as good. After the Great War of 1914–1918 he saw this vulnerability objectified in "mechanisms of matter" and "dark satanic mills," the agents of evil debasing and destroying the world. It is the "terror of history" that now appears in Lawrence's dark and tragic novel, *Women in Love* (1920). Flood, fire, snow, ice are the apocalyptic images that dominate this novel, in which we view the death of civilization brought on by capitulation to a grosser morality. But let Lawrence describe this process of dissolution, found in those remarkable concluding pages of *Women in Love*: "It was a grey day, the third day of greyness and stillness. All was white, icy, pallid. . . . In the distance a slope sheered down from a peak, with many black rockslides." The Lawrence we hear in these words is a prophet who seeks to save the modern world from an immoral destiny.

~ 🦉 ~

There is one novelist whose moral vision contains all worlds. He is our greatest novelist. I am referring to Fyodor M. Dostoevsky, to whom I want now to turn my main attention in the light of some of the critical contexts of my preliminary observations. Dostoevsky defies logical classification and summary, a fact that in itself gives us a clue to his enormous importance. No other novelist is as threatening or as shattering as is Dostoevsky in his impact. No other novelist is his equal as a subtle psychologist of the life of the spiritual world. One can never be the same after encountering the world of Dostoevsky.

Hurling us into unbelievable depths of experience and meaning, it is a world that at times defies language, rational explanations, neat theories and formulas. Even as we begin to understand Dostoevsky's world it suddenly and mysteriously makes a mockery of our conclusions. His world can be likened to a moral and spiritual labyrinth in which, as soon as we think we have found a way out, we realize it is only a small opening into still another dark, descending cave. In Kafka's and in Lawrence's worlds we begin to know what to see, what to fear, what to expect. In Dostoevsky's world strange and unexpected surprises have a way of suddenly snaring us. Such a world finds us unprepared.

There is some truth to Nicholas Berdyaev's remark that Dostoevsky must be read only "in an atmosphere of spiritual manhood." Berdyaev is simply reminding us that Dostoevsky's world is not for a pilgrim but rather for a spiritual wrestler. Dostoevsky's world constitutes an arduous wrestle with and against an uncanny power. Just as one feels that he has finally overcome his adversary, he finds himself astonishingly toppled, needing again to begin another breathtaking effort to disentangle himself and to escape from the power that weighs and presses heavily against him. In Dostoevsky's world there is undiminishing strain and pressure. Inevitably one is pushed towards a border situated somewhere between death and life, victory and defeat, dream and reality, being and nothingness. Held tightly within a suspended time sequence—caught as he is between two awesome forces—he has flashes of a frightening knowledge of himself, of others, of his world, and of the other world.

In his major fiction—in his great quintet, *Crime and Punishment* (1866), *The Idiot* (1868–1869), *The Devils* (1871–1872), *A Raw Youth* (1875), *The Brothers Karamazov* (1879–1880)—he endows place, particularly the city of Saint Petersburg, with an identity that goes far beneath and beyond the physiology of an urban landscape. Place, for Dostoevsky, provides map points, external characteristics that dramatize a special condition or problem such as poverty or isolation. Generally his fictional world mirrors metaphysical qualities; pictorial details are included, cumulatively, so as to help one penetrate metaphysical depths. Hence Dostoevsky employs sensuous elements in order to heighten and color, to body forth, an inner realm.

The material world is a map for the exploration of the spiritual world. How does one converse with the unknown? How does one make his way in that other world once he has entered it? These questions govern and shape Dostoevsky's moral vision. And they again underline the ferocity of struggle, what I have just imaged as a savage wrestle, that Dostoevsky imposes unconditionally upon anyone who dares to enter the world of his fiction. This world is not a linear one but a world without end, which explains the amazing singularity and complexity of each of the worlds of those five, Dostoevsky's last, novels. His world contains everything that is found between heaven and hell. It is self-recognition that we undergo in such a world. To view this world is to feel its impinging strength. Each of the novels represents an intensive and an advancing phase of struggle. In Dostoevsky's multidimensional world we wrestle with the flesh, with powers and principalities. Everything is at stake in this life-and-death struggle.

In Dostoevsky's major novels the city is an inclusive symbolic world that takes on weird shapes and colors and sends forth muffled sounds of anguish; these are the moans and groans of life lived in fear and trembling. His urban world is one of semidark and demon-like tenement houses whose amorphous shadows give the impression of a world that assumes and emits an unending twilight atmosphere. Sordidness, grimness, solitariness, rootlessness become in such a world the substantive conditions that besiege body and soul. A crowded world, it leans mercilessly on its captives, on its victims. Black, sooty buildings; slimy rivers and canals; gray autumn days; "the putrid Petersburg fog" are the constituents of Dostoevsky's "fantastic city." It is a city of nightmare and oppressiveness.

"Tragedy," Dostoevsky wrote, "consists in the consciousness of monstrosity." On its dreary topographical surfaces his world can be studied in terms of nineteenth-century social realism and beyond that, as has been argued, of "the romantic realism" of Balzac or Dickens, who, with Dostoevsky, were the first to realize the potentialities of the milieu and the experience of the city as a subject of fiction, of the city as a new sociological entity. Romanticism comes of age in Dostoevsky's novels as we confront the modern world and as we are compelled to question ourselves. "It asks us [to quote Lionel Trilling] if we are content with ourselves, if we are saved or damned. . . . " This is the overwhelming question that Dostoevsky never ceases to ask. It impels his imagination and stamps his tragic morality, which includes and yet ascends beyond all morality, whether existential, naturalistic, or humanistic. Whatever its paradoxes, it is a morality riveted in a biblical faith that sees the world with humility and charity.

Dostoevsky's vision of evil is never without a counterpart in his vision of salvation. The pull of the profane, though brutally tenacious, is not a unilateral one. Divine possibility—or divine wisdom, as Dostoevsky would no doubt prefer to name it—is never completely absent from a world in which perception of the "dark abyss"—of the abyss of negations—is even half alive. The ongoing struggle between the sacred and the profane permeates Dostoevsky's fictional world. For some of his characters it is a conscious struggle and for others unconscious, but for all of them it is one of deep suffering. One can never ignore the great amount of energy that is spent by Dostoevsky's people. Agitation, both physical and spiritual, is one of their irrevocable characteristics. Even in their most passive state the element of distress, often prompted by that ultimate question Dostoevsky poses at the center of his work, appears relentlessly.

When Dostoevsky's people are not threatened directly by the world around them, they are tormented by nocturnal dreams and psychic discord. And when they are not examining some profound moral problem, it is the problem itself that is examining them. The crystal palace and the anthill image a profane secular world, while the underground images the interior human consciousness, which opposes itself to the world. In their composite unity of fictional form, these images reveal Dostoevsky's conception of "the tragedy of the world." He never stops exploring man's moral "unsightliness." The results of his explorations, as found in his last great novels, register the transformation of his tragic morality into a religious morality.

Crime and Punishment reveals a world of suffocation in which some titanic force has seized one by the throat. It is the death rattle that we hear. Physical properties of this novel underline the impoverishment and the ugliness that end in the killing of life and spirit. Evil is symbolized in a city's sickness. Saint Petersburg can be likened to a dirty prison world—another "house of the dead"—in which its inmates are prone to every thought of escape and freedom at any price. But escape is never concluded and freedom never realized. Self-assertion ends in murder, if not almost in the self-murder of the hero of this novel, Raskolnikov.

A blighted, fearsome atmosphere envelops the world of *Crime and Punishment*: a world of sin, of the boredom of nonbeing, of nausea. Both the physical world of this novel and the human psyche, in their interpenetration, epitomize a living death; Raskolnikov's lodging, for instance, is repeatedly likened to a "coffin." The action takes place in the summer, reinforcing the atmosphere of the city, arid, airless, cramped, gloomy. Moral confusion as a sign of a wrong state of soul is everywhere evident, and is heightened, even indexed, by dimly lit staircases, by foul-smelling taverns. Heat, rain, wind, and lightning assault the flesh. (Shakespeare's words in *Macbeth* come vividly to mind here: "Now o'er the one-half world / Nature seems dead, and wicked dreams abuse / The curtain'd sleep.") Disorder-symbolism extends to eternity itself, which is seen by Svidrigaylov, Dostoevsky's most "calculating tactician of debauchery," as "just a little room . . . something like a village bathhouse, grimy, and spiders in every corner." *Crime and Punishment* is the first of his great quintet in which Dostoevsky earnestly pursues one of his monumental themes and presents one of his direct prophetic warnings: Men of unbelief are haunted men who live in a world with no exit.

In *The Idiot*, Dostoevsky's second major novel, we are pulled into a deeper darkness. Here he gives greater emphasis to an inner, fallen world. Darkness is the overarching image, containing not only the action of this novel but also its sensuality, which ends in murder. Death goes hand-in-hand with "the sickness unto death." Nihilism is in arrogant command; by the end of the novel, whatsoever sacredness, of attitude or of action, exists is routed and annihilated. The main figure, Prince Myshkin, alone and isolated, represents an absolutely powerless innocence for whom an empirical world has nothing but contempt and hatred.

Always preoccupied with the subject of the arrogance of power, Dostoevsky focuses on the power of evil in the world. "From the right of force," he states, "it is not far from the right of tigers and crocodiles." If in *Crime and Punishment* there are glimmerings of repentance, and if the voice of conscience is never completely stilled, in *The Idiot* the impenetrable darkness allows no moment of light. In the terrifying world of this novel we view prisoners of damnation, as if trapped between four walls that, slowly and mechanically, press down on the victims with the sole purpose of crushing them. The external world which Dostoevsky delineates in *Crime and Punishment* is, in *The Idiot*, implicit. That is to say the poetics of the city becomes now the poetics of terror. What we have, in effect, is a demonic mutation, darkly evoked. The evil that is done here is done in darkness, as if too terrible for human eyes. Physical affliction and spiritual deprivation characterize man's venture "down to the depths," there to face head-on the terrible things of the world.

Dostoevsky's aesthetic consciousness was heavily marked by his reading of the Bible, which, as he said, he knew "almost from the cradle." The world of *The Idiot* is Dostoevsky's fictional counterpart of the "bottomless pit" that is described in the Book of Revelation (in verse 2, chapter 9): "And he opened the bottomless pit, and there arose a smoke out of the pit, like the smoke of a great furnace; and the sun and the air were darkened by reason of the smoke of the pit." In his own life, it should be observed, Dostoevsky himself had gone through the furnace of doubt. In *The Idiot* crisis of faith becomes a collective experience of terror.

The novel entitled *The Devils* (also known as *The Possessed*) stands at the mid-center of Dostoevsky's great quintet. And significantly it is the figure of the devil, completely unmasked, on which there is a concentrated focus. The startling powers of Dostoevsky's creative perception illuminate this novel, as he continues his exploration of the world. In this novel his vision surges; it includes the visual elements of the two previous novels and also goes beyond them as Dostoevsky, a master of metaphor, looks into the face not only of the world of evil but also of the prince of that world, Satan. His imagination is at its fiercest point of reference—and of moral rage. It is an unclean, fallen world that he portrays here. He contends with the totality of world-evil, which he renders both in visual and in auditory images. And it is the total effects of Satanism that he seeks to establish.

Dostoevsky's spiritual intuition is perhaps at its highest in *The Devils*, if only because the problem and the experience that he views here are pictured on a gigantic scale. Inevitably any struggle with the devil must be prodigious and all-consuming. Accordingly, in this novel Dostoevsky associates the active power of evil as something lurking in the world and that ignites an unparalleled atmosphere of rapacity, cruelty, bodily pain. Crisis of tragedy and the fury of elements conjoin. This frightful process recalls the summarizing relevance of Shakespeare's words in *King Lear* about the "all-shaking thunder" that "Strike[s] flat the thick rotundity o' the world." *The Devils* is Dostoevsky's most passionate contemplation of the menace of evil that Shakespeare images, and that, in the Book of Job, is shown as that mighty, elemental power which has "gone round about the earth and walked through it." In this novel the world deteriorates into "the vaudeville of devils."

The figure of Satan assumes various faces and human disguises, as seen in the central character of this novel, Stavrogin. Dostoevsky's, and our own, confrontation with Stavrogin is an open confrontation with the full, typical power of evil in the world. Not unlike other diabolic types in the earlier novels, Stavrogin possesses appealing charm, handsomeness, even grandeur, although, to be sure, it is only an atrophied grandeur. The enigma of evil, Dostoevsky is saying, can be fascinating; it can also be terribly misleading and morally fatal. Stavrogin inhabits a world of hideousness, murkiness, fear; often he is linked to the lowest animal life and is imaged as a spider, a vampire, a monster, a wild, clawing beast, a boa constrictor. Children shriek in his presence. Winds hiss and howl. The paths on which he walks are soggy and slippery. He literally dives into the dark abyss. A sinister silence surrounds and a malevolent aura exudes from him. A malignant condition of negation— the negation arising from unbelief—defiles his every action and utterance, or as Dostoevsky writes: "If Stavrogin believes in God, then he doesn't believe that he believes. And if he doesn't believe, then he doesn't believe that he doesn't believe." Whatever and whomever he touches turns into ashes; Stavrogin embodies a burning hell.

Again, in the imagery of this novel, Dostoevsky's poetic qualities are supreme in a Shakespearian sense. The experience of the world of Stavrogin is like the dream of hell that the Duke of Clarence has in Shakespeare's *Richard III*, when "a legion of foul fiends / Environ'd me, and howled in mine ears / Such hideous cries, that with the very noise / I trembling wak'd, and for a season after / Could not believe but that I was in hell." Stavrogin is Dostoevsky's prince of the devils and cosmocrator. Gathered around and inspired by him are lesser satellites, but equally diabolic. Their aims belong to the "algebra of revolution." To overturn mountains, to arouse political troubles, to reduce man into an obedient wretch, to bring unheard-of depravity: these are their obsessive ambitions. "We will proclaim destruction," one of Stavrogin's rebellious dark angels screams. "We'll set fires going. . . . We'll set legends going. . . . Russia will be overwhelmed with darkness, the earth will weep for its old gods. . . . " No words could be more prophetic of the empire of might that Dostoevsky saw devouring the world and turning it into a "furnace of fire."

Dostoevsky's vision of a world cloaked in evil and of man arrested in the dark night of the soul is not a static vision. The meaning of his art does not stop at the infinite edge of darkness. Dostoevsky is not simply a novelist of the last hour. What shines finally in his tragic vision is a moral faith that subsumes and transforms his moral imagination into what Tolstoy calls "religious art." The world of despair and gloom, of sin and dread, as found in *Crime and Punishment*, in *The Idiot*, and in *The Devils*, does not contain the whole of the Dostoevskian world. In the worlds of these three novels, it is, to be sure, a "state of pain" that is one of the main conditions of existence. We are at the point, in fact, where the world is as bad as possible in terms of the range and depth of evil.

For Dostoevsky the world of evil is not an absolute one. There is always the possibility, and the revelation, of the world beyond, at a stage where evil becomes innocence. In the last two novels, *A Raw Youth* and *The Brothers Karamazov*, it is this greater world that is within reach and that holds and conveys the promise of redemption. In these novels we step hesitantly but firmly on holy ground. The temporal abysms of hell are no longer unassailable; the "darkness and the shadow of death" are no longer completely oppressive or spirit-killing. Dostoevsky's last two novels represent a brave leap toward the future, toward the eternal that, as Kierkegaard reminds us, is both the future and the past.

Thus, in these two novels, the world of the past, with its schism, its terror, its demonism, continues to be heard. It is a blasphemous voice that Dostoevsky captures in all of its horror. And yet the voice of the future also now rings more clearly than ever in the world of Dostoevsky. It is a voice which reminds us, as Simone Weil expresses it, that "Faith is the indispensable condition." This voice belongs to Dostoevsky's "messengers of eternity," those mediaries between the world and God.

Though the cityscape of *A Raw Youth* remains harsh and grim, the human experience that transpires here ignites feelings of compassion. Somehow we move upwards in this novel and have glimpses of a better world. Respite, even in the midst of disorder, is now possible. The great spiritual wrestle continues, but the stranglehold of evil is somehow broken, though new dangers and traps are never absent from every new encounter. *A Raw Youth* can be described as the story of a young man gradually awakening to his consciousness of his true relation to his natural father and to his supernatural Father. The renovation of personality is a key factor in this young man's "new life"—of selfhood purified and then liberated from both the "imperial self" and the tyranny of the objective world. The "raw youth" seeks to attain his spiritual identity in a world where "nothing is sacred," or as Dostoevsky was to write in his notebooks: "Disintegration is present everywhere, for everything is falling *apart*, and there are no remaining ties not only in the Russian family, but even simply between people. Even children are apart."

Central to *A Raw Youth* is the recognition of the human need for purgation. The consciousness of God is also allied to this recognition, which in turn is mirrored in the raw youth's search for his lost father and for the absent God. He seeks to find the redeeming love that has eluded him during most of his young life. This fateful deprivation characterizes not only the raw youth but also the young nihilists who appear in the novel. Dostoevsky discloses the never-ending tragedy of a fatherless generation that has lost connection with values, those very values that the raw youth's father has violated or scorned. We have here a morally confused and paralyzed world, appropriately imaged in the novel as a whirlpool.

The role of the profligate father in the life of the raw youth is all-important, and, for Dostoevsky, signifies the consequences of the paternal absence of moral responsibility and how it affects the next generation. Universal moral truths are being emphasized throughout. In the raw youth's father the elements of nature are mixed; passion and compassion collide in his heart, as he, too, slowly sees his own tragic dimension— what he calls his "second self"—in its disordering effects on his own life and on that of his son. The sins of this "second self" intersperse the novel and have a startling impact on the raw youth, who comes, at last, into closer contact with his long-lost father. His dawning recognition of his father's ambivalence and aberrations have, in fact, a purgative counter-effect on the father. In place of murder—and this is the only novel in which the act of murder is absent—we view, in the father, "the gift of tears." Dostoevsky withholds judgment in this novel: Though the father has been both irresponsible and nonresponsible, his fate is not one of malediction. Rather, it is one of spiritual affliction, that sorrowing condition which, to recall Simone Weil again, finds the sufferer "at the foot of the Cross, almost at the greatest possible distance from God."

Distance from God is emphasized, but also shortened, in Dostoevsky's last and greatest novel, *The Brothers Karamazov*. Significantly, the main action occurs in a provincial town (Skotoprigonevsk), far from the musty prison world of Saint Petersburg. Part of the action, too, takes place in a white monastery located at the gates of the town. An alleviating, stronger color contrast is sensitively associated with atmosphere, emotions, or themes, appropriate, it could be said, to Dostoevsky's contention that physical and spiritual beauty can save the world. The darkness symbolism, so pervasive in the preceding novels, is not as pronounced now. The forces of darkness, whether of persons, of places, or of things, are not without their opposing flashes of light, of whiteness and fairness. Those radiant contrasts which form human life and faith itself are distinguishing and differentiating. Struggle, laceration, scoundrelism, rebellion—those by now familiar Dostoevskian subjects—are undeniably present, but so is the growing perception of the "eternal questions." The "Euclidean earthly mind" does not go unchallenged in the world of the Karamazovs.

Dostoevsky's emphasis on the contrasts between the profane and the sacred; between the lecherous father of the Karamazov family, and the old and saintly monk, Father Zossima; between the Karamazovs' house in the center of the town (infested with the rats which the father likes to have for company) and the nearby monastery, with its beautiful flower-beds and serene orderliness, must not go unnoticed. We find ourselves ominously fixed between two worlds, two ways, two voices, two father-hoods. And Dostoevsky moves us to make moral judgments as we view and weigh the drama of two clashing worlds. It is precisely at this point that individual and universal dimensions coincide. The choice between alternatives that we make, the questions that we must answer, the beliefs that we follow, the actions that we take, culminate, Dostoevsky is saying, in murder or in love. "What is hell?" Father Zossima asks, and he goes on to reply: "I maintain that it is the suffering of being unable to love."

Dostoevsky's Russian Orthodox spirituality, embodied in Father Zossima and in the young apprentice monk, Alyosha Karamazov, occupies a major place in this novel. But it is much more than just two religious figures and their spiritual significance that Dostoevsky strives to present. His poetic vision, far too complex for reductionist theories or simplistic conclusions, never ignores the peril and yet the need of penetrating the physical world in order to find ultimate reality. Though Dostoevsky emphasizes the life of belief and holiness, as expressed by Father Zossima, he is also resolutely attuned to the world in all of its frailty. He neither forgets nor underestimates the immediate world that belongs in time and space, even as he recognizes the tenuousness of holiness in its encounter with evil. The moral tensions of his art emerge precisely from this encounter in all its ramifications, and account for the dark colors and torrential passions in Dostoevsky's portrayal of the human world.

The world of the Karamazovs, epitomized by the bestiality of the father, but even more so by the titanic intellectualism of the second son, Ivan, is a fallen world. It is the fate of man in the world of Lucifer which Dostoevsky perceives and renders. Dostoevsky's neglect of the natural world in its iridescence (except as found in several mystical experiences that he includes in his quintet) comes from a tragic view of man trapped in a world that glorifies the rational, the relativistic, the positivistic, and above all, the atheistic. *The Brothers Karamazov* marks the poetic triumph of Dostoevsky's moral and prophetic vision as it dramatizes the spiritual crisis that results from man's belief that his basic and final relationship with things is a material and intellectual relationship.

It is the modern world and its fundamental assumptions about itself that is on trial in Dostoevsky's last novel. As in any crucial trial the questions to be asked (and answered) are of immense consequence. What are we to say about the fact of evil? What are we to do about a world in "confusion and desolation"? What makes Dostoevsky's fiction so demanding is the relentlessness with which such questions are asked, and as they are even more relentlessly dramatized. Inevitably, in the world of Dostoevsky—in the world that is on trial—moral discernment and judgment evolve. *The Brothers Karamazov* contains Dostoevsky's prophecy of evil, and, as in all great prophecy, it enables us to see the evil which is limitless and which turns suffering into violence.

Father Zossima is a witness to the aggressiveness of evil as a force of denial unceasingly building the prison house of unbelief. By teaching that the pain of suffering must be turned into love, Father Zossima is one of the very few characters in Dostoevsky's novels to have escaped from the fate of such a secular prison. His enemy is the archintellectual, the man-god Ivan Karamazov, who defiantly rejects God and refuses salvation; who submits to the tyranny of the world. Even in his death, Father Zossima bears witness against this tyranny, which now seeks to extinguish him with "the breath of corruption." No less than the Evangelist, Dostoevsky knew that another name for Satan is Legion.

~ ෴ ~

The world of Dostoevsky stands in sharp opposition to the modern theories of scientific cosmology. As an artist he approaches and paints the world with an implicitly religious sense. It is his grasp of this religious sense that leads him to certain inviolable criteria of the imagination: He refuses to separate the temporal from the eternal. He insists that man belongs to two orders: to the human, political, historical order and to the divine, eternal order. He discloses time and again that no given life or historical period can escape finiteness, sin, and tragedy. He dramatizes the dreadful tensions that evolve from the collision of these two orders, particularly when man attempts to deny the reality of a divine order. Dostoevsky's novels are essentially about the discord that invades and defiles the human world, when the religious sense is no longer accepted as an intrinsic part of life and when the human act has lost its religious validity.

Dostoevsky's major fiction, in its totality, presents to us an ascending crisis of faith in the modern world. Hence, what he shows with astonishing prophetic power is the great unrest that grips people without belief and that leads them aimlessly up and down dark streets that have no name and no end. In particular what he focuses on is the darkness that he sees increasingly shrouding the life of the soul. Accordingly he portrays physical conditions in terms of a dark chaos, reflecting modern man's spiritual lostness. Of course it is more than an artistic symbolism that Dostoevsky is employing. The fact remains that his is a metaphysical and tragic symbolism, one which contains and exercises a moral conscience. Dostoevsky's "Titans," of course, would do away with such a conscience in order to attain the limitless freedom enabling them to assert that everything is possible and that two and two are five. Before these theories and ideas the world retreats, and it is this retreat that Dostoevsky images in such dark colors and symbols. Chaos, malady, pestilence, madness, murder, blasphemy emblematize for Dostoevsky a world at war.

The world that Dostoevsky reveals is essentially a world of denial, a world without grace, into which his men and women are fatefully "thrown," and in which physical and spiritual suffering prevails. In the Dostoevskian world the quest for self-meaning is invariably a tormenting one since it brings one into direct, naked contact with the deepest currents of his soul. In one way or another Dostoevsky's characters are wrestling with their souls. What results from such an exhausting conflict is either a form of recovery or that of suicide and death. His heroes and, indeed, devils, are desperately, terrifyingly, daringly immersed in their densities—and in the density of the world itself. They move restlessly in a world that seems to have come, or has been brought, to a stop. They seem to have momentarily captured the world and to have made it a prisoner of their ideas. And it is their shadow that enfolds and darkens the world, a fact that perhaps explains the reason why nature in his novels has become an alien. Yet, the world of Dostoevsky does not end at the frontier of nothingness.

Both as a man and as an artist he possessed the "spirit of the gladiator." He knew that tragedy itself was intended to be transcended and transfigured: "Truth dawns in adversity," Dostoevsky wrote in a letter from Siberia (in February 1854). For him the experience of suffering was a dynamic form of purification; inertia, on the other hand, signified cheap consolation. Suffering testifies to the world's imperfection; it should lead to the contemplation of man's limitations and misery. Misery is undoubtedly a preponderant, if not excessive, condition that infects the whole of Dostoevsky's universe. His novels, with a kind of progressive repetition, revolve around and meditate on this condition. He understood that a prophet was concurrently a teacher who must impart his lessons as repeated disciplinary forms of spiritual exercise. And the central lesson that Dostoevsky, as prophet and teacher, keeps repeating in his novels is that which Simone Weil cogently expresses when she writes: "Man's misery consists in the fact that he is not God. Man is continually forgetting this."

D. H. Lawrence describes Dostoevsky as a "marvelous seer," a description that crystallizes the astonishing magnitude of the Russian novelist's vision. As an artist, as a poet—and Dostoevsky spoke of himself as being more of a poet than an artist—he thought in images and was guided by feelings, as his friend Strakhov insisted. In his portrayal of the world it is as a poet that Dostoevsky speaks. In his understanding of the world, in the intrinsic value that he assigns to it and to the men and women who live and die in it, he speaks from a religious ground of being. What must be therefore kept in mind, and stressed, in any attempt to estimate the consummate significance of Dostoevsky's view of the world is that, as a great poet, he accumulates his sensuous perceptions in order to express his spiritual intuitions.

The nature of Dostoevsky's greatness is such that any estimation of his worth can be defined only by asserting that he belongs to the highest constellation of imaginative geniuses that include Dante, Shakespeare, Blake. But not only is he to be included in this constellation. It could also be observed that, if the seismic measure of his importance and relevance is ever to be gauged, these three literary luminaries are included in Dostoevsky. Dante's epic realization of the life of the inward world, Shakespeare's tragic sense of the world, Blake's apocalyptic vision of the world are precisely those realms of imaginative genius that combine and cohere in Dostoevsky's last five novels and that make this world so immense and yet so real that to venture into it is to comprehend The Great Unfathomable. Berdyaev makes far more than just a patriotic claim when he thus declares, "So great is the worth of Dostoevsky that to have produced him is by itself sufficient justification for the existence of the Russian people in the world. . . . "

Moral Discovery

Russell Kirk recalls that as a youth he had purchased in Lansing, Michigan, with his month's allowance, a half set of the works of Joseph Conrad (1857–1924). Later, in his early twenties, while serving in the military, he happened to come across, in Salt Lake City, Utah, the missing half of that broken set, and acquired it out of his private's pay. His appreciation of Conrad's writings endured to the end of his life. In 1993, when his *Politics of Prudence* was published, Kirk returned to Conrad for a parting salute to a novelist who has exceptional appeal to readers interested in the literature of politics.[1]

In calling attention to Conrad's importance, Kirk must also have had in mind those higher values and virtues he ascribed to the moral imagination, which for Kirk aspires "to the apprehending of right order in the soul and right order in the commonwealth."[2] Utilizing the power of the word and the requisite imaginative responsibility, the artist can play an active role in orienting a reader toward something higher, in growing wings to overcome gravity. The artist, in short, has the capacity to fulfill the function of visionaries who also can serve as shepherds of the peoples. The artist's impact can thus contain both a moral and a redemptive element. It is precisely in this sense that Conrad's greatest novels engage the reader in the moral life; and "hold truth enough," as Conrad's narrator in *Under Western Eyes* (1911) observes, "to help the moral discovery which should be the object of every tale." Yet moral discovery is never detached from the moral reality which Conrad unceasingly confronts and which he recreates with astonishing intensity as he takes the reader into "the heart of darkness" and all its perils. In Conrad's fiction, moral discovery must ultimately emerge from moral reality in the extended form of moral courage. This triple process constitutes what one critic calls "the morality of Conrad's imagination." "At the center of vision, then, Conrad locates a profound and desperate opposition be-

---

[1](Bryn Mawr PA: Intercollegiate Studies Institute, 1993) 73.
[2]*Eliot and His Age: T. S. Eliot's Moral Imagination in the Twentieth Century* (New York: Random House, 1971) 7-8.

tween disintegration and the creative engagement stirred to life in his reader."[3] So writes Daniel Melnick in words that further clarify the nature of Conrad's moral imagination, what it is and does, what it leads to and results in.

Conrad's novel *The Secret Agent* (1907) particularly illustrates not only his moral universality but also his moral indictment of the betrayal of order, which a civilized society needs for its existence. His view of "the natural sensibilities of mankind" in this novel, in the context of what he calls "the moral squalor of the tale," is unyielding in "its unsparing indignation and underlying pity," as Conrad wrote in his "Author's Note," published later, in 1920, which pinpoints his aims in writing *The Secret Agent.* Perhaps no other of his novels better confirms George Orwell's assertion that Conrad's most memorable passages and scenes deal with the sea, but that his most mature insights emerge "when he touches dry land."[4]

The Secret Agent records the disintegration, with all the manifold consequences, of both the human community and the human soul. The "personages" who live and move, darkly and sinisterly, in this "monstrous town" variously typify the "revolutionary spirit" that possesses and transforms them into "the devils" of Dostoevsky's novel by that name. No less than the Russian novelist, Conrad has no sympathy for anarchists, applying to them an "ironic method," in "the earnest belief that ironic treatment alone would enable me to say all I felt I would have to say in scorn as well as pity," as he wrote in his note. In relating the story "to its anachronistic end of utter desolation, madness, and despair," he goes on to say, "I have not intended to commit gratuitous outrage on the feelings of mankind." At the heart of Conrad's imaginative genius is the impersonalizing intelligence, the disinterestedness, that gives to his fiction its ability to record what "is fundamental, what is enduring and essential," as Conrad wrote in the preface to *The Nigger of the Narcissus* (1897), and "by the power of the written word, to make you hear, to make you feel—it is, before all to make you *see*."

The Secret Agent evokes the dramatic range and depth of Conrad's moral concerns. A novel of rigorous moral exploration, it forces one to

[3]Daniel Melnick, "The Morality of Conrad's Imagination: *Heart of Darkness* and *Nostromo*," in *Joseph Conrad*, ed. and with an introduction by Harold Bloom, Modern Critical Views series (New York: Chelsea House, 1986) 117.

[4]*As I Please, 1943–1945*, vol. 3 of *The Collected Essays, Journalism, and Letters of George Orwell*, ed. Sonia Orwell and Ian Angus, 389 (New York: Harcourt, Brace, Jovanovich, 1968).

see the things of the world that one has hitherto not seen, or has refused to see, or has feared to see. As such this novel also helps a reader to gain some semblance of "moral discovery" and, in the process, to discern more sharply the deeper meanings of life viewed in the context of assertions that have a confluent and recurrent motif in *The Secret Agent*: "This ain't an easy world"; "life doesn't stand much looking into"; "it may be good for one not to know too much." Conrad's "ironic method" is a dominant and even a passional aspect of this novel; his use of irony becomes, in Thomas Mann's phrase, "a form of morality." The ironic method employed in *The Secret Agent* serves as a contradictory outcome of the novel's happenings—the conscious failure of the novel's men and women to avoid confronting the hard facts of existence, or as Conrad writes: "They refrained from going to the bottom of facts and motives." *The Secret Agent* shows, inexorably, a profound contrast between man and his hopes, fears, wishes, and undertakings and a dark, inflexible fate. Or to put it another way, Conrad's ironic treatment attains his special aim to dislodge the illusions of those who, avoiding or disregarding the data of human existence, embrace false or safe conceptions and remain trans-fixed in the gulf between appearance and reality. The moral momentum and gravity of this novel are to be observed in the stripping away of cherished illusions. Moral discovery triumphs in this process.

The world we encounter in this novel, set in London in the winter and spring of 1886, is draped in shadows and grime, which Conrad likens to a "descent into a slimy aquarium." The first chapter of *The Secret Agent* puts us in contact immediately with a sordid world and people. What we see here and those we meet embody what is morally slothful, evidenced early on in the appearance of Adolf Verloc, shop owner in Soho and *agent provocateur*: "His eyes were naturally heavy; he had an air of having wallowed, fully dressed, all day on an unmade bed." Indolence and idleness seem to shroud his persona, "undemonstrative and burly in a fat-pig style." Even the streets he walks, in pursuit of his devious political purposes, bring into relief Verloc's inner and outer condition. Here, in the midst of "London's topographical mysteries," Verloc has come to a foreign embassy, which employs him as a secret operative, to meet Privy Councillor Wurmt, *Chancelier d'Ambassade*, whose own weary and melancholy presence heightens the purpose of this meeting of two men harboring a purely destructive aim to create social disorder: "the occurrence of something definite which should stimulate their [the police's] vigilance"; "the accentuation of the unrest" through a "series of outrages." Immediately following this initial phase of the meeting, Verloc is then taken to the private room of Mr. Vladimir, first secretary, a smooth and witty favorite in society circles, who quietly but firmly centers on the type of dynamite outrage Verloc is to perpetuate with the help of other anarchists-terrorists: blowing up Greenwich Observatory, "of the first meridian." The foreign official, Russian no doubt, believes that such an outrage would push England to adopt stern political measures of suppression of political crimes: "This country," he insists, "is absurd with its sentimental regard for individual liberty. . . . "

The Secret Agent portrays no single, genuine hero, concentrating instead on a grouping, mostly anarchists, of characters. Conrad's portrayal throughout is steadfast in its objectivity as he seeks to focus on men and women as "shams," without principles and without any loyalty to first principles; and throughout the focus is on moral breakdown, its features and consequences. The novel has, in effect, a parabolic thrust that helps one see through the anarchists in their repulsiveness and degeneracy; indeed, their slothfulness is always magnified, with graphic emphasis on physical extremes, as in the case of Michaelis, "the ticket-of-leave apostle," "with an enormous stomach," as well as in the case of Verloc himself, whose face and figure disclose a "fat-pig style": "He's fat—the animal," Mr. Vladimir thinks to himself during their meeting. They lack precisely that discipline, inner and outer, that society requires if it is to rise above a protoplasmic state.

The discerning moral faculty, as Conrad believed and showed, enables one to discriminate judgmentally between qualities of existence, thought, and character; to distinguish between vice and virtue. *The Secret Agent* depicts both the absence and the entailing costs of this faculty. From a moral angle, *The Secret Agent* is the most fearless of Conrad's novels; his controlled contempt for the anarchists, and for moral lethargy and indifference, is undeviating. Invariably the novelist's moral responsibility is on display. No doubt T. S. Eliot had this dynamic in mind when insisting that Conrad (along with Hawthorne and Dostoevsky) possesses and enacts the "essential moral preoccupation. . . . Evil is rare, bad is common. Evil cannot be perceived but by a very few."[5] *The Secret Agent* has both a ferocity and a momentum of vision in its exposure of agents of moral laceration. Its "dark vision of megalopolis," of London, goes hand-in-hand with its dark vision of moral and spiritual inertia, of stagnancy, with the horrors of which Conrad confronts the reader, who is pressed by Conrad to enlist a profound moral effort in detecting and

---

[5]F. O. Matthiessen, *The Achievement of T. S. Eliot: An Essay on the Nature of Poetry* (London/New York: Oxford University Press, 1958) 24.

gauging the horrors. *The Secret Agent*, in many respects, becomes a kind of catechetical novel, that is, one of moral education.

~ ❧ ❧ ~

For Conrad, the anarchists, who are among the main figures in his novel and whom we first find gathered in the parlor of Verloc's house, personify moral corruption and negation. Whether Conrad is viewing Michaelis, the "ticket-of-leave apostle of humanitarian hopes," or Karl Yundt, the old terrorist, or Comrade Alexander Ossipon, the principal writer of revolutionary leaflets, he depicts them as odious human beings, ugly and malevolent in both demeanor and their abstract discussions, which blend fully with London and its "enormity of cold, black, wet, muddy, inhospitable accumulation of bricks, slates, and stones, things in themselves unlovely and unfriendly to man." From them we can expect nothing of substance or meaning; their common language is one of personal, social, and moral rot. They have no reverence for moral value or for the virtue of loyalty that Conrad reveres. Their world is an abyss of negations, without acceptance or affirmation or any possibility of growth or ascent. Circumvention and circuitousness are its main reference points. It is Stevie, the half-witted brother of Winnie, Verloc's wife, who provides here the image of the world of the anarchists. While seated quietly at a deal table, in the kitchen adjacent to the parlor where the anarchists are meeting, he is to be seen "drawing circles, circles, circles; innumerable circles . . . a coruscating whirl of circles . . . suggest[ing] . . . cosmic chaos. . . . " *The Secret Agent* reveals the chaos in life that honors no value, no principle, no virtue, no tradition. And the anarchists are breeders of chaos, of "that old confusion, which we call chaos, wherein without order, without fashion, confusedly lay the discordant seeds of things," to recall here an old definition.[6]

The Secret Agent is a collective symbol of chaos. Both the revolutionists and the legal and political authorities respect no central value or discipline. They are "hollow men" who exert no moral effort or judgment, preferring to drift in the world. In all matters, their minds and bearing seem to go in circles. Indeed, once the attempted bombing of the observatory takes place, when Stevie, delegated by Verloc as the carrier of the bomb, trips and is blown to pieces, the Assistant Commissioner of Police,

---

[6]See the second definition of "Chaos," in *The Oxford English Dictionary*, ed. James A. H. Murray et al. (London: Oxford University Press, 1933; repr.: 1961) 2:173.

and head of the Special Crimes Department, shows no appreciation of his renowned subordinate, Chief Inspector Heat, in tracking down the culprits—"his appreciation . . . excluded all notion of moral confidence." Human interrelations and discourse throughout lack sincerity at all levels, even as there is a common refusal to address the nexus of cause and effects. Chief Inspector Heat actually uses Secret Agent Verloc by providing him with police protection in exchange for information regarding revolutionaries, their networks, plans, and activities. Moral integrity is an unaffordable luxury, as Conrad brings out in these words spoken by the Chief Inspector to his superior: " 'I must do my work in my own way. . . . When it comes to that I would deal with the devil himself, and take the consequences. There are things not fit for everybody to know.' "

From top to bottom people personify secrecy. The "great personage," Sir Ethelred, who holds political power, meets with the Assistant Commissioner concerning the bomb outrage, and stresses, "don't go into details. I have no time for that. . . . Spare me the details." (In this respect, he is not different from Winnie Verloc, whose "philosophy consisted in not taking notice of the inside of facts.") Moral responsibility and moral action require effort of attention and decision, and in *The Secret Agent* these needs are shunned. Conrad shows us the profound costs of such shunning in the light of fear, apathy, indifference, expediency. And here Conrad addresses the human situation, even as he answers those who pursue the comfort of illusions. Sir Ethelred discloses the political dimension of moral laxity; political leadership, Conrad seems to be saying, can be notoriously shallow and insincere. The Assistant Commissioner, of course, seeks help from "The Personage" in restraining Chief Inspector Heat from protecting a double agent like Verloc. Such protection, he reports, leads to "some species of authorized scoundrelism" blatantly ignoring "the work of anarchism." He seeks, and receives, permission to investigate the circumstances of the bomb outrage personally, knowing as he does that the address on Stevie's clothing, "the only piece of material evidence" discovered and reported by Heat, may lead him to the bottom of the affair. The Assistant Commissioner thereupon proceeds to go to Mr. Verloc's shop, at 32 Brett Street, "sullen, brooding, and sinister."

Conrad's image of the descent into a subterranean world is vividly rendered in his detailed portrayal, at the very middle of the novel, of Mrs. Verloc's mother when she moves to an almshouse. Determined not to burden her daughter and Verloc any longer, and hoping above all that her removal would insure her son Stevie's place in living with his devoted sister, the mother leaves Brett Street. This harrowing journey is likened to a journey in a "Cab of death,"—"Crawling behind an infirm horse . . . on wobbly wheels and with a maimed driver on the box," all this taking place at "night, the early dirty night, the sinister, noisy, hopeless, and rowdy night of South London." This grim journey enters a realm in which, as the mother reflects, "everything decays, wears out . . . the rule of decay affecting all things human and some things divine." The entire scene, which Conrad evokes in a language of pathos, further accentuates the absence of light in a novel in which everything is suffused in murky shadows and in eerie circumstances afflicting life and soul. Conrad's men and women "dwell in the thick of darkness" to recall here a biblical image of "the power of darkness." "It was a bad world. Bad! Bad!" exclaims an agitated Stevie at one point as he contemplates intuitively the scene of "human and equine misery" once the removal to the almshouse has been completed. In the meantime, "the smell of fried fish" permeates the scene and atmosphere—the street like "a slimy aquarium from which the water had been run off."

In the novel's total situation moral darkness torments both man's inner and outer worlds, both body and soul. The men who drift or wallow in this darkness by refusing "not to know too much," who refuse, that is to say, to make any moral effort, thus choose to live in a moral and spiritual vacuum. Conrad, it is interesting to note, dedicated *The Secret Agent* as "this simple tale of the XIX century" to H. G. Wells. It would be more correct to call it a moral tale in which the novelist portrays the results of moral affliction and of life that has no moral center or worth. The refrain "put out the light, and then put out the light" is heard again and again in the novel. Indeed, the only character in the novel aware of impoverishing moral and social conditions is an utterly helpless and expendable Stevie: "You could do anything with that boy, Adolf. . . . He would go through fire for you," Mrs. Verloc exclaims to her husband. Dialogue in the novel, one is often reminded, is muffled, joyless, cruelly detached, a slave of secrecy. Its primary aim is that of always avoiding the reality of truth—"disinclined to look under the surface of things," as Conrad writes.

Any revelation of truth emerges with difficulty, circuitously, as when Chief Inspector Heat, relieved of the case of the bomb outrage, arrives one evening at the "shop of shoddy wares" with the express purpose of speaking privately to an absent Verloc. It is on this particular occasion that Mrs. Verloc gradually learns the news of Stevie's death in Greenwich, unreported by her husband, who seemed to be guarding the incident with the kind of secretiveness appropriate to his work. Heat now shows her, and Winnie identifies, the label sewn on the inside of Stevie's coat with the Brett Street address written in marking ink. Verloc's return to the shop at exactly this point adds to the suspense and fatefulness of the revelation. The two men go into the parlor to discuss matters, as a startled and aroused Mrs. Verloc listens to their conversation through the door's keyhole. Now she "heard nothing but murmurs, whose mysteriousness was less nightmarish to her brain than the horrible suggestions of shaped words. . . . Mrs. Verloc pressed her ear to the keyhole; her lips were blue, her hands cold as ice, and her pale face, in which the two eyes seemed like two black holes, felt to her as if it were enveloped in flames."

For Winnie, truth, no less than life, *ain't easy*, she having to recognize the cruel and irreducible fact that her husband had enlisted Stevie to carry the bomb in the attempt to blow up Greenwich Observatory, the task delegated to Verloc by Mr. Vladimir. The intense "agitation of rage and despair" fixed her pose into one of "perfect immobility." One realizes, too, that Winnie's sole reason for marrying Verloc, in the first place, was her belief that he would be a devoted guardian of Stevie. But Stevie, of course, carrying a detonator supplied by the Little Professor, had stumbled against the root of a tree and fell, "blown to fragments in a state of innocence and in the conviction of being engaged in a humanitarian enterprise." Winnie's habit of not taking notice of the inside of facts has now been equally sundered, even as her notion of marital stability has been destroyed. She now experiences not only the death of a brother but also the death of a marriage—of a husband, the consummate Secret Agent, who, she feels, had betrayed "a genuine wife" and "a genuine brother-in-law," as he had betrayed many others, in England and abroad, during the period of eleven years he acted as a secret agent. The death of Stevie marks, for Winnie, the death of an illusion, as she drops "the gold circle of the wedding ring" into a dustbin.

From this point on the novel moves dramatically to its concluding scenes and chapters (particularly the eleventh chapter, "one of the most astonishing triumphs of genius in fiction," declares F. R. Leavis[7]). The emphasis in this chapter is on Verloc, not only on some of his inner thoughts regarding the fateful happening, but also on some of the thoughts he expresses to his wife, who is shuddering and hiding her face in her hands. "I didn't mean any harm to come to the boy," he insists, for in fact he never expected Stevie to stumble within five minutes of being left to himself. Verloc, too, is a victim of illusion, believing fully in "being loved for himself." Clearly he never understood the depth of his wife's

---

[7]*The Great Tradition: George Eliot, Henry James, Joseph Conrad* (London: Chatto & Windus, 1960) 214.

love for her brother, "since it was impossible for him to understand it without ceasing to be himself." Illusions, even the simplest ones, do not easily vanish, as another of Verloc's assertions shows: "Do be reasonable, Winnie. What would it have been if you had lost me?" The unfolding events in *The Secret Agent*, particularly in the concluding chapters, illustrate remarkably the truth of what Joyce Cary, in *Art and Reality*, writes about the moral dimension of art: "A novelist creates a world of action and therefore he has to deal with motive, with morality. . . . The story gives the meaning, the morality."[8]

~ ❦ ❦ ~

The effects of moral blindness, as the lives and fates of Adolf and Winnie Verloc demonstrate, are staggering. His belief that he has been loyal to his employers, to the cause of social stability, and to his affection embodies grand illusions for which he pays with his life. Clearly both husband and wife have been dishonest with each other, masking their motives in the most insidious ways: "They refrained from going to the bottom of facts and motives." During their marriage of seven years, he has kept his activities secret from her; and she has never fully admitted to him that she married him only to provide home and security for young and vulnerable Stevie. Winnie thus feels herself to be a betrayed woman; he, the victim of an unexpected catastrophe that ends his career—he is somewhat over the age of forty—as a secret agent, and now suddenly making him subject to "the knife of infuriated revolutionists." But his career never meant anything to her, and she knew very little about its complexion and needs. What she did know was that she had to insure Stevie's security at any cost. And the man who now is speaking, her husband, she sees as one who took her brother away from his home *and* from her to murder him. Her "militant love" and care for Stevie are even likened to a big battle, which she has lost because of her husband.

Throughout this agonizing and muted evening encounter Mrs. Verloc fixes her solitary thoughts on Stevie: "The poor boy had been taken out and killed. The poor boy was dead." And she reaches this unalterable conclusion: "There was no need for her to stay there, in that kitchen, in that house, with that man—since the boy was gone for ever." The entire encounter is exhausting for Verloc, who flings himself on the sofa in the parlor, overcome by his wife's "sulking in that dreadful overcharged silence." Winnie, for her part, "remained irresolute, as if scrupulously

---

[8](New York: Harper & Brothers, 1958) 149, 154.

aware of something wanting . . . for the formal closing of that transaction."

This "closing" comes with catastrophic vengeance in the final pages. No amount of quoting or summarizing can do justice to what unfolds in the story of the Verlocs as all their idols of illusion come crashing down. A tragic poetry triumphs here, of a Shakespearian magnitude. Verloc "reposing [on the sofa] in that pathetic condition of optimism induced by an excess of fatigue," invites Winnie to come and join him, with that peculiar tone that has "the note of wooing." But their love is in essence a corrupt love. Little does he realize her hatred for him, or the power of clarity and cunning and purposefulness that dictates her every thought and gesture of revenge. A macabre suspensefulness permeates this scene, "the formal closing," as Winnie Verloc, who even assumes an uncanny resemblance to Stevie, passes on toward the sofa, where Verloc "was lying on his back and staring upwards." What he sees, almost in chiaroscuro, has frightening impact on him: "He saw partly on the ceiling and partly on the wall the moving shadow of an arm with a clenched hand holding a carving knife." It is now too late for him to dodge the death blow from a woman who "had gone raving mad—murdering mad," as she enacts, with steely clarity and fierce determination, "Stevie's urgent claim on her devotion." "The knife was already planted in his breast," Conrad writes. "It met no resistance on its way. . . . Mr. Verloc, the Secret Agent, turning slightly on his side with the force of the blow, expired without stirring a limb in the muttered sound of the word 'Don't' by way of protest."

The death of Adolf Verloc marks still another death of illusion. Conrad merges these two states of death with the "Tic, tic, tic" of the clock that Winnie hears, in the mystery of time, and the dark drops of blood that she sees, in the fact of extinction, falling on the floorcloth. A now frightened but comprehending Winnie ("afraid of the gallows") beholds the sight of her husband: "He was nothing," as we are again reminded by Conrad that illusions and nothingness are synonymous, that illusion ends in nothing. Winnie's own fate, as recorded in these last pages, dramatizes, by reemphasizing, the consequences of illusion. As such her ending merges as a kind of fictional constatation, that is, as a process of verification. Winnie has thoughts of death, or of escape abroad. The note of nothingness in the novel resounds: "She had nothing. . . . She was alone in London: and the whole town of marvels and mud, with its maze of streets and its mass of lights, was sunk in hopeless night, rested at the bottom of a black abyss"—the abyss of negations one might add.

Her chance meeting on the street with Comrade Ossipon, "the robust anarchist" inordinately "interested in women," reinforces the constatation. The instinct of self-preservation prompts Winnie to see Ossipon as "a radiant messenger of light." But Ossipon's motives are neither sincere nor benevolent: He is thinking of material benefits, the business value of the shop and the amount of money the widow of Mr. Verloc has in the bank. Ossipon still labors under the misapprehension that it was Verloc who died in Greenwich Park, as he skeptically eyes Mrs. Verloc, "veiled in a black net," hanging on his arm, and entreating him to join her in an immediate flight to the Continent. Increasingly he feels "himself losing his footing in the depths of this tenebrous affair. . . . But there was the rest. These savings. The money!" His hunger for "the money"—"We revolutionaries are not rich," he exclaims—prompts him to propose that they take the 10:30 train from the Waterloo Station to Southampton, the boat leaving there for France at about midnight. But Winnie insists that they return first to the shop on Brett Street in order to shut the door, which she had forgotten to do earlier. And so they now return together, he thinking opportunely that she might have left the money in the drawer. The light in the parlor, where Verloc lies dead on the sofa, not having been put out, she asks the revolutionist to tend to this task, even pushing him forward into the parlor.

Discovering Verloc's body, Ossipon rids himself of his misapprehension, and even sees himself as a victim of madness. The full sight of Verloc's body makes him retch violently. Now, too, he realizes that Winnie is Verloc's executioner, though he is also "terrified out of all capacity for belief or disbelief in regard to this extraordinary affair." Terror fills him as she begs him to help her, thinking that she possibly has another knife, this time for him. And only now does he realize it was Stevie, "the degenerate—by heavens!" who got killed. Desperate for a savior, she now entrusts him with the new pigskin pocketbook containing the money Verloc had given to her to tide her over until he finished a probable jail sentence, a consequence he saw as inevitable for his actions as a secret agent. Ossipon, in any case, accompanies her to the Waterloo Station for the train that would then take her to Southampton and the cross-Channel boat for France.

Author of a medical pamphlet, lecturer on the social aspects of hygiene to working men's clubs, admirer of Cesare Lombroso's theories on the psychology of the criminal, especially the relation between a criminal's physical constitution and his pathological nature, Ossipon views Winnie "scientifically" as an atavistic criminal: "the sister of a degenerate, a degenerate herself—of a murdering type." Eventually they enter one of the empty compartments of the train, which soon begins to move. "He felt the train roll quickly, rumbling heavily to the sound of the woman's loud sobs, and then crossing the carriage in two long strides he opened the door deliberately and leaped out." Comrade Ossipon, anarchist, "flush of safe banknotes as never before in his life," makes his escape—a savior neither to Winnie Verloc nor to mankind. His actions further exemplify the truth of the words of one critic, Chull Wang: "What the anarchists are doing in the society is an outrageous betrayal of humanity."[9] Of the fate of Winnie Verloc we finally learn from these last lines of a paragraph in a newspaper account, now ten days old, under the caption, "Suicide of Lady Passenger from a Cross-Channel Boat": "An impenetrable mystery seems destined to hang for ever over this act of madness or despair."

~ ❦ ~

The concluding chapter of *The Secret Agent* finds Ossipon and the Professor, "the Perfect Anarchist," together in the latter's shoddy room. Their discussion in the room and then during their omnibus ride to and the time they spend in the Silenus Restaurant underlines the moral debasement that the anarchists and their actions personify. The Professor wants to exterminate first "the great multitude of the weak" as the source of the world's problems, with only the Professor remaining as a saving force. Ossipon, on the other hand, speaks of eternity as "a damned hole." The entire conversation is no less morose than their immediate surroundings. Ossipon is in a state of total confusion and knows not where he is going, not even thinking of adding to his "collection of women." The note of nothingness rings out again in the penultimate paragraph of the novel: "Comrade Ossipon walked without looking where he put his feet, feeling no fatigue, feeling nothing, seeing nothing. . . . " The "incorruptible Professor" is also seen, in the very last paragraph, "averting his eyes from the odious multitude of mankind. He had no future." His thoughts, Conrad tells us, "caressed the images of ruin and destruction," as he walked "terrible in the simplicity of his idea calling madness and despair to the regeneration of the world."

---

[9]See chap. 4, "The Secret Agent," of Chull Wang, "Betrayal and Moral Imagination: A Study of Joseph Conrad's Five Major Works" (diss., University of Maryland, 1990). I am indebted to Dr. Wang for his many and rich insights into Conrad's views and treatment of moral issues in the major novels (*Lord Jim, Nostromo, The Secret Agent, Under Western Eyes,* and *Victory*).

From a dramatic point of view *The Secret Agent* could have ended, powerfully, with the murder of Verloc. But such an ending would be too simplistic in its melodrama. A moral tale requires dramatic commentation that more directly involves the reader in deliberation and judgment, appropriate to the purpose and scope of a moral tale. In the last two chapters of *The Secret Agent*, which form a kind of coda, Conrad is making sure that his reader will not be lulled by the visual power and verbal magic of the novel. There are serious lessons that have to be registered, and moral judgments that have to be crystallized with absolute decisiveness of meaning. Conrad's allegiance to the moral imagination receives added confirmation here. Clearly he is aware that a reader should not "walk in darkness," and that it is the novelist's task to help the reader pass beyond "the shadow line" in facing up to ultimate moral issues.

In the working of the revolutionary mind Conrad recreates the abstract and perverse forms of ideology, which Russell Kirk defines as "a passionate endeavor to overthrow the spiritual and moral order."[10] Conrad enables a modern reader to see anarchism as the consummation of nihilism and its program of absolute denial and rejection of life and spirit. The ideology of anarchism, as this novel's events and outcome bear out, completes and advances nihilism to its ultimate point of negation through destruction. Anarchy is what comes beyond nihilism: the final outrage, the final debasement, the final apostasy. Anarchy can thus be called the final movement of revolution and terror, as one astute interpreter observes, in short, the end-stage when anarchism brings the movement which nihilism began to its logical conclusion.[11] Indeed, the anarchists in *The Secret Agent* represent a subhumanism in which madness and despair prevail and rule.

In *The Secret Agent* Conrad is neither preacher nor propagandist; he is a master of art-speech, intuitively and tensively responsive to social and moral issues, which he renders in plot, action, scene, dialogue, character. "The function of the novelist," again to recall Joyce Cary, "is to make the world contemplate and understand itself, not only as a rational being but as experience of value, as a complete thing."[12] Joseph

---

[10]*Enemies of the Permanent Things: Observations of Abnormity in Literature and Politics* (LaSalle IL: Sherwood Sugden, 1969) 164.

[11]Eugene (Fr. Seraphim) Rose, *Nihilism: The Root of the Revolution of the Modern Age* (Forestville CA: Fr. Seraphim Rose Foundation, 1994) 88.

[12]Joyce Cary, "Morality and the Novelist," in *Selected Essays*, ed. A. G. Bishop (New York: St. Martin's, 1976) 153.

Conrad fulfills this function, this responsibility, in *The Secret Agent*. If Conrad is concerned with the order of human destiny, he is also concerned with the order of the human soul. *The Secret Agent* gives us an astonishing picture of what has gone wrong with the order of the soul in the "antagonist world" in which "the imperative of relevance" discards life of the soul. The "sordid surroundings and moral squalor of the tale," to use Conrad's words, "lie simply in the outward circumstances of the setting." It is as a moral tale that *The Secret Agent* enters and illuminates the inward terrain.

In the writing of this novel, Conrad insisted, "I was simply attending to my business. . . . with complete self-surrender"—in other words, with complete concentration, purposefulness, seriousness, honesty. These qualities, which are the stuff of the moral imagination, command a great novelist to speak to our time, to our condition, to our conscience—and to our soul.

Spiritual Heroism

During the past twenty years, ever since the publication of *The Gulag Archipelago*—the first of three volumes in English translation appeared in 1973—Aleksandr Solzhenitsyn (b. 1918) has been subjected to sharp criticism in the West. The intelligentsia frequently brand him as a moral fascist. These denigrators can best be described, to apply his own words, as "advanced people," "smatterers." For the most part, they are liberal ideologues who are deeply, but not surprisingly, disturbed by Solzhenitsyn's savage indictment, in *The Gulag Archipelago*, of Marxism-Leninism. His nonfictional, or publicistic, writings in particular—for example, his *Letter to the Soviet Leaders* (1974) and *A World Split Apart* (1978)—and his worldview in general are early examples of what we now designate as not being politically correct. He has chosen to reject what the liberal mind finds requisite and sacrosanct in the doctrine of unlimited material and social progress, in Enlightenment thought and absolute reason, in utopian and millennial dreams of a worldly paradise.

Solzhenitsyn has chosen, that is to say, to embrace the religious idea, the moral life and ethical life, in their Christian contexts and ramifications. His indictment of Communism is inherently a metaphysical indictment of the modern secular world itself. It is an indictment of a totalitarian system, of a political process, that reduces human beings to things and, in effect, disinherits them morally and spiritually. Communism crystallizes, for Solzhenitsyn, a crisis of modernism in which "men have forgotten God." As such Communism is emblematic of an inclusive titanism that, Solzhenitsyn insists, has its origin in "the flaw of a consciousness lacking all divine dimension." Modernism signifies imprisonment of mind and spirit in uniform ideology, of which the Marxist-Leninist system is the overarching model. Solzhenitsyn belongs to that small and brave band of visionaries who find in political and social disorder the absence of spiritual principles and religious belief. Above all, he exposes the dangers and consequences of modern sociopolitical ideology in an "era of systems, institutions, mechanisms and statistical averages," as Vàclav Havel expresses it.

Consistently and courageously, Solzhenitsyn has focused on the evils of ideology in the modern world; has shown how ideology violates the laws of a moral universe. This defiance, this "dissidence," made him an enemy not only of the Soviet Union but also of liberal and radical groupings in the West. The culmination of a modernism that negates man's moral and spiritual meaning, the Soviet system epitomized for him the modern world in all of its extremisms. In the Soviet system, in short, Solzhenitsyn was to discern a modernism adrift—an unchecked modernism triumphantly proclaiming the death of God, of the soul, of all moral categories and criteria, and of human uniqueness. As Solzhenitsyn indicates in his critical writings, Communism is the apex of a modernism beginning in the Renaissance and developing in concrete forms from the Enlightenment of positivism and scientism. The Russian Revolution of 1917 was to continue and to consummate, in the most dramatic historical ways, the French Revolution of 1789, as the "Red Wheel," in Solzhenitsyn's words "rolls onward, lit by the conflagration, / unrestrained / unstoppable, / crushing everything in its path."[1]

What the liberal mind in the West has found so objectionable in Solzhenitsyn is not so much his diagnosis of the bankruptcy of the Soviet system per se, but rather his total rejection of the modern liberal *Zeitgeist* that Communism was to enact at the most inhumane levels. Solzhenitsyn ultimately exposes the debasement of modernism, of the modern myths of unlimited experimentation and advances. His *oeuvre* reveals the Soviet face of modernism in all its intrinsic terror and cruelty. The liberal mind, especially as it is embodied in the "terrible simplifiers," denies the sovereignty of any absolute standards, choosing as it does to travel on the road to ease and expediency and to chase unceasingly the illusion of an earthly paradise. His metaphysics—his insistence on the needs of the soul, on repentance and self-limitation, on the moral virtues—are to the liberal mind an abomination. It can neither tolerate nor in any way accept Solzhenitsyn's stress on a transcendent realm of reality.

At one time largely receptive to and even admiring of Solzhenitsyn's mythopoetic genius, his fictive imagination and forms, the liberal mind instinctively rejects his worldview, his principles of order, his spiritual affirmations. At that point of his witness when Solzhenitsyn was to speak out on the eternal questions affecting human destiny, openly challenging ideologues of modernism who spurn religion and metaphysics, he was to seal his fate in terms of how liberals reacted to his "warning to the West." In the beginning they were willing to accept the genius of his art,

---

[1]Quoted from "Aleksandr Solzhenitsyn," in *European Writers: The Twentieth Century*, ed. George Stade (New York: Knopf, 1990) 13:3210a. Alexis Klimoff is the author of the concise and helpful entry on the Russian writer.

but in time they would reject the "living principle" of his vision in its totality: the wonderful fusion of art and thought that pushes the imagination beyond style and technique—that, in short, activates the full powers of vision in their full moral thrust and pertinence. "To create today," Albert Camus tells us, "is to create dangerously. And publication is an act, and that act exposes one to the passions of an age that forgives nothing."[2] Solzhenitsyn exemplifies Camus's perception of the artist who heeds a higher calling and speaks to the human condition judgmentally, morally, spiritually.

In essence, then, Solzhenitsyn addresses himself to the ideology of modernism—of malaise, decadence, disorder. Ideology, Russell Kirk reminds us, "is the politics of passionate unreason," which is precisely what Solzhenitsyn condemns. Inevitably he has had to pay the price of his challenge to the liberal mind-set as the reigning ideology in modern times. In Solzhenitsyn we have not only a poet but also a prose writer, a man of letters, a visionary who assays the crisis of values as a crisis of consciousness. His vision is so piercing and troubling, so censorial of modern secular society and culture, of "a world split apart," that inevitably a challenged liberal power center strikes back, angrily and desperately. Clearly Solzhenitsyn has unsettled the liberal mind more than any other writer in this century. His is an absolute censure of the liberal superstructure—its sacred texts, doctrines, agents, architects. "In the end, his kind of conservatism, like that of his *ancien régime* predecessors, strikes me as unconvincing."[3] Thus writes the Harvard historian Richard Pipes, his words representative of the animosity against Solzhenitsyn among liberal American intellectuals, who doubtlessly view him as one of their sternnest critics and judges.

To correct the recurring misunderstandings and misinterpretations of the Russian writer's work and thought is the major aim of Professor Edward Ericson's *Solzhenitsyn and the Modern World* (1993). To reappraise and revalidate his reputation and influence is still another, ancillary aim. As such this is a worthy book, with a worthy subject and a worthy purpose. It is a singularly comprehensive book, painstakingly researched and argued with courage and conviction, as one would expect from the

---

[2]"Create Dangerously," in *Resistance, Rebellion, and Death*, trans. Justin O'Brien (New York: Knopf, 1961) 251.

[3]This sentence appears in Professor Pipes's review of *A World Split Apart* in *Encounter* 52/6 (June 1979): 56.

author of an earlier, well-received study, *Solzhenitsyn: The Moral Vision* (1980),[4] and who, with Solzhenitsyn's cooperation, also abridged *The Gulag Archipelago* (1985) in one volume. This new book is characterized by critical strenuousness and discrimination. Its exposition and commentation show an acuteness of insight that emerges from concentrated reflection and analysis. Clarity of expression and lucidity of thought are reciprocating qualities that empower its style and content. Solzhenitsyn could not have a more gifted American commentator.

Especially admirable is the sense of devotion to critical and historical truth that Ericson brings to his book and that engages the reader's attention. Here we have a critic who has uncompromising principles and values, as well as sincerity and fortitude. His book helps to restore Solzhenitsyn's meaning to the modern world, even as it becomes for readers who are subjected to ideological brainwashings in the house of intellect an uncommonly restorative critical experience. In fact, the book should occasion rejoicing among those readers who care about principles and values incessantly derided in liberal and intellectual circles. To these readers Ericson's book will convey the stimulus and the courage to endure in the face of a monolithic liberal establishment that shapes public opinion and policy. Ericson's portrayal of Solzhenitsyn vindicates the Russian's relevance to our civilization. By the time one has reached the last page of the book one knows that the liberal mind does not have the last word concerning either Solzhenitsyn's prophetic vision or his prophetic importance. Surely we owe a great deal to Ericson for what he has done in this timely book and also for providing us with an inspiring example of authorial integrity and critical perspicacity. No less than Solzhenitsyn himself, Ericson gives us hope that the human spirit cannot be made a permanent prisoner in the gulag, political or intellectual.

That "we should develop our soul" before we do anything else in life is ultimately Solzhenitsyn's basic premise. And it is one that most antagonizes the liberal mind. If, therefore, Solzhenitsyn is fundamentally an "anti-ideologist," his work, as Ericson shows, has the final virtue of taking us beyond ideology: beyond, that is, the oppressive borders of secular, gnostic, and progressivist ideologies seeking to substitute a political religion of immanentism for a supertemporal religion of transcendence. In striving to preserve "unspoiled, undisturbed and undistorted the image of eternity with which each is born," Solzhenitsyn defies the anthropocentrism that is at the vortex of the liberal faith. This defiance

---

[4]See my review in *Christianity and Literature* 30/1 (Fall 1981): 68-71.

inevitably invites the liberals' hostility to Solzhenitsyn, and to all others who question anthropocentric postulates. And it has led to the politicizing of Solzhenitsyn criticism and to the consequential distortions of his thought. His critical fate echoes that of Simone Weil and of T. S. Eliot, two earlier conservative visionaries who dared to champion a religious and spiritual perspective. Thus, Simone Weil's Christian Hellenism and her unrelenting allegiance to "the supernatural power of the sacraments" have long ignited liberal critics' trivialization of her metaphysical views, as my examination of Robert Coles's *Simone Weil: A Modern Pilgrimage* in part 1, "Advocates of Debasement," seeks to show. In T. S. Eliot's case, one sees no end to liberals' mauling of his sociological writings—for example, *The Idea of a Christian Society* (1940) and *Notes towards the Definition of Culture* (1948).[5] Clearly the "enemies of the permanent things" are notorious for their wrath, and their attack on "the dark side of Solzhenitsyn" as "reactionary, authoritarian, and charismatic" is both typical and symptomatic of how "the men of the Enlightenment" react to any criticism of the liberal credo.

Ericson meets head-on the attacks on Solzhenitsyn with irrefutable arguments. He is no apologist but a defender who looks at the total record with critical and historical astuteness. His documentation, both notes and works cited, encompasses fifty printed pages, and he makes no accusations or claims without the support of his sources. Ericson conclusively debunks some of the bad myths that have been concocted regarding Solzhenitsyn's opinions. That he is "a reluctant democrat" rather than an antidemocrat is a point that Ericson also makes with considerable argumentative force: "Solzhenitsyn laments the weakness of the modern West, but never does he attribute the cause of it to democracy. To secularism, atheism, materialism—yes. But not to democracy." That, in addition, Solzhenitsyn is a militant "Russian nationalist" is, as Ericson reveals, an unfounded charge, and one that ignores (or flagrantly misconstrues) the moral foundation of Solzhenitsyn's insistence on "self-limitation as the supreme principle for every individual and nation." Robert Conquest rightly remarks that *Solzhenitsyn and the Modern World* is the "most definitive" work on the Russian writer's impact and views.

For Solzhenitsyn the condition of the soul is the key to some of the major problems with which the Russian people must wrestle: "The healing of our souls!" he declares in his *Letter to the Soviet Leaders.*

---

[5]See my discussion, "T. S. Eliot and the Critique of Liberalism," in *The Courage of Judgment* (Knoxville TN: University of Tennessee Press, 1982) 85-108.

"Nothing now is more important to us after all we have lived through, after our long complicity in lies and even crimes." An extremely impressive section in Ericson's book is his analysis of Solzhenitsyn's *Rebuilding Russia: Reflections and Tentative Proposals* (1991). Here he carefully clarifies what Solzhenitsyn is saying and also argues that his remedies for Marxist-Leninist disasters are both realistic and pragmatic. The following paragraph is worth quoting in full, for it underscores the special qualities of Ericson's critical insight and orientation:

> Solzhenitsyn's advice to reject the party system of politics is not the only point on which his ideas are akin to those of the American Founding Fathers. . . . He has often spoken with open admiration about early American democracy, particularly because he discovers there a recognition that human beings are morally responsible before God to order a good society. Post-Enlightenment ideologies have led societies away from this fundamental condition of the moral universe. . . . Clearly, Solzhenitsyn believes that Russia today can learn more about a wholesome democracy from early America than from contemporary America. It would be a curious provincialism of present-mindedness—or, perhaps, a zealotry for the doctrine of progress—to hold that every single deviation in American democracy from its original pattern marks an unquestionable improvement.

Ericson's concluding chapter evaluates the extent and the depth of Solzhenitsyn's influence. The role of *The Gulag Archipelago* in the collapse of the Soviet Union is perhaps his greatest accomplishment. Yet, as Ericson emphasizes, his contribution has an influence of ascending magnitude: "Like a stone dropped in a pond, Solzhenitsyn's influence is seen first in the Gulag itself, then in Russia as a whole, then in the larger Communist bloc of nations, then rippling out through the whole world." Such is his achievement, Viktor Astafyev states, that this "'greatest writer of our time'" is also "'a hero of the spirit.'"[6] Ericson's book vindicates this high praise. Whether it is the religious revival now occurring in Russia, or the ways in which Solzhenitsyn has inspired, for instance, Václav Havel, the Czech playwright and political statesman, the French "New Philosopher" Bernard-Henri Levy, or David Walsh, the American political scientist and author of *After Ideology*, which I discuss at the beginning of the third part of this book—in addition to his impact on all those who are concerned with the moral breakdown and the massive dehumanization

---

[6]Quoted in Edward E. Ericson, Jr., *Solzhenitsyn and the Modern World* (Washington DC: Regnery Gateway, 1993) 343.

in the Western world—Ericson shows how profound Solzhenitsyn has been in his influence. As Ericson writes:

> If many intellectuals have turned a deaf ear in his direction, he is not without influence upon his contemporaries. . . . Solzhenitsyn will leave the world better than he found it. Whether we have read him or not, whether we revile him or honor him, he has affected our lives. And he has affected them for good.

It is the supreme value of Edward Ericson's book that it enables a reader to appreciate Solzhenitsyn not only as a moral thinker but also as a prophetic visionary writer—as one who, seeing more than he should see, speaks forth the deepest truths about human experience and destiny. The modern scientific world, which in Simone Weil's words is "perfectly compatible . . . with absolutely everything except what is authentically spiritual,"[7] too often ignores prophetic truths. Invariably a prophetic writer like Solzhenitsyn has to confront both the wall of indifference and the fury of rejection, as he tenaciously pursues his prophetic mission with an immediate and yet ultimate sense of involvement, attentiveness, concern.[8] Solzhenitsyn honors and continues that illustrious line of prophetic writers which, in the realm of poetry, includes Virgil, Dante, Milton, and Blake, and which, in the halls of fiction, counts Tolstoy as prophet of the flesh and Dostoevsky as prophet of the soul. Aleksandr Solzhenitsyn is a prophet of the modern world whose central warning cannot be ignored or silenced except at the greatest peril: "Nothing worthy can be built on a neglect of higher meanings and on a relativistic view of concepts and culture as a whole."[9]

---

[7]Quoted from "Scientism—A Review," in *The Simone Weil Reader*, ed. George A. Panichas (New York: David McKay Co., 1977) 296-97.

[8]See Abraham J. Heschel's *The Prophets* (New York/Evanston: Harper & Row, 1962); and also Cecil Maurice Bowra, "The Prophetic Element," in *In General and Particular* (Cleveland/New York: World Publishing, 1964) 223-40. Sir Maurice Bowra's essay, originally his presidential address to the English Association, 1959, deals with poetry and prophetic vision.

[9]Aleksandr Solzhenitsyn, "The Relentless Cult of Novelty and How It Wrecked the Century," *The New York Times Book Review*, 7 February 1993, 17. The translation of the text of Solzhenitsyn's acceptance remarks, upon receiving the medal of honor for literature from the National Arts Club in New York City, is by his sons, Ignat and Stephen.

Orientation toward Something Higher

Two modern American teachers and critics who can now be honored as Sages and, indeed, included among the *Sacri Vates*, are Irving Babbitt and Richard Weaver. One who in any way studies two recently reissued books, Babbitt's *Character and Culture: Essays on East and West* (1940; 1995) (originally titled *Spanish Character and Other Essays*) and Weaver's *Visions of Order: The Cultural Crisis of Our Time* (1964; 1995) will need very little convincing as to the appropriateness of the sapiential ascription. To read these books again, or even for the first time, is to make contact with men of vision who are quintessentially men of wisdom. Perhaps at no time of our history do we have more urgent need for wisdom than now. For the wisdom we gain here is both salvific and restorative; it enables us to climb the ladder of illumination. Babbitt likens this process to "the ascending path of insight and discrimination"; Weaver describes it as the need to "have something ascending up toward an ultimate source of good." This moving upward requires strenuous effort, and its rewards are to be found in the higher experiential contexts of what is self-cleansing and self-disciplining.

Moral indolence and apathy, both Babbitt and Weaver stress, are forces of gravity that need to be quelled if one is to fly beyond the nets of naturalism and temperamental excesses. Such ascent, Babbitt stresses, is an intrinsic part of the "aspiration to rise above the impermanent." He sees this entire process in the light of individual character, and especially as to how this process relates to its making. Also emphatically aware of individual character, Weaver examines it in direct relation to the larger cultural picture, to what he designates as "the discriminations of a culture." It can be said that Babbitt addresses first and foremost the problem of man, of individual character and destiny; Weaver, the problem of culture—"the cultural crisis of our time." To make this particular contrast is not to lessen Babbitt's larger civilizational concerns, even as his magisterial book *Democracy and Leadership* will thoroughly indicate. Still, in Babbitt the voice we hear is mainly that of the teacher speaking to his students. "For Babbitt's service as teacher," Austin

Warren writes of his Harvard mentor, "transcended his doctrine." If Babbitt begins with *anthropos*, and Weaver begins with *paideia*, both ultimately meet in absolute allegiance to *humanitas*, which in the end allies them in their search for *aristeia* of character and culture.

Of Weaver, Russell Kirk remarks, with characteristic pungency and insight: "Meant to expose and restrain the illusions of our century, his books and his teaching were instruments for action." He goes on to say that, for Weaver, order was an "austere passion: the inner order of the soul, the outer order of society." These words could equally apply to that great conservative mind in the earlier years of the twentieth century, Babbitt. Neither Babbitt nor Weaver ceased to seek after principles of order in a century of disorder. For Babbitt the Great War of 1914–1918 emblematized the symptoms and portents of modern disorder, even as he, an admirer of Aristotle, goes back to Jean-Jacques Rousseau as the primary architect of the scheme of disorder in the modern world in the form of unchecked romanticism. For Weaver, World War II unmasked the spirit of disorder, and he, an admirer of Plato, goes back to William of Ockham (1285–1349) as a progenitor of disorder in the form of nominalism. To view Babbitt and Weaver together, in continuity, so to speak, is to view two visionary thinkers deeply concerned with the order of a humane civilization and the order of human character. In their conjoining perceptions and interpretations of the rhythm of disintegration and the schism of the soul they centered on the crisis of modernism as a crisis of disorder.

What especially ties together these two thinkers is their defense of the idea of the personal realm and the sociocultural realm. And what both sought to find as a coalescing force in the two realms was the element of stability, or that integral metaphysical force which checks the impulse of disorder that never ceases to assault life. Their writings, whatever the differences in style and in specificities of emphasis, are responsive to the virtue of character—the character of man, the character of culture, the character of the polity. For them character signifies discipline of responsibility, the moral sense and burden of responsibility, to be more exact. And for them such discipline predicates a categorical need for standards in direct relation to what Babbitt calls an "enduring scale of values" and a "clear-cut scale of moral values." No modern American critics have been more aware of an interdependent need for discipline and standards than Babbitt and Weaver. Babbitt views this double need in terms of man's discovery of the path that leads to human growth, maturity, edification. Travelling on this path mandates effort and choice of direction, or as Babbitt cogently describes it in one of his essays, "Interpreting India to the West" (1917):

> On the one hand is the ascending path of insight and discrimination. Those who take it may be termed the spiritual athletes. On the other hand is the descending path towards the subrational followed by those who court the confused reverie that comes from the breakdown of barriers and the blurring of distinctions and who are ready to forego purpose in favor of "spontaneity"; and these may be termed cosmic loafers.

Weaver, in his own vision of order, is writing along these same lines of thought, with respect to the principle of distinction, when he declares: "In order to have meaningful status we must have something ascending toward an ultimate source of good." In ancient times, it was Plato who viewed the need and possibility of standards in the light of what he called the problem of the One and the Many. Once again, Babbitt is to the point here: "Unless there is something that abides in the midst of change and serves to measure it, it is obvious that there can be no standards." Babbitt and Weaver were to indict the arch tendency in modern times as the tendency to drift in centerless, undisciplined, anarchic ways. In this tendency Babbitt saw the manifestation of disorder in the form of anarchy, and Weaver, in the form of presentism. And for both disorder was rooted in what Weaver perceived, in words that echo those of Babbitt, as "the confusion of categories" and indifference, or hostility, to "transcendental ideas":

> The greatest weakness of a function-oriented culture is that it sets little or no store by the kind of achievement which is comparatively timeless—the formation of character, the perfection of style, the attainment of distinction in intellect and imagination. These require for their appreciation something other than keen senses; they require an effort of the mind and the spirit to grasp timeless values, to perceive the presence of things that extend through a temporal span.

Clearly, Babbitt and Weaver were reacting, with intense and total concern, to the main issues of contemporary life as expressed in literature, politics, education, and religion. And on these issues they spoke out candidly, consistently. In many ways they were diagnosticians of modern social order in rapid and mindless retreat from a faith in first principles and first causes—in "the law of the spirit," "the law of measure" steadily being supplanted by a "new dualism based on the myth of man's natural goodness." Babbitt and Weaver associated this retreat with the forces of aggressive anarchy and revolution assaulting the foundations of Western civilization, and especially its humanistic tradition. These forces, secular and gnostic, as well as decadent and ideological in orientation and intent, conspire to bring about, in Weaver's words, "the progressive demotion of man." These are precisely the forces that now embody the nihilism that pervades the basic categories of life and discards all semblance of the truth of the inner life. Babbitt and Weaver rendered in their own particular eras the ongoing stages of modern disequilibrium and deorientation which have now reached a point of no return. In their rendering of what Babbitt sees as a modern world "treading very near the edge of sudden disaster," one hears the prophetic voice crying out with the urgency and the fearlessness that belong to the ethical prophet's mission.

We hear this voice in the final paragraph of the final essay, "The Reconsideration of Man," in *Visions of Order*, Weaver speaking here with genuine vatic intensity about culture as an intermediary between man and his highest vocation, which he also reminds us is a matter of spirit:

> There is always in a cultural observance a little gesture of piety, a recognition that there are higher demands on man along with the lower. While culture is not a worship, and should not be made a worship, it is a kind of orienting of the mind toward mood, a reverence for the spirit on secular occasions.

And in Babbitt, too, the prophetic voice can be heard with equal intensity of attention to what Rabbi Abraham J. Heschel has called "the application of timeless standards to particular situations" and "an interpretation of a particular moment in history." Babbitt writes:

> As for the typical modern, he is not only at an infinite remove from anything resembling renunciation, but is increasingly unable to accept the will to refrain from anything else on a basis of mere tradition and authority. Yet the failure to exercise the will to refrain in some form or degree means spiritual anarchy. A combination such as we are getting more and more at present of spiritual anarchy with an ever-increasing material efficiency— power without wisdom, as one is tempted to put it—is not likely to work either for the happiness of the individual or for the welfare of society.

As teachers in the highest moral and civilizational sense, Babbitt and Weaver believed in the education of the whole human personality— intellect, character, mind, and soul. (Babbitt's first book, *Literature and the American College* [1908], argued forcefully for what Claes Ryn, in his discerning introduction to *Character and Culture*, calls a "reinvigorated humanistic curriculum and discipline as a way of reversing the decline of Western life and letters.") To the very end of his life and career, Babbitt's preoccupation with educational issues never wavered. And, no less than Babbitt, Weaver argued vigorously the case for humane letters. In a celebrated essay, "Up from Liberalism" (1958–1959), he wrote in words echoing Babbitt's own, "[O]ur education will have to recover the lost vision of the person as a creature of both intellect and will." "Gnostics of Education," the longest essay in *Visions of Order*, and inspired by Eric Voegelin's *The New Science of Politics* (1952), conveys the essence of Weaver's educational thought and views.

~ ❦ ❦ ~

Both in Babbitt's and in Weaver's writings, educational problems have an intrinsic bearing on their major ideas and thought. Their opinions are directed not only to their students in the classroom but also to their auditors at large. Their own teaching experiences doubtlessly helped to inspire and even define their educational thought, even as they treated educational issues as a significant part of the modern cultural scene. What they witness in the realm of education inevitably affects, even molds, their view of society and culture, and, of course, the human condition in the modern age. And what they have to say about education, whether diagnostic, censorial, or corrective, is clear and direct, singularly constructive and not cynical. In their educational ideas one finds the saving qualities of measure, prudence, humility. It is the teacher as sage who discourses here, guided in lecture and text by a sense of proportionateness and by a need, in Babbitt's words, "to glimpse the total symmetry of life and with reference to this symmetry to maintain some degree of poise and centrality." And here, too, one has the privilege of listening to a true humanist, in contradistinction to our modern specialists, the Napoleons of solution, with their overemphasis and glitz.

Babbitt and Weaver illustrate a common concern and a common witness to the crisis of education in the twentieth century and the accelerating diminution of humane values and humane learning. Babbitt largely examines the causes of educational malaise; Weaver is responding to effects. Their writings on education constitute a united front against what Russell Kirk speaks of as the decadence of higher learning in America. In their discernments we have an astonishing portrayal of the theories and movements that have contributed to our educational plight, today epitomized by anarchic and nihilistic conditions at all levels of American education. Babbitt's essay on "President Eliot and American Education" (1929) remains indispensable testimony for anyone who seeks to understand some of the basic reasons why American education has been floundering for many decades now. One will want to reflect on what Babbitt has to say, with such a timely ring of truth and perception, in these representative observations:

> The humanitarian idealism based on the faith in progress will be found on analysis to be either utilitarian or sentimental. Practically, in education as elsewhere, a utilitarian and sentimental movement has been displacing traditions that are either religious or humanistic.

> In the absence of human purposes, what has triumphed is the purpose of the utilitarian. A multitude of specialties . . . has taken the place not only of the selection of studies in the old curriculum but of the selective principle itself. Education has become increasingly miscellaneous and encyclopaedic.

> At the bottom of the whole educational debate . . . is the opposition between a religious-humanistic and a utilitarian-sentimental philosophy. This opposition, involving as it does first principles, is not subject to compromise or mediation. Those who attempt such mediation are not humanists but Laodiceans.

Babbitt's indictment of a raw and uncivilized pragmatism afflicting education returns us to his endorsement of Matthew Arnold's contention that our democracy is too much concerned with quantity and not quality. American democracy has obviously chosen to enforce, in an imperial manner, quantified reductionisms in the shape of what Babbitt calls "naturalistic disintegration," as part of the effort to legislate equality and uniformity. And a sham liberalism, as Babbitt reminds us in *Democracy and Leadership*, by not distinguishing between moral and material progress, has misled modern man to place ironclad faith in organization, efficiency, machinery: in short, in utilitarian and utopian schemes that have now emerged in the adulterated metaphysics of a New Morality and a New Age. Inevitably these schemes produce the momentum of subversions that affects the educational realm. Weaver addresses these subversions in his essay "Gnostics of Education," updating Babbitt's earlier critical testimony by giving to it a more current garb and idiom. That is to say, he helps take Babbitt's testimony beyond pragmatism by bringing it into contact with an educational system now gradually annexed by those he dubs "radical doctrinaires and social faddists." Weaver, in other words, provides us with a picture of educational dissimulation, *in extremis*, as it advances from pragmatism to ideology.

For Weaver, as for Babbitt, the central function of education is twofold: to form character and to preserve culture. But this function, he asserts, has been seriously impaired by the growth of progressivist educational philosophy in the hands of "revolutionaries" and "in the form of a systematic attempt to undermine a society's traditions and beliefs through the educational establishment." These revolutionaries, he goes on to say, have a vision of a "new future" totally unlike and even hostile to the past. They seek, above all, to nullify a vision of order that Weaver associates with the classical and Judaeo-Christian patrimony of the West. Among the aims of these revolutionaries he counts the methodical erasure of a common body of knowledge, of accepted truths, of standards, of authority as the most crippling. The following observation, written more than thirty years ago, and strikingly reechoing Babbitt, underlines Weaver's perception of the kind of ideology that today dominates educational thought and practice: "The student is to be prepared not to save his soul, or to inherit the wisdom and usages of past civilizations, or even to get ahead in life, but to become a member of a utopia resting on a false view of both nature and man." Weaver connects this modern subversive educational movement by way of historical descent with the Gnosticism of the first and second centuries A.D., the main goal, then and now, being to restructure humane values and concepts in terms suited to an "enlightenment" that boasts of being above creation, and that also vows that the material universe in and of itself is the real source of evil. The educationists of the new order, Weaver contends, parallel the Gnostics of antiquity in promulgating "a kind of irresponsibility to the past and to the structure of reality in the present."

The Rousseauism of Babbitt thus assumes in Weaver the shape of Gnosticism; the consequences for both are epitomized in disorder. Certainly what Weaver has to say in the following statement regarding the deification of man and the radicalization of the whole system of ethics into something that becomes categorically man-centered has definitive parallel, in language and in thought, in Babbitt's *Rousseau and Romanticism* (1919):

> The Gnostic belief was that man is not sinful, but divine. The real evil in the universe cannot be imputed to him; his impulses are good, and there is no ground for restraining him from anything he wants to do. . . . By divinizing man, Gnostic thinking says that what he wants to do, he should do.

Present-day gnostics of education, Weaver further observes, and again further confirming Babbitt's views, reject the existence or relevance of any moral absolutes as these affect and determine rightness from wrongness. Modern educators, hence, show little or no regard for an existent reality, but rather for "mastery of methodology"—for the technique and the technicism that currently hold sway in educational agenda. What Weaver is obviously criticizing is exactly the modern temper, and process, that Babbitt saw as the shifting of a value system increasingly controlled by the metaphysicians of the Many who have defeated the metaphysicians of the One; who have defeated, in short, the acceptance of what must be a central premise in grappling strenuously with the problem of the One and the Many that Babbitt describes in these words: "if there is no principle of unity in things with which to measure the manifoldness and change, the individual is left without standards and so falls necessarily into anarchic impressionism."

In his examination of modern education, in particular, and of culture, in general, it can be said, Weaver traces the consequences of what happens to the human world when there is no principle of unity and, in turn, no standards. He singles out in the process of what he depicts as "the dark night of the mind" the effects of unlimited democracy, about which Babbitt has trenchant things to say in his essay on "The Problem of Style in a Democracy," composed originally as an address to the American Academy of Arts and Letters, November 10, 1932, included in *Character and Culture*. Weaver argues that "When democracy is taken from its proper place and is allowed to fill the entire horizon, it produces an envious hatred not only of all distinction but of all difference." This contention, though in a more contemporary vein, continues Babbitt's argument that "Another and far graver error is to seek, like the egalitarian democrat, to get rid of the selective and aristocratic principle altogether. The cult of the common man that the egalitarian democrat encourages, is hard to distinguish from commonness." Any reflecting on the following sentences in the chapter "Democracy and Standards," in *Democracy and Leadership*, should remind one that Irving Babbitt and Richard Weaver finally speak in one voice:

> The democratic contention that everybody should have a chance is excellent provided it means that everybody is to have a chance to measure up to high standards. If the democratic extension of opportunity is, on the other hand, made a pretext for lowering standards, democracy is, insofar, incompatible with civilization.

Babbitt and Weaver focus on John Dewey's extensive role in the "denigration of the intellect," and see in his exaltation of activity over thinking a ruinous departure from the great body of traditional knowledge and the wisdom of the race. Babbitt sees Dewey's influence in a national tendency among educators to insist on "the doctrine of service" at the expense of culture and civilization, and of character and the inner life. Weaver sees Dewey's impact on educational theory and policy as one that above all discards the significant place of the concepts, signs, and symbols through which man has created cultural achievement. The results bring about an extreme and expansive secularization and with it the arrogant dismissal of moral, spiritual, and religious principles, especially as these inhere in the virtue of piety and the role it plays in "the discipline of the negative," as Weaver expresses it and then goes on to add, again evoking Babbitt's thinking and idiom: "Effective education often demands the rigorous suppressing of a present, desultory interest so that we can focus on things that have a real, enduring, and sanctioned interest. Indeed, this is identical with the act of concentration." In remarkably prophetic ways, then, Babbitt and Weaver perceived not only the growing eclipse of excellence throughout American education, but also the breakdown of authority. This process of decomposition, which Weaver connects with "the substitution of fantasy for historicity," and which Babbitt was to connect with reverie, "this imaginative melting of man into outer nature," is quintessentialized in Weaver's picture of the teacher in America under incessant and heavy attack:

> The teacher is not to be viewed as one in authority commissioned to instruct, but as a kind of moderator whose function is merely to conduct a meeting. Especially resented is the idea that the teacher has any advantage of knowledge or wisdom which entitles him to stand above his students. This would be a recognition of inequality, and equality must reign, *ruat caelum*!

Inevitably Babbitt and Weaver are reproving the rise of political ideology as it afflicts not only American character and culture, but also the organic conception of man and his world. Political ideology becomes, in effect, the haven of the "enemies of the permanent things." Man, Babbitt and Weaver insist, may be classified as a political animal, but political activity is neither his nor his culture's highest expression, or as Weaver declares: "He [man] is also a contemplative animal, and a creature with aesthetic and cultural yearnings. His very restlessness is a sign that he is a spiritual being with intimations about his origin and destiny." *Character and Culture* and *Visions of Order* have, in effect, the power of reminding us that Babbitt and Weaver wrestled unceasingly with the primary questions. They particularly lamented Americans' growing submission to what Babbitt terms a "cheap contemporaneousness," and what Weaver designates as "the belief that only existence in the present can give significance to the thing." This belief inevitably denies the place of memory as that which, Weaver submits, "directs one along the path of obligation" and keeps "us whole and consistent in opposition to that contrary force which is dissolution." Here, too, Babbitt's words are equally pertinent: "If the individual condemns the general sense, and trusts unduly his private self, he will have no model; and a man's first need is to look up to a sound model and imitate it."

"It is the critic's business," Babbitt writes, "to grapple with the age in which he lives and give it what he sees it needs." These words best define the critical calling not only of Babbitt but also of Weaver, and underline the courage a true critic needs to establish a moral ethos in examining life, literature, and thought. Babbitt and Weaver never deviated from their critical calling, even as their writings show a centrality and a consistency that invest their standards and outlook with an integrity of purpose and vision. To the dignity of literature they join the dignity of criticism. What will most impress readers of these two books is the moral seriousness and responsibility, as well as the moral measure, which Babbitt and Weaver record in their writings, and which in turn make them profoundly credible as critics who have something important to say about the human condition, and inevitably to say something of value about the "war in the cave," that unending struggle in man between good and evil. No less than the moral imagination, moral criticism has the capacity to make men and women better in their cities in that special context Babbitt apprehends when he stresses that the indefinite future progress of humanity is unequal to the immediate definite progress of the individual.

The problems that Babbitt associates with "the present contagion of commonness" and its impact on cultural life are problems that Weaver addresses remedially. For Babbitt the loss of a sense of proportion, especially as seen in the uncharted growth of specialization, constituted a severe crisis of culture inherent in the crisis of modernism. And for Weaver the loss of historical consciousness is tantamount to his fear that persuasive speech, as an "ethics of rhetoric," is to be displaced by mere communication. Both critics speak as one in rejecting what Weaver calls "the principle of pure relativism for cultures." And both are profoundly aware of a modern world that, through its machine culture, has fallen into idolatry. "But the road away from idolatry," Weaver observes, "remains the same as before: it lies in respect for the struggling dignity of man and for his orientation toward something higher than himself which he has not created."

What best reconciles life and letters? This question much preoccupied both critics, and both emphasized the role of the ethical faculty in judging cultural forms. Truly ethical art is at once imaginative and decorous, Babbitt insisted, noting in *Rousseau and Romanticism* that

The presence of the ethical imagination whether in art or life is always known as an element of calm. . . . But it is only with reference to some ethical centre that we may determine what art is soundly recreative, in what forms of adventure the imagination may innocently indulge.

Weaver is no less insistent on the need for ethical apprehensions of sociocultural creations and forms that are imposed but that are not worth the cost and have no real validity:

So it is that when a culture falls to the worshipping of the forms it has created, it grows blind to the source of cultural expression itself and may engender perverse cruelty. The degeneration may take the form of static arts, of barbarous legal codes in defense of conventions, or the inhuman sacrifice exacted by a brilliant technology. At some point, its delight in these things has clouded over the right ethical and other determinations of life.

Modern Western culture and society, Babbitt and Weaver agreed, can be increasingly identified by its tyranny of forms, equipped with a new language and new clothes, and driven by an oppressive bureaucracy and a new technology. For both critics, Americans' easy acceptance of and subservience to these reifying forms instanced the sharp intellectual and spiritual decline of a nation and its people. "[A]ny granting of moral status and imperative force to form in its spatiotemporal embodiment is a sign of danger," Weaver warned. The only way a culture, he went on to say, can be kept from "'worshipping monuments of its own magnificence,'" thus becoming repressive and destructive even in the midst of great achievements, is to recognize and preserve what he calls "allocations of the spirit": "For if man is a cognitive, aesthetic, ethical, and religious creature, he must maintain some rights of office among these various faculties." No less than Babbitt, Weaver observed a pronounced tendency to extremism in American life, and he repeatedly warned against this tendency as he saw it asserted in all aspects of American society and culture. At the heart of this extremism he viewed a growing pattern of disorder in reckless deviations from the sacred path that Babbitt saw as leading to peace, poise, and centrality. Weaver especially lamented the modern world's "general exaltation of means over ends," as people more and more "feel a loyalty toward means which leave them indifferent to ends." "The more secular society grows," he warned, "the more dominant this attitude is likely to become."

Babbitt's enemies have liked to think that he left no followers or allies and that he exerted little or no influence after his death in 1933. Such are, everywhere and always, the fantasies of the liberal mind. No two books, separated in date of publication by over twenty years, more forcefully repudiate these fantasies than *Character and Culture* and *Visions of Order*. In their basic themes and ethos, these books demonstrate astonishing continuity and correlation. In their warnings regarding the health of American character and culture, they depict a shared indictment of tendencies that have progressively led a nation and its people to chase after the heresies and the illusions that have no purpose other than that of destroying both the idea of value and humane civilization.

Babbitt discerned and identified the modern malaise as it was developing and spreading with cruel rapidity. His teachings and writings sought to chart those regions of modernism that held the greatest danger for modern man. Critical fortitude, steadfastness, and patience character-ize his life and work. He pressed on with his mission, his calling, to the end, refusing to be stranded, like others, on "the heights of despair." For Babbitt the law of humility was endless. With Edmund Burke he believed that it is at the root of all other virtues that involve first principles. "Nothing will avail short of humility," Babbitt insisted, standing, as he does, at the fountainhead of the dissident critical spirit that modernism and all its sectaries could not mute. "In the closing years of the twentieth century," Ryn observes, "it is evident that Irving Babbitt will go down in history as one of his country's original and seminal intellects." One could go so far as to say that the crisis of modernism, as it now slides with a vengeance into a postmodern stage of decadence and nihilism, cannot be fully grasped or resisted without an understanding of Babbitt's achieve-ment.

Even to ponder a few pages from Babbitt's *oeuvre* each day can be a valuable exercise for anyone who wants to be rescued from contemporary negators of the moral life and the ethical life: from, in a word, the technologico-Benthamite forces of gravity. Ultimately Babbitt's thought has a good influence, imparting as it does soundness and sanity, good sense, reasonableness, direction, balance—reverent qualities that actively oppose the disordering extremes that modern life legislates indiscrimi-nately. He was truly a critical genius who was for too long misunder-stood and misrepresented, unrecognized and unrewarded by his countrymen. But abroad, especially in the Orient, he was esteemed as an American sage and saint who wrought a noble reconciliation of East and West, of Confucius and Aristotle, of Buddha and Christ.

Nowhere in his published writings does Weaver acknowledge straightaway Babbitt's influence or praise its significance—perhaps because great thinkers prefer their own counsel and seek to protect and preserve their own sovereignty of mind and thought. On one occasion when Weaver does mention Babbitt's name (along with Paul Elmer More's), in an essay entitled "Agrarianism in Exile" (1950), it is on a disparaging note that, following T. S. Eliot and Allen Tate, simply restates "the fallacy of humanism." In "its admission of a theism," Weaver writes, Agrarianism is "unafraid to step beyond the phenomenal world," whereas the New Humanism "assumed that man could find his destiny through a discriminating study of his own achievements." At the time of Weaver's composition of "Agrarianism in Exile," it hardly needs saying, Babbitt's achievement had not as yet been honestly estimated so as to disprove many of his critics' attacks on his ideas as lacking the idea of transcendence, of the absolute, of a total awareness. Yet, as *Visions of Order* shows so conclusively, Weaver had pondered his Babbitt, reacted to his ideas, and even used his language. Indeed, as a young graduate student he had studied his Babbitt in order to complete a master's thesis in English, in the spring of 1934, at Vanderbilt University, under the direction of John Crowe Ransom. That thesis was entitled "The Revolt Against Humanism," and in it he voiced doubts about the "creed of the genteel tradition" later articulated in "Agrarianism in Exile."

But when one chooses to go beyond the early and disingenuous criticisms of Babbitt and the New Humanism, which had no doubt brushed Weaver's generation, one will discover that Babbitt's moral impact was deep and lasting, even as any critical comparison of *Character and Culture* and *Visions of Order* will prove. Yes, differences in critical orientation are there, but the affinities and the similarities, the visionary sperma, the larger moral concerns and spiritual purposes, are also very much there, transcendently. The passage of time—Babbitt had been dead for more than three decades when *Visions of Order* saw print—had softened some of the immediate intellectual tensions and hostilities, personal animosities and regional differences, that had clouded Babbitt's contribution. His central message to modern man, his wise teachings, and the universality of his vision could hardly escape either the interest or the respect of a great inheritor and continuer: Richard Weaver was, after all, fighting the new-old battles, now even more perilous in their outcome, in which Babbitt had fought valiantly and selflessly, in the front lines, in the fledgling years of the twentieth century.

In his unrelenting labors to provide correctives to the fragmentation and excesses of the modern world, Babbitt had penetrated to its heart of darkness. *Visions of Order*, in its remarkable way, pays tribute to Babbitt's enduring legacy and relevance. Babbitt neither desired nor expected to be acknowledged for his contribution to life and letters. There is, really, no need to cite him by name: His ideas have both implicit and beneficent consequences, and cannot be routinely relegated to footnotes. Weaver is among those "keen-sighted few" who attest to Irving Babbitt's permanence of value in the order of the "permanent things."

Keepers of the Flame

In *The Conservative Intellectual Movement in America since 1945*, George H. Nash has this to say about *Modern Age*:

> It immediately became the principal—indeed, the only—scholarly medium deliberately designed to publish conservative thought in the United States.
>
> . . . [It] was primarily oriented toward the traditionalist or new conservative segment of the revival. . . . *Modern Age* . . . filled a desperate need . . . [as] the principal quarterly of the intellectual right.[1]

The first issue appeared in the summer of 1957; its founding editor was Russell Kirk, a man of letters and the author of *The Conservative Mind*, which has become a classic. Henry Regnery, a distinguished, independent Chicago publisher, and David S. Collier, trained as a political scientist at Northwestern University (where he was a pupil of William M. McGovern and of Kenneth Colegrove) assisted Kirk in the founding. When Kirk resigned as editor in 1959, as Nash observes, "he had established what he wanted: a dignified forum for reflective, traditionalist conservatism."

The editorial continuity of *Modern Age*, no less than the original graphic design and format, remains unbroken, despite destined changes in editorship. Eugene Davidson, formerly an editor and then director of the Yale University Press, succeeded Kirk and served as editor in 1960–1970; in turn he was succeeded by Collier, who remained as editor until his unexpected death on November 19, 1983. The literary editors of *Modern Age* have been, in the following order of succession: Richard M. Weaver, a professor of English at the University of Chicago and the author of the celebrated book *Ideas Have Consequences*; J. M. Lalley (1896–1980), a journalist and for many years an editorial writer for and book review editor of *The Washington Post*; and George A. Panichas, a teacher and moralist critic, since 1962 a professor of English at the University of Maryland. Upon Collier's death, Panichas assumed editorship of the journal.

---

[1](New York: Basic Books, 1976) 144-45.

Originally bearing the subtitle "A Conservative Review," *Modern Age* was first sponsored by the Foundation for Foreign Affairs, Inc., of Chicago, which brought out the first nine issues (volume 1, number 1 [Summer 1957] through volume 3, number 3 [Summer 1959]). The Institute for Philosophical and Historical Studies, Inc., also of Chicago, then took over publication of *Modern Age*, beginning with volume 3, number 4 (Fall 1959). The Institute brought out all the thirteen succeeding issues of the journal until volume 7, number 1 (Winter 1962–1963), when sponsorship again reverted to the Foundation for Foreign Affairs and the subtitle became "A Quarterly Review." Beginning with the Fall 1976 issue of *Modern Age* (volume 20, number 4), The Intercollegiate Studies Institute, Inc., of Bryn Mawr, Pennsylvania, and now of Wilmington, Delaware, became the publisher.

It should be noted, too, that for twenty years Chicago remained as the editorial base of the journal. Russell Kirk and Henry Regnery had in fact hoped that *Modern Age* would serve as an intellectual forum for "the culture of the Middle West, and the heart of the United States generally." This hope, however, did not materialize, for in content and orientation *Modern Age* ultimately transcended any regional identity or parochial affiliation, becoming on a national and even international level a part of a larger program of conservative thought. Of the founding of *Modern Age*, Regnery later recalled:

In 1957 . . . Camelot, the New Frontier, the Great Society, the Vietnam War, the "Hippie and Drug Culture" of the sixties were all in the future, as were many of the political and social problems that loom so large today—the deficit, inflation, unemployment, exhibitionist homosexuality and pornography with the decline of standards associated with them, to mention only a few and to say nothing of the very different and far more dangerous power relationships in the world around us. Liberalism, then as now, was the dominant influence in communications and in the colleges and universities . . . but was being seriously challenged: Friedrich A. Hayek's *The Road to Serfdom* had appeared in 1945, Richard M. Weaver's *Ideas Have Consequences* in 1948, and in 1951 William F. Buckley appeared on the scene with the publication of *God and Man at Yale* and founded his magazine *National Review* four years later. It was the publication, and success, of Russell Kirk's *The Conservative Mind* in 1953 that brought the various elements of opposition to liberalism together and was the decisive factor in the founding of *Modern Age*.[2]

Since its inception *Modern Age* has become a veritable treasure house of conservative thought and opinion and has attracted contributors renowned for their writings and ideas. Among those seeking to define the concepts and principles of conservatism were M. E. Bradford, George W. Carey, Bertrand de Jouvenel, John Dos Passos, Paul Gottfried, Harry V. Jaffa, Willmoore Kendall, Frank S. Meyer, Robert Nisbet, José Ortega y Gasset, Stanley Parry, and Eliseo Vivas. Among those writing on conservative thinkers and expositors were John Chamberlain, John P. East, Byron C. Lambert, Marion Montgomery, Claes G. Ryn, and Peter J. Stanlis. In addition, on the cultural role of art, one will discover notable essays by Martin Buber, Donald Davidson, Robert Drake, W. E. Hocking, Folke Leander, Mario Pei, Herbert Read, and Austin Warren; on the significance and value of the Judaeo-Christian tradition and patrimony, Will Herberg, John Courtney Murray, Wilhelm Röpke, Leo R. Ward, Frederick Wilhelmsen, and René de Visme Williamson; on educational issues, James Burnham, W. T. Couch, Max Picard, Stephen M. Tonsor, and Eric Voegelin. No less significant have been crucial essays on Karl Marx's work and thought by William Henry Chamberlin, David J. Dallin, Thomas Molnar, Philip E. Moseley, and Gerhart Niemeyer; on the anatomy of terror and revolution, C. P. Ives, Felix Morley, and Francis Russell. Essays pertaining to the roots of American order have been written by Harry Elmer Barnes, Clare Boothe Luce, Andrew Lytle, Forrest McDonald, and Francis Gorham Wilson. Even a cursory listing of the names can hardly register the breadth and the depth of the subjects and issues explored year in and year out by writers and thinkers of great reputation and influence.

No statement better defines the aims of *Modern Age* than the opening editorial, "Apology for a New Review," in the summer 1957 issue. It remains as applicable today as when it first appeared. That the journal is called, in the very first sentence, "a journal of controversy" is especially pertinent, given the conditions inciting its publication at a time when liberal and radical journals of opinion, always in preponderance, generated an "orthodoxy of enlightenment." That, as the editorial stresses, *Modern Age* was hardly in the mainstream of American social and political thought and action, essentially reformist and progressivist in orientation, summarizes those conditions crying for the publication of a "con-

---

[2]"The Fourth Editorship," *Modern Age* 28/1 (Winter 1984): 2.

servative quarterly." The adjective in this phrase, often paradoxical to many, is directly encountered in this paragraph of definition:

> By "conservative," we mean a journal dedicated to conserving the best elements in our civilization; and those best elements are in peril nowadays. We confess to a prejudice against doctrinaire radical alteration, and to a preference for the wisdom of our ancestors. Beyond this, we have no party line. Our purpose is to stimulate discussion of the great moral and social and literary questions of the hour, and to search for means by which the legacy of our civilization may be kept safe.[3]

As the "Apology" expresses it, "*Modern Age* intends to pursue a conservative policy for the sake of a liberal understanding." It is the moral constituents of this "conservative policy" that epitomize the standards of discrimination differentiating the editorial ethos of *Modern Age* from that of other journals of opinion in America. The editorial admits that there is a widespread absence of serious reading in the nation, a bleak fact underscoring the point that a serious (and simultaneously conservative) journal of opinion is not likely to exert great influence over national policy or the conditions of American life and civilization. "But for all that," the editorial goes on to say, "modern society cannot endure—and its survival is immediately in question—without discussion among thinking men." These words announced the aspiration of "a new review" and adverted to the values that a "conservative review" seeks to convey, to promulgate, so as to "reach the minds of men who think of something more than the appetites of the hour." If the aims of the journal have been bold, they have not been quixotic, as the editorial discloses in these words:

> We are not ideologists: we do not believe we have all the remedies for all the ills to which flesh is heir. With Burke, we take our stand against abstract doctrine and theoretic dogma. But, still with Burke, we are in favor of principle.[4]

"We hope to revive the best in the old journalism and to mold it to the temper of our time." This statement poses the kind of challenge that an independent "conservative review" faces. How will it be possible to reconcile the mission of such a review, as a conservator of the great tradition of "permanent things," with the urgencies of cruel history and of an age in swift transition and expanding crisis? Encouraging critical examination and discussion of national and international issues has been a

---

[3]"Apology for a New Review," *Modern Age* 1/1 (Summer 1957): 2.
[4]Ibid.

long-standing aim of *Modern Age*. If the ethos of this "conservative review" has been moral in perspective, it has also been humanistic. From the beginning *Modern Age* has defended the "idea of value" as it relates to the concept of the *honnête homme*.

Traditions and values that actively resist the tyranny of collectivist principles are what inform the conservative viewpoints expressed in the journal and at the same time provide the reminding evidence of the force of truth that one finds in Paul Elmer More's words: "We are intellectually incompetent and morally responsible: that would appear to be the last lesson of life." It is the considered response to both the significance and the ramifications of More's contentions that *Modern Age* has exercised its conservative articles of faith on both a diagnostic and a corrective plane. That these articles of faith signify, in Burke's words, "the dissidence of dissent" points to the degree of concern that the journal shows regarding the need to oppose a majoritarian leveling that has produced decadent phenomena in American life and culture—the unchecked romanticism, positivism, and gnosticism emerging from the arrogances of "telluric revolt" (to use Hermann Keyserling's expression). This opposition has been conducted in accordance with the purposive function of a "conservative review" and of a "principled conservatism," as Frank S. Meyer has designated it.

A major editorial task has been that of confronting pervasive deculturation, statism, endless shifts and drifts of the climate of opinion, and the various forms of the moral collapse in the Western world. The character and the conscience of *Modern Age* are clearly identified in terms not only of the contributors themselves, "a worthy company" indeed, but also of the subjects they explore and assess. Conservative standards of discrimination are upheld by Americans and Europeans who share a sympathy of vision and who, concerned with the *why* of things as well as the *what*, protest against those conditions of life without principles, of "life without prejudice," as Weaver puts it. That remnant of conservative scholars, or what Eliseo Vivas calls the "intellectual *guerrilleros* of the right," is for a journal that seeks for a moral identity (and centrality), and also seeks to create a conservative valuation (and validation), its life source, giving it its authentic function, if not its prophetic voice. The properties of that function and the tone of that voice have been totally consistent with the *desiderata* that Niemeyer poses in these words:

> In the shallowness of liberal and socialist humanism, we must rediscover the depth of being and of history. In the process we must first learn, and then teach, to recognize distinctions between truth and perversion, rationality and semirationality, philosophy

and ideology. We need great figures whose personal lives are an eloquent alternative to liberal relativism. . . . We need orators who can call the bluff, and decry the false plausibility, of the ideologists, positivists, and humanist moralists. We need lawgivers who can translate deep convictions into public rules.[5]

Pluralistic, pragmatic, and collectivist tendencies that are dominant in "the promise of liberalism" and sanctioned by "creative sceptics in defense of the liberal temper," as the philosopher-politician T. V. Smith once expressed the mission of his liberal allies, often characterize modern American civilization. The challenging of this liberal *Zeitgeist* and of the ideologues who support the *volonté générale* is graphically registered in the pages of *Modern Age*. One must inevitably reflect, in viewing this challenge and ideological struggle, on how the journal and its contributors, without an academic base (or, better, a privileged and often affluent sanctuary), without munificent foundation grants, without popular support and instant revenues, without a heavily financed visibility, have survived.

It is not far-fetched to image the function and mission of those connected with the journal as a dissident enterprise. Indeed, those who have been associated with *Modern Age* have often been made to feel as dissidents. This fate is unavoidable when a journal hews closely to paradigms of conservative acceptances in the contexts of what Weaver speaks of not only as "belief in the primacy of ideas and values" but also as "visions of order." As a journal of opinion *Modern Age* has sought to maintain commitment to first causes and first principles and reverence for moral constants and universals. It has sought to diminish the Marxizing imperialisms and the technologico-Benthamite habits of mind besieging all areas of life in the twentieth century. In its strict adherence to these purposes and commitments, *Modern Age* has tried to exemplify the meaning of what Voegelin speaks of as "the consciousness of principles."

Although no single religious viewpoint or affirmation prevails either in editorial policy or among the contributors, the Judaeo-Christian tradition has the largest shaping influence in the perspectives that are enunciated in the journal. *Modern Age* epitomizes precisely the traditional religious position as opposed to the liberal agnosticisms that T. S. Eliot pinpoints when he writes:

We, on the other hand, feel convinced, however darkly, that our spiritual faith should give us some guidance in temporal matters;

---

[5]"A Remarkable Conservative Presence," *Modern Age* 20/1 (Winter 1976): 5-6.

that, if it does not, the fault is our own; that morality rests upon religious sanction, and that the social organization of the world rests upon moral sanction; that we can only judge of temporal values in the light of eternal values.[6]

At a time of history that has seen an overwhelming crisis of faith *Modern Age* has defended religious traditions, siding with the supernatural against the natural, with permanence against relativism, with an apostolic orthodoxy against heresy, with the idea of cultural unity in religious faith, as opposed to faith in secular utopias. Thus, what can be termed a metaphysics of transcendence defines the chief spiritual concerns of the journal.

In *Modern Age* the conservative ethos is substantively communicated in relation to basic categories of thought. The main criterion for judging the human condition is inextricably tied to cause and effect, not means and ends. If there is one edict that molds and monitors the editorial standards of *Modern Age*, it is that which endorses unconditionally the qualitative element. Maintaining a hierarchy and a scale of values and stressing man's duties and then man's rights have been a central editorial purpose. In holding to a conservatism at once selective, synthesizing, and assimilative, *Modern Age* has disclosed a consistent toughness and a tenacity of belief. Overcentralization, bureaucratization, the expansion of "new deals" and "fair deals," of "new frontiers" and "great societies," social planning and social engineering—these are, for *Modern Age*, acute imperialistic tendencies in the "liberal temper" and governance that transpose into faults, inner and outer, individual and social. The progressivism of representative democracy in its proliferating forms and dimensions, then, has been under severe censorial inspection in *Modern Age*. It is not that the concept of democracy incurs disapproval, but rather the excesses of a majoritarian society as these transform into indiscrimination, relativism, indiscipline, and disorder.

Modern Age stands for the mobilizing of the moral virtues as forms of both the exterior life and the interior life. Political philosophy no less than political theory that underestimates the moral meaning of existence inevitably is worthless. Though profoundly concerned with the condition of American society, *Modern Age* is not restricted to parochial issues. Its perspective, generalist and universal, is ultimately rooted in the larger world. Even as it has been loyal to the need for adhering to "the idea of

---

[6]"Catholicism and International Order," in *Essays Ancient and Modern* (London: Faber & Faber, 1936) 113-14.

diversity in conservative thought," *Modern Age* has never succumbed to divided allegiances or vague romanticizing impulses that characterize a vulgar contemporaneousness. Its conservative principles have been absolute in their rejection of the "new morality of drifting." Those very principles of a critical conservatism and of a "principled conservatism" are planted in a symbiosis of moral effort and disciplinary virtues forming the bedrock of tradition, which, as Austin Warren notes, "emphasizes the shared inheritance as embodied in institutions—all organized, continuous, and more or less coherent expressions of values and ideals."[7]

In the end, the critical function of *Modern Age* can be described as serious, judgmental, moral, prescriptive; it is concerned with the character and conscience of individual man and also of society and culture. That the crisis of civilization is essentially a crisis of spirit is a phenomenon that *Modern Age* vigilantly observes. In its emphasis on this truth the journal adheres to a spiritual centrality. Going beyond political and socioeconomic arrangements of an essentially mechanomaterial cast, it is anchored in metaphysical concepts and convictions. This is not to say that it discards temporal considerations, but rather that it looks for eternal values and permanent truths. Moral effort and moral conversion precede programmatic and material experiments. Principles, not possibilities, are priorities that govern the human prospect.

What differentiates *Modern Age* from other journals of opinion is precisely its metaphysical acceptances as these govern its conservative aims and outlook. At no time has the journal failed to take a stand on issues affecting the condition and the measure of man. Invariably, matters of conduct, conscience, and character, in their total relation to life, literature, and thought, receive strict attention in *Modern Age*. The standards are consonant with those articles of a conservative's faith that More delineates in these words:

> Despite the clamour of the hour he will know that the obligation to society is not the primal law and is not the source of personal integrity, but is secondary to personal integrity. He will believe that social justice is in itself desirable, but he will not hold that it is far more important to preach first the responsibility of each man to himself for his own character. He will admit that equality of opportunity is an ideal to be aimed at, but he will think this is a small thing in comparison with the universality of duty. In

---

[7]"Tradition and the Individual," *Modern Age* 27/1 (Winter 1983): 82.

his attitude towards mankind he will not deny the claims of sympathy, but he will listen first to the voice of judgment.[8]

In placing the organic interconnections between the economic, the political, the philosophical, and the religious essences that comprise the conditions of existence, *Modern Age* adheres to the principles of restraint, of discipline, of control implicit in Burke's statement: "There is no qualification for government but virtue or wisdom, actual or presumptive." Burke's words belong to an old and great tradition, if not of the old criticism, which has attracted, in the pages of *Modern Age*, definers and defenders of the idea of continuity. Above all, how are those two venerable words of virtue and wisdom, dedicated to the law of measure and the life of reverence, to be preserved at an ignoble hour when other venerable words, encouraging both inspiration and aspiration—loyalty, honor, nobility, honesty, generosity—have been equally compromised by the forces to which the idea of value is meaningless? Simone Weil's belief that "language is no longer equipped for legitimately praising a man's character" comes to mind here. With the corruption of language, the unchecked drift of modern civilization has hastened towards nihilism. For what principles of faith and certitudes of order can operate in a society in which relativism is placed in a commanding position? In a deep sense, then, *Modern Age* is devoted to the tradition of what Matthew Arnold calls "the grand style" that is connected with an "elevation of character," a "noble way of thinking and behaving," and a "dealing with great things."

Arnold's phrases help to identify not only the concerns of *Modern Age* but also the psychology and philosophy of its critical aims—and its *raison d'être*. If many of its writers and reviewers are academics, *Modern Age* rejects narrow academic specializations. The journal does not speak exclusively to (or for) the academy but rather to "man thinking." Its approach is interdisciplinary and transdisciplinary. Implicit in the responsibilities of such an approach is the necessity for making connections between the dynamic forces and energies of human life and the standards of the tradition to which Arnold alludes. The journal's reverence for the idea of tradition, for a return to origins, absorbs the idea of conservatism and points to what is inclusive and transcendent in character and orientation. For *Modern Age*, to quote the words of Father Yves Congar, "the word tradition connotes something more than mere

---

[8]"The New Morality," in *Aristocracy and Justice*, Shelburne Essays 9th ser. (vol. 9) (Boston/New York: Houghton Mifflin, 1967 [©1915]) 216.

conservatism; something deeper is involved, namely, the continual presence of a spirit and of a moral attitude, the continuity of an ethos."[9]

If one can discern in the mass of American life a heightening state of blankness, of cultural decline, one can also discern in the American intellectual community an ascending habit of disloyalty to the idea of value. Ortega y Gasset is again to the point here when he observes: "[A] characteristic of our times is the predominance, even in groups tradition-ally selective, of the mass and the vulgar. Thus, in the intellectual life, which of its essence requires and presupposes qualification, one can note the progressive triumph of the pseudointellectual, unqualified, unquali-fiable, and, by their very mental texture, disqualified."[10] A contemporary of Ortega's, Julien Benda, applied a celebrated phrase, *la trahison des clercs*, to the tendency that the Spanish philosopher identified. In American intellectual and sociopolitical life it is the gravity and the extent of this breakdown that one finds continually examined in *Modern Age*. Indeed, no better diagnostic index to the conditions afflicting American society can be found than in its pages.

If crisis and revolution are representative of the modern world, there are two other closely related destructive processes that, as Voegelin has observed, are inescapable in their consequences: the fragmentation of science through specialization and the deculturation of society. Their con-sequences have been of deep concern to *Modern Age*. Especially noticeable in these destructive processes is the glorification of the social collective and the diminution of the nature of man. Empirical as opposed to meta-physical priorities color all questions of existence. In effect, both the bibli-cal view and the classical ideal, foundations of the Spirit that they are, re-treat before this phenomenon. The Great War of 1914–1918, the Russian Revolution of 1917, and World War II constitute epochal manifestations of the terrors of debasement wrought in a megatechnic world. With the culmination of each of these disasters, what Simone Weil calls "the em-pire of might" has attained its continuing confirmation, its profane ontol-ogy, as it were. The struggle for order, in other words, gives way to the forces of disintegration, not only materialistic but also ideological, pro-gressivist and positivist, liberal and socialist, Marxist and Freudian, that now take civilization "beyond nihilism." The moral meaning of man, soci-ety, and history withers as these forces annul that sapiential concept of

---

[9] Yves Congar, *The Meaning of Tradition*, trans. A. N. Woodrow (New York: Hawthorn, 1964) 7.

[10] José Ortega y Gasset, "The Coming of the Masses," in *The Revolt of the Masses* (New York: Norton, 1957 [1932]) 16.

man, society, and history that Voegelin identifies in these words: "Every society is burdened with the task, under its concrete conditions, of creating an order that will endow the fact of its existence with meaning in terms of ends divine and human." The ongoing mission of *Modern Age*, it could be said, resides in Voegelin's concept of the structure of order.

The consequent need to find remedies against the disorder of the time through philosophical and critical inquiry points to one of the original needs leading to the founding of *Modern Age*. From the beginning the journal has viewed its function, intellectually and politically, as well as socially and culturally, as one that is predominantly diagnostic and corrective, seeing things in their causes and facts in their connections. Whatever the uncertainties and the paradoxes of the modern situation, they accentuate a need for order. If historical uncertainties and metaphysical paradoxes often lead to experimental social and political solutions, rooted in mere sentiment, in empty rhetoric, in illusions, or in utilitarian experiments, the need for order presupposes disciplinary virtues and exacting paradigms of character. In the end it all comes down to the question of transcendent permanencies, of hierarchies, their acceptance and affirmation. A rigorous loyalty to these permanencies accents the loyalty of *Modern Age* to *historia sacra* and, in turn, to a civilized world of dignity, reason, and order. That history has meaning, that the world makes sense, that man has redeeming worth: these are, for *Modern Age*, absolute concepts to be defended absolutely against sophistic and gnostic forces of disorder. Once again Voegelin helps to clarify a basic moral and philosophical concern defining the scope and the purpose of *Modern Age*: "The truth of order has to be gained and regained in the perpetual struggle against the fall from it; and the movement toward truth starts from a man's awareness of his existence in untruth."[11]

One of the crucial aspects of the critical function that *Modern Age* seeks to fulfill lies in the review of books. The evaluative discussion of new books, and the reconsideration of old books, that have been ignored or scanted, are central tasks of any journal of opinion. Yet in many academic journals and in the popular press one does not find the standards of discrimination essential to a proper evaluation of books of critical and cultural significance, particularly books that convey a conserva-

---

[11]For his understanding of transcendence and his view of spiritual, or "paradigmatic," history, see Eric Voegelin's *Order and History*, in 5 vols. (Baton Rouge: Louisiana State University Press, 1956–1987): 1. *Israel and Revelation* (1956); 2. *The World of the Polis* (1956); 3. *Plato and Aristotle* (1957); 4. *The Ecumenic Age* (1974); 5. *In Search of Order* (1987).

tive and moral sensibility. The literary establishment, moreover, remains largely loyal to liberal oracles like John Dewey and Bertrand Russell, and to heresiarchs like Herbert Marcuse, B. F. Skinner, Georg Lukács, Jacques Derrida. And it continues to minimize the moral imagination and moral criticism, even as it manifestly minimizes both humanistic principles of *paideia* rooted in tradition and the unity of spiritual life that a Christopher Dawson and a T. S. Eliot defend. Empirical, liberal-radical, and revisionist-turned-deconstructionist habits of mind and opinion too often and expediently determine the treatment, reputation, and fate of new books and of the popular successes, the so-called "best sellers" that one finds listed in the *New York Times Book Review* week after week. What is alarming about these reviewing practices and the climate of opinion that they foment is not only the limiting selection of nonserious and noncritical literature to be reviewed, but also the limiting of reviewers to those who adhere safely to a party line of relativistic criticism.

Relevance, a specious word that has been certified by liberal pundits, has become a procedural standard in discussing national policy and in seeking cultural consensus. All too often such a spurious standard has enjoyed complete demagogic success, especially in the late 1960s and 1970s when American civilization experienced serious social and cultural problems. These were barren years when *Modern Age* was one of the few journals publishing essays and reviews that went against the American grain and challenged the "democratization of personhood" that liberal and radical leaders championed. These were years of danger and unreason when, as one alarmed critic termed it in *Modern Age*, "*meta*-barbaric man now dances and fornicates in the streets."[12] In more nearly normal circumstances, of course, such a declaration would be deemed hyperbolic, designed for literary effect. But even a random visual examination of American street scenes in a "morbid democracy" in the 1960s and 1970s would corroborate the sorry spectacle described by the alarmed critic.

Only the passage of time and disinterested critical assessment will fully vindicate the writings in *Modern Age* protesting the debasement of national character that, in these two decades, seemed of no threat to acclaimed gurus, political and religious leaders, jurists, educators, columnists, television commentators, and nationally prestigious newspapers and journals of opinion whose common admonition was summed up in two words, "Right on!" No admonition could more betray the habits of order

---

[12]George A. Panichas, "The Cult of Mediocrity," *Modern Age* 15/4 (Fall 1971): 424.

that Walter Bagehot connects with "the settled calm by which the world is best administered." If there ever was any need for exonerating even the existence of a journal of opinion like *Modern Age*, it was in the 1960s and 1970s, dishonest and hedonistic decades when, as its writers warned, the abandonment of the idea of value and the disregard for moral responsibility rendered an impasse in American civilization.

"From the element of unity in things to the element of diversity": Irving Babbitt's words describing a basic shift in principles bear repeating. His words encompass a crisis of civilization and also define the kind of social and moral transvaluation that many in the American intellectual community have accepted, even as they have been increasingly content, as Wilhelm Röpke asserts, to allow "incidentals [to] recede behind the essential, the variables behind the constants, the ephemeral behind the permanent, the fluctuating behind the durable, the fleeting moment behind the era."[13] This disarray, as it affects life not only in a sociopolitical but also in a cultural and literal sense, goes unchecked. It underlines modern man's disregard of "the tragic sense of life," as well as of "a tragic wisdom." Insofar as the tragic dimension connotes a sense of an ending, or *telos*, it conflicts with an uncritical optimism. That even religious leaders and theologians now subscribe to and propagate this optimism indicates how serious is the shift in principles and values. Disarray is in essence the failure to locate a center of values, which is in turn the rejection of what Voegelin calls "paradigmatic" history, that is, of spiritual history or tradition. This process of rejection, with its disordering results, causes a crisis of existence, particularly evidenced as a weakening of the spiritual fiber, or as Father Stanley Parry observes in his essay "The Restoration of Tradition," a most distinguished contribution of its kind to appear in *Modern Age*, "Civilization itself—tradition— falls out of existence when the human spirit itself becomes confused."[14]

Conservatism, as Russell Kirk reminds us, is in essence a way of looking at the human condition. Such a conservatism is predicated on an understanding of the relation between philosophy and practical politics, between *theoria* and *praxis*, between idea and reality. *Modern Age* has sought for the attainment of this understanding; its pursuit has been fundamentally dispassionate in discrimination and judgment. What one finds in examining the journal as a whole is a comprehensive conservatism preoccupied with the total human condition. Behind its valuation lies an

---

[13]Wilhelm Röpke, *The Social Crisis of Our Time*, trans. Annette Jacobson and Peter Jacobson (Chicago: University of Chicago Press, 1950) 1.

[14]*Modern Age* 5/2 (Spring 1961): 129.

endemic preoccupation with the idea of conservation and continuity: "The first duty of society is the preservation of society." Walter Bagehot's words epitomize the origin of that preoccupation. Honoring and sustaining that preoccupation are infinitely difficult in an age addicted to the doctrines of progress, reform, and freedom, and of all that comes under the heading of "open society." When the scale of values and the meaning of value have been drastically altered, the conservative's task is further complicated. To admit this is not to diminish in any way the fortitude of those writers who have helped to mold the ethos of *Modern Age*. This ethos has been applied philosophically, morally, politically, with consistency and, when necessary, with severity.

Modern Age has not relaxed its moral attention to the critical problems of civilization at a time when inattention has characterized responses to matters of human and cultural importance. Indeed, the nature of freedom itself has been both distanced and distorted by a temporal concern with delimiting the boundaries of freedom. In such circumstances freedom assumes a purely empirical guise impervious to the metaphysical dimension. "Moral freedom is simply this freedom to hold by attention," Josiah Royce writes, "or to forget by inattention, an Ought already present to one's finite consciousness."[15] No other words better express the moral imperative as it has been defended in *Modern Age*. The presence of the Ought helps to locate and measure the condition of the moral order, especially in the framework of what constitutes attention and responsibility.

Materialistic doctrine has increasingly displaced the attention and judgment that form an integral and active part of moral sensibility. Moral consequences are ignored or discounted; in effect, moral order and order of meaning are removed from the realm of reality. Just how catastrophic this process can be is illustrated by Eliseo Vivas in a discussion of books "by and on Marcuse," an *enragé* who, in the 1960s and 1970s, captured the allegiance of the intellectual left. Vivas, and *Modern Age*, could hardly ignore the threat that a radical guru and dogmatist like Marcuse presents to the moral order; could hardly ignore

> Marcuse's conception of human destiny as envisaged in his repugnant secularistic *Erlösungslehre*: the psychological-ethical hedonism which he preaches . . . [his] total lack of piety towards past human achievements, the absurdity of a mind that claims to have found the final solution for man's problems, the dystopian

---

[15]Josiah Royce, *Nature, Man, and the Moral Order*, vol. 2 of *The World and the Individual* (New York/London: Macmillan, 1901) 360.

dream of a state in which human beings regress into pleasure-seeking animals.[16]

The survival of *Modern Age* in no way alters the fact that, especially in the literary and academic worlds and in the judiciary, a genuine conservative metaphysic tends to trail in the dusty rear. Insofar as in modern society gnostic and uncritical habits of mind are predominant, it cannot be expected that the genuinely conservative metaphysic will find an easy passage. In American society since World War II it is precisely what is antithetical to restraints at all levels of life that has gained ascendancy. The "promise of a millennium," when man has at last entered the "gates of Eden," epitomizes the messianism characteristically preached by liberal theorists "swayed by sensations, and not by principles," to quote de Tocqueville. What Peter Viereck writes is also to the point here:

> Whereas the liberal and rationalist mind consciously articulates abstract blueprints, the conservative mind embodies rather than argues; its best insights are almost never developed into sustained theoretical works equal to those of liberalism and radicalism.[17]

The conservatives' reverence for intangible yet permanent things—for the things of the spirit, as it were—goes counter to the materialistic drives of the modern world and the anthropology of a largely atheistic humanism that now assume an obscene character and a program reducing the world to a theory.

Increasing surrender in the twentieth century to the demands of "historical necessity" embodies the sad fate of large parts of modern society. It further underlines retreat from a tradition of political philosophy which expresses what Leo Strauss, reconciler of classical and biblical views and beliefs, calls "the character of ascent" and of the related qualitative search for piety and wisdom. Marxism in particular embodies a political process that rejects the element of virtue that is essential to the best political order. The anti-Marxist position of *Modern Age* has been unyielding. Both Marxist politics and Marxist philosophy have been the subject of extensive criticism, even as American foreign policy has also been extensively examined in terms of its perception (or its lack of perception) of the dangers of Marxist doctrine. The French Revolution of 1789 and the Russian Revolution of 1917, as well as the consequent rise of the Jacobin

---

[16]*Modern Age* 15/1 (Winter 1971): 88.

[17]"Conservatism," in *The New Encyclopaedia Britannica: Macropaedia* (Chicago: Encyclopædia Britannica, Inc., 1985) 27:476.

and Bolshevik dictatorships, have often been viewed as manifestations not only of "revolutionary terror" but also of the spirit of modern totalitarianism. Conservative scholars in *Modern Age* have refused to accede to the so-called Marxist "aim of the transcendence of domination."

If *Modern Age* has followed a supposedly "hard-line" approach, as some of its liberal critics have charged, the political and spiritual catastrophes of post-1917 history would seem to vindicate such an approach. "Our present system is unique in history," Aleksandr Solzhenitsyn writes in *From under the Rubble* (1974), "because over and above its physical and economic constraints, it demands of us total surrender of our souls, continuous and active participation in the general, conscious *lie*." *Modern Age* has refused to participate in this lie exactly for the reasons that Solzhenitsyn stresses: "No one who voluntarily runs with the hounds of falsehood, or props it up, will ever be able to justify himself to the living or to posterity, or to his friends, or to his children."

Not long after the end of World War II, Whittaker Chambers (1901–1961) was one of the few brave men to direct our attention to the metaphysical dimension, and to the deeper psychology, of Marxism. Tearing away any veil of illusion that he once had regarding the Marxist doctrine, he was able to say straight out that in our time there is a great conflict between two irreconcilable faiths—Communism and Freedom. When Chambers declares, in his moving "Foreword in the Form of a Letter to My Children," in *Witness* (1952), that the two world wars did not end the crisis of civilization, but raised its ideological tensions to a new pitch, and that "All the politics of our time, including the politics of war, will be the politics of this crisis," he focuses precisely on a matter that occupied *Modern Age* from the beginning. As such the journal has long been critical of those prevailing policy advisors, political leaders, and liberal academics who refuse to recognize that, as Solzhenitsyn puts it, the West "finds itself in a crisis, perhaps even in mortal danger." That crisis and that danger embody the struggle between human freedom and totalitarianism, between a way of life that seeks to affirm faith in human dignity and any collectivist doctrine that results in tyranny and the slave mentality. With Eric Voegelin, then, *Modern Age* affirms that "the truth of man and the truth of God are inseparably one." This affirmation, this choice, points to the principles of faith and order that shape the substance of *Modern Age*'s editorial principles and commitments.

As modern gnosticism and "leftist-horizontalism" have gained ascendancy, the mission of *Modern Age* has become more urgent in terms of conserving civilized values and verities. Where habitual compromise has informed the thought and policy of the American intelligentsia and of political leadership, *Modern Age* has stalwartly identified the fallacies and the inbreeding of the liberal *Zeitgeist*. To reiterate, the mission of *Modern Age* has been sustained by a generous welcome to its pages of writers from all parts of the United States and from Europe. From the beginning, as Anthony Harrigan has observed, "*Modern Age* introduced a wider, more comprehensive intellectual tradition than existed in New York and Boston."[18] In this tradition one discovers a common allegiance on the part of the journal's contributors: dedication to a higher and ever demanding task—"the task of intellectual and moral preparation and restoration."

"For a conservatism of ignorance, like a liberalism of ignorance, is a curse to society; while a conservatism of reflection is a counterbalance to a liberalism of reflection." Thus wrote Kirk back in 1955 in *Commonweal*. That "counterbalance" was, with the founding of *Modern Age* in 1957, to become the major and restorative task of the journal. Its essays and reviews have from the beginning been engaged in the active implementation of this task. For its contributors the journal was to become, in Marion Montgomery's words, "a house where we gather periodically in complementary encounters." In *Modern Age*, then, it has been a conservative minority that has spoken, animated, as Kirk observes, by "their love of right reason" and their desire "to inform and persuade, rather than to indoctrinate in secular dogmas." *Modern Age* has, in effect, sought to define and preserve a conservative ethos. Not social reform per se but moral struggle constitutes a working principle of order in this ethos. Or, to put it another way, the conservative ethos revolves around a particular disposition, which Michael Oakeshott describes as follows:

> To be conservative is to be disposed to think and behave in certain matters; it is to prefer certain kinds of conduct and certain conditions of human circumstances to others; it is to be disposed to make certain kinds of choices."[19]

That *Modern Age* has appeared without interruption since 1957 records both an act of survival and an occasion for gratification. But this statement should in no way be taken as self-congratulatory. "Conservative intellectual victories not intimately tied to a genuine reorientation of imagination and character," Claes G. Ryn warns, "are likely to be precari-

---

[18]"*Modern Age* in a Changing World," *Modern Age* 26/3-4 (Summer/Fall 1982): 351.

[19]"On Being Conservative," in *Rationalism in Politics and Other Essays* (London/New York: Methuen, 1981 [1962]) 168.

ous and easily reversible."[20] The fight for "lost causes" never ends, insofar as that fight is inextricably tied to organic metaphysical and socio-historical dialectics, which John Kenneth Galbraith, elder statesman of the American left, identifies in these words: "Ever since [Franklin D.] Roosevelt, liberals have assumed the solidity and even the sanctity of our basic positions." Among these positions he lists Keynesian macroeconomic management of the economy, welfare programs, minority rights, and a more equitable distribution of income. Such an enumeration of goals underlines the presuppositions and prepossessions of the liberal doctrine. It is one of the functions of the conservative scholar to provide a counteraction to a programmatic "metastatic" faith, the faith of "an abiding liberal," to use Galbraith's own caption. Conspicuously absent from this faith, *Modern Age* has persisted in saying, is a concern with the order of the soul as this order relates to the order of the republic. In this absence are found the roots of spiritual crisis. For the conservative scholar this crisis—and it is, in the end, a crisis of disorder—generates the substance of his quarrel with the liberal dialectic, with what Claude Levi-Strauss calls "the dialectic of superstructures."

Contemplating the contemporary social and moral situation, Isaac Bashevis Singer laments: "The daily news tells us again and again that, with all his knowledge and with all his refined ways, modern man remains the wildest animal." He declares that too many people passively accept the moral decay of the time and respond to the present crisis of civilization with indifference. He goes on to emphasize: "There is a time when man must say what he considers important." These words should trouble the conscience and alert us to the distempers of a civilization that, individually and collectively, negate the axiomatic principles of character that dignify and sanctify the moral meaning of man. During the past four decades the conservative scholar has spoken out on fundamental issues in *Modern Age*: He has said *what he considers important*. To the psalmist's perennial question, "If the foundations be destroyed, what can the righteous do?" the conservative scholar gives reply. His testimony, no less than his witness, inscribes the pages and informs the ethos of *Modern Age*, which to this day remains, indefatigably, what its founding fathers intended it to be, "an American protest against the illusions of the age," and a bulwark against the "enemies of the permanent things."

---

[20]"American Intellectual Conservatism: Needs, Opportunities, Prospects," *Modern Age* 26/3-4 (Summer/Fall 1982): 313.

The Courage to Go On

In her essay on "Morality and Literature," which originally appeared in French in 1944, Simone Weil complains bitterly regarding the modern phenomenon of "the usurpation by writers of the function of spiritual guidance." She asserts that only a few great geniuses among writers—Homer, Aeschylus, Sophocles, Dante, Shakespeare, Racine, Dostoevsky—can perform this high function effectively. In their works, she goes on to say, we have contemplations that contain the genuine kind of inspiration which can guide human beings, particularly in times of intellectual decadence and spiritual impoverishment. Her essay concludes with these words: "For this inspiration, if we know how to receive it, tends—as Plato said—to make us grow wings to overcome gravity."

What in effect Simone Weil is stressing here is the establishment of standards that not only the writer but also the reader must mutually satisfy. For the writer this need is tied to the dictates of the moral imagination; and for the reader it is tied to making moral discovery and moral ascent from "the experience of literature." We need writers, Simone Weil the Christian Platonist is saying, who can responsibly and integratively, as well as intellectually and spiritually, help and inspire us to surmount the traps of our own secularity.

The proliferation of false art and false inspiration is now writ large in the "Best Sellers" lists of our Sunday newspapers and, scandalously, in the reading requirements of our colleges and universities. Anything that smacks of a "great tradition" or that has both moral and ethical ingredients and loyalties, let alone metaphysical presuppositions, is not looked on with favor; is not "politically correct," to use that by now all too worn phrase. Clearly, we neither encourage nor sanction the kind of paradigms which Simone Weil no doubt has in mind. We are hell-bent on deconstruction, and the "directors of conscience" we tend to choose are those who create and celebrate menacing solipsisms. In the academy the required focus is on the irreverent—on the mediocre and egalitarian, with standards of discrimination mercilessly sacrificed or abandoned in the name of change, progress, equality, popularity—and on what Irving Babbitt calls an "indefinite progression in unreason."

Undergraduate courses on the literature of AIDS and graduate courses on "Sacred Monsters," that is, writers like T. S. Eliot who are scornfully placed "outside the range of normal human behavior," are now taking center stage as the core curriculum is being scuttled and as clinical and ideological concerns take over. Professors of literature now and too often constitute a fifth column of enormous power and influence and their actions inevitably prompt one to ask, Who will save imaginative literature from the professors? Clearly aware of these conditions, the late Isaac Bashevis Singer, that "last teller of tales," declared: "The various schools and 'isms' of literature were invented by professors. Only small fish swim in schools."

There are many ways, to be sure, that we can be saved from professors' isms, and from the "commercial novel-makers" they institutionally enshrine for purposes that are radically removed from the supreme excellence of art form and from any genuinely human and moral vision of existence. The entropic, the solipsistic, the nihilistic, the relativistic: these are the major elements and proclivities of the writings of many contemporary American novelists imprisoned by and ultimately allegiant to a pluralistic culture. Theirs is a dismal surrender to the "antagonist world," as well as a notorious inability to attain any transcendent perspective. Sadly, our academic critics and their commanding allies in the literary establishment refuse to acknowledge these conditions that characterize the moral breakdown of imaginative literature as we encounter it in its proliferation.

Here and there, to be sure, we do hear strong voices of critical dissent. Among these the voice of Professor John W. Aldridge—his critical efforts are examined in part 2, under the title "A Corrective to Darkening Counsel"—has remained consistently honest and clear; his diagnostic critiques as found, for instance, in *The American Novel and the Way We Live Now* (1983) are especially relevant, and one cannot read words like the following without expressing gratitude to their author for his refusal to accept the monolithic critical valuations that abound and echo in what we read:

> [I]t is a characteristic of some of our best and most serious fiction that in it both the ideal and the reality of individual self-discovery and transcendence as central thematic preoccupations have been replaced by a dark fantasy in which prophecy and paranoia join to project a horror of universal conspiracy and mass apocalypse.

No doubt Aldridge's words are viewed by our minimalist commissars of literature as heresy, and within the academy those who in any way defend humane letters are often penalized, humiliated, or exiled. What we find so grimly inescapable in the republic of letters today is a view of life and literature that disdains criticism as the pursuit of virtue, choosing instead to advance the idea of desanctification. This profane process dominates our society and culture and becomes a certified attitude at every level of existence, in word and work, going beyond the nightmare visions of a Huxley or Orwell. In short, what we now see all around us is a kind of intellectual totalitarianism that has one major goal, the final "enfeeblement of the sense of value," to use Simone Weil's phrase.

Our teachers, critics, and writers, even our ministers of the Word and our legislators, it seems, are now firmly committed to the eradication of the great words like virtue, nobility, honor, honesty, generosity—words that, as Simone Weil points out, legitimately define and praise human character and conscience. "The fate of words," she writes, "is a touchstone of the progressive weakening of the idea of value, and although the fate of words does not depend upon writers one cannot help attributing a special responsibility to them, since words are their business." The present state of language, whether oral or written, abundantly underscores this decomposition.

But, as it is becoming dangerously evident, in the academy, in the book review supplements, in periodical literature in general, and in the electronics culture, those who shape opinion and have a big educative role and influence not only condone but also espouse the mediocrity that now reaches such dangerous proportions. Increasingly, common agreement is synonymous with the common denominator. Dissident opinions and judgments have only a peripheral impact. Indiscrimination becomes the pervasive condition of intellect; becomes, in short, ignorance itself and thus the great equalizer and quantifier. The discipline of criticism is viewed as elitism, which is intolerable to the majoritarian mind. Thus, expanding emphasis on multicultural studies is symptomatic of the leveling process that affects the whole social fabric. Little or no attempt is made to indicate gradations of value and achievement to differentiate between sham and truth, between good and bad, or, indeed, even between good and evil. Students now awarded baccalaureate degrees go through an entire educational process without forming any judgmental perception that, say, a Henry James is infinitely superior to a Jerzy Kosinski.

Evading moral issues and moral judgments becomes the monomania of teachers and students alike. The hierarchy of value no less than the idea of value becomes an object of ridicule, and silencing anyone who resists the "new Jacobinism," as Claes G. Ryn terms it, becomes a national pastime. To remind one of intrinsic differences is anathema. Ours is, then, a society in which the descending motion of the multitude is accounted better than the upward tendency of the few. Transcendence is still another great word banished from the lexicon of American life, still another victim of the decanonization that has been arrogantly perpetrated in recent years by Marxists, deconstructionists, behaviorists, feminists, critical theorists.

Who, then, can protect us from the "irrational empiricists"? On whom can we rely to guide us to a viable and ennobling understanding of the great words, the certitudes, that give higher meaning to life and enable us to leap over the obsessive nihilisms and perversities that dominate the view of life proclaimed by so many writers? Certainly neither the literary nor the academic establishments will help us to emerge from the cruel and marshy deeps of contemporary imaginative literature, and to put us into contact again with the great words and the virtues and criteria which result. Who, to repeat, will help us to grow wings to overcome gravity?

Again it is Simone Weil who reminds us that the task is never hopeless, that great words and great visions endure to the end of time itself, that the writings of authentic genius are alive and remain available to us: "Their contemplation is the ever-flowing source of an inspiration which may legitimately guide us." There is no need for any one of us to remain a slave of the obscurantist writers and critics and educators who have steadily betrayed the first principles of their high vocation. And, indeed, there is no need for any one of us to remain under the shadow of the malignant god Belphegor any longer than we choose to. We maintain *stasis* only so long as we want to, provided we are also willing to accept the real possibility of seeking a counterpoise to the situation in which we find ourselves. By no means should we capitulate to the demon of dissolution that now reigns in the halls and the texts of higher learning. Babbitt rightly reminds us, as very few major American critics would now dare to remind us, that "a necessary preliminary to any valid construction, must be a sound diagnosis of existing ills."

Symptomatic of these ills, as the great American novelist Willa Cather (1873–1947) trenchantly observes in her *On Writing* (1949), is the capitulation of artists to abstractions and creeds and to the urge to graft art into a science and make it sociological and psychological. Contemporary writers, critics, and students of literature, deliriously caught up in the tidal wave of political ideology, would do well to ponder Willa Cather's small classic for its meditative views and insights—for its wisdom, a word one rarely encounters these days in the American scene. What she has to say should trouble us about the ugly politicization of arts and letters. She addresses some of her remarks to the literary radicals who, in her time and now in our own, distort the true function of art in their demands for change and reform, and who, making "a career of destroying the past," merely offer us "contempt for the old."

In *On Writing* Willa Cather discloses critical vision that is miraculously free from the tyranny of abstractions and creeds that abound in the assigned texts of Foucault, Derrida, Eagleton, de Man, Hartman, Fish—the darlings of the academy who accelerate the downward motion, if not the death, of literature. In this connection, the following extract from a graduate course description (English 666. Readings in Modern Literary Theory: Reading of the Basic Texts of Contemporary Narrative Theory), at present being given in a major state university, serves as a symptom and portent:

> Starting with definitions of narrative, we move from Vladimir Propp to his structuralist and poststructuralist critics, Levi-Strauss, Barthes, Greimas. Anglo-American narratology is sampled through Kermode, Hayden White, Chatman, etc. as found in the 1979 Chicago Conference on Narrative. Theories of feminist writing and cinema will be met in the work of Teresa de Lauretis. Phenomenological and reader-response theory will be centered on Iser and Ricoeur. The work of Greimas and Eco introduces a semiotics of narrative which must be compared to companion works in anthropology, linguistics, and cognitive science.

To put these dark and dreary formulations of a professor of English, who is so pitiably bereft of any fineness of literary sense, side by side with the following quotation from Willa Cather's ennobling views "On the Art of Fiction"—it is a marvel of critical power—is to grasp just how deep the study of literature has sunk in the academy:

> Writing ought either to be the manufacture of stories for which there is a market demand—a business as safe and commendable as making bread or breakfast foods—or it should be an art, which is always a search for something for which there is no market demand, something new and untried, where the values are intrinsic and have nothing to do with standardized values. The courage to go on without compromise does not come to a writer all at once—nor, for that matter, does the ability. Both are phases of natural development.

Surely we should be thankful for great imaginators and great under-standers who, like Willa Cather, cannot be fooled about fundamentals; who help rescue us from falling terminally into the pits our professors of literature never stop digging—or for that matter, from all those cheaply manufactured "masterpieces" that, in Willa Cather's words, keep "bumping down upon us like trunks pouring down the baggage chutes from an overcrowded ocean steamer." Willa Cather reminds us that, somehow, we need to oppose the devaluation of the great words; that we need not enter that strange twilight world of a secular gnosticism that now prevails. At a time when the literati are so discouraging and faith-killing, never failing to boast that nothing matters and nothing has value, and when novelist, teacher, and critic become ardent champions of impiety and infidelity, we need more than ever to hear "the old moral harmonies." We need, too, to hear the voices of reconnection and reaffir-mation—otherwise all is lost, all is *nada*.

One cannot do better, then, than to return to the works of "authentic genius," to the guiding voice and vision of a Willa Cather who bravely ratifies her creed of art in words that postmodernists revile: "Religion and art spring from the same root and are close kin. Economics and art are strangers." These are also words that help identify the fountainhead of Willa Cather's sapiential qualities of art, and that lead one sensitive critic to remark, "she loved faithfulness. It was her preferred climate. It was a climate in which she could breathe."

This faithfulness throbs fervently in her novel *Death Comes for the Archbishop*, which was first published in 1927, but which eludes the profound disenchantment of those bleak years following World War I. (In her book of contemplative essays, *Not under Forty* [1936], Willa Cather asserts that, in 1922, "the world broke in two.") It is a novel that is rooted in the "permanent things"; the candles of belief flicker brightly and warmly in its chronicle of two Catholic missionary priests from France, Father Jean Marie Latour and Father Joseph Vaillant, who labor mightily in New Mexico at the midpoint of the nineteenth century. Devotion and reverence are virtues that suffuse their work and that define its moral goodness in all of its power. The story of their daily lives inspires and cleanses at once and provides spiritual paradigms that present-day readers desperately need. The old verities empower the novel's mood and rhythm and shape its vision. A poetry of faith and a commensurate poetry of language shape and define the novelist's narrative vision as it is delineated against a backdrop of cruciform trees, conical hills, and old mission churches in the mountains and desert.

"In lonely, sombre villages in the mountains," Willa Cather wrote in a candid and warmhearted letter concerning the composition of *Death Comes for the Archbishop*, "the church decorations were sombre, the martyrdoms bloodier, the grief of the virgin more agonized, the figure of Death more terrifying." Indeed, in this novel an extraordinary percipience of divine otherness emerges. Inspiration stamps each page, startlingly removing us from those contemporary gnostic writers who insist that there is no ultimate "reason" for valuing anything; or as Matthew Arnold wrote in one of his "Fragments" (1876): "Our aspiration quits us, not our need. / The unrest of youth departs; we cease to search. . . . "

This novel depicts moral struggle as it transforms into insight and, above all, humility. Indeed, no other virtue better characterizes Father Latour, the Apostolic Vicar to New Mexico, than humility. In him, all the great words vibrate, challenging as they do our nominalist preconceptions. Those commentators who choose to praise only Willa Cather's poetry of place—her magnificent portrayal of the southwest landscape—miss the metaphysical depths of her vision in this novel. They miss, that is to say, the full and powerful significance of Willa Cather's words to an old friend, "Faith is a gift." The expression of this faith in this novel is, in fact, an offshoot of the religious sense which she affirms and which makes her vision and craft at once palpitant and sacramental. And it is precisely the religious sense, as it pervades *Death Comes for the Archbishop*, that saves this novel from the negations that ravage so much of contemporary literature. Her celebration of the power and truth of belief inheres in and controls its tensive rhythms of existence. No sentimentalism or illusion clouds this novel; Willa Cather's spiritual realism is disinterested as she captures the world in all its glory and tragedy.

Death Comes for the Archbishop exemplifies a "conservative vision" in observing those classical restraints that Willa Cather deemed essential to the art of fiction. For her the novel must be stark and unfurnished, as she stressed in one of her most important critical essays, "The Novel Démeublé." The novelist, she states, should excise "meaningless reiterations concerning physical sensations" and "leave the room as bare as the stage of a Greek theatre," or as that house into which "the glory of the Pentecost descended"; proper cleansing and purifying, then, leave "the scene bare for the play of emotions, great and little." "The higher processes of art," she further insists, "are all processes of simplification." Her words here, in fact, help point to the nature of the greatness that lies in her novel and that, above all, comes from the quality of reverence which infuses Willa Cather's total achievement.

As an implicit dimension of the religious sense, reverence is the feeling that kindles respect and awe for the transcendent, for what lies outside one's immediate world; that redeems us from our presentness and awakens us to the divine mystery of life. Reverence is the intuitive recognition of the supertemporal and the supermundane that raises—incarnates—word and work to higher levels of meaning and perception. It has the power of "discerning of spirits." As the victory of the sacred over the profane, it accents the journey on the upward path. Creative writers who possess the gift of reverence communicate its spiritual authenticity with a detachment, a lucidity, a radiance, and a humility that elevate language to the height of contemplation. By no means does this process signify an escape or a mystical flight from the body of mankind. Rather, it marks the union of body and soul, of flesh and spirit, when language itself becomes a language of reverence. In *Death Comes for the Archbishop* the religious sense molds a language of reverence, and also specifies the fundamental ethos of the novelist.

This reverence enables Willa Cather to disclose how genuine self-examination and self-transcendence lift her characters to a glory now foreign to merchants of abstraction and insignificance. It can perhaps be asserted that reverence is the spiritual hero of *Death Comes for the Archbishop*. Or, to put it another way, this is a novel of reverence. This reverence pervades the prose, as well as the land and the people of the novel. Friendships, separations, and deaths are bathed in their full living reality, never romanticized or fantasied. Disillusionment, doubt, isolation, sadness, and fear unflaggingly tug at the hearts and souls of the major characters, but angst is arrested in Willa Cather's reverent vision, which she conveys with unusual narrative economy and honesty.

Again and again this reverence emerges in numinous language and episodes, which attain great poetic intensity and feeling. Reverence endows this novel with an ascending order and beauty, memorably rendered in unforgettable scenes often involving Father Vaillant and Father Latour, the main actors in this drama of two priests, one complementing and ampiflying the persona of the other, who share a lifetime of heroic strivings and sacrifices in their missionary work in the New World.

An outstanding example of the reverence that lies at the heart of Willa Cather's novel and colors its mood and setting, and, indeed, its human complexities, occurs in the concluding pages. We have reached that point in the story when Father Vaillant, now Bishop Latour's Vicar, is preparing to extend his missionary work to Colorado, in a primitive, lawless part of the Rocky Mountains where wandering gold miners are recklessly digging for fortunes in gold. It is clear that a considerable change will now affect the lives of the two priests. For Father Vaillant the new assignment means a new challenge, which he welcomes. "But it was the discipline of his life to break ties; to say farewell and move on into the unknown." Bishop Latour, in particular, has a premonition that this change signals permanent separation:

> As a Bishop, he could only approve Father Vaillant's eagerness to be gone, and the enthusiasm with which he turned to hardships of a new kind. But as a man, he was a little hurt that his old comrade should leave his old companion without one regret. He seemed to know, as if it had been revealed to him, that this was the final break; that their lives would part here, and that they would never work together again.

In these pages, fraught with emotional revelation, we also learn how much Father Latour needed the companionship of Father Vaillant, friends since their boyhood in France. It is the aristocratic Father Latour who shows himself to be the more sensitive, the more lonely, the more needing, the more vulnerable, emotionally, of the two friends. Willa Cather renders human complexities with commensurate poetic power, with narrative genius, with a stark compassion that is real and discerning. And here, too, Father Vaillant's own persona is no less drawn with comparable interest and insight. He is in every way Father Latour's opposite, at least on the surface—tougher, harder, more rugged, more direct:

> He was short, skinny, bowlegged from a life on horseback, and his countenance had little to recommend it but kindliness and vivacity. . . . His skin was hardened and seamed by exposure to weather in a bitter climate, his neck scrawny and wrinkled like an old man's. A bold, blunt-tipped nose, positive skin, a very large mouth—the lips thick and succulent but never loose, never relaxed, always stiffened by effort or working with excitement.

In sharp contrast, Father Latour is a "man of severe and refined tastes," tall, reserved, handsome, aristocratic in bearing and family background, more formal and reticent:

> His manners, even when he was alone in the desert, were distinguished. He had a kind of courtesy toward himself, toward his beasts, toward the juniper tree before which he knelt, and the God whom he was addressing.

But he is also more prone to moods of lassitude and melancholy, even self-questioning, at times "going through one of those periods of coldness and doubt which, from his boyhood, had occasionally settled down upon his spirit and made him feel an alien, wherever he was." Willa Cather's portrayal of the two priests never becomes simplistic or vaporous characterization. She portrays qualitative distinctions in all their mystery, and renders the deep and hidden facets of interpersonal relations in all their subtlety. An imaginative integrity, which Henry James associates with a transcendent "disinterestedness," is poignantly at work in the novel, always taking us back to Willa Cather's metaphysic of art, to the virtue of reverence that inheres in and intensifies the magnitude of her vision and craft.

Thus, to return here to those pages in the text describing the parting of the ways of two priests who together have exalted in their missionary work, in their long pilgrimages, and in shared dangers, we witness a full demonstration of Willa Cather's "true vocation for imaginative writing." Father Vaillant, "whose life was to be a succession of mountain ranges, pathless deserts, yawning canyons and swollen rivers," and who is now so "wholly absorbed in his preparations for saving souls in the gold camps" that he is "blind to everything else," begins unconsciously to reflect on those differences that separate his life from that of Father Latour's. Slowly but forcibly he sees the "fine personality" of the first Bishop of New Mexico in all of its distinctions. This mood of reflection, emerging as it does from a humane and moral conscience, resonates on the afternoon of the next day, when we find Father Vaillant, having concluded all preparations for his departure, seated at the Bishop's desk, writing letters to his brother and sister in his native France, explaining the nature of his new missionary work: "He wrote rapidly and jerkily, moving his lips as well as his fingers."

Father Latour now enters the study and asks whether Father Vaillant will be taking his mule Contento with him to Colorado. (This mule is one of two cream-colored mules—the other is called Angelica—that Father Vaillant had managed years before to extricate as gifts from a rich Mexican, Manuel Lujon, who owned a rancho near Bernalillo, New Mexico. The two mules had served well the two priests in the course of their ceaseless missionary journeys.) The significance of the pending separation is captured in the short exchange between the two priests; the scene is quietly but fatefully dramatic in disclosing the interior feelings of both men.

> "I did not mean to interrupt you, Joseph, but do you intend to take Contento with you to Colorado?"
> Father Joseph blinked. "Why certainly. I had intended to ride him. However, if you have need for him here —"

"Oh no. Not at all. But if you take Contento, I will ask you to take Angelica as well. They have a great affection for each other; why separate them indefinitely? One could not explain to them. They have worked long together."

The novelist conveys here the symbolic import of this conversation, poetically caught in wonderfully dramatic nuances, as we now discern the inexorable meaning of their parting—its finality and the inevitable consequences it has in the lives of two friends. A narrative quietude is crucially telling at this point, as the reader also fathoms the two priests' apprehension of the solitariness associated with the priestly vows to God and to His holy service. This apprehension, unspoken and couched in the pain of sadness, further heightens the deepest human and universal feelings that sometimes do not venture to articulate travail, which has to be suffered quietly and bravely, with solemn resignation and brave acceptance. The immediate scene thus comes to a symbolic close that memorably epiphanizes the rising emotional momentum of the announced separation as its drama has irreversibly unfolded:

> Father Vaillant made no reply. He stood looking intently at the pages of the letter. The Bishop saw a drop of water splash down upon the violet script and spread. He turned quickly and went out through the arched doorway.

The dénouement is equally compelling as the reader enters—both compassionately and understandingly—the innermost reaches of each man's emotional world. It is now sunrise of the next morning as Father Vaillant, riding Contento, and his helper, riding Angelica, set out on a new missionary journey. The brilliant particulars of this scene weigh heavily and vividly on the memory:

> They took the old road to the northeast, through the sharp red sand hills spotted with juniper, and the Bishop accompanied them as far as the loop where the road wound out on the top of one of these conical hills, giving the departing traveller his last glimpse of Santa Fé. There Father Joseph drew rein and looked back at the town lying rosily in the morning light, the mountain behind it, and the hills close about it like two encircling arms.
>
> "*Auspice*, Maria!" he murmured as he turned his back on those familiar things.

We have, in the above passage, a twin sense of ending and of new beginnings as two priests press on in their spiritual pilgrimage, the imaging theme in *Death Comes for the Archbishop*. In its emotional, moral, and spiritual overtones, this passage brings to mind Willa Cather's longtime admiration of John Bunyan's *The Pilgrim's Progress*, which she first read avidly in her youth, even reading it eight times in one winter and learning to recite long sections from it; its influence on her writings was to remain resonant and indelible. As a testament of faith, it is a passage that vibrantly recalls the words of Bunyan's Shepherds on the Delectable Mountains:

> "These mountains are Immanuel's Land, and they are within sight of his city, and the sheep are also his, and he laid down his life for them."

Any additional commentary here would be inadequate in fully measuring the nobility of Willa Cather's vision as it is so exactingly realized in *Death Comes for the Archbishop*. The specific episode that has been examined should be enough to prompt a reader to turn attentively to the entire text of the novel and to experience the reverence that imbues and refines the novelist's vision. This entire process ultimately elevates and sacralizes the meaning of human character and becomes a moral process of discovery and ascent. It also transcribes "the idea of the holy," which contemporary fiction chooses so often to reduce to a world in which, according to novelist Pete Dexter, National Book Award winner in 1988 for his novel *Paris Trout*, "Violence is a great shaping thing. It shapes what follows for everybody."

Death Comes for the Archbishop refuses to confuse the categories of the sacred and the profane and in effect also provides an orienting sense of spiritual nobility. "There is such a thing in life as nobility," Willa Cather said, "and novels which celebrate it will always be the novels which are finally loved." The two priests in the novel enact precisely this nobility that impels one to go beyond the walls of personality and soar upwards so as "to reach ever higher levels of attention," in Simone Weil's words. This is a novel about two great souls in search of the "supernatural good" and in sight of that "other world." In this novel of the very highest genius we make contact with a novelist who is acutely aware of the needs of the soul and who helps us resist the world we experience in all the fury of its downward pull—a world without faith, without hope, without aspiration, without God. And throughout we hear the voice of Willa Cather speaking out with a reverence etched in wondrous beauty and clarity, telling us that there is absolutely no power on earth that can keep us from growing wings to overcome gravity.

In Steady Ascension

With the turn of the century and the coming of a new millennium, the hope arises that the Age of the New Barbarians will flounder upon its misconceptions, its lack of roots and stability, its disregard for essential human values, its failure of faith in the human spirit, and that a renaissance will occur, a return to tradition, to the ancient beliefs that have always sustained the human spirit. Still the question arises: Where can the way through be found, down what path, behind what door? The answer, of course, is that there presently exist, for those who choose to follow them, many avenues to redemption, to spiritual recovery, to transcendence. None offers more than the poet Czeslaw Milosz. A descendant of a Polish-speaking family, Milosz was born in 1911 in Szetejnie, Lithuania, which then belonged to Russia. He is a renowned Polish poet, "one of the greatest poets in our time, perhaps the greatest," according to the late Joseph Brodsky. He is also a great Eastern European man of letters. Many of his poems, novels, essays, and translations, originally written in Polish, have been translated into English. In 1980 he received the Nobel Prize in literature.

Both as a poet and as a man of letters, Milosz sees his true vocation as one that contemplates Being. His is a moral vision which he most often conveys in the form of moral meditations. He never ceases to explore and reflect on the human condition in terms of the reality of nature and the reality of history. The meaning of human destiny and the human actions that shape this destiny come under close scrutiny in his writings. Matters of character and conscience are of deep moral concern to him, which he addresses in their individual and collective significances. Refusing to ignore the metaphysical and religious constituents of human existence, he asserts: "I am searching for an answer as to what will result from an internal erosion of religious beliefs."

A "child of Europe," he remains a firsthand witness to the major crises of the twentieth century: the disenchantment in the 1920s following the first Great War; the economic slump in the 1930s, and the growing threat of Nazism and Fascism; the abominations of the second Great War; the scourge of Stalinism after 1945, especially in Eastern Europe; the protest movements in the 1960s and the birth of democratic opposition to totalitarian tyranny in the 1970s; and the democratic triumphs in the late 1980s. Throughout his experience of all these epochal events Milosz has given his testimony with exceptional honesty and dignity, never trying to cover up the debasement of the modern human spirit. Though he is by no means a "thoughtless optimist," he finds hope in poetry and affirms a steady movement from human affliction to salvation to redemption.

Nowhere does he make this note of hope more emphatic than in his "Nobel Lecture" with which one of his volumes of essays closes, *Beginning with My Streets: Essays and Recollections* (1991). In this lecture, in which he lays bare his "memory of wounds," he speaks of a "profound transformation" that is occurring and that "it is probable that in spite of all horrors and perils, our time will be judged as a necessary phase of travail before mankind ascends to a new awareness." These are brave words, brave hopes, and come from one who discerns the "spiritual vacancy, isolation of the individual, the minatory character of civilization as a whole," as well as from one who sees twentieth-century man stripped of absolutes, having only "[t]he starry sky above, *no* moral law within." That Milosz is steeped in the writings of Fyodor Dostoevsky and Simone Weil, on both of whom he has written with much insight, is made manifest in his worldview. He neither trusts nor hides in the world of illusion and sentiment, and is as much aware of the snares of illusion as is an earlier Polish exile, the Joseph Conrad who renders "the curse of consciousness" in novels like *Nostromo* (1904) and *Victory* (1915).

Milosz's moral vision is a transcendent vision, ever aware of, because also a part of, both the human depravity and the human greatness enacted in our time. For Milosz the metaphysical element of transcendence is deepened by the virtue of humanity. It is the moral quality of humility, of understanding that precedes revelation—as a "precarious balance of opposites"—that reverberates in these lines from the poem "Winter" (found in *Unattainable Earth* [1986]):

> I passed judgment on that. Though marked myself.
> This hasn't been the age for the righteous and the decent.
> I know what it means to beget monsters
> And to recognize in them myself.

The union of these two qualities makes possible a statement that contains these significant words:

> Those who are alive receive a mandate from those who are silent forever. They can fulfill their duties only by trying to reconstruct precisely things as they were and by wresting the past from fictions and legends.

The shaping spirit of this union ultimately saves Milosz not only from arrogance but also from "nihilistic temptation" and enables him to communicate the wise insights that make him a humane man of letters who unhesitantly confesses his "respect and gratitude for certain things which protect people from internal disintegration and from yielding to tyranny." Such protection, Milosz reminds us, is anchored in the discipline of continuity, of connection, of community. And in Milosz himself we are, as the writings collected in *Beginning with My Streets* eloquently confirm, in contact with a poet and man of letters who possesses the historical sense and insists that "Man is history, historical memory."

What Simone Weil speaks of as "deracination," José Ortega y Gasset, as "deorientation," and Erich Heller, as "disinheritance" are conditions that Milosz views as representative of modern civilization. Since the eighteenth century, he believes, we have increasingly become captives of the material and scientific world, "that realm of spiritual pain such as is borne and must be borne by the crippled man." This is the realm that William Blake calls Ulro, the "deepest night," the "Sea of Satan," the "Grave." In the twentieth century, in particular, Milosz believes, "the land of Ulro" manifests "the utter failure of secular humanism, a failure sponsored by the very successes of that same humanism." Milosz's view of the world harbors a hard realism; and he describes poetry as a "passionate pursuit of the Real." No sentimentality, or escapism, no excessive promise, no utopian dream or "fuzzy syncretism" cloud Milosz's discernment of human existence in all of its inherent paradox, ambiguity, contradiction. As a poet and man of letters, Milosz testifies to the palpitant relevance of what the Polish novelist and diarist Witgold Gombrowicz (1904–1969)—to whom he devotes an incisive essay in his book—depicts in these words: "The difference between the writers of Eastern and Western Europe consists in that the first know that man can do anything to man." (Here some readers will also recall these fearsome words by Conrad, "Poland's English genius," in *Victory*: "The world is a bad dog. It will bite you if you give it a chance. . . . ")

Unfailingly, Milosz identifies himself as a Polish poet. "The true home of the Polish poet," he asserts in *The Witness of Poetry*, containing his "Charles Eliot Norton Lectures at Harvard University, 1981–1982," "is history, and though Polish history is much shorter than that of Greece, it is no less rich in defeats and lost illusions." (Milosz makes this geographical reference at the point when he is discussing the modern Greek poet from Alexandria, Constantine Cavafy, and his poems as "meditations on the past.") This history also instances for Milosz what he speaks of as "an encounter of an European poet with the hell of the twentieth century." In his poem entitled "Farewell," dated "Kraków, 1945," he tells us something about this encounter and conveys the anguish of a Polish poet who, to recall Anna Akhmatova's words, has "To walk with a candle and howl":

> From life, from the apple cut by the flaming knife,
> What grain will be saved?
> My son, believe me, nothing remains.
> Only adult toil,
> the furrow of fate in the palm.
> Only toil,
> nothing more.[1]

Clearly the "historical imagination" vibrates in Milosz's consciousness; the offshoots and shimmer of that imagination have a way of returning us to the memory of "the fathers" and of "the things." "For at every moment," he writes, "whether we admit it or not, we are in the power of those who lived before us. Where there is no memory, both time and space are a wasteland; the trees and rocks speak to us, but we do not understand them. Only through memory can we learn to understand their speech."

For Milosz the mission of the artist and the function of art have far-reaching moral significance. When one studies not only this collection of essays but also earlier prose writings like *The Captive Mind* (1953), *Emperor of the Earth* (1977), and *The Land of Ulro* (1984), one meets the man of letters inspecting and measuring the moral meaning of art and life, of art and reality, of art and history. *Beginning with My Streets* further bears out and enriches Milosz's burden of vision and its moral foundations. One could even say that there is not a paragraph in which Milosz's moral sense and moral responsibility, in confluence, do not illuminate the substance of his thought, his search for meaning, for values:

> It is not literature's task to provide answers; it is sufficient if it poses questions. No doubt. But the author seeks answers, for if he were not seeking, he would not pose the questions; the reader is also seeking.

His spiritual honesty bursts forth again and again with startling force and transparency, as when he declares that the writer who aspires to enchant people is prone to compromises and following fads:

---

[1]Unless otherwise noted in the text, all the poems quoted are from Czeslaw Milosz, *The Collected Poems, 1931–1987* (New York: Ecco Press, 1988).

When I say "Not to enchant anybody," I mean that I follow my own need for order, for rhythm and form—here, now, before my own piece of paper—and I use them as weapons or as instruments against chaos and nothingness.

Milosz's preoccupation with the writer's need to pose questions, to seek answers, to make judgments, to define decisions, to take a stand and also be right underscores the intensity of moral struggle:

But what does poetry have in common with being right? A whole lot. The arrangement of words implies choice, choice implies deliberation, and behind your words lurks a silent judgment about the many human matters you have dealt with. If in your judgment (conscious, semiconscious, or unconscious) you are right, you will break through the cocoon of generally accepted opinions in your epoch; the others, however, will become trapped in them.

The writer, the thinker, he insists, should not get lost in abstractions or hide in illusions. ("The best cure for illusions is hunger, patience, and obedience," Milosz states in his poem "1945.") Historical events and circumstances do not allow one to swallow the magic "pill of Murti-Bing" that relieves one from individual responsibility:

The years of the Second World War were a moment of shock and nakedness. The horror of events was so enormous that few poets in history have had to face anything like it; it compelled them to either undertake a total reassessment or recognize the meaninglessness of art. Reality did not deal kindly with the theories of aesthetes.

No single sentence better epitomizes Milosz's grasp of the responsibility of writers and of the power of words than this in the essay titled "A Poet Between East and West":

Language, liberated from aims and duties, seeks to speak by itself to itself.

Moral strength characterizes Milosz's writings and also makes us profoundly aware of a poet and man of letters who categorically rejects the "devaluation of the world, such as is found in contemporary nihilism." In his writings, in his vision, we thus come face to face with one who belongs to that line of great modern moral artists which includes Albert Camus, who, it is worth mentioning, was helpful to Milosz when he left Stalinist Poland for Paris in 1951 and whose friendship enabled Milosz

to "survive in the labyrinth of the West."[2] Of Milosz it can be said, as
Jean-Paul Sartre said of Camus in an obituary tribute back in 1960, that
"through his dogged rejections he reaffirmed, at the heart of our epoch,
against the Machiavellians and against the Idol of Realism, the existence
of the moral issue."

In *Beginning with My Streets* Milosz portrays his continuing "search
for self-definition" in a world that swings desperately between despair
and faith, between his perception in the late 1940s that "Before us lies the
heart of darkness," and his "thankfulness" in the late 1980s that

> You gave me gifts, God-enchanter.
> I give you thanks for good and ill.
> Eternal light in everything on earth.
> As now, so on the day after my death.

No less than the Camus who insists that "One must accept everything.
Between yes and no," and who believes the artist "will seek help in
hope," Milosz demonstrates comparable patience and endurance. That
Milosz is a suffering witness to history; that he is also terribly aware of
the "insoluble contradiction" which exists in the world and which ultimately lies between gravity and grace; that he is besieged and yet formed
by historical circumstances and conditions: these are factors that impact
on the reach and import of his vision. They also emphasize the development and direction of his work as a whole, stretching from the purely
intellectual to the philosophical to the meditational. "The aim of Milosz's
poetry," Madeline G. Levine writes, "has been the exploration of man's
moral predicament in an often diabolical world."[3]

But Milosz is not so much a moralist as he is an indefatigable moral
prober of the human condition. "[O]ntological contemplation is my very
essence," he declares. He probes religious problems without at the same
time being a religionist; to be more exact, he is a metaphysical "poet of
pity and anger" who possesses a "dialectical mind" that holds "opposing
truths in tension." When the Nobel Prize was awarded to Milosz, the presentation of the Swedish Academy included these words: "In both an outward and an inward sense he is an exiled writer, a stranger for whom
physical exile is really a reflection of a metaphysical—or even religious—
spiritual exile applying to humanity in general."

---

[2]See Herbert R. Lottman, *Albert Camus: A Biography* (Garden City NY:
Doubleday, 1979) 418n.16.

[3]Madeline G. Levine, *Contemporary Polish Poetry, 1925–1975*, Twayne World
Authors (Boston: Twayne, 1981) 54.

The apocalyptic note rings out strongly in Milosz's *oeuvre*: pain, disillusion, suffering, *dolor* are etched in his vision, in his poetry of incantation, and the images of great moral disasters, as found in these stinging lines from his 1947 poem "The Spirit of Laws," are ineradicable in his memory:

> From the cry of children on the floors of stations beyond time,
> From the red scars of two wars on the forehead,
> I awoke under the bronze of winged monuments,
> Under the griffins of a Masonic temple
> With the dying ash of a cigar.

This stanza brings to mind, again, the truth of Albert Camus's words, "Nobody, I think, can ask [my generation] to be optimists." Yet Milosz's apprehension of the great ethical void, no less than Camus's, does not overwhelm him, does not throw him into the nets of nihilism. An interior moral strength saves him from such a fatal capitulation. Milosz agrees with Camus that one should not expect from the modern writer "complete solutions and high morals," and also shares Camus's faith in human possibility ("the womb of the negative is kept open") and in the concomitant need not "to bow down to pestilences." Indeed, Milosz believes that "for rebirth to occur, one first has to enter the heart of darkness"; in his poem "Central Park," included in his first volume of poems published in exile, *Light of Day* (1953), the element of possibility resonates:

> Gazing calmly upon force, we know
> That those who wish to rule the world will pass,
> And we realize that it is not always necessary
> To live with knife or gun in hand.
> The cunning of weapons turns to misfortune
> And strong winds tear standards to tatters,
> But glory, our heritage from Greece,
> Will last as long as mankind lasts.

To speak of Milosz's moral vision, born of struggle, is also to speak of his eschatological vision, influenced by his readings and reflection on Blaise Pascal, Emmanuel Swedenborg, Lev Shestov, Sergei Bulgakov, Simone Weil, and especially his relative Oscar Milosz (1877–1939), the French poet, Lithuanian by birth, whose mystical and eschatological speculations helped shape Milosz's rejection of materialistic scientism. Not surprisingly, then, Milosz's admission that "I belong to those who believe in *apokatastasis*," the Greek word for "reinstatement," points to the indomitable spiritual transcendences that ennoble his life and thought. Nor is it surprising, in this connection, that he acknowledges mystical faith in the teleological view expounded by that "first systematic theologian," one of the great Christian Platonists of ancient Alexandria, Origen: "the consummation and restoration of all things," when "God shall be all in all."

Milosz's "representative man," as he tells us in *The Land of Ulro*, emerges from tradition, unlike, say, Samuel Beckett's, who "comes from nowhere." The source of his poetry, he further insists, has religious roots in "my childhood, which was a childhood of carols, Month of May devotions, vespers. . . . " And as would be expected from Milosz's "Polish inheritance," and specifically his Roman Catholicism, he acknowledges the existence of good and evil, even as he condemns the surrender of so many moderns to noncommittal, areligious, and aphilosophical perspectives. "I feel a profound gratitude," Milosz declares, "that there is *Una Sancta Catholica Ecclesia*. . . . " His religious ideas, it should be stressed, have also been deeply influenced by the Dostoevsky who maintains that man must choose between God and the devil, and also by the Simone Weil who, posing the vexing problem of necessity and determinism, asserts: "God consigned all phenomena without exception to the mechanism of the world"; "necessity is the veil of God." In the end Milosz confirms the truth of Flannery O'Connor's words, "To try to disconnect faith from vision is to do violence to the whole personality, and the whole personality participates in the act of writing."

To be sure, his religious position is one that is keenly attuned to the heightened doubts and contradictions of the modern world, and catches the dangerous and destructive tensions that have pushed many writers in our time from "the hands of God" into spiritual homelessness, into the vacuum of disinheritance, and, finally, into "the camp of the Man-god." But for Milosz there is not the dead end of spiritual negation embodied in Beckett's "texts of nothingness." Statism no less than solipsism is a condition that he sees as being cowardly. The movement of life, he claims, consists of "successive renewals and incarnations." His writings in effect tellingly remind us that he is a modern man of letters who accepts his place in time with a strong feeling of responsibility:

> But I feel closer to the view that man lives in time and in some way has to build those eternal and lasting values out of time. Time is given to man for his use. But he should not allow himself to be completely carried away by time, because then he will be lost in relativism and utter fluidity and be smashed to bits.[4]

---

[4]Ewa Czarnecka and Aleksandr Fiut, *Conversations with Czeslaw Milosz*, trans. Richard Lowrie (San Diego: Harcourt, Brace, Jovanovich, 1987) 181.

His words here are representative of sharpness and clarity of mind, of intellect, of moral seriousness. They are words, too, that reflect a vision that is sinewy and deliberate in temper, tone, breadth. Invariably in his writings we make contact with a man of letters who transposes experience into words and who has contended determinedly with the great historical and metaphysical issues of the modern age.

He is far more than simply "one of those polymathical Europeans," as he is sometimes assumed to be by American commentators. Clearly, Milosz challenges a superficial assumption such as this, speaking as he does, inclusively, on the highest intellectual, political, literary, and spiritual level. His positions and judgments are not defiled by the kind of one-dimensional ideological orientation that cripples the work and thought of influential European writers like Georg Lukàcs (1885–1971), the Hungarian Marxist critical theorist who swore loyalty to Lenin's "materialism and empirocriticism," and Jacques Derrida (b. 1930), the French poststructuralist whose "strategy of deconstruction" leads many American academics and their deluded students into the smelly marshes of nihilism.

To English-speaking readers Milosz no doubt poses difficulty of comprehension. His is a sensibility centered in a world and in a place and time foreign to Americans, or at least hard to recognize or identify with historically. The reckless growth of secularist humanist ideologies, and increasingly antitraditionalist, antimetaphysical, and antihistorical habits of thought and mind, no doubt compound this difficulty. Sadly, too, the intellectual and spiritual legacy of ancient Israel, Greece, and Rome is eroding in contemporary Western civilization, and this is precisely the legacy of which Milosz is a brave conservator and celebrator. In particular the classical and biblical constituents of Milosz's vision distinctly separate him from the specious forms of an antinomian romanticism that dominates the present-day academy and cultural life. In some ways Milosz invites from an audience the kind of antipathy or skepticism that, in an earlier era, greeted a great Spanish man of letters, Don Miguel de Unamuno (1864–1936). For no less than Unamuno of *"el sentimiento trágico de la vida en los hombres y los pueblos,"* the Milosz of the "unattainable earth" opposes a self-sufficient rationalism, scientism, and devaluation of "holiness of being." His poem "On Prayer," with its religious and sapiential overtones, is much to the point here:

> You ask me how to pray to someone who is not.
> All I know is that prayer constructs a velvet bridge
> And walking it we are aloft, as on a springboard,
> Above landscapes the color of ripe gold
> Transformed by a magic stopping of the sun.

That bridge leads to the shore of Reversal
Where everything is just the opposite and the word *is*
Unveils a meaning we hardly envisioned.
Notice: I say we; there, every one, separately,
Feels compassion for others entangled in the flesh
And knows that if there is no other shore
They will take that aerial bridge all the same.

For English-speaking readers the difficulty of appreciating an Eastern European writer can measurably diminish when one places Milosz alongside T. S. Eliot (1888–1965), revered modern poet, critic, and man of letters. Both Eliot and Milosz depict the consequences of their removal from their native realm. Both give witness to the historical exigencies of modern history and to the crisis of modernism as a whole, to what Oscar Milosz terms "an age of jeering ugliness." Both enunciate a conservative vision rooted in the moral imagination and in the great religious and spiritual traditions of Western civilization. Both are responsive to actions and tendencies that shake the foundations of faith and life in the West. Both are intensely engaged in moral and ethical questions, as these are often provoked by those moderns whom Eliot sees as plagued by "the demon of doubt," chasing furiously "after strange gods." Both attest to the constant and fateful interconnection of economic, political, philosophical, and religious problems. Both present their critiques of a profane liberalism with unyielding fortitude. Both condemn those collectivist policies and programs that Simone Weil images as the Great Beast of social idolatry, which Eliot sees in the light of a modern industrial and scientific world in which "we become mechanized in mind, and consequently attempt to provide solutions in terms of *engineering*, for problems which are essentially problems of *life*."[5]

Of course, these correspondences should not lead us to think that Eliot and Milosz possess an internal, organic equivalence as writers. Such a claim would admit to an oversimplification of the true role of the poet as a man of letters who exercises the full play of what Eliot terms "constant surveillance" and shows a steady attentiveness to the "cultural map." In Eliot the note of weariness ("when time stops and time is never ending"), of disillusion, compelled by "the disorder, the futility, the meaninglessness, the mystery of life and suffering," is always there, as he slowly makes his way "through the cold dark and empty desolation" to the point when he can declare that "Only through time is time con-

---

[5]T. S. Eliot, "The Man of Letters and the Future of Europe," *The Sewanee Review* 53/3 (Summer 1945): 338.

quered." Milosz's catastrophism actuates Eliot's view of the "human predicament," especially as found in those troubling facets of twentieth-
century life that Eliot, in "Burnt Norton," sees

> In a dim light: neither daylight,
> Investing form with lucid stillness
> Turning shadow into transient beauty
> With slow rotation suggesting permanence
> Nor darkness to purify the soul
> Emptying the sensual with deprivation
> Cleansing affection from the temporal.
> Neither plenitude nor vacancy.

For Eliot and Milosz human order and dignity are matters of almost
terrifying concern that lend urgency to their poetry and prose. And as
poets and men of letters they are equally concerned with the total process
of denial and affirmation and its effects on all civilizational levels.
Generational and geographical elements divide and yet connect and continue their witness as men of letters. The substance of Eliot's work and
thought first emerged in the years immediately before the Great War and
particularly in "the years of *l'entre deux guerres*." Indeed, the publication
of *Four Quartets* in 1943 marked his "farewell to poetry." Milosz, it can
be said, extends and toughens the function of the man of letters in a postwar, post-Christian world. Thus the Munich of September 1938, which for
Eliot "brought a profounder realisation of a general plight," becomes in
Milosz the immediate experience of the inferno of totalitarianism. He
speaks experientially as "a poor Christian [who] looks at the ghetto":

> Slowly, boring a tunnel, a guardian mole makes his way,
> With a small red lamp fastened to his forehead.
> He touches buried bodies, counts them, pushes on,
> He distinguishes human ashes by their luminous vapor,
> The ashes of each man by a different part of the spectrum.

In Milosz, experience shapes the vision and vision recreates the
experience. Modernism *in extremis* constitutes the terrain of battle for him,
and his reports come, as it were, from the Eastern front, from "the land
of Ulro." "One can well imagine," he writes, "the effect . . . of having
one's gravest forebodings borne out; of wartime Warsaw and that
postwar spectacle when suffering, by then routine, was to be experienced
in even stronger doses. . . . " Such a world signified for Milosz the
diminution of human possibility, and also negated the ideal that the
Lithuanian city of Wilno, now Vilnius, always held for him:

Wilno was where I passed my boyhood, thinking that my life would develop along quite ordinary lines; it was only later that everything in that life began to turn upside down. So Wilno became a reference mark for me—of possibility, the possibility of normalcy.

Czeslaw Milosz has looked the empire of might directly in the face and has shown that all its power and principalities are not invincible. A man of letters, he has wrestled fiercely with men of arms. In a time of spiritual disintegration he has sought to defend those first principles that "faceless men" cynically and brutally discard. For Milosz there are always luminous moments in the midst of the general breakdown of civilization when a man can still find his soul. In the "biting frost," when "all is cold and gray," Milosz hears "bells in winter."

Rightly, the Polish critic Stanislaw Baranczak finds in the fabric and texture of Milosz's achievement the supreme element of transcendence. "His entire career," he observes, "can be seen as a process of steady ascension."[6] But here it is best to allow Milosz to speak for himself, to give his own testimony of conscience, "my yes and no," as a poet and man of letters whose living witness and words link us to the past and to the future and help us grow wings to overcome gravity:

> If disintegration is a function of development, and development a function of disintegration, the race between them may very well end in the victory of disintegration. For a long time, but not forever—and here is where hope enters. It is neither chimerical or foolish. On the contrary, every day one can see signs indicating that now, at the present moment, something new, and on a scale never witnessed before, is being born: humanity as an elemental force conscious of transcending Nature, for it lives by memory of itself, that is, in History.[7]

---

[6]"Czeslaw Milosz," in *European Writers: The Twentieth Century*, ed. George Stade, 2 vols., European Writers 10 and 11 (New York: Scribner, 1990) 1:2929.

[7]Czeslaw Milosz, *The Witness of Poetry*, Charles Eliot Norton Lectures 1981–1982 (Cambridge MA: Harvard University Press, 1983) 116.

A Selected Bibliography
of Sources

The following list of books and other references is presented here, first, to supplement and to amplify the general documentation found in the text and in the footnotes; and, second, to give a reader further direction in locating and clarifying the source and the context of a particular quotation or reference. This list, I hope, should also enable a reader to see at a glance the sources I have relied on and selected as most germane to my subject matter in its latitude and in its depth.

A reader who wants to place an individual essay in the book in its specific time frame should consult the "Bibliographical Note"—pages 291-92, above—which provides full information regarding original title, date of publication, pagination, and the name of the journal in which the essay first appeared.

Aldridge, John W. *The American Novel and the Way We Live Now*. New York and London: Oxford University Press, 1983.

_____. *Classics and Contemporaries*. Columbia MO and London: University of Missouri Press, 1992.

_____. *Talents and Technicians: Literary Chic and the New Assembly-Line Fiction*. New York: Charles Scribner's Sons, 1992.

Allen, Alexander V. G. *The Continuity of Christian Thought: A Study of Modern Theology in the Light of Its History*. Boston: Houghton, Mifflin and Co., 1884.

Arnold, Matthew. *Culture & Anarchy: An Essay in Political and Social Criticism*. New York: Macmillan, 1924; 1869.

Babbitt, Irving. "Buddha and the Occident." In *The Dhammapada*. Translated from the Pāli by Irving Babbitt. New York and London: Oxford University Press, 1936; New York: New Directions, 1965.

_____. *Democracy and Leadership*. Boston and New York: Houghton Mifflin Company, 1924; Indianapolis: Liberty Classics, 1979.

_____. *Irving Babbitt: Representative Writings*. Edited and with an introduction by George A. Panichas. Lincoln and London: University of Nebraska Press, 1981.

_____. *Literature and the American College: Essays in Defense of the Humanities*. Boston and New York: Houghton Mifflin Co., 1908; Chicago: Gateway Editions/Regnery Gateway, Inc., 1956; Clifton NJ: Augustus M. Kelley, 1972; Washington DC: National Humanities Institute, 1986.

_____. *The Masters of Modern French Criticism.* Boston and New York: Houghton Mifflin Co., 1912; New York: Farrar, Straus, and Co., 1963; Westport CT: Greenwood Press, 1977.

_____. *The New Laokoon: An Essay on the Confusion of the Arts.* Boston and New York: Houghton Mifflin Co., 1910.

_____. *On Being Creative and Other Essays.* Boston and New York: Houghton Mifflin Co., 1932; New York: Biblo and Tannen, 1968.

_____. *Rousseau and Romanticism.* Boston and New York: Houghton Mifflin, 1919; New York: Meridian Books, 1955; Austin: University of Texas Press, 1977; New York: AMS Press, 1978.

_____. *Spanish Character and Other Essays.* Edited by Frederick Manchester, Rachel Giese, and William F. Giese. Boston and New York: Houghton Mifflin Co., 1940. (Later published under the title *Character and Culture: Essays East and West.* With an introduction by Claes G. Ryn and with an index to Babbitt's collected works. New Brunswick CT and London: Transaction Publishers, 1995.)

Barzun, Jacques, editor. *The Selected Writings of John Jay Chapman.* New York: Farrar, Straus and Cudahy, 1957.

_____. *Teacher in America.* Garden City NY: Doubleday & Company, 1954; 1945.

Bell, Bernard Iddings. *Crisis in Education: A Challenge to American Complacency.* New York: McGraw-Hill Book Company, Inc., 1949.

Benda, Julien. *The Betrayal of the Intellectuals.* Translated from the French by Richard Aldington. With an introduction by Herbert Read. Boston: Beacon Press, 1955; 1927.

Berdyaev, Nicholas [Nikolai Berdiaev]. *Dostoevsky.* Translated from the Russian by Donald Attwater. Living Age Books. Cleveland and New York: Meridian Books/World Publishing Company, 1957; 1934.

_____. *The Fate of Man in the Modern World.* Translated from the Russian by Donald A. Lowrie. New York and Milwaukee: Morehouse Publishing Co., 1935. Reprint: Ann Arbor paperbacks AA59. Ann Arbor: University of Michigan Press, 1961.

Bloom, Harold, editor. *Joseph Conrad.* Edited and with an introduction by Harold Bloom. Modern Critical Views. New York: Chelsea House Publishers, 1986.

Bonhoeffer, Dietrich. *The Cost of Discipleship.* Translated from the German by R. H. Fuller. With some revisions by Irmgard Booth. New York: Macmillan Publishing Co., Inc., 1963; 1937.

Bowra, Cecil Maurice. *The Prophetic Element.* English Association (Great Britain) Presidential Address, September 1959. London: Oxford University Press, 1959. Reprinted in C. M. Bowra. *In General and Particular.* Essays and Addresses. Cleveland: World Publishing Company, 1964.

Bredvold, Louis I., and Ralph G. Ross, editors. *The Philosophy of Edmund Burke: A Selection from His Speeches and Writings.* With an introduction by the editors. An Ann Arbor Paperback. Ann Arbor: University of Michigan Press, 1967.

Buber, Martin. *At the Turning. Three Essays on Judaism.* New York: Farrar, Straus, and Young, 1952. Also in Hebrew: *Be-mashber ha-ruah.* Jerusalem: n.p., 1953.

_____. *Eclipse of God: Studies in the Relation between Religion and Philosophy.* New York and Evanston: Harper & Row, Publishers, 1952.

_____. *Pointing the Way: Collected Essays.* Edited and translated by Maurice S. Friedman. New York: Schocken Books, 1974; 1957.

_____. "The Silent Question: On Henri Bergson and Simone Weil." In *The Writings of Martin Buber*. Selected, edited, and introduced by Will Herberg. Cleveland and New York: Meridian Books/World Publishing Company, 1956.

Burckhardt, Jacob. *Reflections on History*. Translated from the German by M. D. Hottinger. With an introduction by Gottfried Dietze. Indianapolis: Liberty Classics, 1979; 1905. First English edition with above translation published in London: George Allen & Unwin, Ltd., 1943.

Burke, Edmund. *Reflections on the Revolution in France*. Edited and with an introduction by Conor Cruise O'Brien. Harmondsworth/Middlesex: Penguin Books, 1968; 1790.

_____. *Selected Writings and Speeches*. Edited by Peter J. Stanlis. Chicago: Regnery Gateway, 1963.

Burnham, James. *Suicide of the West: An Essay on the Meaning and Destiny of Liberalism*. Washington DC: Regnery Gateway, 1985; 1964.

Camus, Albert. *The Myth of Sisyphus and Other Essays*. Translated from the French by Justin O'Brien. New York: Vintage Books/Random House, 1955; 1942.

_____. *Notebooks 1935–1942*. Translated from the French, and with a preface and notes, by Philip Thody. New York: Modern Library, 1965; 1962.

_____. *The Rebel: An Essay on Man in Revolt*. Translated from the French by Anthony Bower. With a foreword by Sir Herbert Read. New York: Vintage Books/Random House, 1956; 1951.

_____. *Resistance, Rebellion, and Death*. Translated from the French and with an introduction by Justin O'Brien. New York: Alfred A. Knopf, 1961.

Canavan, Francis. *The Pluralist Game: Pluralism, Liberalism, and the Moral Conscience*. Lanham MD: Rowman & Littlefield, Publishers, Inc., 1995.

Carlyle, Thomas. *On Heroes, Hero-Worship, and the Heroic in History*. New York: Dodge Publishing Co., 1841.

Cary, Joyce. *Art and Reality: Ways of the Creative Process*. World Perspectives 20. New York: Harper & Brothers, 1958.

_____. *Selected Essays*. Edited by A. G. Bishop. New York: St. Martin's Press, 1976.

Cassirer, Ernst. *An Essay on Man: An Introduction to a Philosophy of Human Culture*. Garden City NY: Doubleday & Company, Inc., 1953; 1944.

_____. *Symbol, Myth, and Culture: Essays and Lectures of Ernst Cassirer, 1933–1945*. Edited by Donald Phillip Verene. New Haven CT and London: Yale University Press, 1979.

Cather, Willa. *Death Comes for the Archbishop*. Vintage Classics. New York: Vintage Books, 1990; 1927.

_____. *Not under Forty*. Lincoln and London: University of Nebraska Press, 1988; 1922.

_____. *On Writing: Critical Studies on Writing as an Art*. New York: Alfred A. Knopf, 1949.

Chalmers, Gordon Keith. *The Republic and the Person*. Chicago: Henry Regnery, 1952.

Chambers, Whittaker. *Ghosts on the Roof: Selected Journalism of Whittaker Chambers, 1931–1959*. Edited by Terry Teachout. Washington DC: Regnery Gateway, 1989.

_____. *Witness*. South Bend IN: Regnery Gateway, Inc., 1979; 1952.

Christensen, Damascene. *Not of This World: The Life and Teaching of Fr. Seraphim Rose, Pathfinder to the Heart of Ancient Christianity.* Forestville CA: Fr. Seraphim Rose Foundation, 1993.

Coles, Robert. *Simone Weil: A Modern Pilgrimage.* Radcliffe Biography Series. Reading MA: Addison-Wesley Publishing Company, Inc., 1987.

Congar, Yves. *The Meaning of Tradition.* Translated by A. N. Woodrow. New York: Hawthorn Books, 1964.

Conrad, Joseph. *The Nigger of the Narcissus.* In *Tales of Land and Sea.* Introduction by William McFee. Garden City NY: Hanover House, 1953. Original: Garden City NY: Doubleday, Page & Co., 1897.

_____. *Nostromo. A Tale of the Seaboard.* With a foreword by F. R. Leavis. Signet Classic CT-28. New York: New American Library, 1960. Original: Garden City NY: Doubleday, Page, 1904.

_____. *The Secret Agent: A Simple Tale.* Doubleday Anchor Books A8. Garden City NY: Doubleday & Co., Inc., 1955. Original: New York and London: Harper & Brothers, 1907.

_____. *Under Western Eyes.* With an introduction by Morton Dauwen Zabel. Doubleday Anchor Books A323. Garden City NY: Anchor Books, 1963. Original: New York and London: Harper & Brothers, 1911.

Crunden, Robert M., editor. *The Superfluous Men: Conservative Critics of American Culture, 1900–1945.* Austin and London: University of Texas Press, 1977.

Curtius, Ernst Robert. *Essays on European Literature.* Translated from the German by Michael Kowal. Princeton: Princeton University Press, 1973.

Czarnecka, Ewa, and Aleksandr Fiut, editors. *Conversations with Czeslaw Milosz.* Translated by Richard Lowrie. San Diego: Harcourt Brace Jovanovich, 1987.

Davidson, Donald. *Still Rebels, Still Yankees and Other Essays.* With an introduction by Lewis P. Simpson. Baton Rouge: Louisiana State University Press, 1972.

Dawson, Christopher. *The Judgment of the Nations.* New York: Sheed & Ward, 1942.

_____. *Understanding Europe.* New York: Sheed and Ward, 1952.

Dewey, John. *Liberalism and Social Action.* New York: Capricorn Books, 1963; 1935.

Dickstein, Morris. *Gates of Eden: American Culture in the Sixties.* New York: Basic Books, Inc., Publishers, 1977.

Dietze, Gottfried. "The Americanization of the Mind." *Modern Age* 32/1 (Winter 1988): 21-26.

Dostoevsky, Fyodor. *The Brothers Karamozov.* Translated from the Russian by Constance Garnett. With an introduction by Marc Slonim. New York: Modern Library, 1929, 1950. Original, 1879–1880.

_____. *Crime and Punishment.* Translated from the Russian, with an introduction, by David Magarshack. Harmondsworth/Middlesex and Baltimore: Penguin Books, 1951. Original, 1866.

_____. *The Devils.* [*The Possessed.*] Translated from the Russian, and with an introduction, by David Magarshack. Harmondsworth/Middlesex and Baltimore: Penguin Books, 1953. Original, 1871–1872.

_____. *The Idiot.* Translated from the Russian, with an introduction, by David Magarshack. Harmondsworth/Middlesex and Baltimore: Penguin Books, 1955. Original, 1868–1869.

_____. *Letters of Fyodor Michailovitch Dostoevsky to His Family and Friends.* Translated from the Russian by Ethel Colburn Mayne. New York: Macmillan Company; London: Chatto & Windus, 1914.

_____. *A Raw Youth.* Translated from the Russian by Constance Garnett. New York: Macmillan Company, 1916. Original, 1875.

Eliot, T. S. *After Strange Gods: A Primer of Modern Heresy.* London: Faber and Faber Limited, 1934.

_____. *Collected Poems, 1909–1935.* New York: Harcourt, Brace and Company, 1936.

_____. *Christianity and Culture.* (Comprising *The Idea of a Christian Society* [1940] and *Notes towards the Definition of Culture* [1948].) New York: Harvest Books/ Harcourt, Brace & World, Inc., 1968.

_____. *Essays Ancient and Modern.* London: Faber and Faber, 1936.

_____. *Four Quartets.* New York: Harcourt, Brace and Company, 1943.

_____. "The Man of Letters and the Future of Europe." *The Sewanee Review* 53/ 3 (Summer 1945): 333-42.

_____. *Selected Essays.* New York: Harcourt, Brace & World, Inc., 1960.

_____. *To Criticize the Critic and Other Writings.* New York: Farrar, Straus & Giroux, 1965.

_____. "War Memorial Address, at Milton Academy, Milton, Massachusetts, 3 November 1948: Leadership and Letters." *Milton Bulletin* 12/1 (February 1949): 5-16.

Emerson, Ralph Waldo. *English Traits, Representative Men, and Other Essays.* London: J. M. Dent, Ltd.; New York: E. P. Dutton and Co., 1908; 1856; 1850.

_____. *Lectures and Biographical Sketches.* Boston: Houghton, Mifflin, 1895.

_____. *The Portable Emerson.* Selected and arranged, with an introduction and notes, by Mark Van Doren. New York: Viking Press, 1946.

Ericson, Edward E., Jr. *Solzhenitsyn and the Modern World.* Washington DC: Regnery Gateway, 1993.

_____. *Solzhenitsyn: The Moral Vision.* With a foreword by Malcolm Muggeridge. Grand Rapids MI: William B. Eerdmans Publishing Co., 1980.

Florovsky, Georges. "Three Masters: The Quest for Religion in Nineteenth-Century Russian Literature." In *Mansions of the Spirit: Essays in Literature and Religion*, edited by George A. Panichas, 157-79. New York: Hawthorn Books, Inc., Publishers, 1967.

Forster, E. M. *Abinger Harvest.* London: Edward Arnold & Co., 1953; 1910.

_____. *Howards End.* London: Edward Arnold & Co., 1951; 1910.

_____. *A Passage to India.* London: Edward Arnold & Co., 1947; 1924.

_____. *Two Cheers for Democracy.* New York: Harcourt, Brace & Co., 1951.

Grene, Marjorie. *Dreadful Freedom.* Chicago: University of Chicago Press, 1948.

Guardini, Romano. *The End of the Modern World: A Search for Orientation.* Translated from the German by Joseph Theman and Herbert Burke. Edited and with an introduction by Frederick D. Wilhelmsen. New York: Sheed & Ward, 1956.

_____. *Power and Responsibility: A Course of Action for the New Age.* Translated from the German by Elinor C. Briefs. Chicago: Henry Regnery Company, 1961; 1951.

Gurney, Stephen. *British Poetry of the Nineteenth Century.* New York: Twayne Publishers, 1993.

Havel, Vàclav. *Open Letters: Selected Writings, 1965–1990.* New York: Vintage Books, 1992.

Heidegger, Martin. *Basic Writings, from* Being and Time *(1927) to* The Task of Thinking *(1964).* Edited, with a general introduction and introductions to each selection, by David Farrell Krell. New York: Harper & Row, Publishers, 1977.

Heschel, Abraham J. *The Prophets.* New York and Evanston: Harper & Row, Publishers, Inc., 1962.

Hindus, Milton. *Irving Babbitt, Literature, and the Democractic Culture.* New Brunswick CT and London: Transaction Publishers, 1994.

Hubben, William. *Four Prophets of Our Destiny: Kierkegaard, Dostoevsky, Nietzsche, Kafka.* New York: Macmillan Company, 1952.

Hulme, T. E. *Speculations: Essays on Humanism and the Philosophy of Art.* Edited by Herbert Read. With a foreword by Jacob Epstein. New York: Harcourt, Brace and Company, n.d.; 1924.

Jaki, Stanley L. "Science and the Future of Religion." *Modern Age* 33/2 (Summer 1990): 142-50.

James, Henry. *Letters.* Volume 1. *1843–1875* (1974). Volume 2. *1875–1883* (1975). Volume 3. *1883–1895* (1980). Volume 4. *1895–1916* (1984). Edited by Leon Edel. Cambridge MA: Harvard University Press, 1974–1984.

Jaspers, Karl. *Man in the Modern Age.* Translated from the German by Eden and Cedar Paul. Garden City NY: Doubleday and Company, 1957; 1931.

_____. *Tragedy Is Not Enough.* Translated from the German by Harald A. T. Reiche, Harry T. Moore, and Karl W. Deutsch. Boston: Beacon Press, 1952; 1947.

Jesus-Marie, Pere Bruno de, O.C.D., editor. *Satan.* With an introduction by Charles Moeller. New York: Sheed & Ward, 1952.

Johannesen, Richard L., Rennard Strickland, and Ralph T. Eubanks, editors. *Language Is Sermonic: Richard M. Weaver on the Nature of Rhetoric.* Baton Rouge and London: Louisiana State University Press, 1970.

Kafka, Franz. *Dearest Father: Stories and Other Writings.* Translated from the German by Ernst Kaiser and Eithne Wilkins. New York: Schocken Books, 1954.

Kazin, Alfred. *The Inmost Leaf: A Selection of Essays.* New York: Harcourt, Brace, 1955, pbk. 1979; New York: Noonday Press, 1959; repr. Westport CT: Greenwood Press, 1974.

_____. *On Native Grounds: An Interpretation of Modern American Prose Literature.* Garden City NY: Doubleday & Company, Inc., 1956; 1942.

Kierkegaard, Søren. *The Living Thoughts of Kierkegaard.* Presented by W. H. Auden. A Midland Book. Bloomington and London: Indiana University Press, 1963; New York: David McKay Company, Inc., 1952.

Kirk, Russell. *Academic Freedom: An Essay in Definition.* Chicago: Henry Regnery Company, 1955.

_____. *America's British Culture.* New Brunswick CT and London: Transaction Publishers, 1993.

_____. *The Conservative Mind: From Burke to Eliot.* Seventh revised edition. Chicago and Washington DC: Regnery Books, 1986; 1953.

_____. *Decadence and Renewal in the Higher Learning.* Chicago: Regnery Gateway, 1978.

_____. *Edmund Burke: A Genius Reconsidered.* With a foreword by Roger Scruton. Wilmington DE: Intercollegiate Studies Institute, 1997; 1967.

_____. *Eliot and His Age: T. S. Eliot's Moral Imagination in the Twentieth Century.* New York: Random House, 1972.

_____. *Enemies of the Permanent Things: Observations of Abnormity in Literature and Politics.* La Salle IL: Sherwood Sugden & Co., Publishers, 1984; 1969.

_____. *John Randolph of Roanoke: A Study in American Politics, with Selected Speeches and Letters.* Chicago: Henry Regnery Co., 1964; 1951.

_____. *The Politics of Prudence.* Bryn Mawr PA: Intercollegiate Studies Institute, 1993.

_____. *Redeeming the Time.* Edited and with an introduction by Jeffrey O. Nelson. Wilmington DE: Intercollegiate Studies Institute, 1996.

_____. *The Roots of American Order.* With an epilogue by Frank Shakespeare. Washington DC: Regnery Gateway, 1991; 1974.

_____. *The Sword of Imagination: Memoirs of a Half-Century of Literary Conflict.* Grand Rapids MI: Eerdmans Publishing Co., 1995.

_____. *The Wise Men Know What Wicked Things Are Written on the Sky.* Washington DC: Regnery Gateway, Inc., 1987.

Krasnov, Vladislav G. *Solzhenitsyn and Dostoevsky.* Athens: University of Georgia Press, 1980.

Lawrence, D. H. *Letters.* Edited and with an introduction by Aldous Huxley. London: Heinemann, 1935.

_____. *Phoenix: The Posthumous Papers.* Edited and with an introduction by Edward D. McDonald. New York: Viking Press, 1932.

_____. *The Rainbow.* London: Methuen, 1915.

_____. *Women in Love.* London: Martin Secker, 1920.

Leavis, F. R. *Anna Karenina and Other Essays.* London: Chatto & Windus, 1967.

_____. *The Common Pursuit.* London: Chatto & Windus, 1952.

_____. *The Great Tradition: George Eliot, Henry James, Joseph Conrad.* London: Chatto & Windus, 1960.

_____. *The Living Principle: "English" as a Discipline of Thought.* London: Chatto & Windus, 1975. New York and Oxford: Oxford University Press, 1975.

Levine, Madeline G. *Contemporary Polish Poetry, 1925–1975.* Twayne's World Authors 586: Poland. Boston: Twayne Publishers, 1981.

Lindbom, Tage. *The Myth of Democracy.* With an introduction by Claes G. Ryn. Grand Rapids MI: Eerdmans Publishing Co., 1996.

Lippmann, Walter. *The Public Philosophy.* Boston: Little, Brown, 1965; 1955.

Lossky, N.O. *The World as an Organic Whole.* Translated from the Russian by Natalie Duddington. London: Humphrey Milford/Oxford University Press, 1928.

Lottman, Herbert R. *Albert Camus. A Biography.* Garden City NY: Doubleday, 1979.

Manchester, Frederick, and Odell Shepard, editors. *Irving Babbitt: Man and Teacher.* New York: G. P. Putnam's Sons, 1941.

Marcel, Gabriel. *The Mystery of Being.* Volume 1. *Reflection & Mystery,* translated by G. S. Fraser (1950). Volume 2. *Faith & Reality,* translated by René Hague (1951). The Gifford Lectures, University of Aberdeen, 1949–1950. Chicago: Henry Regnery Company, 1960; 1950, 1951.

Matthiessen, Francis Otto. *The Achievement of T. S. Eliot: An Essay on the Nature of Poetry.* London and New York: Oxford University Press, 1958.

_____. *The Responsibilities of the Critic: Essays and Reviews.* Selected by John Rackliffe. New York and London: Oxford University Press, 1952.

Meyerhoff, Hans. "Contra Simone Weil." In *Arguments and Doctrines: A Reader of Jewish Thinking in the Aftermath of the Holocaust.* Selected and with introductory essays by Arthur A. Cohen. New York: Harper & Row, 1970.

Milosz, Czeslaw. *Beginning with My Streets: Essays and Recollections.* Translated from the Polish by Madeline G. Levine. New York: Farrar, Straus and Giroux, Inc., 1991.

_____. *The Collected Poems, 1931–1987.* New York: Ecco Press, 1988.

_____. *Emperor of the Earth: Modes of Eccentric Vision.* Berkeley and Los Angeles and London: University of California Press, 1977.

_____. *The Land of Ulro.* Translated from the Polish by Louis Iribarne. New York: Farrar, Straus and Giroux, Inc., 1984; 1977.

_____. *The Witness of Poetry.* Charles Eliot Norton Lectures 1981–1982. Cambridge MA and London: Harvard University Press, 1983.

Mochulsky, Konstantin. *Dostoevsky: His Life and Work.* Translated from the Russian, and with an introduction, by Michael A. Minihan. Princeton: Princeton University Press, 1967; 1947.

Molnar, Thomas. "Tradition and the Mechanical Eden." *Modern Age* 36/3 (Spring 1994): 244-50.

More, Paul Elmer. *Aristocracy and Justice.* Shelburne Essays volume 9. Boston and New York: Houghton Mifflin, 1915.

_____. *Christ the Word.* Volume 4 of *The Greek Tradition.* Princeton: Princeton University Press, 1927.

_____. *The Demon of the Absolute.* New Shelburne Essays volume 1. Princeton: Princeton University Press, 1928.

_____. *The Drift of Romanticism.* Shelburne Essays volume 8. Boston and New York: Houghton Mifflin, 1913.

_____. *A New England Group and Others.* Shelburne Essays volume 11. Boston and New York: Houghton Mifflin, 1921.

_____. *On Being Human.* New Shelburne Essays volume 3. Princeton: Princeton University Press, 1936.

Murray, Gilbert. *Tradition and Progress.* Boston: Houghton, Mifflin Company, 1922.

Nash, George H. *The Conservative Intellectual Movement in America, since 1945.* Updated edition. Wilmington DE: Intercollegiate Studies Institute, 1996. First edition: New York: Basic Books, 1976.

Nietzsche, Friedrich. *The Portable Nietzsche.* Selected and translated, with an introduction, prefaces, and notes, by Walter Kaufmann. Viking Portable Library. New York: Viking Press, 1954.

Nigg, Walter. *The Heretics.* Edited and translated by Richard Winston and Clara Winston. New York: Alfred A. Knopf, Inc., 1962. Reprint: New York: Dorsett, 1990.

Nin, Anaïs. *Incest: From a Journal of Love: The Unexpurgated Diary of Anaïs Nin.* San Diego: Harcourt Brace Jovanovich, Publishers, 1992.

Nisbet, Robert. *Roosevelt and Stalin: The Failed Courtship.* Washington DC: Regnery Gateway, 1988.

Oakeshott, Michael. *Rationalism in Politics and Other Essays.* London and New York: Methuen & Co., Ltd., 1962.

O'Connor, Flannery. *Mystery and Manners: Occasional Prose of Flannery O'Connor.* Selected and edited by Sally and Robert Fitzgerald. New York: Farrar, Straus & Giroux, 1969.

Ortega y Gasset, José. *The Dehumanization of Art and Other Essays on Art, Culture, and Literature.* Translated by Helene Weyl. Princeton NJ: Princeton University Press, 1968; 1925.

_____. *The Mission of the University.* Translation and introduction by Howard Lee Nostrand. Princeton NJ: Princeton University Press, 1944; 1930.

_____. *The Revolt of the Masses.* Authorized translation from the Spanish. New York: W. W. Norton and Company, 1932; 1930.

_____. *Some Lessons in Metaphysics.* Translated by Mildred Adams. New York: W. W. Norton and Company, 1969; 1966.

Orwell, George. *As I Please, 1943–1945.* Volume 3 of *Collected Essays, Journalism, and Letters of George Orwell.* Edited by Sonia Orwell and Ian Angus. New York: Harcourt, Brace Jovanovich, 1968.

Panichas, George A. *The Burden of Vision: Dostoevsky's Spiritual Art.* Grand Rapids MI: Eerdmans Publishing Co., 1977; Chicago: Gateway Editions, 1985.

_____. *The Courage of Judgment: Essays in Criticism, Culture, and Society.* With a foreword by Austin Warren. Knoxville: University of Tennessee Press, 1982.

_____. *The Critic as Conservator: Essays in Literature, Society, and Culture.* Washington DC: Catholic University of America Press, 1992.

_____. "Foreword," in *The Courage of Judgment: Essays in Criticism, Culture, and Society,* by Austin Warren, ix-xiii. Knoxville: University of Tennessee Press, 1982.

_____, and Claes G. Ryn, editors. *Irving Babbitt in Our Time.* Washington DC: Catholic University of America Press, 1986.

_____, editor. *Irving Babbitt: Representative Writings.* Edited and with an introduction by George A. Panichas. Lincoln and London: University of Nebraska Press, 1981.

_____, editor. *Modern Age: The First Twenty-Five Years. A Selection.* Indianapolis: Liberty Press, 1988.

_____. *The Reverent Discipline: Essays in Literary Criticism and Culture.* With a foreword by G. Wilson Knight. Knoxville: University of Tennessee Press, 1974.

_____, editor. *The Simone Weil Reader.* New York: David McKay Company, Inc., 1977. Wakefield RI and London: Moyer Bell, 1994.

Pelikan, Jaroslav. *The Vindication of Tradition.* New York and London: Yale University Press, 1984.

Picard, Max. *The Flight from God.* Translated by Marianne Kuschnitzky and J. M. Cameron, with a note on Max Picard by Gabriel Marcel and an introduction by J. M. Cameron. Humanist Library. Chicago: Henry Regnery Co., 1951.

_____. *Hitler in Our Selves.* Translated from the German by Heinrich Hauser. With an introduction by Robert S. Hartman. Hinsdale IL: Henry Regnery Company, 1947.

_____. *The World of Silence.* Translated by Stanley Godman. Humanist Library. Chicago: Henry Regnery Co., 1952.

Pieper, Josef. "Tradition: The Concept and Its Claim upon Us." *Modern Age* 36/3 (Spring 1994): 217-28.

Polanyi, Michael. "On the Modern Mind." *Encounter* 24/5 (May 1965): 2-20.

_____. *Personal Knowledge: Towards a Post-Critical Philosophy.* Chicago: University of Chicago Press, 1958.

Quasten, Johannes. *Patrology.* Volume 2 of *The Ante-Nicene Literature after Irenaeus.* Utrecht and Antwerp: Spectrum Publishers, 1953.

Rahv, Philip. *Literature and the Sixth Sense*. Boston: Houghton Mifflin Co., 1969.

Regnery, Henry. *The Cliff Dwellers: The History of a Chicago Cultural Institution*. Evanston IL: Chicago Historical Bookworks, 1990.

_____. *Creative Chicago: From* The Chap-Book *to the University*. Introduction by Joseph Epstein. Evanston IL: Chicago Historical Bookworks, 1993.

_____. *A Few Reasonable Words: Selected Writings*. With an introduction by George A. Panichas. Wilmington DE: Intercollegiate Studies Institute, 1996.

_____. *Memoirs of a Dissident Publisher*. New York: Harcourt Brace Jovanovich, 1979.

_____. *Russell Kirk: An Appraisal*. Mt. Pleasant MI: Clarke Historical Library, Central Michigan University, [1980]. (15 pages.)

Röpke [Roepke], Wilhelm. *The Social Crisis of Our Time*. Translated from the German by Annette Jacobson and Peter Schiffer Jacobson, with a new introduction by William F. Campbell and a foreword by Russell Kirk. The Library of Conservative Thought. New Brunswick CT and London: Transaction Publishers, 1991, ©1992. First English edition: "Based on the 5th edition of the Swiss original (1948) with only slight alterations made for the American and British readers." Chicago: University of Chicago Press, 1950. Original, 1942.

Rose, Eugene (Fr. Seraphim). *Nihilism: The Root of the Revolution of the Modern Age*. Forestville CA: Fr. Seraphim Rose Foundation, 1994.

Royce, Josiah. *The Philosophy of Loyalty*. New York: Macmillan Company, 1908.

_____. *The World and the Individual*. Gifford Lectures 1899, 1900. Two volumes. 1. *The Four Historical Conceptions of Being*. 2. *Nature, Man, and the Moral Order*. New York and London: Macmillan, [©1899, 1901].

Ryn, Claes G. *The New Jacobism: Can Democracy Survive?* Washington DC: National Humanities Institute, 1991.

_____. *Will, Imagination, and Reason: Irving Babbitt and the Problem of Reality*. Chicago and Washington DC: Regnery Books, 1986.

Sartre, Jean-Paul. "Tribute to Albert Camus." In *Camus: A Collection of Critical Essays*. Translated by Justin O'Brien. Edited by Germaine Brée, 173-75. Englewood Cliffs NJ: Prentice-Hall, Inc., 1962.

Schmemann, Alexander. "On Solzhenitsyn." In *Aleksandr Solzhenitsyn: Critical Essays and Documentary Materials*. Edited by John B. Dunlop, Richard Haugh, and Alexis Klimoff. New York: Collier, 1975.

Singer, Isaac Bashevis, and Richard Burgin. *Conversations with Isaac Bashevis Singer*. Garden City NY: Doubleday & Co., Inc., 1985.

Solzhenitsyn, Aleksandr I. *The First Circle*. Translated from the Russian by Thomas P. Whitney. New York: Harper & Row, 1968.

_____. *The Gulag Archipelago, 1918–1956: An Experiment in Literary Investigation*. Three volumes. Translated from the Russian by Thomas P. Whitney. New York: Harper & Row, (1) 1973, (2) 1975, (3) 1978.

_____. *Letter to the Soviet Leaders*. Translated from the Russian by Hilary Sternberg. New York: Harper & Row, 1974.

_____. *The Mortal Danger: How Misconceptions about Russia Imperil America*. Second edition. Translated from the Russian by Michael Nicholson and Alexis Klimoff. New York: Harper & Row, 1981; 1980.

_____. *Nobel Lecture*. Translated by F. D. Reeve. New York: Farrar, Straus and Giroux, Inc., 1972.

_____. *Rebuilding Russia: Reflections and Tentative Proposals*. Translated and annotated by Alexis Klimoff. New York: Farrar, Straus and Giroux, 1991.

_____. "The Templeton Address." *National Review* (22 July 1983): 873-76.

_____. *A World Split Apart: Commencement Address Delivered at Harvard University, June 8, 1978*. Translated by Irina Ilovayskaya Alberti with help from Alexis Klimoff. New York: Harper & Row, 1978.

Stade, George, editor in chief. *European Writers: The Twentieth Century*. Two volumes. European Writers 10 and 11. New York: Scribner, 1990.

Tate, Allen. *Essays of Four Decades*. Chicago: Swallow Press, Inc., 1968.

Tillich, Paul. *The Shaking of the Foundations*. New York: Charles Scribner's Sons, 1948.

Tocqueville, Alexis de. *Democracy in America*. Garden City NY: Doubleday Anchor, 1969; 1835–1839.

Tonsor, Stephen J. "Conservatives as a Creative Minority." *Modern Age* 40/1 (Winter 1998): 7-14.

Trilling, Lionel. *The Experience of Literature: A Reader with Commentaries. Fiction*. New York/Chicago/San Francisco/Toronto: Holt, Rinehart and Winston, 1967.

_____. *The Last Decade: Essays and Reviews, 1965-75*. Edited by Diana Trilling. New York and London: Harcourt Brace Jovanovich, 1977.

_____. *The Liberal Imagination: Essays on Literature and Society*. New York: Viking Press, 1950.

_____, editor. *The Portable Matthew Arnold*. Harmondsworth/Middlesex: Penguin Books, 1949.

Turgenev, Ivan Sergeyevich (alternately Turgenef, Ivan Sergheievitch). *Fathers and Sons. A Novel*. Translated from the Russian (*Ottsy i deti*, 1862) with the approval of the author by Eugene Schuyler. New York: Leypoldt & Holt, 1867. Translated from the Russian by Constance Garnett. London: William Heinemann, 1895. Translated by Avril Pyman. London and New York: J. M. Dent; Dutton, 1921. (In Great Britain entitled *Fathers and Children*.)

_____. *Sincerity and Authenticity*. Cambridge: Harvard University Press, 1972.

Viereck, Peter. *Conservatism Revisited: The Revolt against Revolt, 1815–1949*. New York and London: Charles Scribner's Sons, 1949; 1950.

Vivas, Eliseo. *The Artistic Transaction, and Essays on Theory of Literature*. Columbus: Ohio State University Press, 1963.

_____. *Contra Marcuse*. New York: Dell Publishing Company, 1972.

_____. *Creation and Discovery: Essays in Criticism and Aesthetics*. New York: Noonday Press, 1955.

_____. *The Moral Life and the Ethical Life*. Chicago: University of Chicago Press, 1950.

Voegelin, Eric. *Anamnesis*. Translated and edited by Gerhart Niemeyer. Notre Dame IN and London: University of Notre Dame Press, 1978.

_____. "Immortality: Experience and Symbol." *Harvard Theological Review* 60 (1967): 236-79. Repr. in *Published Essays, 1966–1985*. Volume 12 of *The Collected Works of Eric Voegelin*. Edited and with an introduction by Ellis Sandoz. Baton Rouge and London: Louisiana State University Press, 1990.

_____. *The New Science of Politics: An Introduction*. Chicago: University of Chicago Press, 1952.

_____. *Order and History*. Five volumes. 1. *Israel and Revelation* (1956). 2. *The World of the Polis* (1957). 3. *Plato and Aristotle* (1957). 4. *The Ecumenic Age* (1974).

5. *In Search of Order* (1987). Baton Rouge and London: Louisiana State University Press, 1956–1987.

Walsh, David. *After Ideology: Recovering the Spiritual Foundations of Freedom*. San Francisco: HarperSanFrancisco, 1990. Second edition. Washington DC: Catholic University of America Press, 1995.

Wang, Chull. "Betrayal and Moral Imagination: A Study of Joseph Conrad's Five Major Works." Ph.D. dissertation, University of Maryland, 1990.

Warren, Antonia J., editor. "Austin Warren (1899–1956): Letters from Five Decades." *Modern Age* 33/4 (Summer 1991): 326-45.

Warren, Austin. *Connections*. Ann Arbor: University of Michigan Press, 1970.

_____. *The Courage of Judgment: Essays in Criticism, Culture, and Society*. Foreword by George A. Panichas. Knoxville: University of Tennessee Press, 1982.

_____. *In Continuity: The Last Essays of Austin Warren*. Introduced and edited by George A. Panichas. Macon GA: Mercer University Press, 1996.

_____. *The New England Conscience*. Ann Arbor: University of Michigan Press, 1966.

_____. *New England Saints*. Ann Arbor: University of Michigan Press, 1956.

_____. *Rage for Order: Essays in Criticism*. Ann Arbor: University of Michigan Press, 1948.

_____. *Teacher & Critic: Essays by and about Austin Warren*. Edited by Myron Simon and Harvey Gross. Los Angeles: Plantin Press, 1976.

Weaver, Richard M. *Ideas Have Consequences*. Chicago: University of Chicago Press, 1948.

_____. *Life without Prejudice and Other Essays*. Chicago: Henry Regnery, 1965.

_____. *Visions of Order: The Cultural Crisis of Our Time*. With a foreword by Russell Kirk. Baton Rouge: Louisiana State University Press, 1964.

Weil, Simone. "The *Iliad*, Poem of Might." In *Intimations of Christianity among the Ancient Greeks*. Edited and translated by Elisabeth Chase Geissbuhler, 24-55. London and New York: Routledge & Kegan Paul, 1957. Reprinted in *The Simone Weil Reader*, edited by George A. Panichas, 153-83. New York: David McKay Company, Inc., 1977; Mt. Kisco NY: Moyer Bell, 1977, 1985; New York: Dorset Press, 1981.

The Iliad; or, The Poem of Force. Translated by Mary McCarthy. Pendle Hill pamphlet no. 91. Wallingford PA: Pendle Hill, 1956; Iowa City IA: Stone Wall Press, 1973. Reprinted as "The *Iliad*, or, The Poem of Force," in *Simone Weil: An Anthology*, ed. Sîan Miles, 182-215. London: Virago, 1986.

_____. *The Need for Roots: Prelude to a Declaration of Duties toward Mankind*. Translated by Arthur Wills. With a preface by T. S. Eliot. New York: G. P. Putnam's Sons, 1952.

_____. *The Simone Weil Reader*. Edited by George A. Panichas. New York: David McKay Company, Inc., 1977; Mt. Kisco NY: Moyer Bell, ©1977, 1985; New York: Dorset Press, 1981; Wakefield RI and London: Moyer Bell, 1994.

White, George Abbott, editor. *Simone Weil: Interpretations of a Life*. Amherst: University of Massachusetts Press, 1981.

Wilson, Edmund. *The Shores of Light: A Literary Chronicle of the 1920s and 1930s*. New York: Noonday Press, 1967; 1952.

Index

sky on, 26); Eric Voegelin on, 147
Politics (Dwight McDonald): and Simone Weil, 131
Politics of Prudence, The (Russell Kirk): on Joseph Conrad, 214; significance of, 155
Pope, Alexander: on chaos, 91; a moral poet, 116
Potsdam Conference, the: aftermath of, 128
Pound, Ezra: on T. S. Eliot, 105; and Henry Regnery, 125, 130
Power: of affliction, x; of ascent, x; of aspiration, x; of negations, x
Prairie Folks (Hamlin Garland): and Chicago publishers, 137
Prairie Songs (Hamlin Garland): and Chicago publishers, 137
Prejudice: life without, 253; Richard M. Weaver on, 253
Presentism: and continuity, xiv
"President Eliot and American Education" (Irving Babbitt): its indispensable testimony, 239-40
Presley, Elvis: a cult hero, 33
"Problem of Style in a Democracy, The" (Irving Babbitt): on the proper place of democracy, 242
Proceedings of the American Historical Association: and Martin Van Buren, 181
Profane spirit, the: and continuity, xiii; of criticism, x; and modernism, x; and negation, x, xiii. *See also* Luciferism, Satan
Prophecy: William Blake's prophetic writings, 234; and Dante, 234; of "Dover Beach," 4; of *A Passage to India*, 4; and John Milton, 234; of "The Second Coming," 4; of the soul, 234; and Leo Tolstoy, 234; and Virgil, 234; Prophets: of extremity, 101; of the flesh, 234; Hebrew, xix, 3; of Israel, 147; the minor prophets, 65; Simone Weil on, 65
Propp, Vladimir: critics of, 271; and Greimas, 271; and Claude Levi-Strauss, 271
Protestantism: of Irving Babbitt, 83, 84;

of Simone Weil, 72
Providence, R. I.: Austin Warren's home in, 119-20
Prufrock and Other Observations (T. S. Eliot): and the Great War, 108-109
Psalmist, the: on God, 185
Psalms, the: Simone Weil on, 65
Pseudo-Religion and the Modern Age (Seraphim Rose): *see Kingdom of Man and the Kingdom of God, The*
Pynchon, Thomas: Morris Dickstein on, 39; successors of, 167

Racine, Jean: spiritual guidance of, 267
"Radcliffe Biography Series, The": and Robert Coles, 66
Rage for Order (Austin Warren): part of a critical trilogy, 110
Rahv, Philip: on T. S. Eliot, 107
Rainbow, The (D. H. Lawrence): and D. H. Lawrence's paradisal world, 201
Randolph of Roanoke, John: Russell Kirk on, 152
Ransom, John Crowe: Robert M. Crunden on, 40-41; Richard M. Weaver's thesis advisor, 247
Raw Youth, A (Fyodor M. Dostoevsky): profligate father in, 208-209; and purgation, 207-208; and spirit of place, 202
Read, Herbert: and *Modern Age*, 251
Reagan, Ronald: *Where's the Rest of Me?*, 181
Rebuilding Russia (Aleksandr Solzhenitsyn): Edward Ericson on, 233
Reductionism: agents of, 56-61; and John Bunyan, 59; and Edmund Burke, 59; and Dante, 59; Stanley L. Jaki on, 186; and Henry James, 59; and John Milton, 59; quantitative, 186; of Aleksandr Solzhenitsyn, 59; and Sophocles, 59; Eric Voegelin on, 59; and Richard M. Weaver, 59
"Reflections Concerning the Causes of Liberty and Social Oppression" (Simone Weil): Robert Coles on, 69
"Reflections on the Right Use of School Studies with a View to the Love of God" (Simone Weil): on academic

Growing Wings to Overcome Gravity.
Criticism as the Pursuit of Virtue.
by George A. Panichas

Mercer University Press, Macon, Georgia 31210-3960.
Isbn 0-86554-606-1. Pick number: MUP/H457. (Casebound.)
Isbn 0-86554-618-5. Pick number: MUP/P177. (Perfectbound.)
Text and interior designs and composition by Edmon L. Rowell, Jr.
Covers and jacket designs by Mary Frances Burt.
Camera-ready pages composed on a Gateway2000 386/33C
    and an AOpen BG45-AP5VM via dos WordPerfect 5.1
        and WordPerfect for Windows 5.1/5.2
            and printed on a LaserMaster 1000.
Text font: Palatino (Adobe Systems, ©Linotype AG).
Display font: Present Script (Adobe Systems, ©Linotype AG).
Printed and bound by McNaughton & Gunn, Inc., Saline, Michigan 48176,
    via offset lithography on 55# Writers Natural.
Casebound: Smyth sewn and cased into B grade cloth with one-hit gold foil
    on spine and c. 4 and with 80# natural endsheets.
Dust jacket printed 4-color process on 80# Litholabel and layflat film laminated.
Perfectbound: notched and glued into c1s 10-pt. stock
    printed four-color and layflat film laminated.
                        [November 1999 / 300 + 1M]

101399elr.